ANDRE AGASSI
PAMELA ANDERSON
MICHAEL BALLACK
ANTONIO BANDERAS
BORIS BECKER
DAVID BECKHAM
BONO
BORAT
RICHARD BRANSON
ADRIANO CELENTANO
BILL CLINTON
GEORGE CLOONEY
JOAN COLLINS
COLUMBO
SEAN CONNERY
DANIEL CRAIG
LARA CROFT
PENELOPE CRUZ
JAMIE LEE CURTIS
JOHNNY DEPP
DANNY DEVITO
LEONARDO DICAPRIO
ROGER FEDERER
SARAH FERGUSON
CLARK GABLE
RICKY GERVAIS
WHOOPI GOLDBERG
MICHAIL GORBATSCHOW
STEFFI GRAF
HUGH GRANT
LEWIS HAMILTON
DARYL HANNAH
ERICH HONECKER
ANTHONY HOPKINS
MICHELLE HUNZIKER
MICHAEL JACKSON
SAMUEL L. JACKSON
GÜNTHER JAUCH
ANGELINA JOLIE
INDIANA JONES
OLIVER KAHN
MIROSLAV KLOSE
KEVIN KURANYI
LADY GAGA
UDO LINDENBERG
SOPHIA LOREN
DIEGO MARADONA
ANGELA MERKEL
LIZA MINNELLI
JACK NICHOLSON
OZZY OSBOURNE
SARAH JESSICA PARKER
CAMILLA PARKER BOWLES
LUCIANO PAVAROTTI
PABLO PICASSO
LUKAS PODOLSKI
HARRY POTTER
PRINCE AUGUST VON HANNOVER
PRINCE CHARLES
PRINCE WILLIAM
QUEEN ELIZABETH II
GORDON RAMSAY
LIONEL RICHIE
JULIA ROBERTS
RONALDO
CRISTIANO RONALDO
CLAUDIA SCHIFFER
GERHARD SCHRÖDER
MICHAEL SCHUMACHER
ARNOLD SCHWARZENEGGER
SEBASTIAN SCHWEINSTEIGER
BRITNEY SPEARS
SYLVESTER STALLONE
GWEN STEFANI
SHARON STONE
RUDI VÖLLER
ANDY WARHOL
BRUCE WILLIS
AMY WINEHOUSE

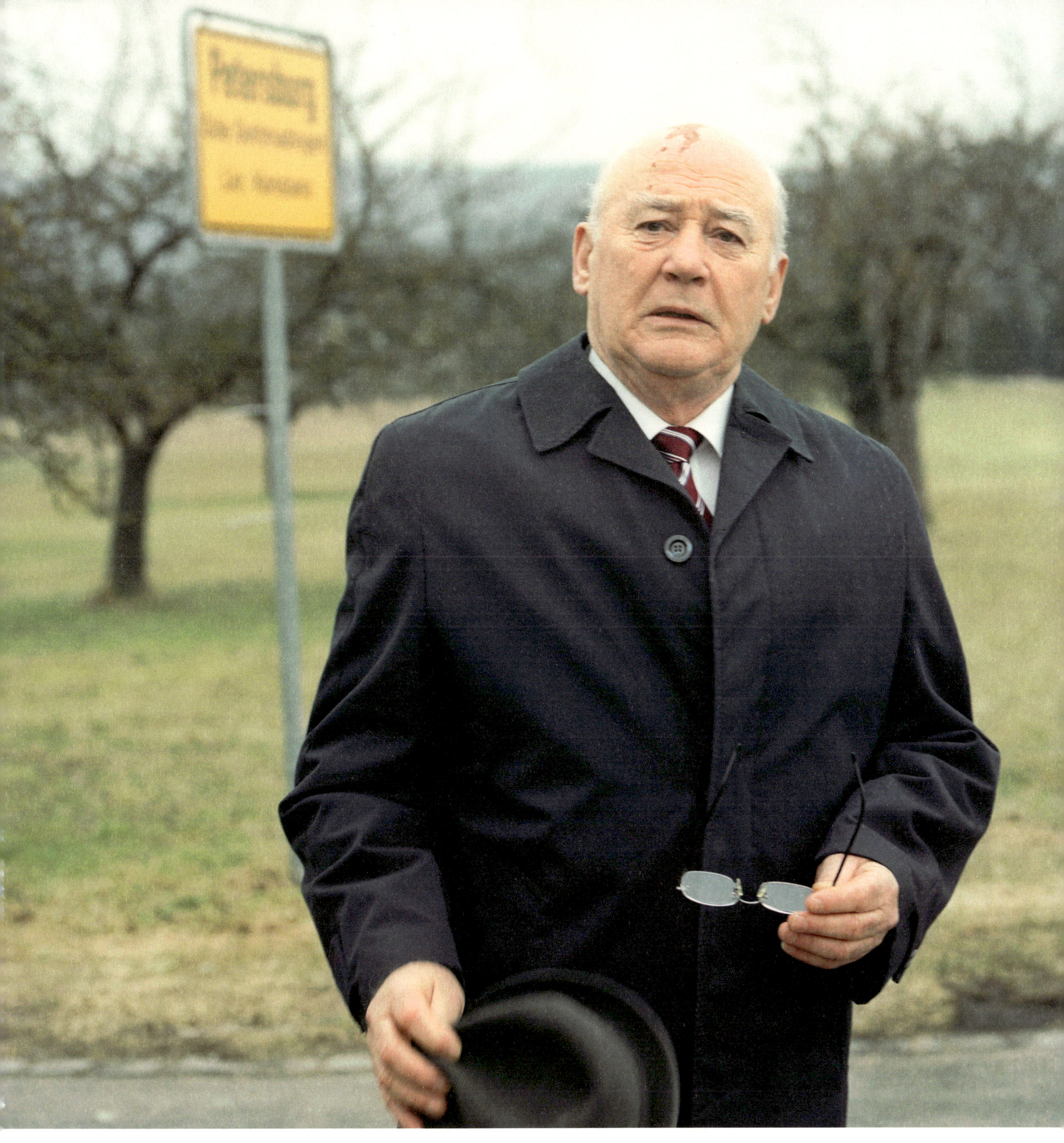

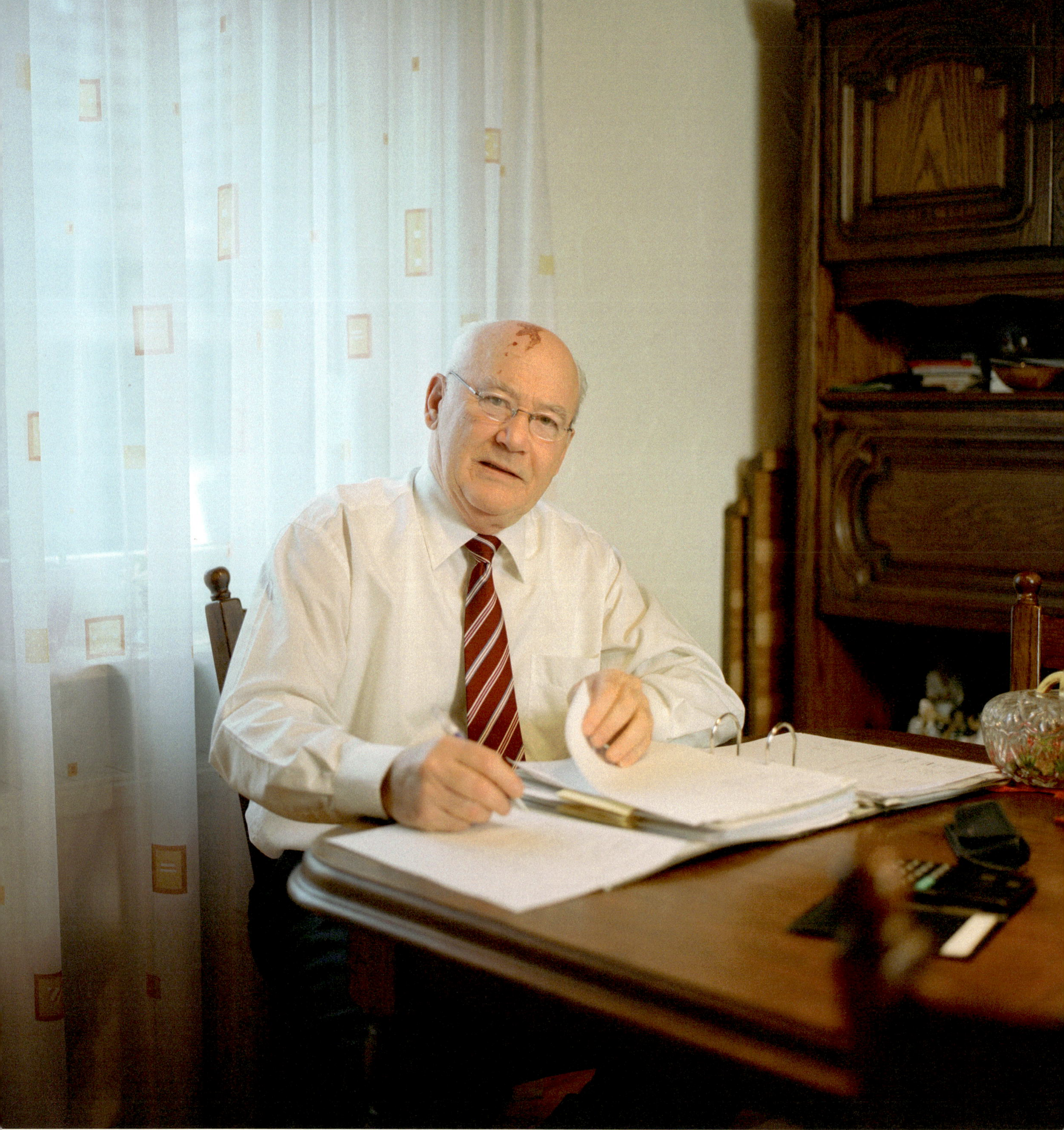

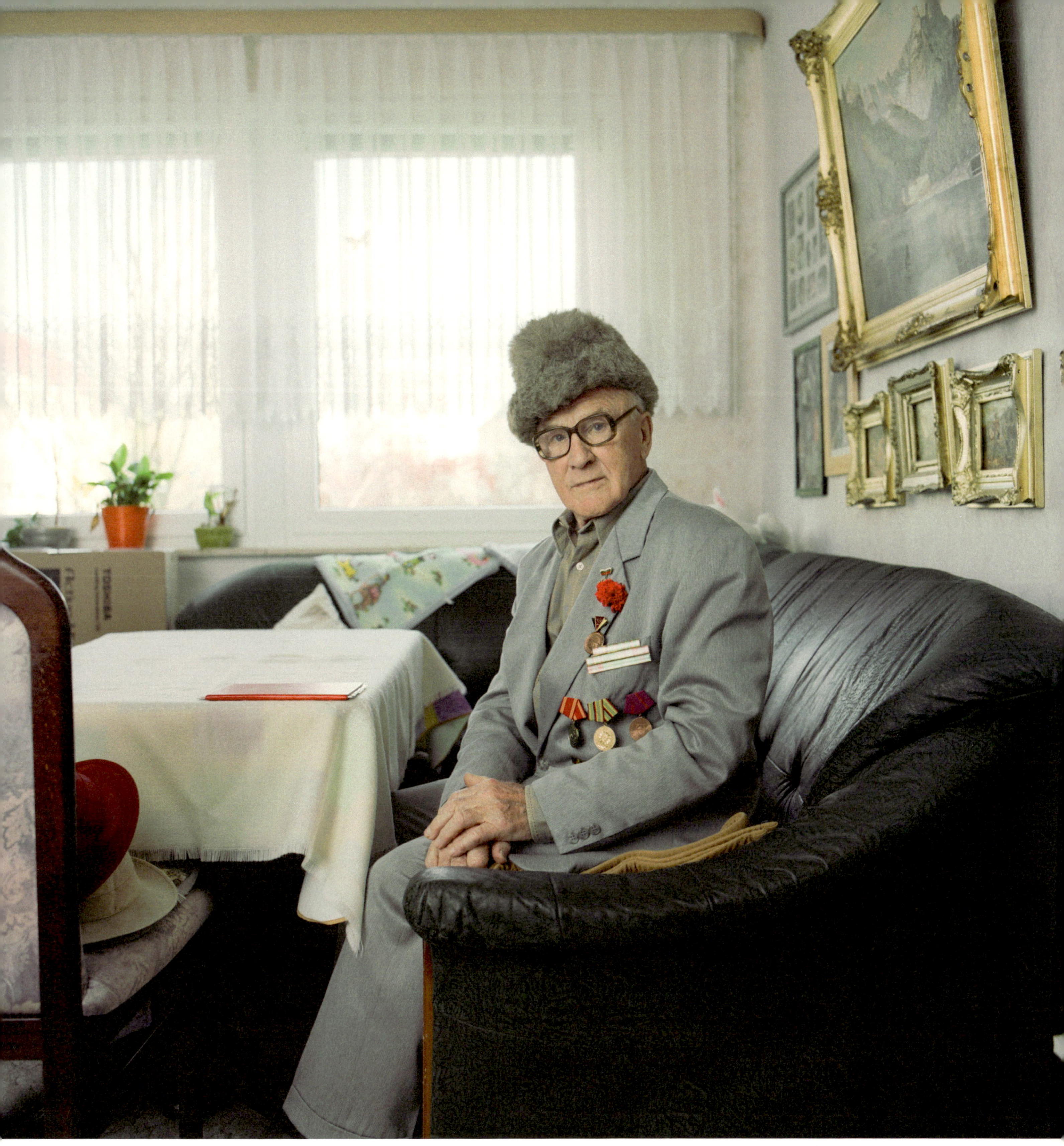

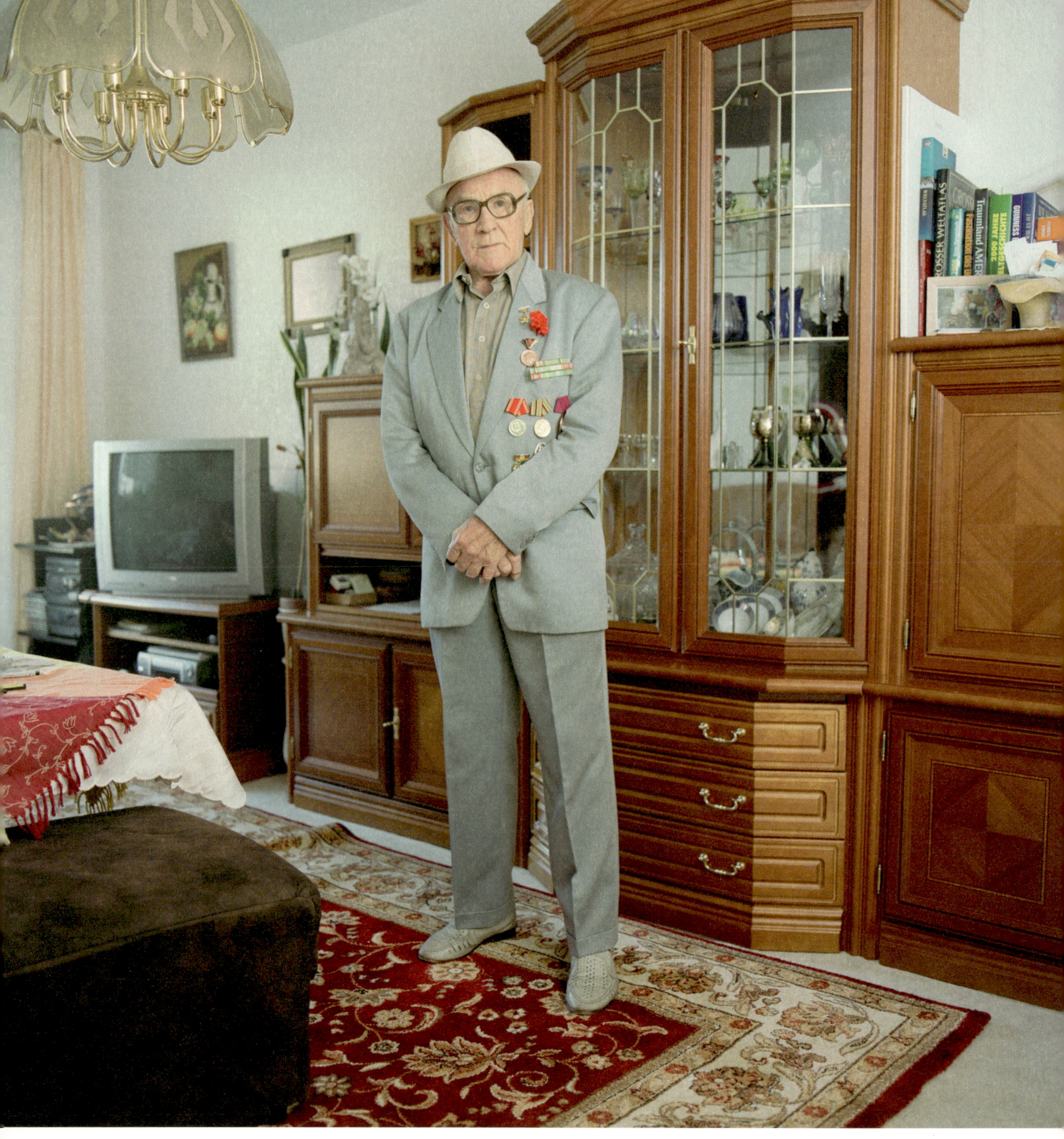

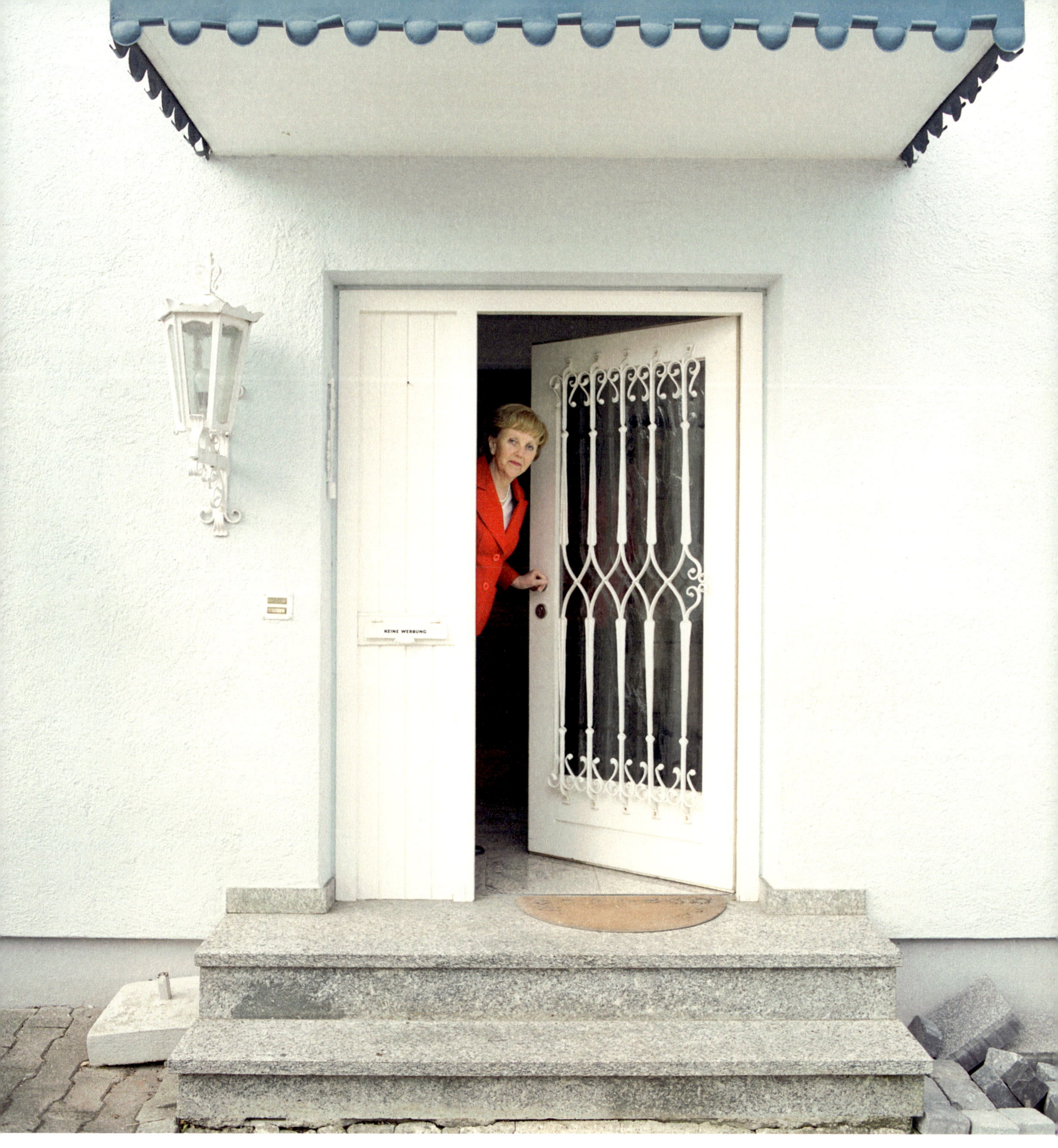
KEINE WERBUNG

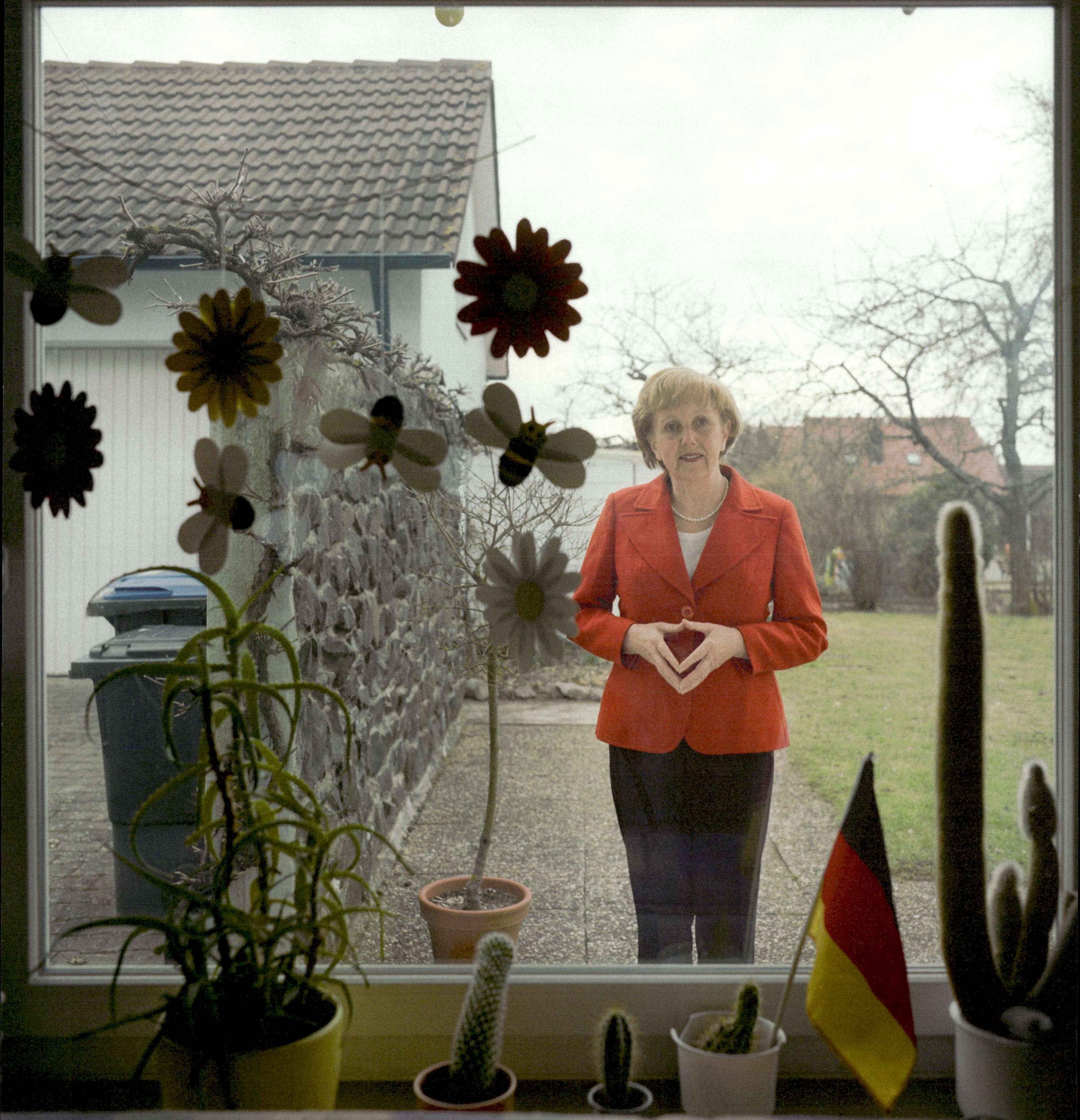

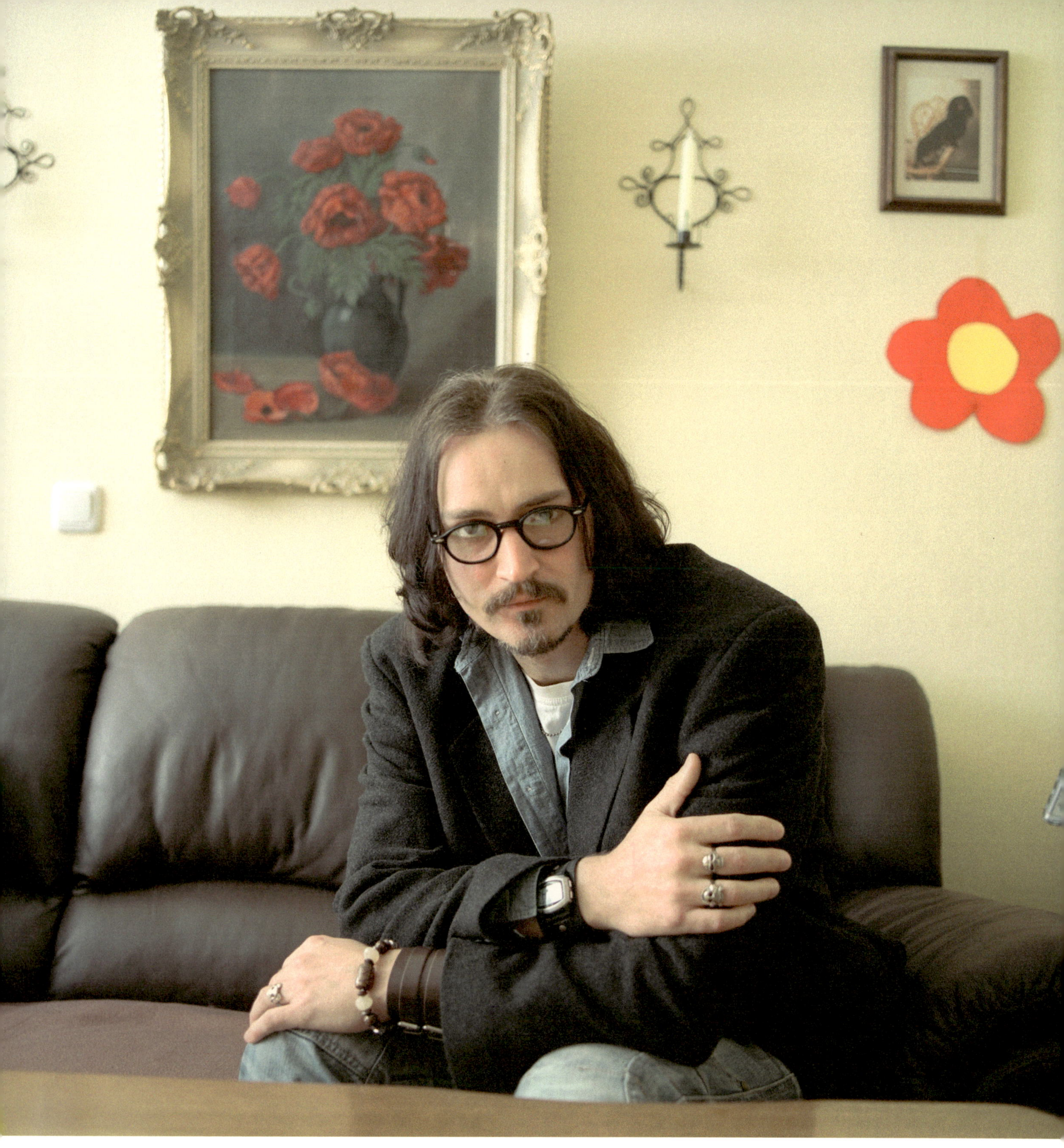

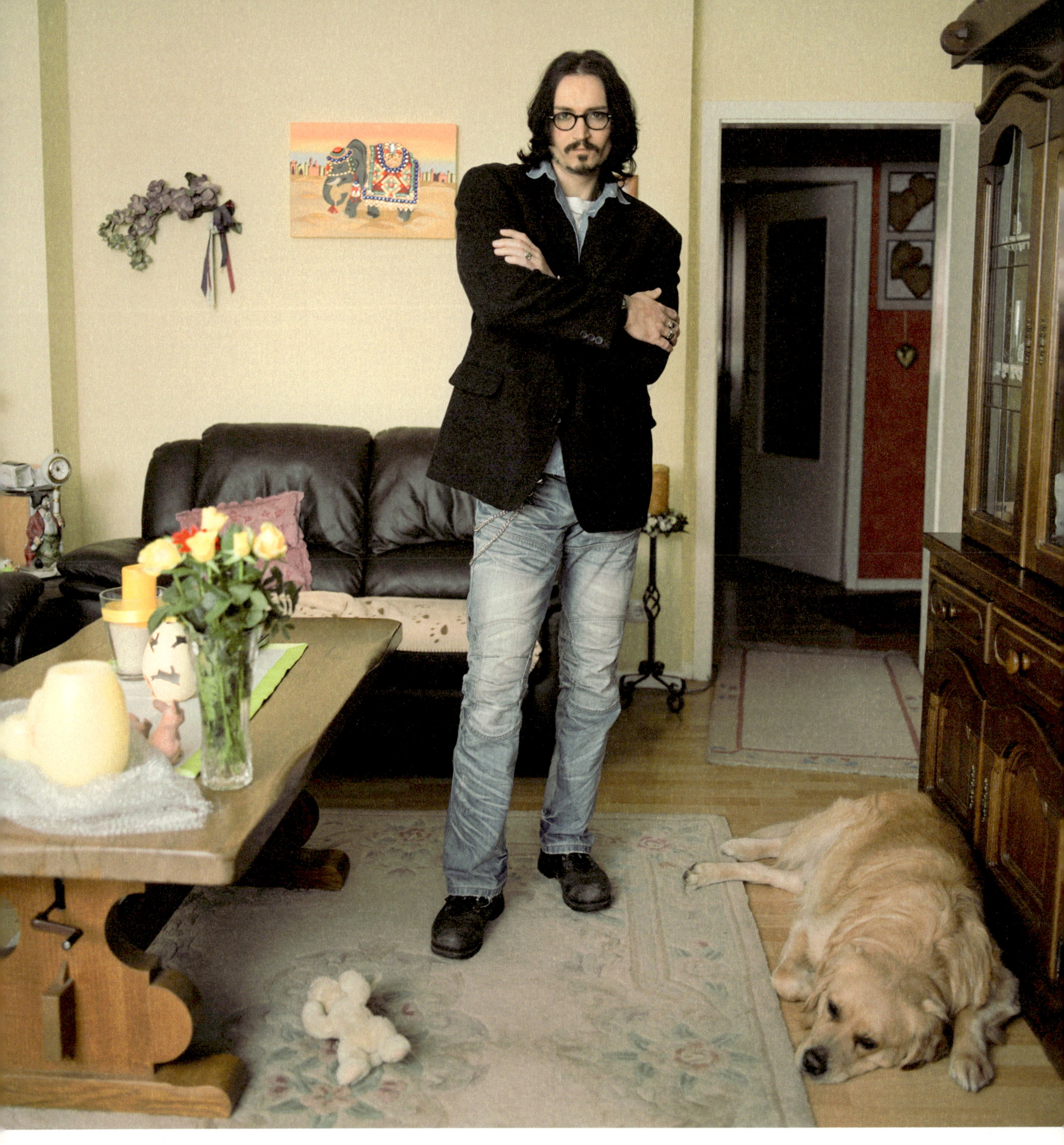

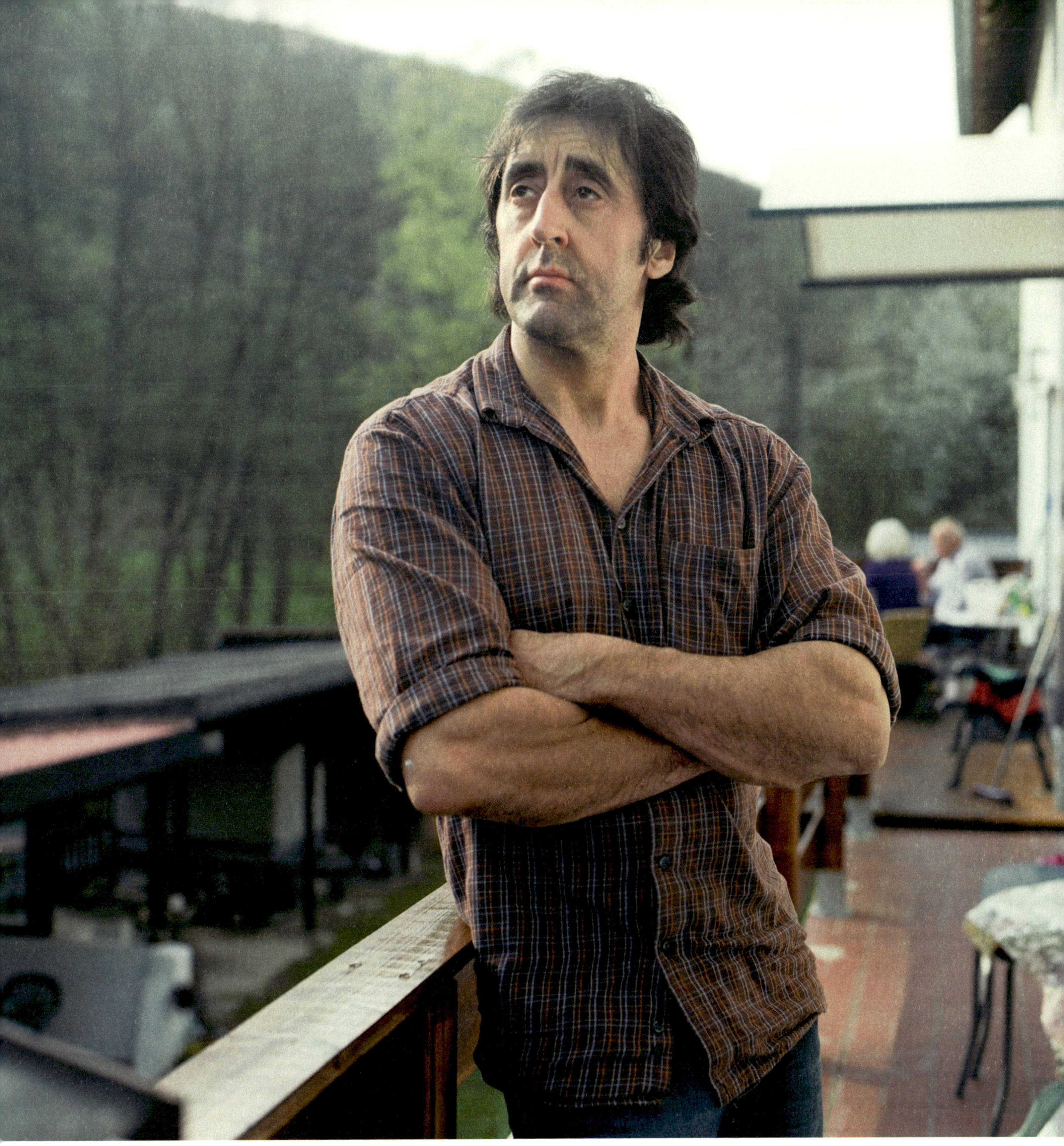

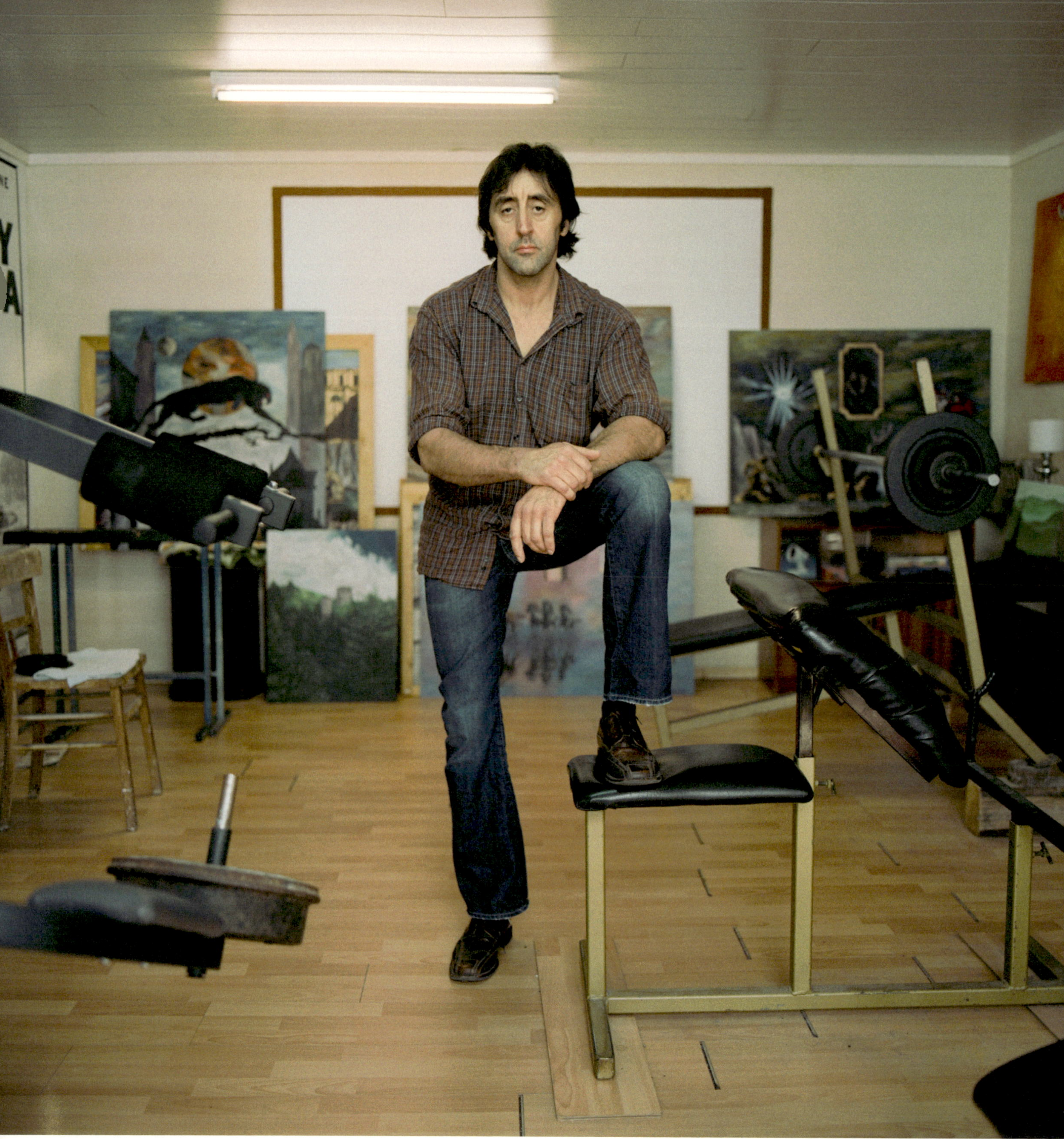

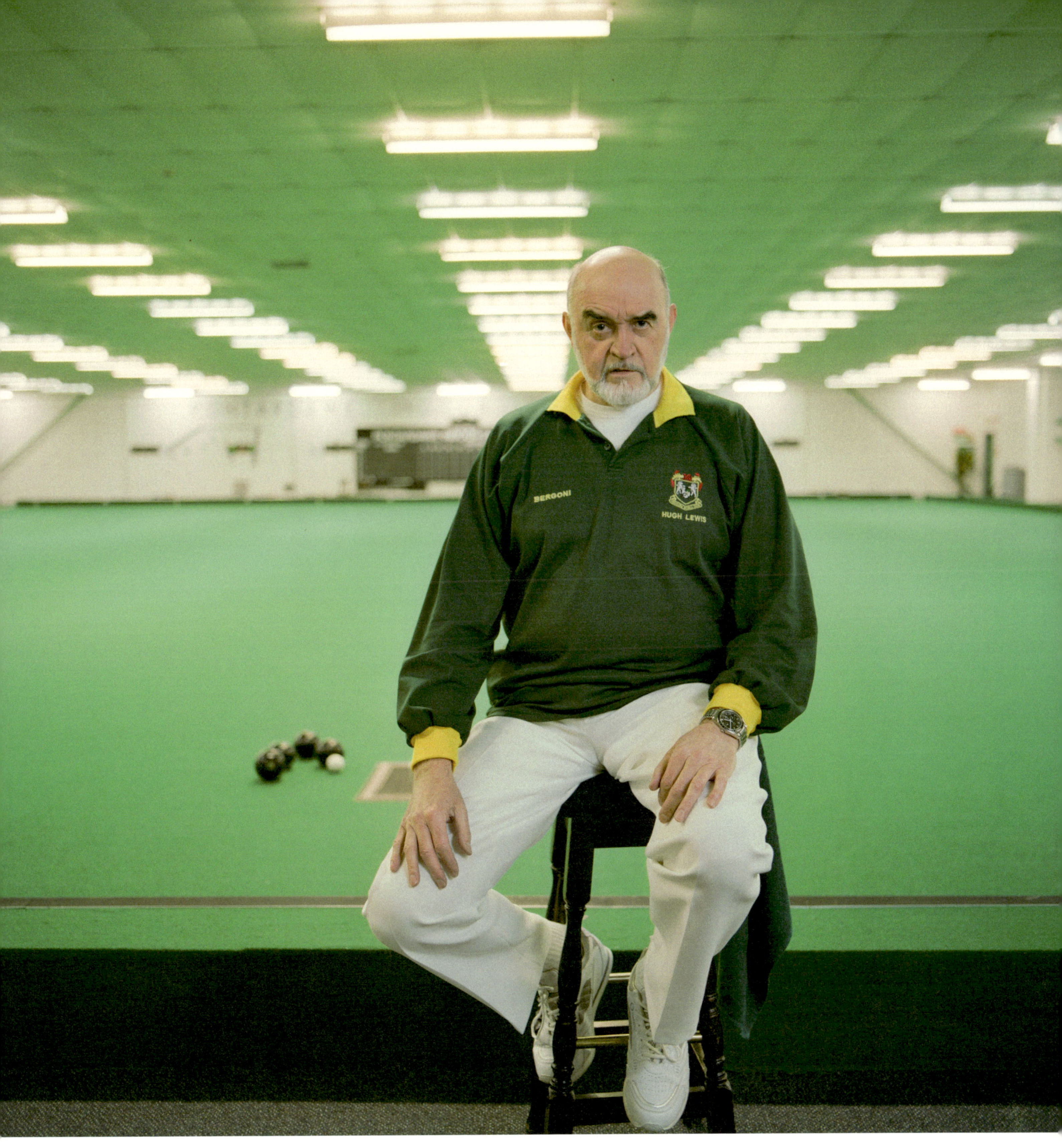

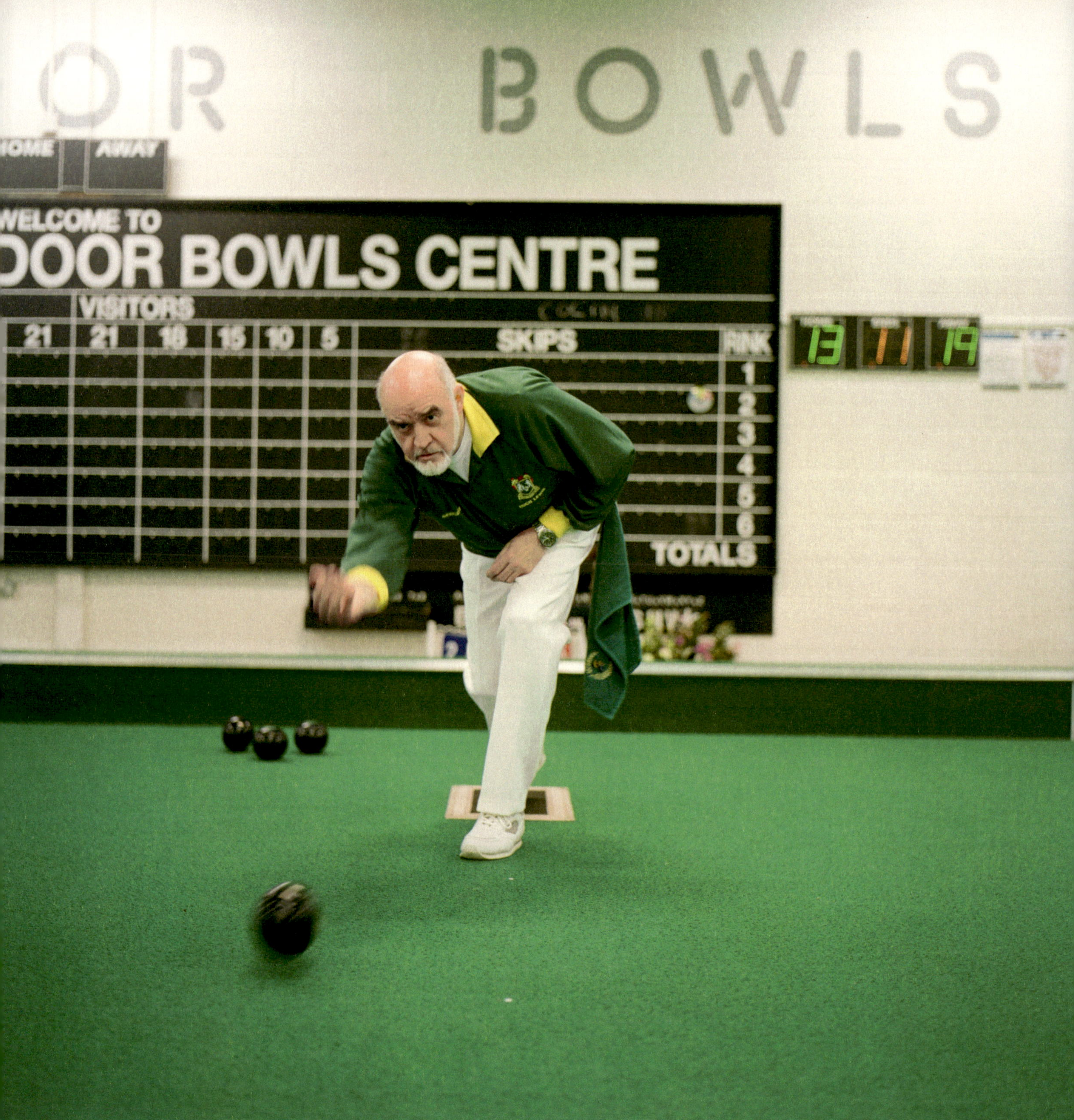
OR
BOWLS
HOME AWAY
WELCOME TO
DOOR BOWLS CENTRE
VISITORS
21 21 18 15 10 5
SKIPS
RINK
1
2
3
4
5
6
TOTALS
13 11 19

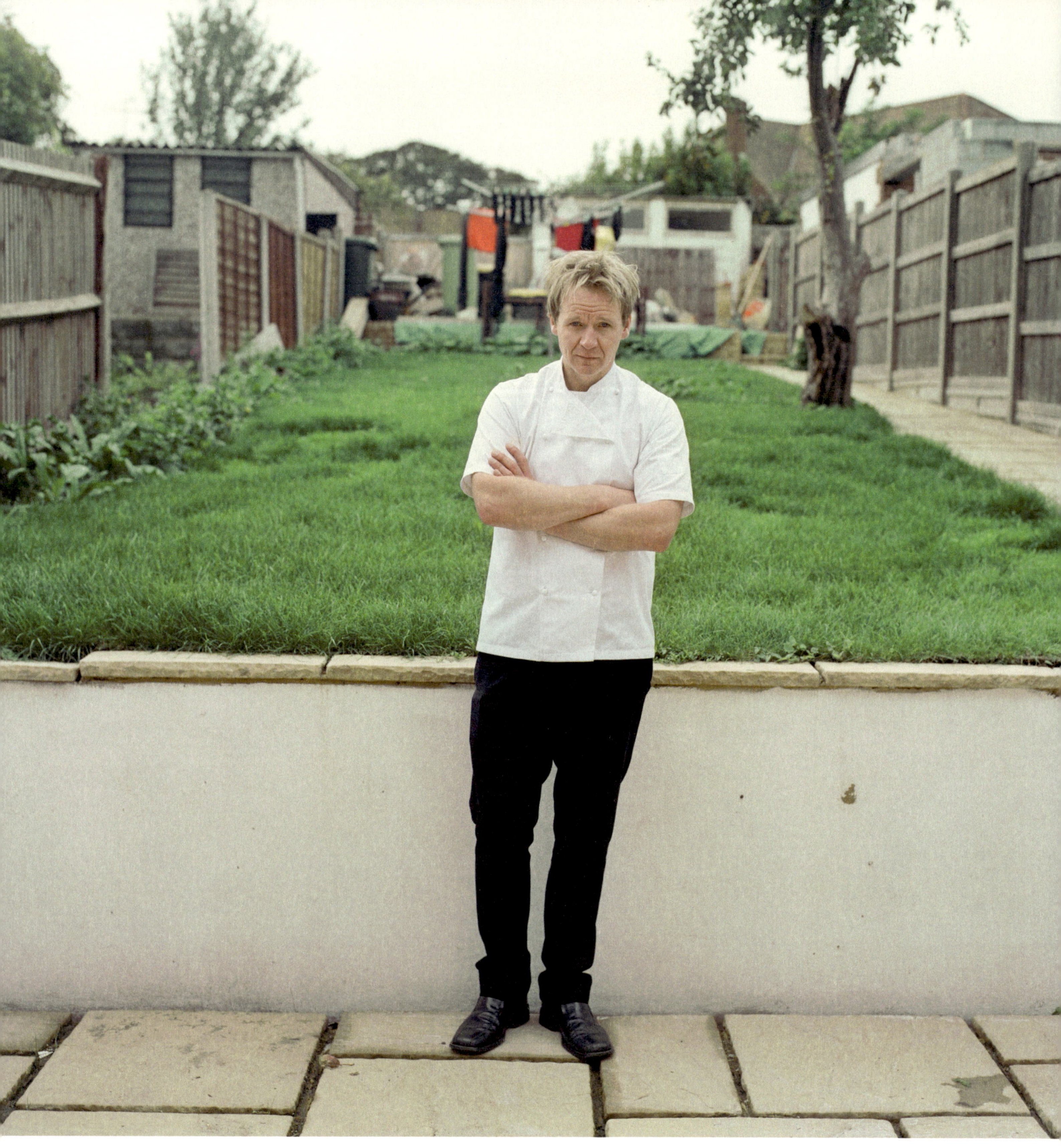

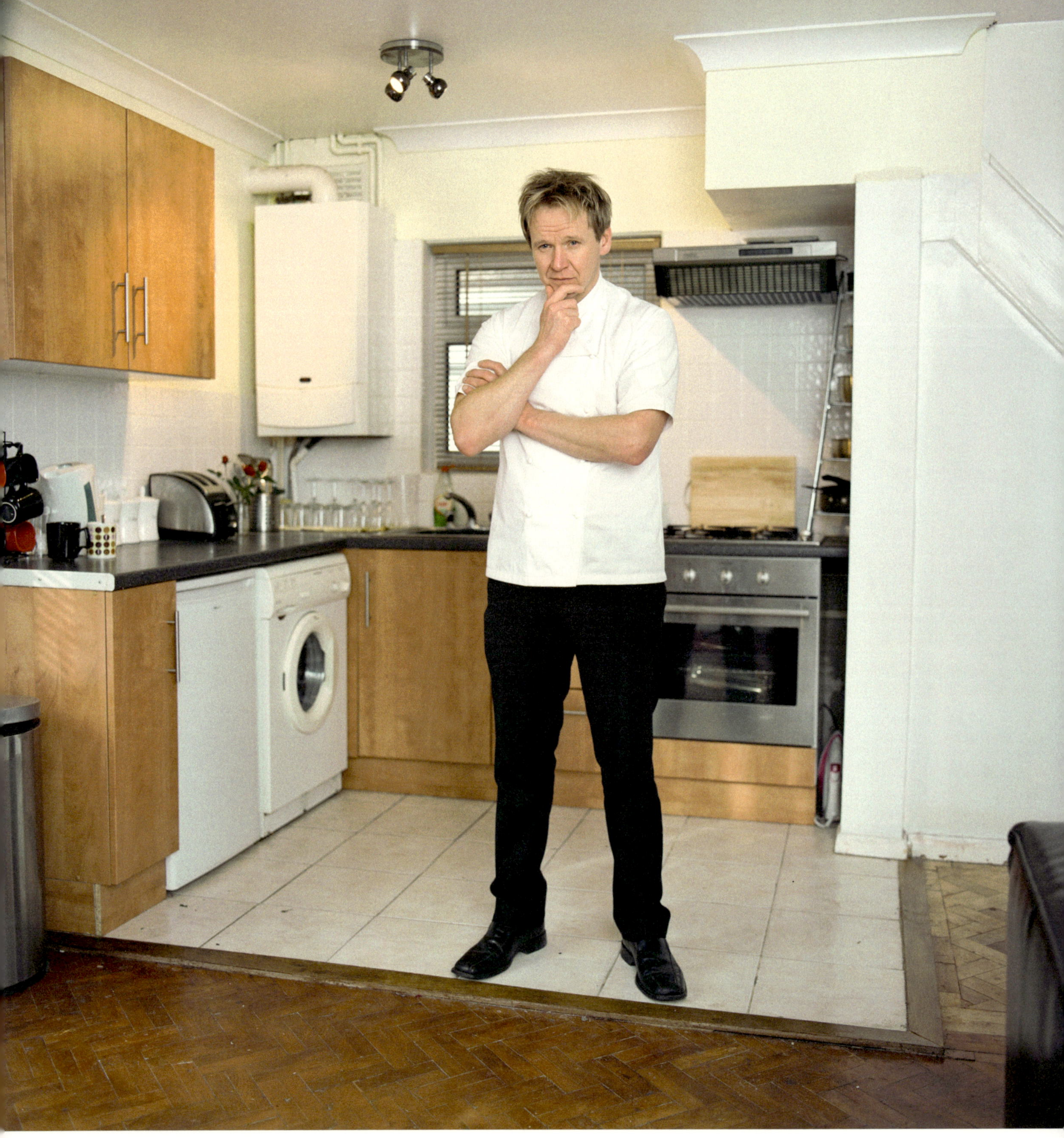

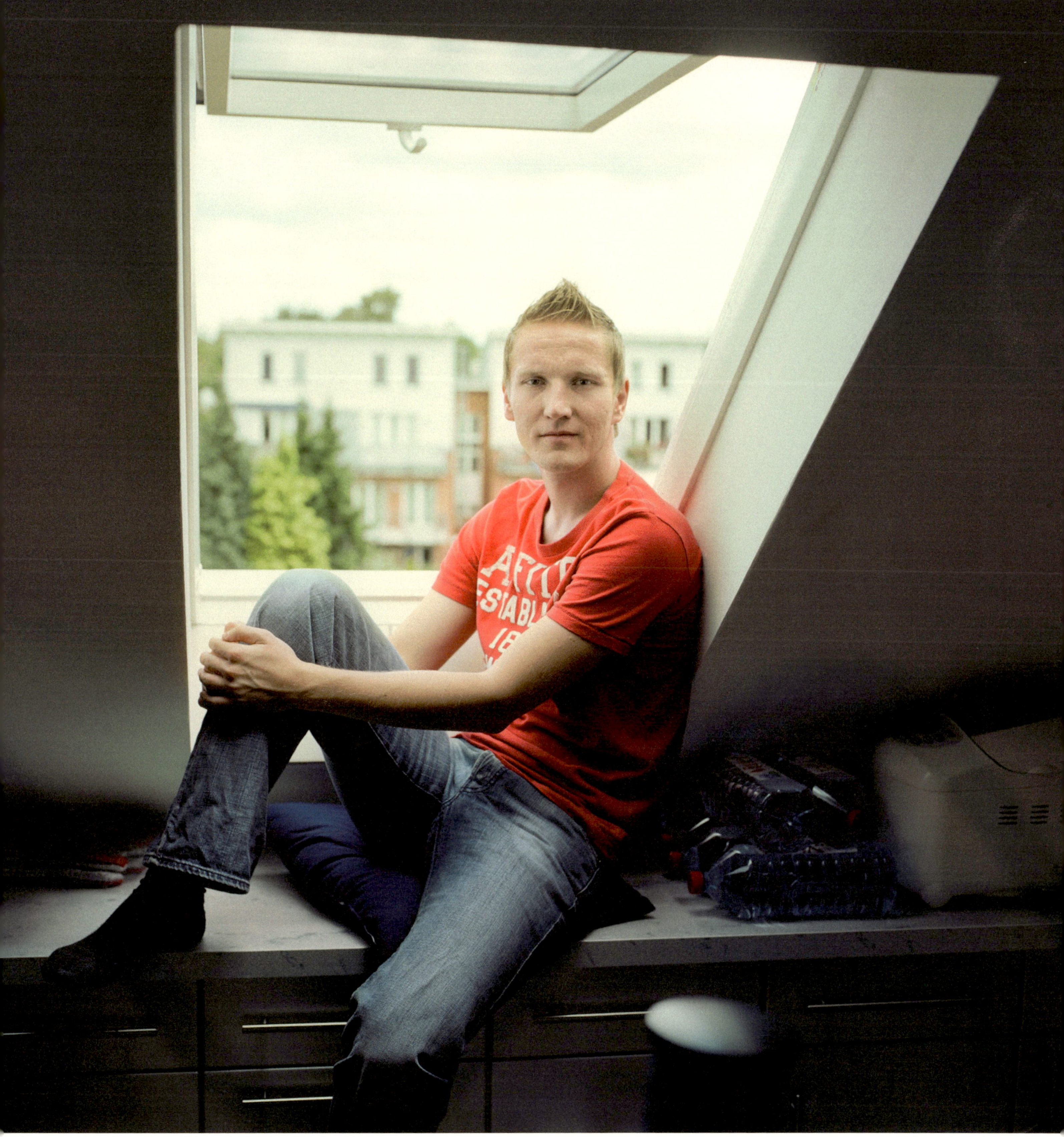

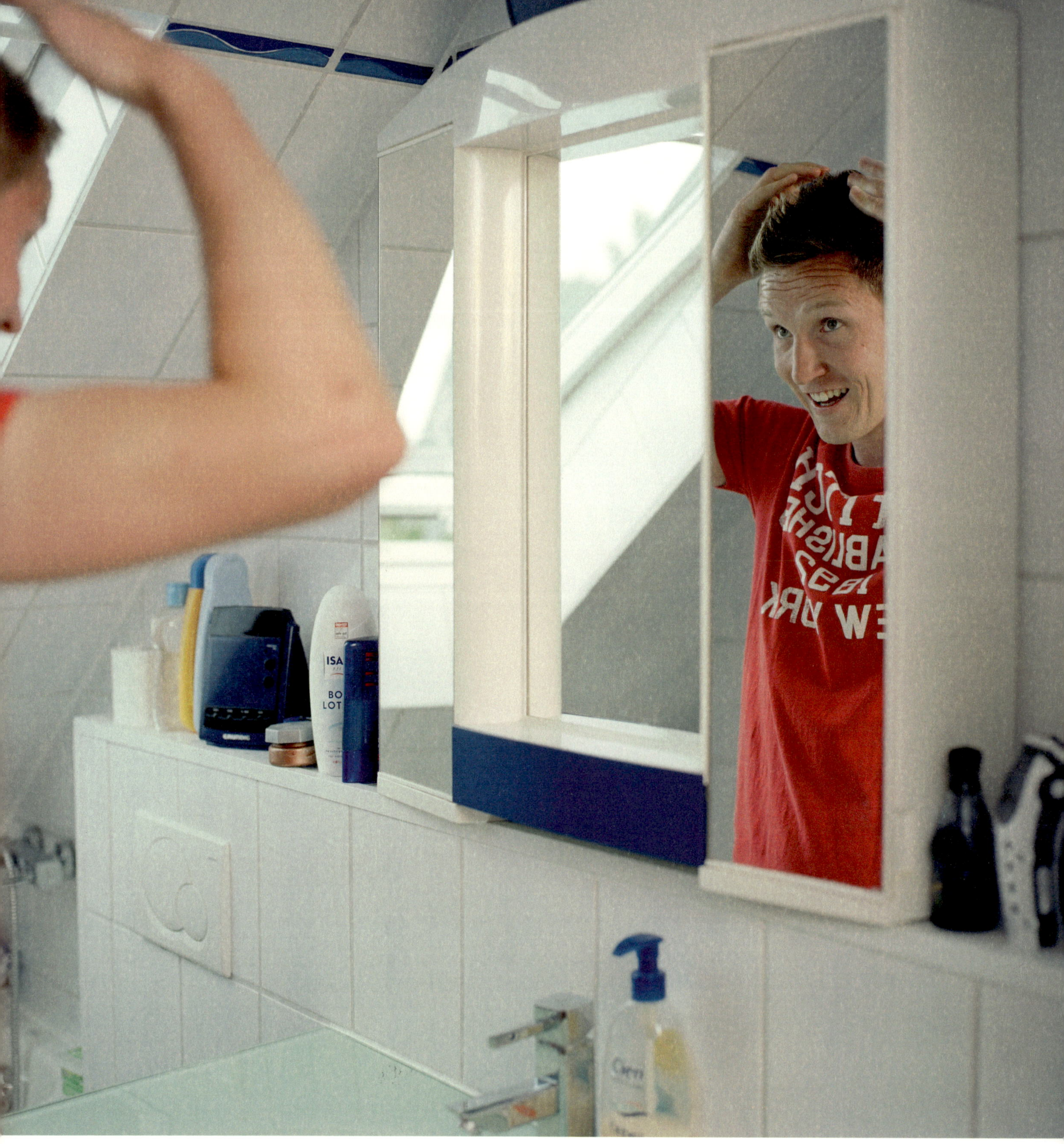

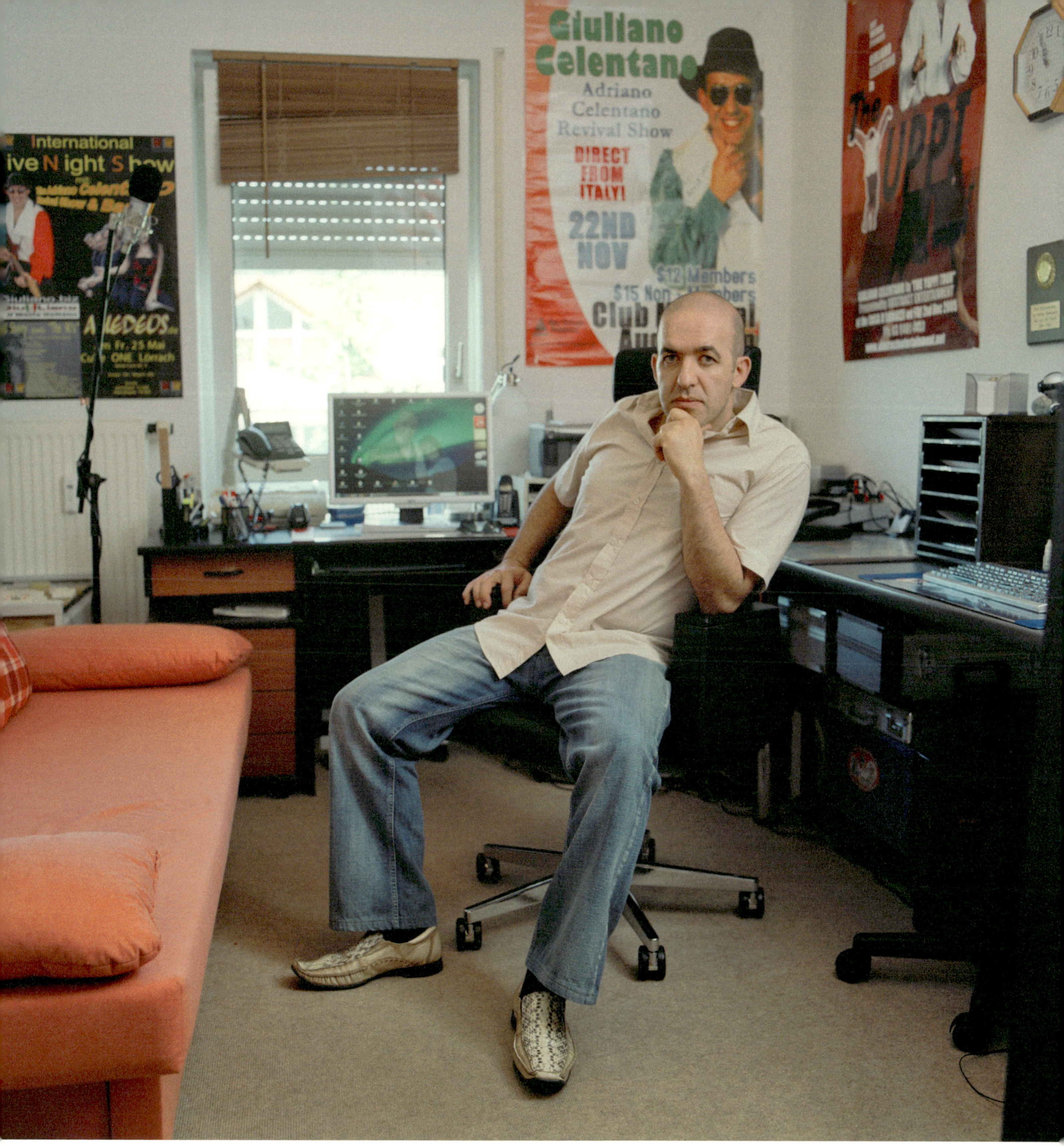

International
ive Night Show
Giuliano Celentano
Adriano
Celentano
Revival Show
DIRECT
FROM
ITALY!
22ND
NOV
$12 Members
$15 Non - Members
Club

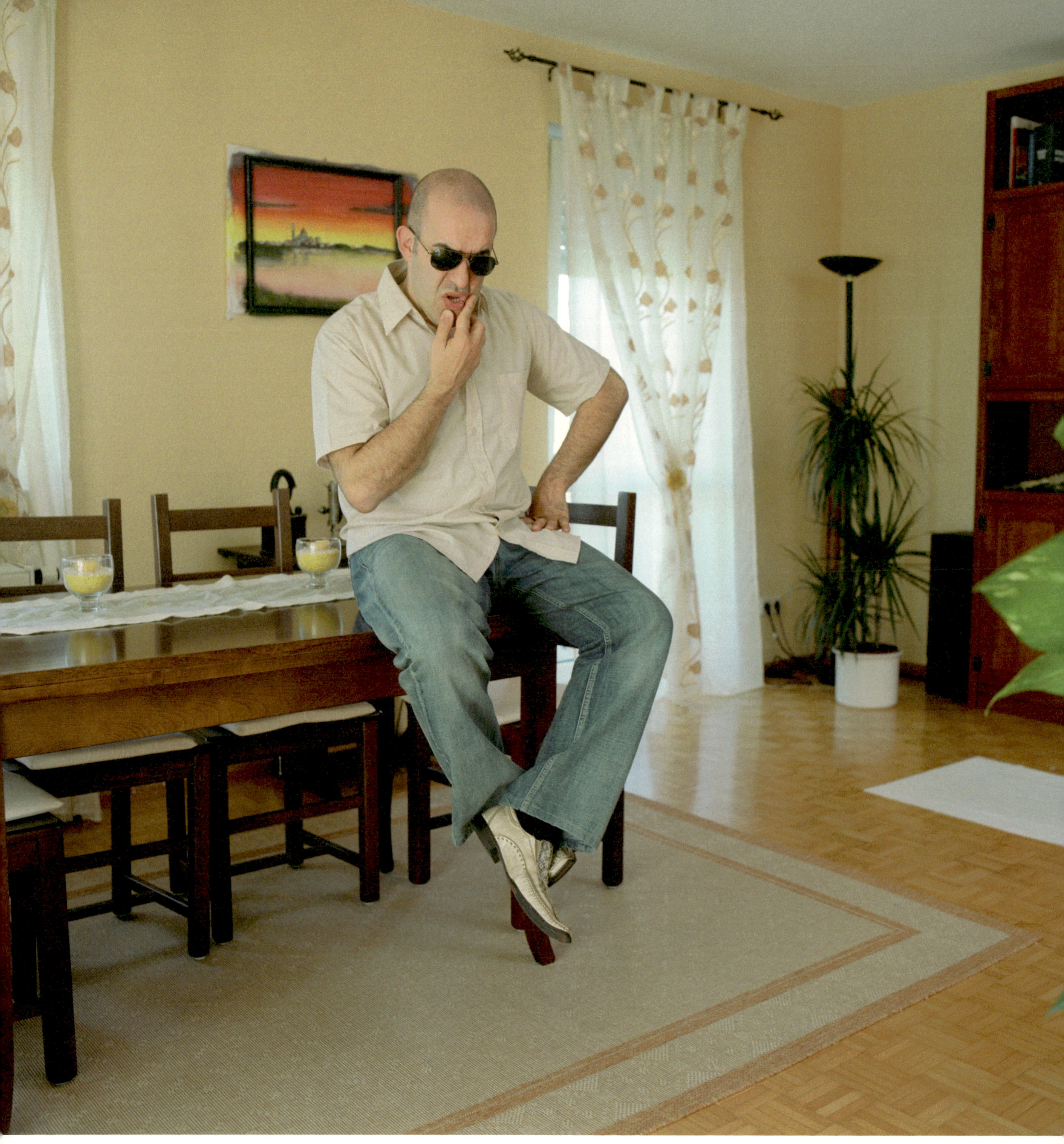

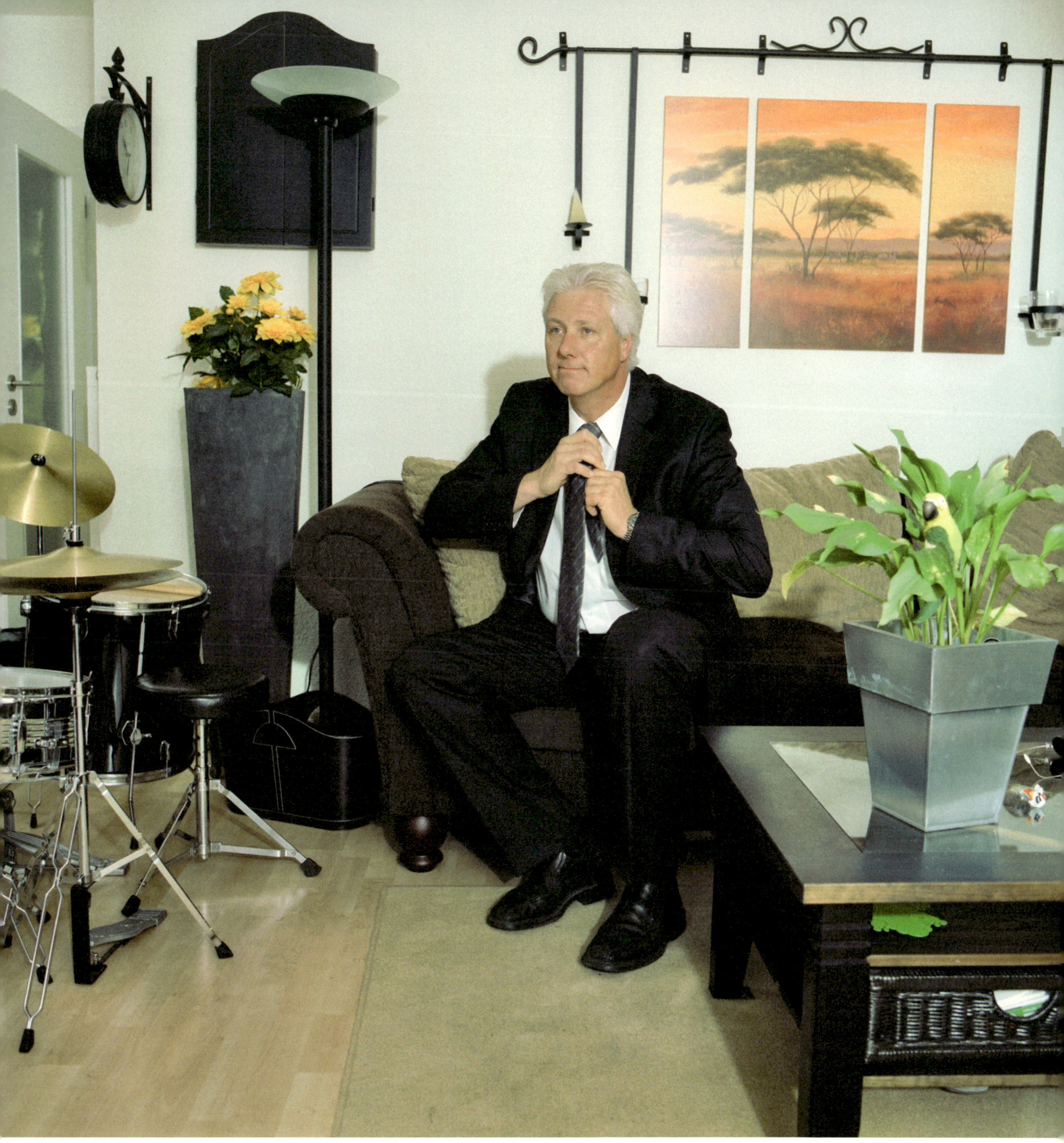

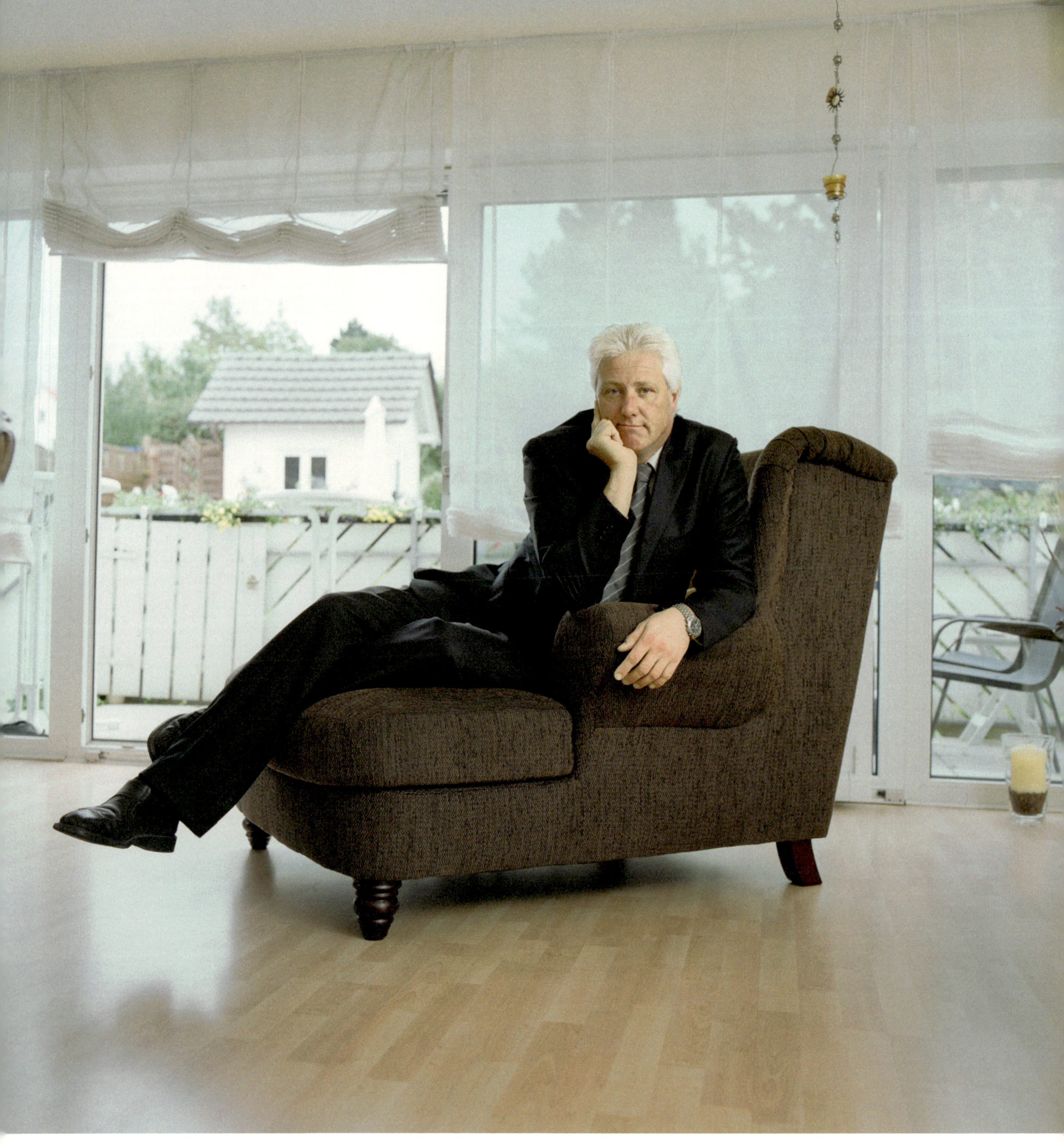

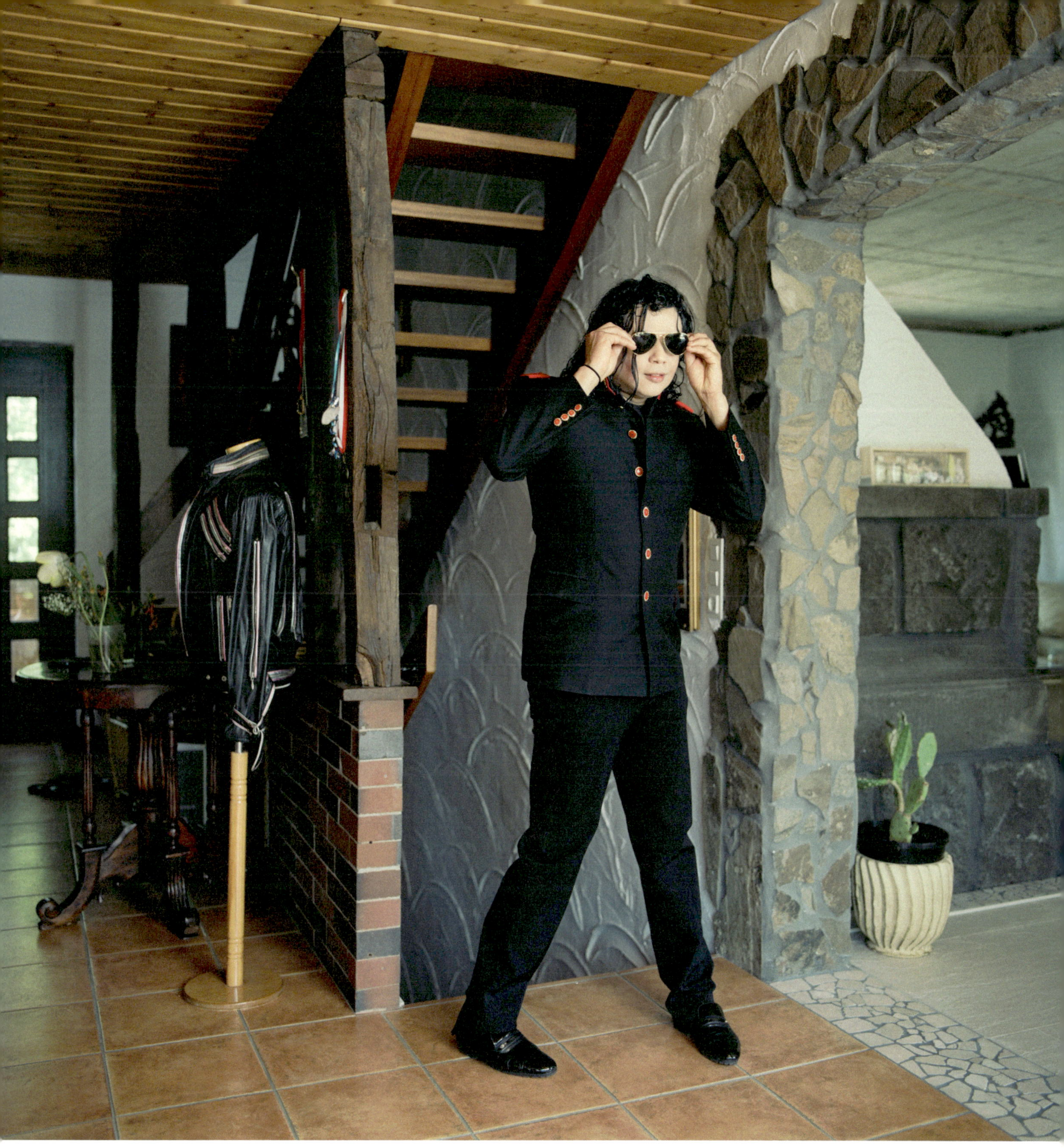

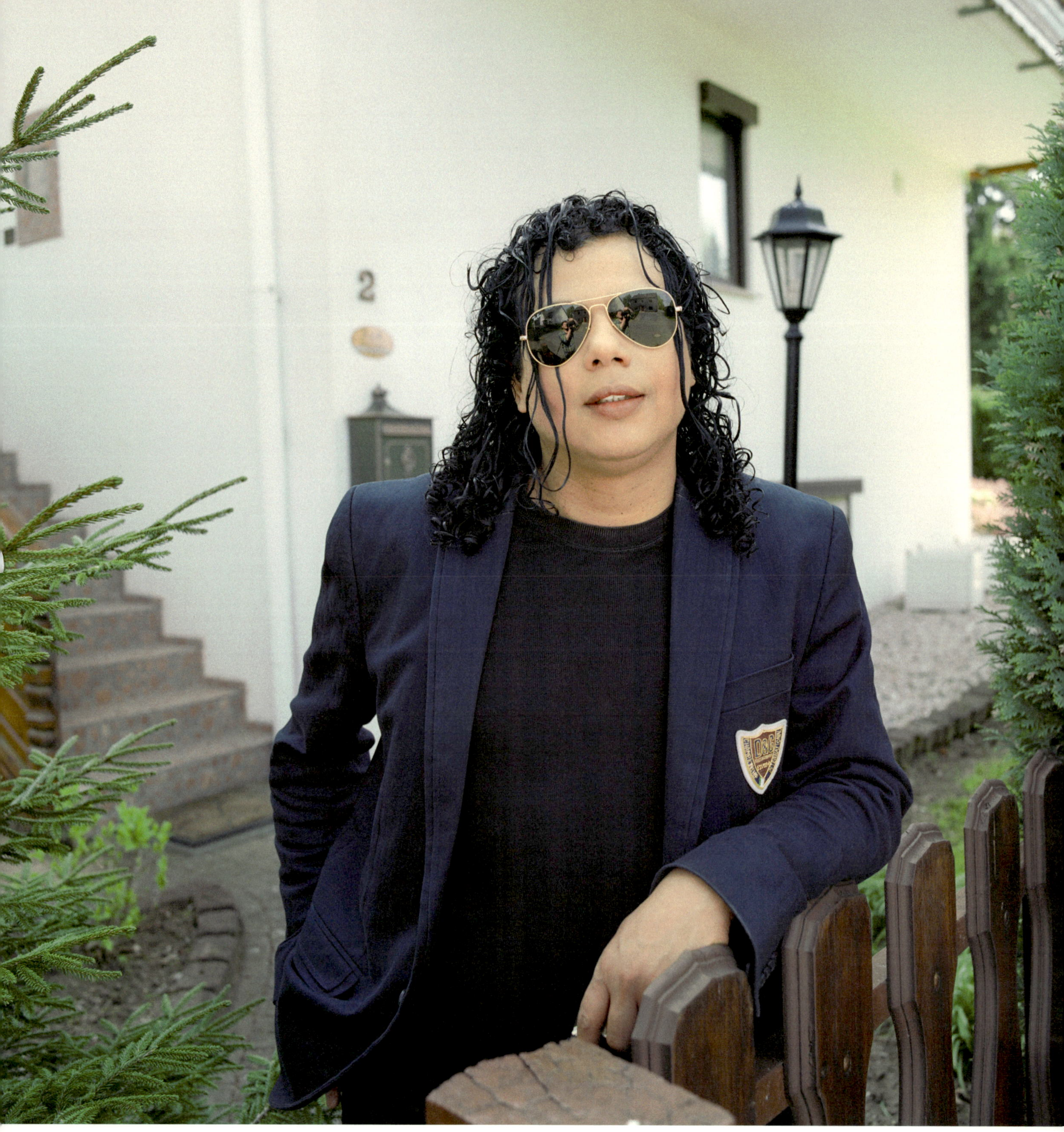

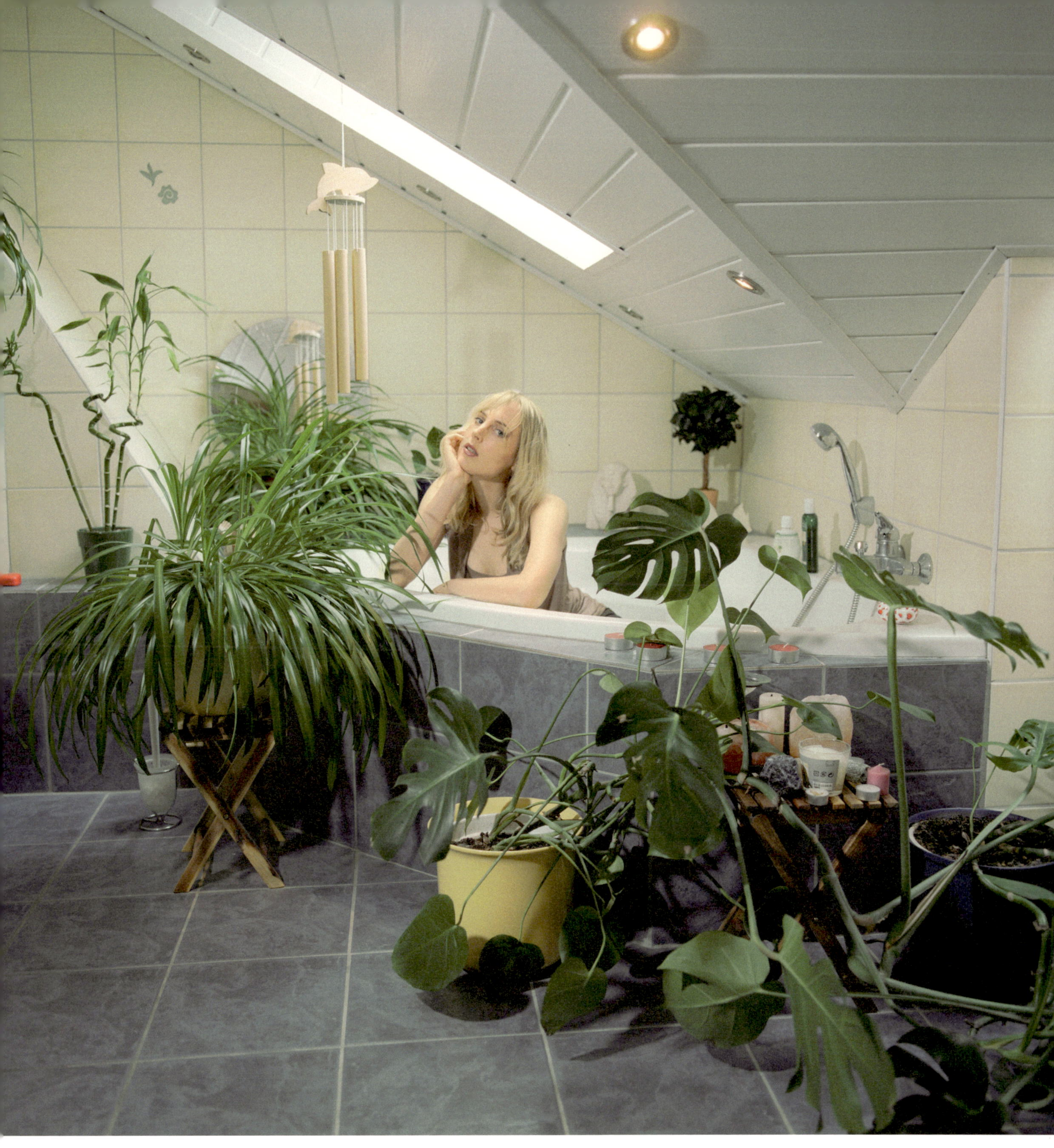

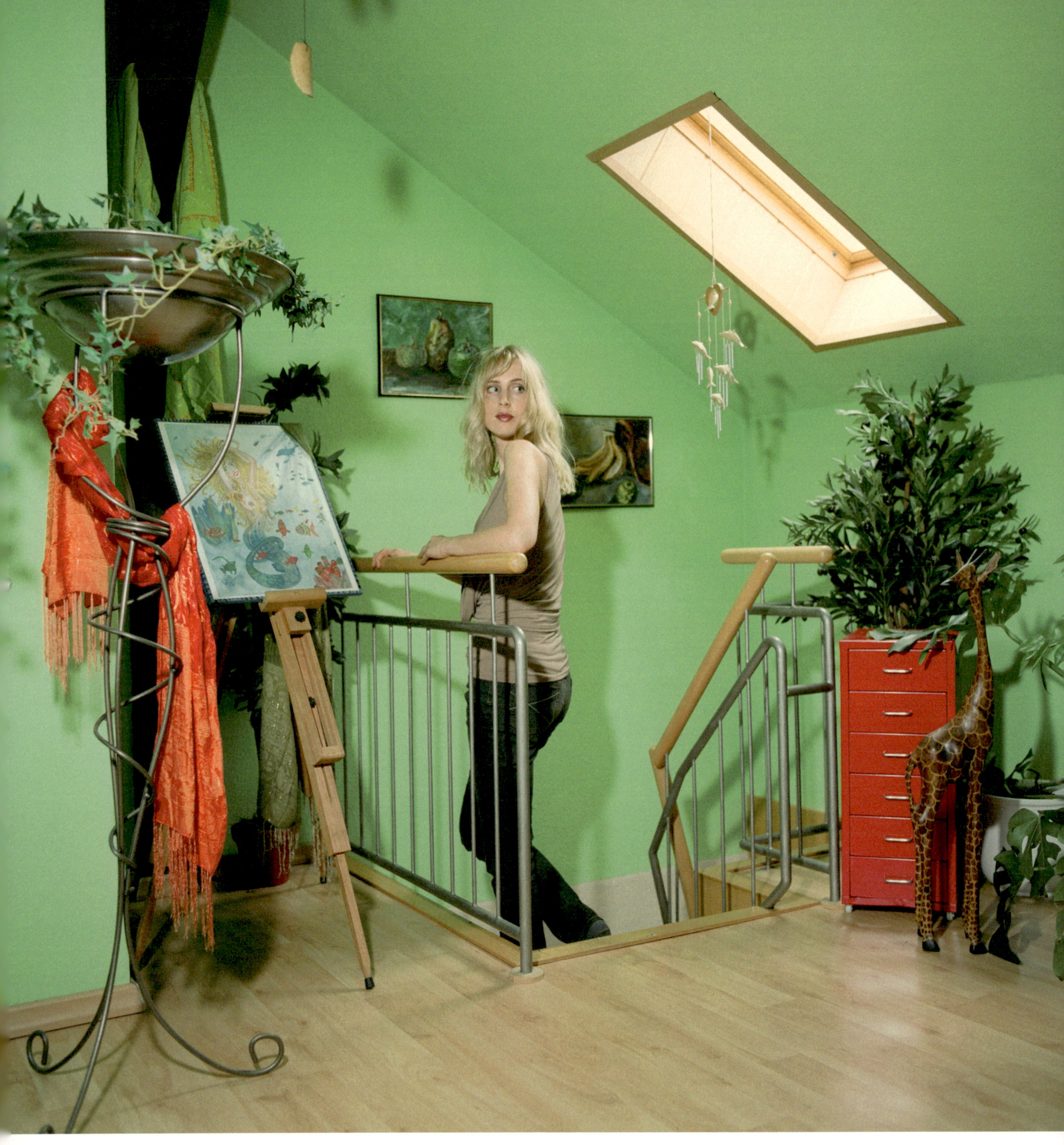

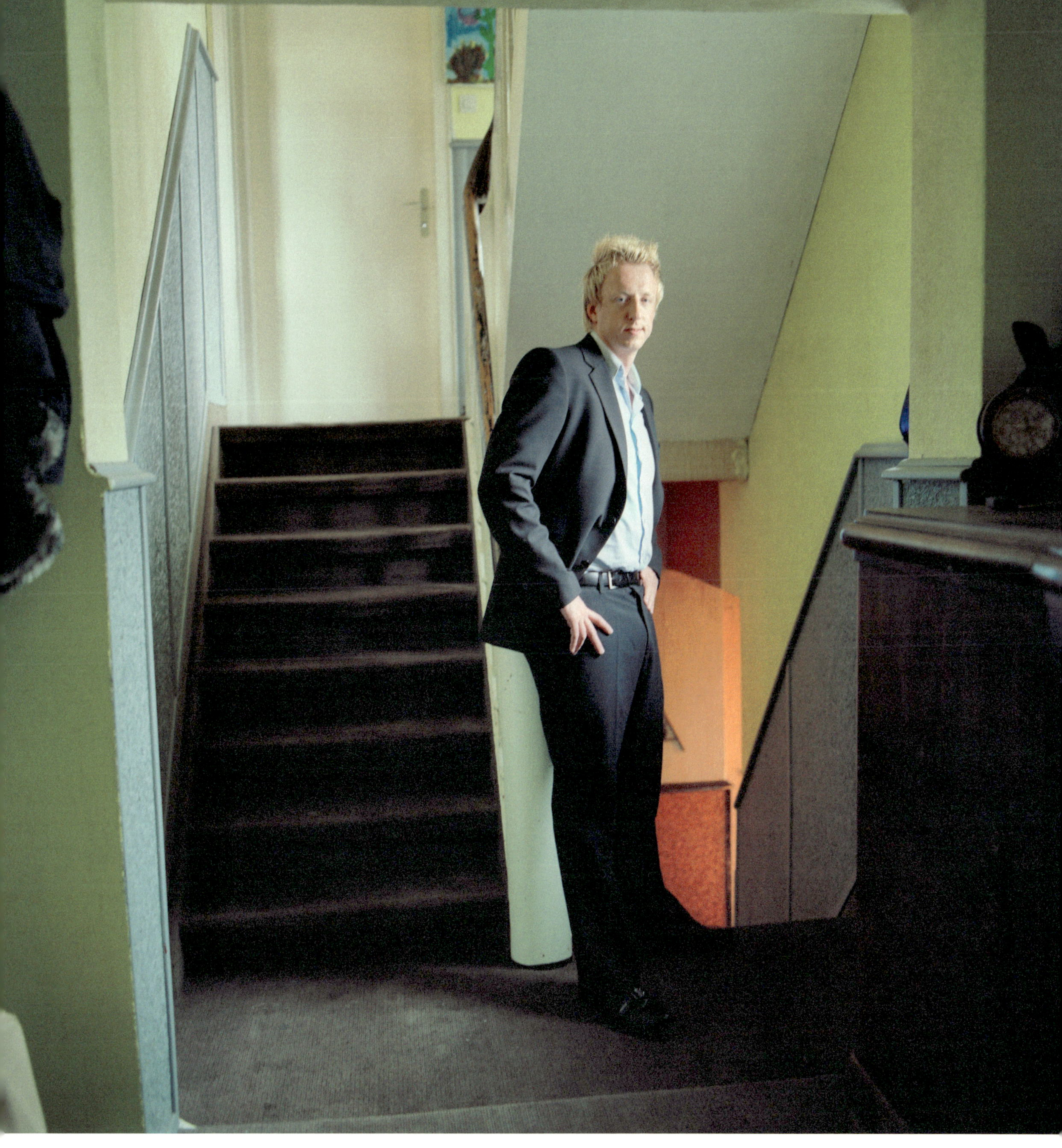

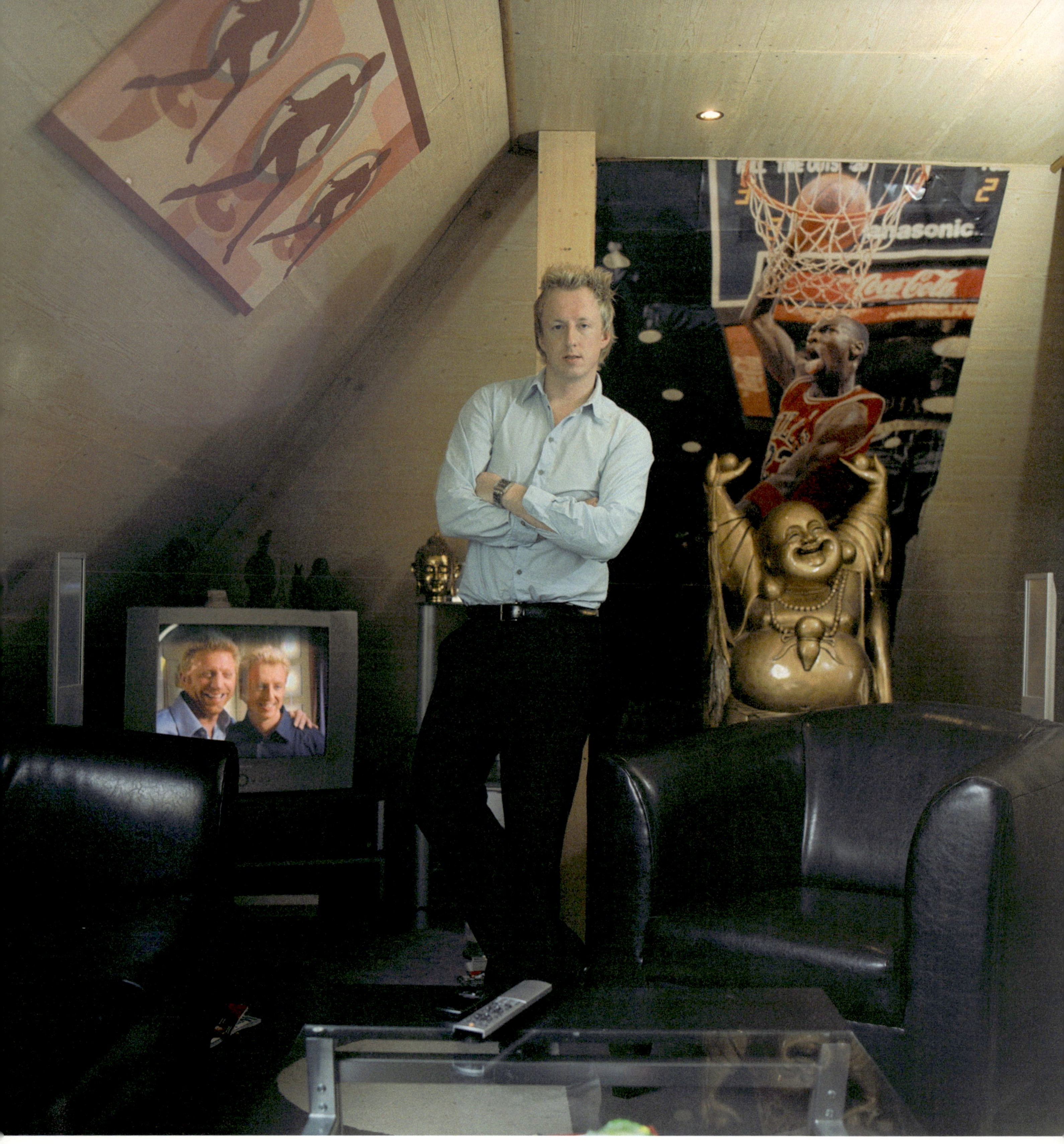

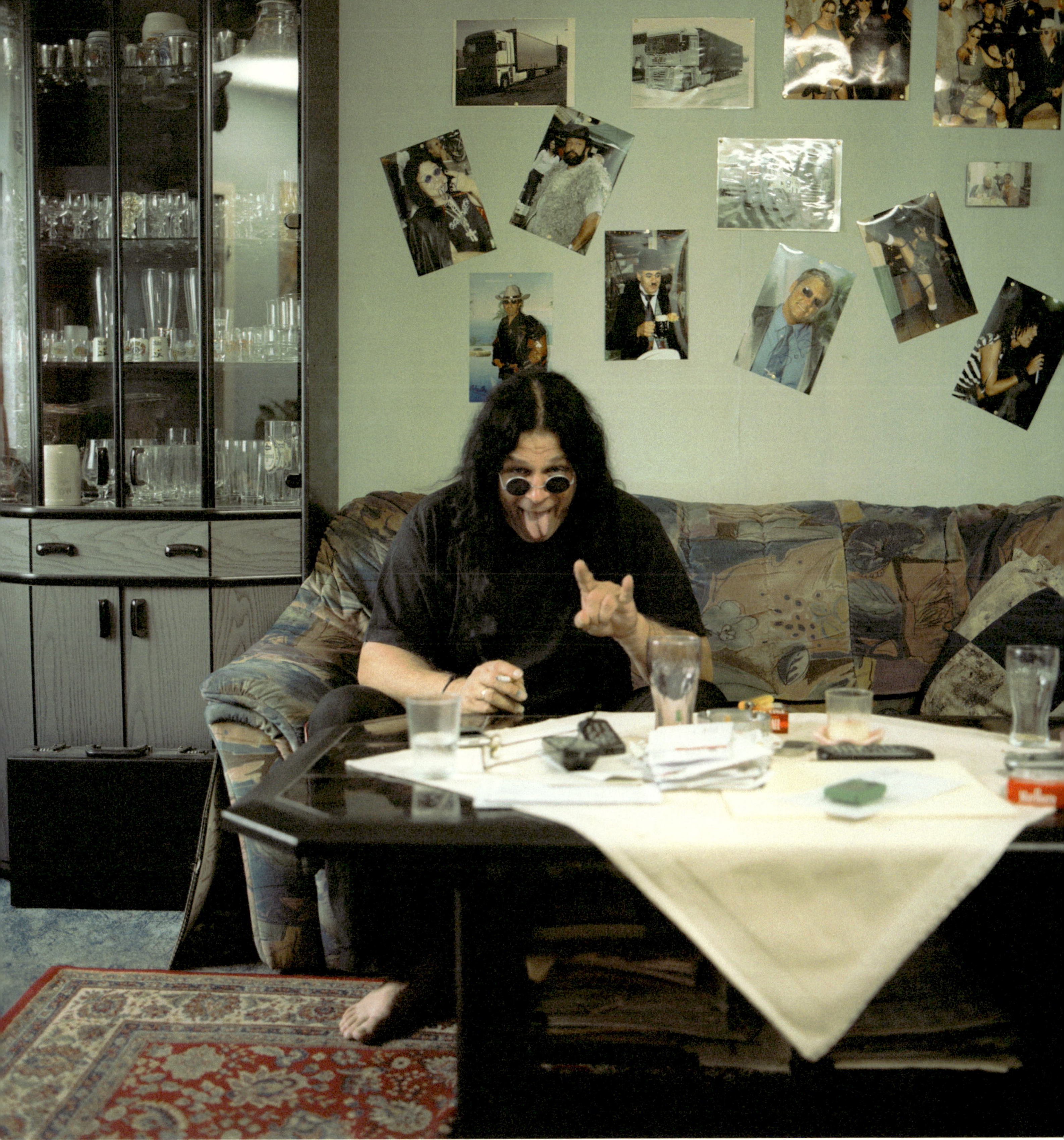

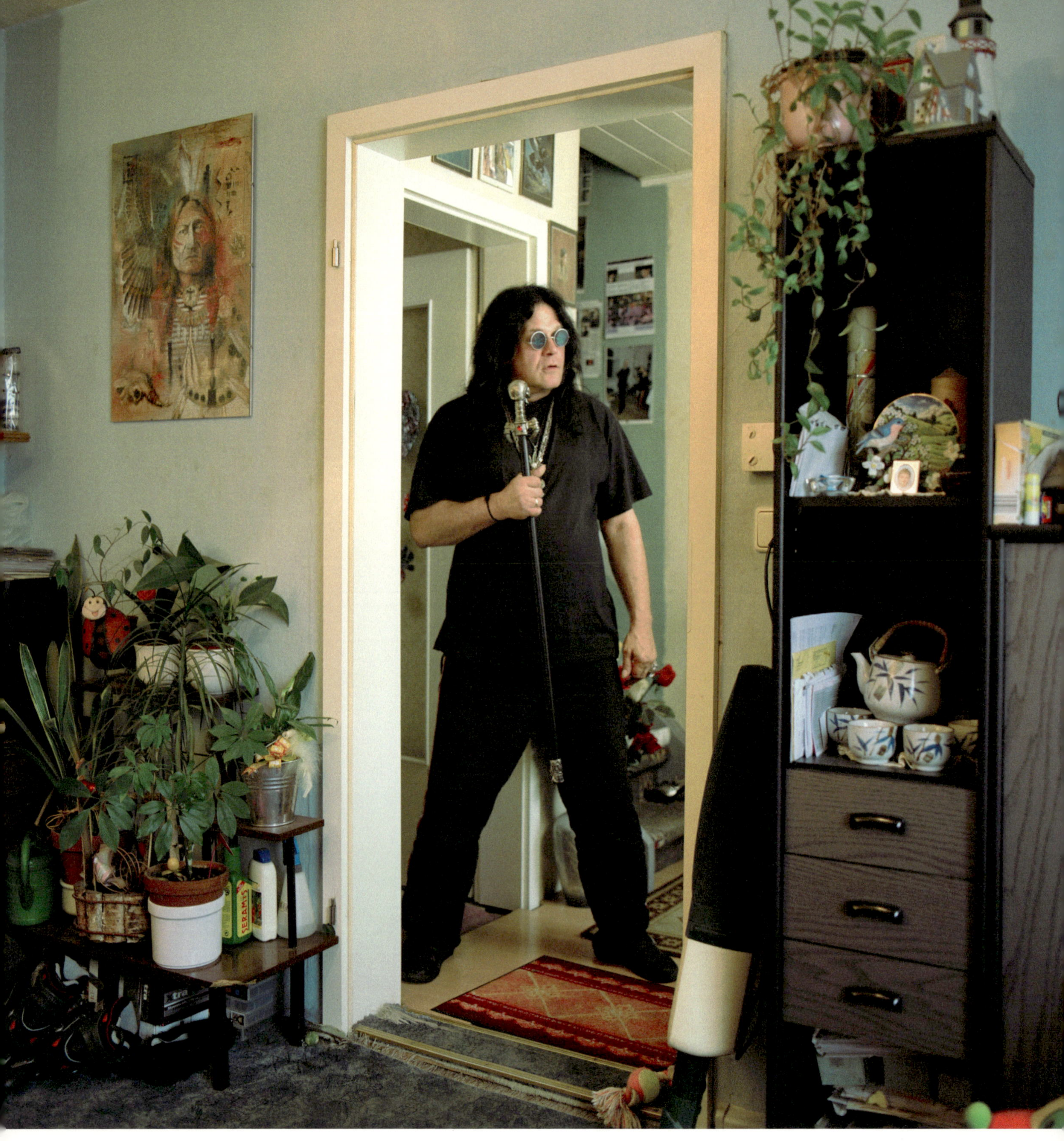

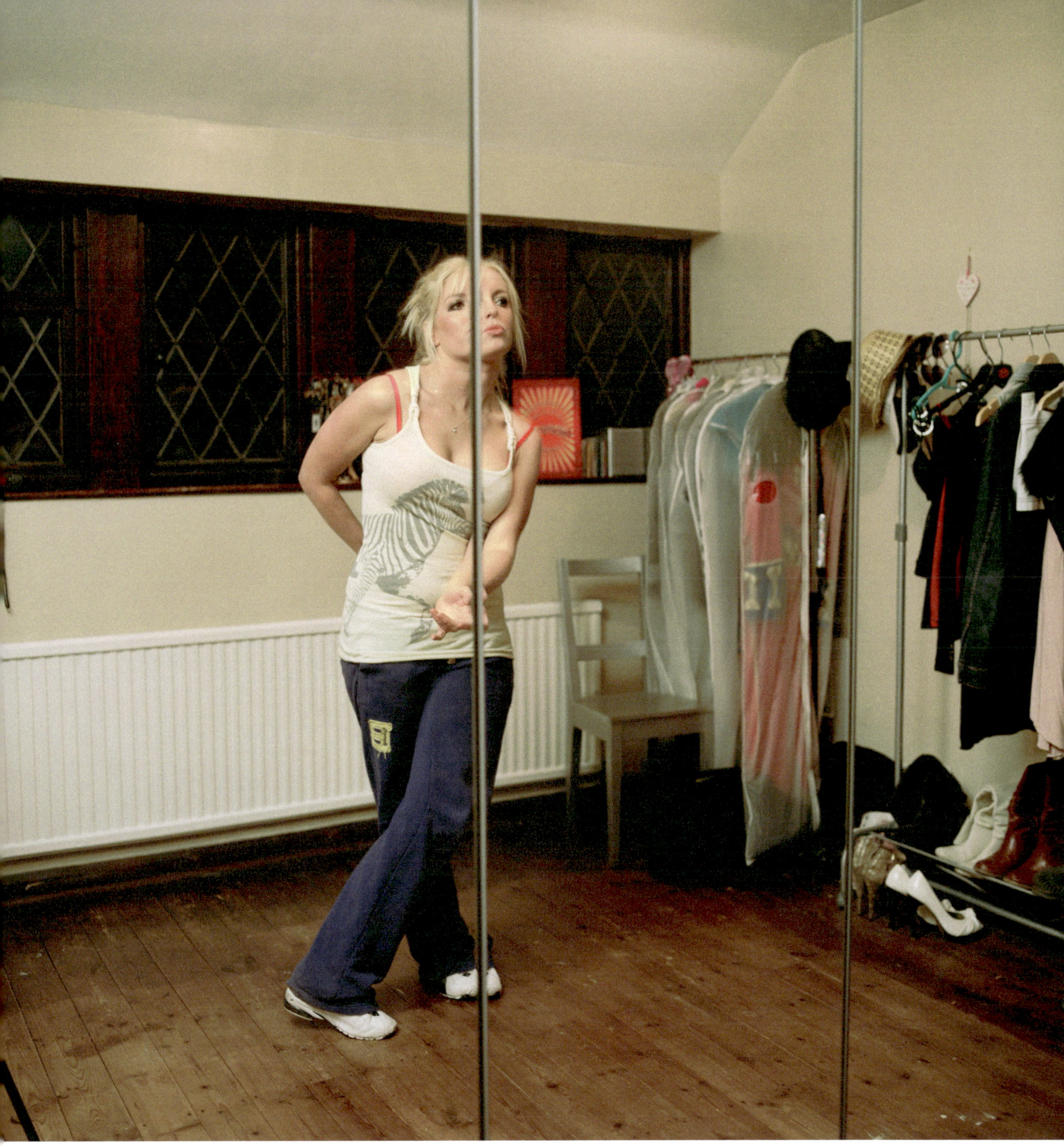

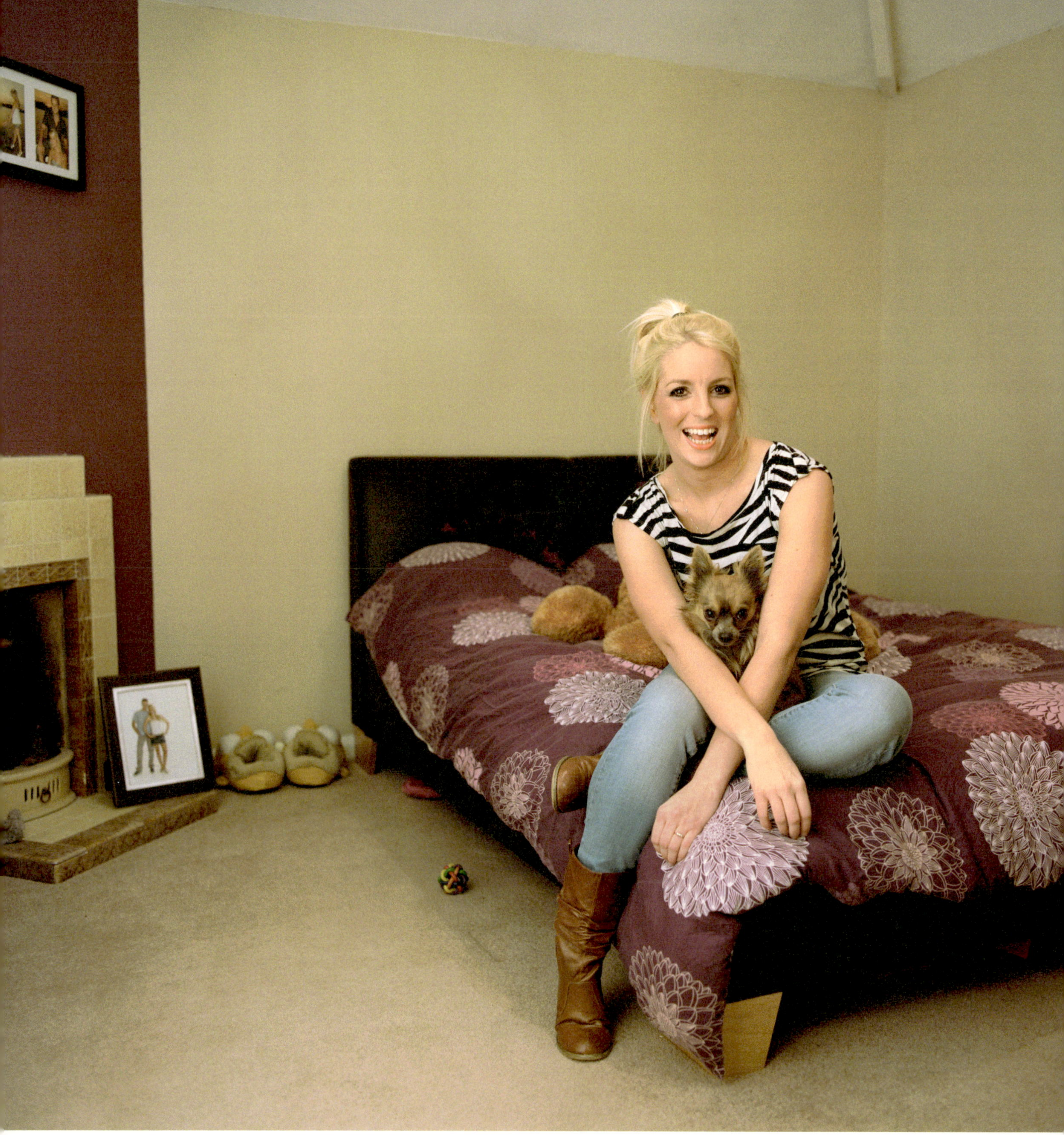

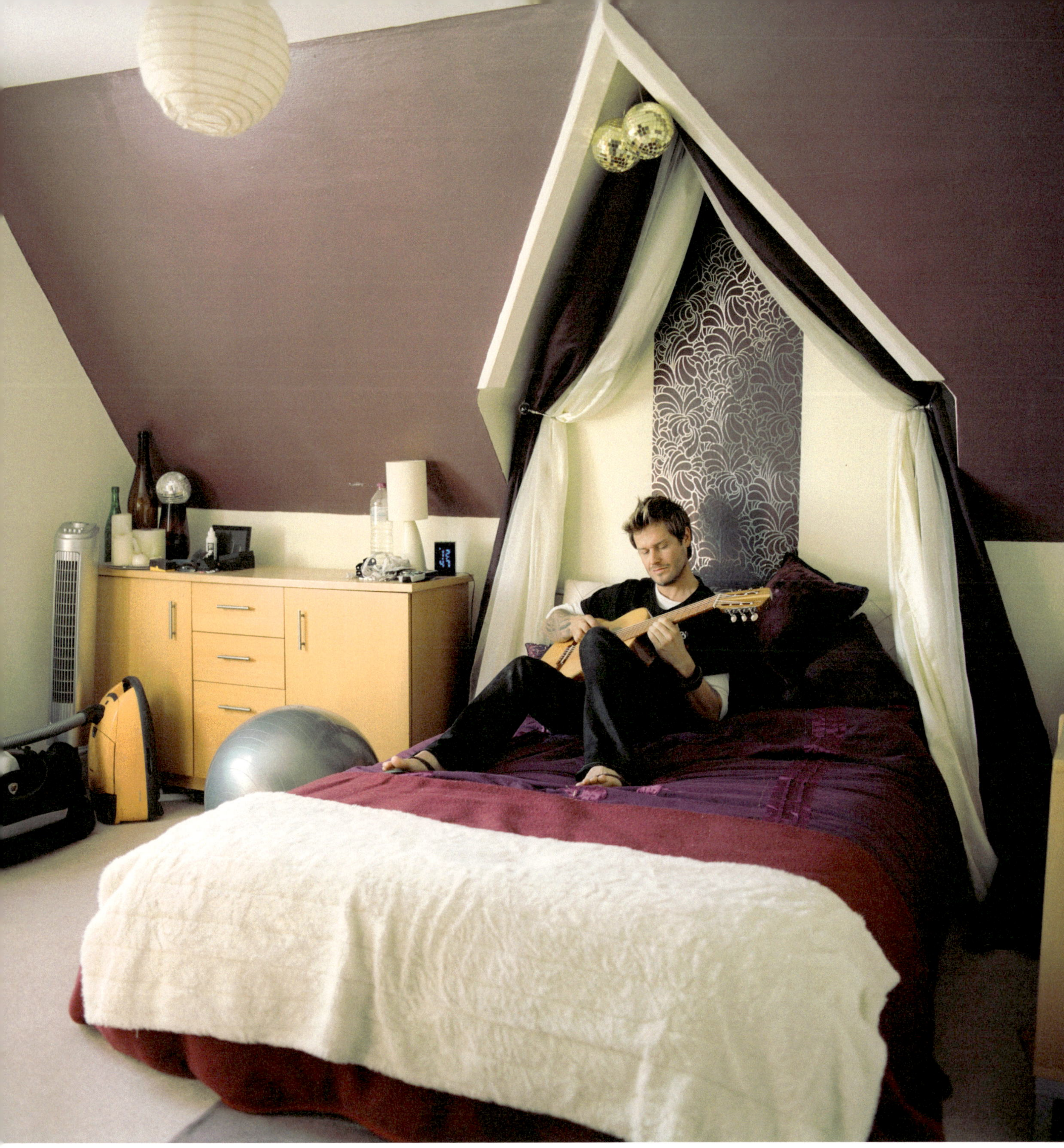

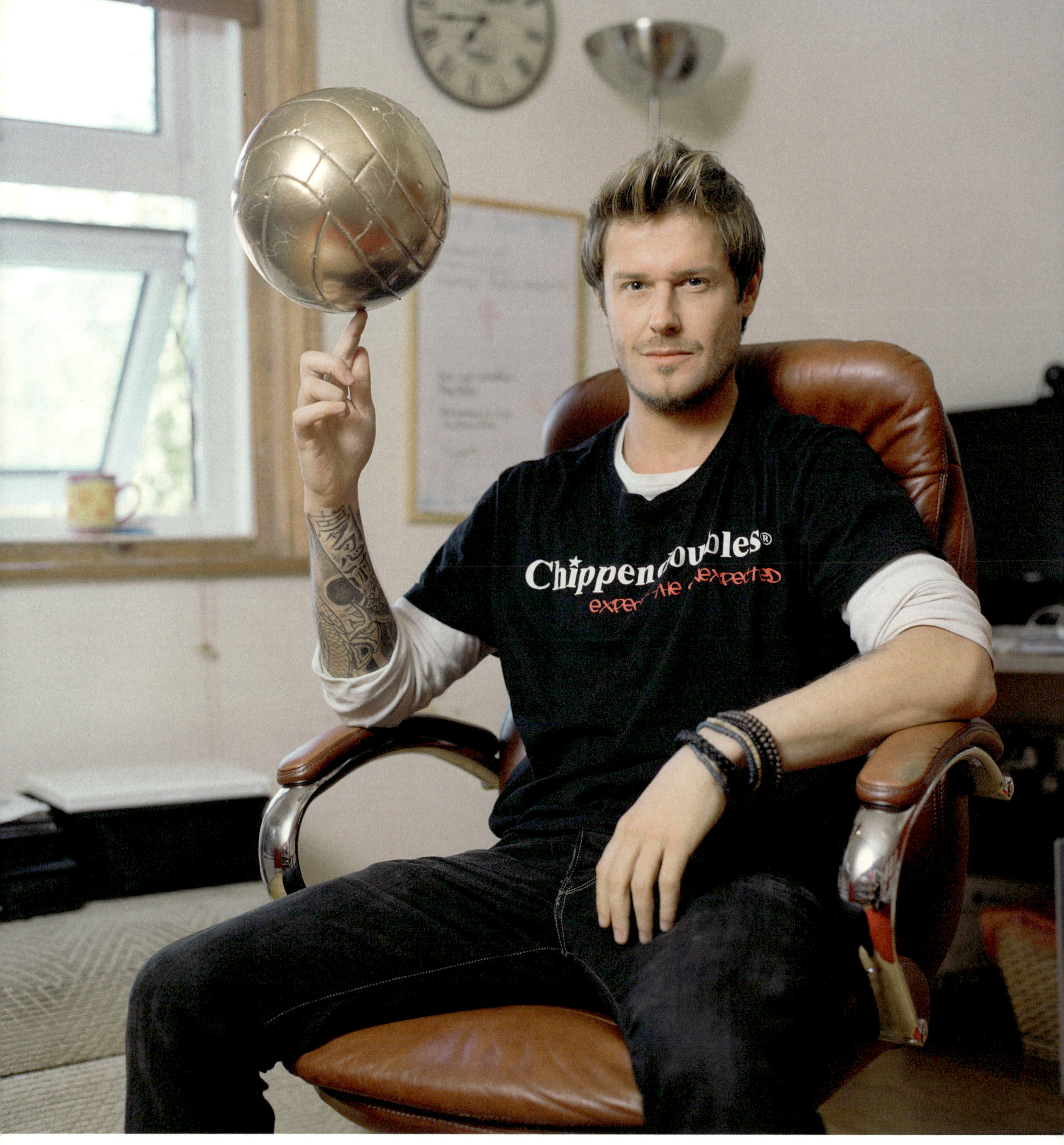

Chippendoubles®
expect the unexpected

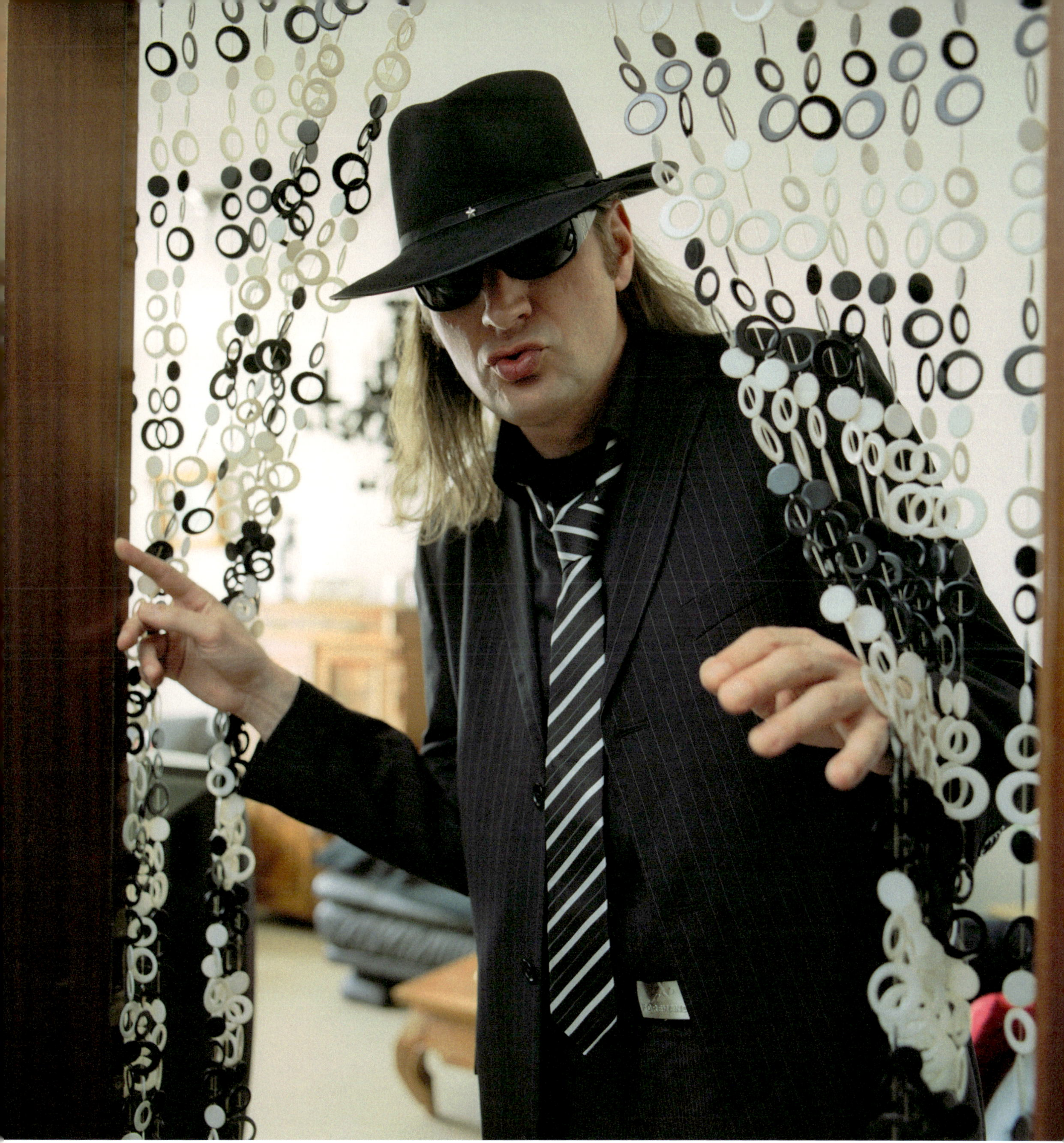

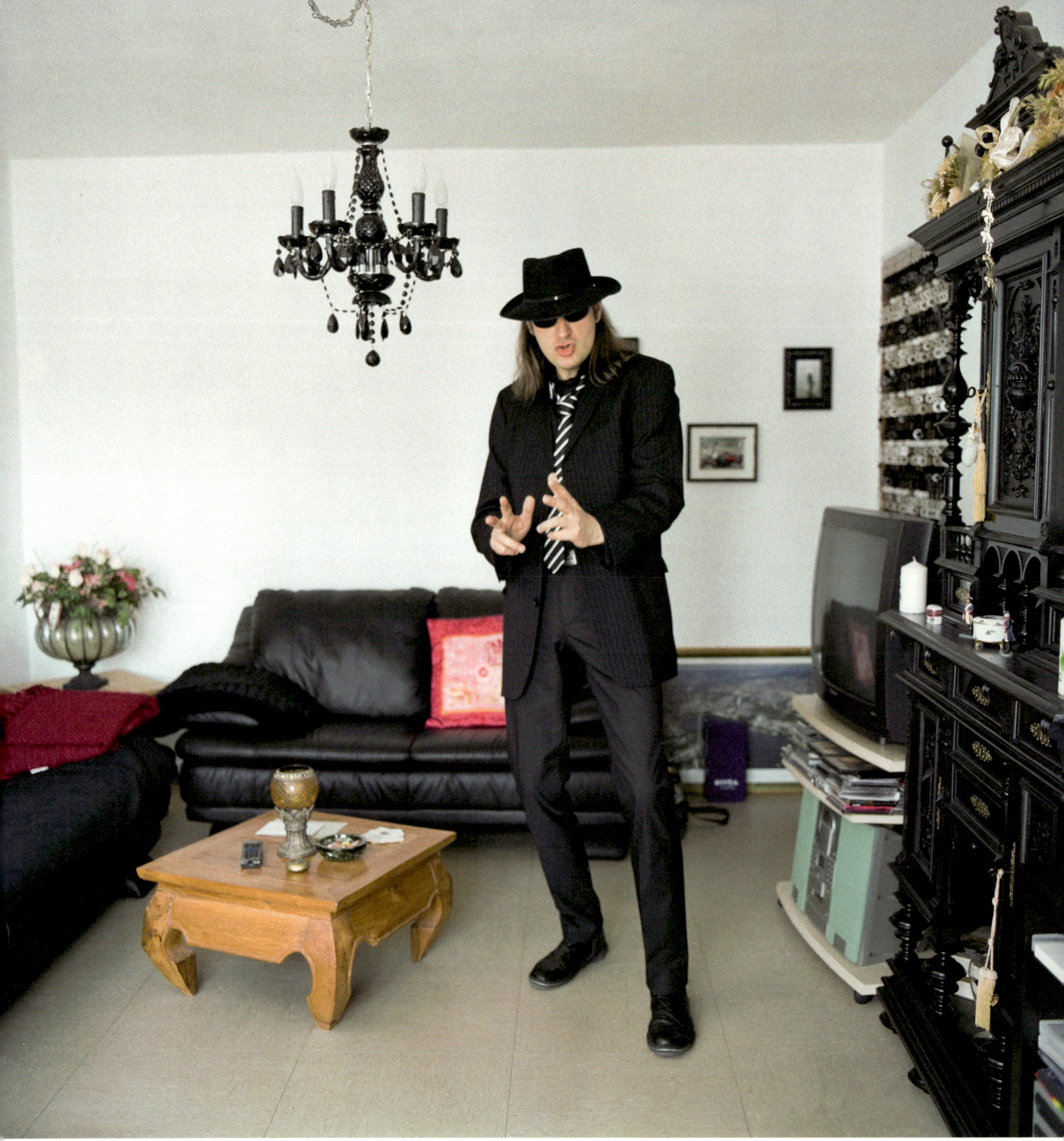

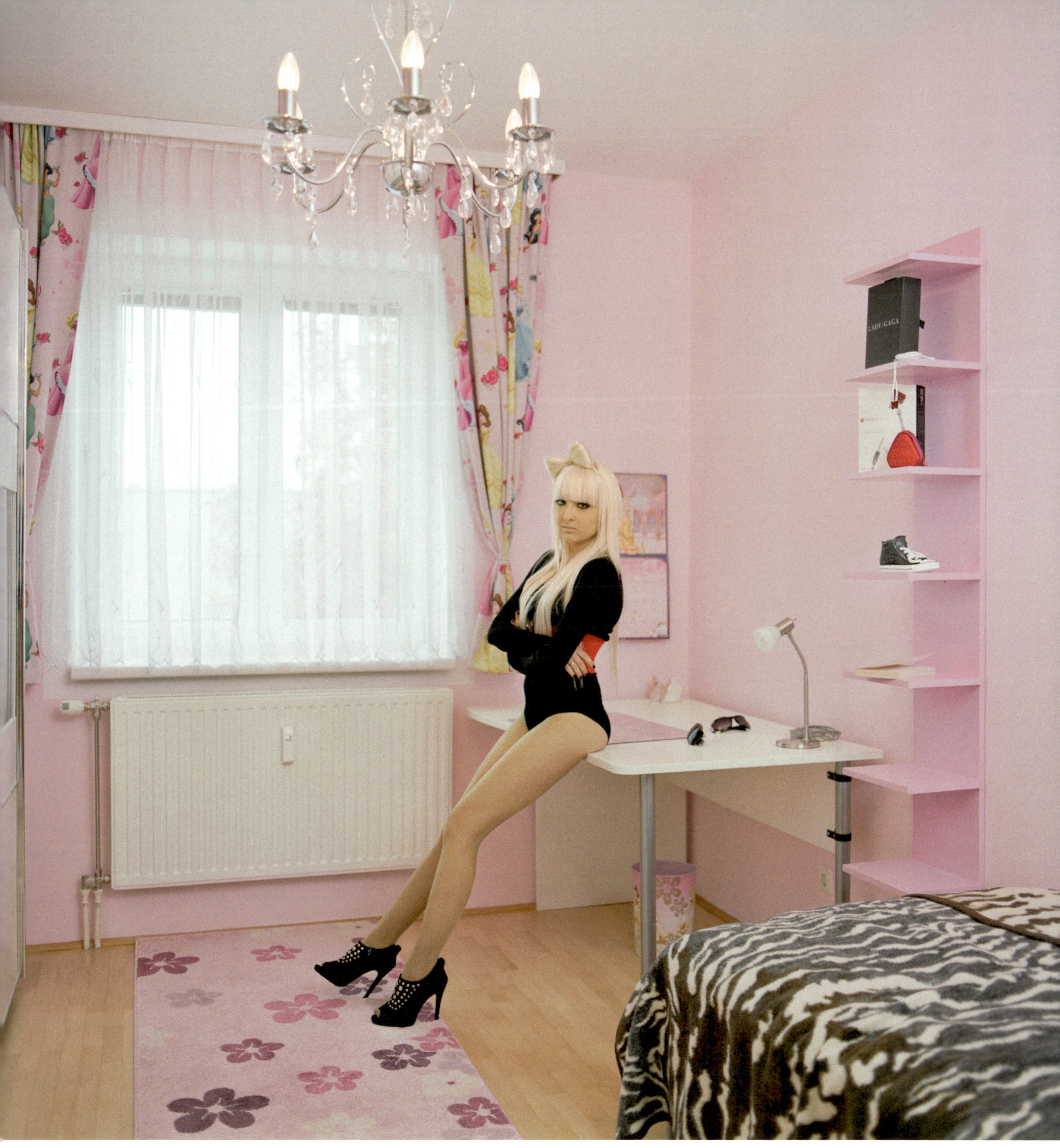

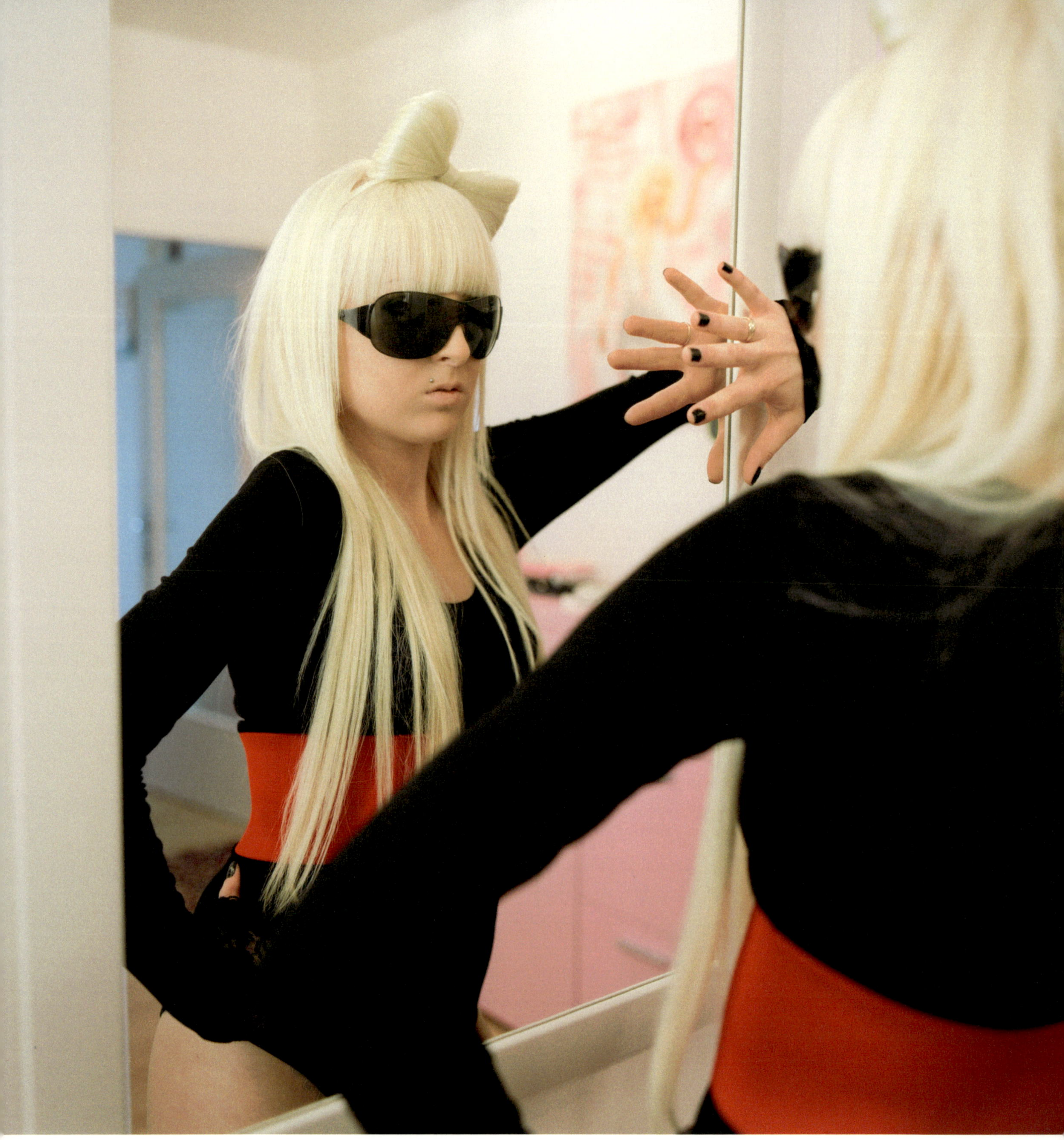

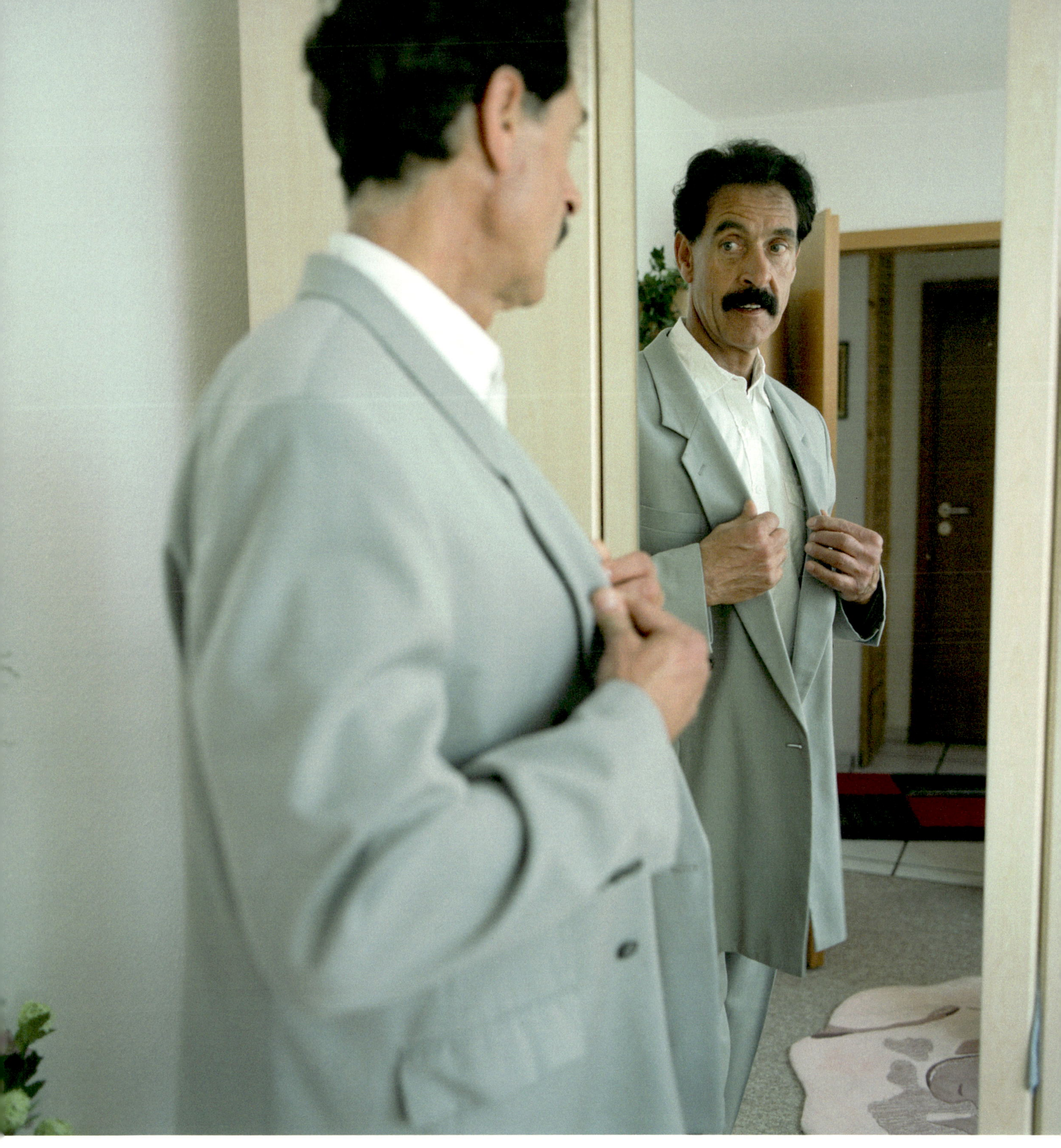

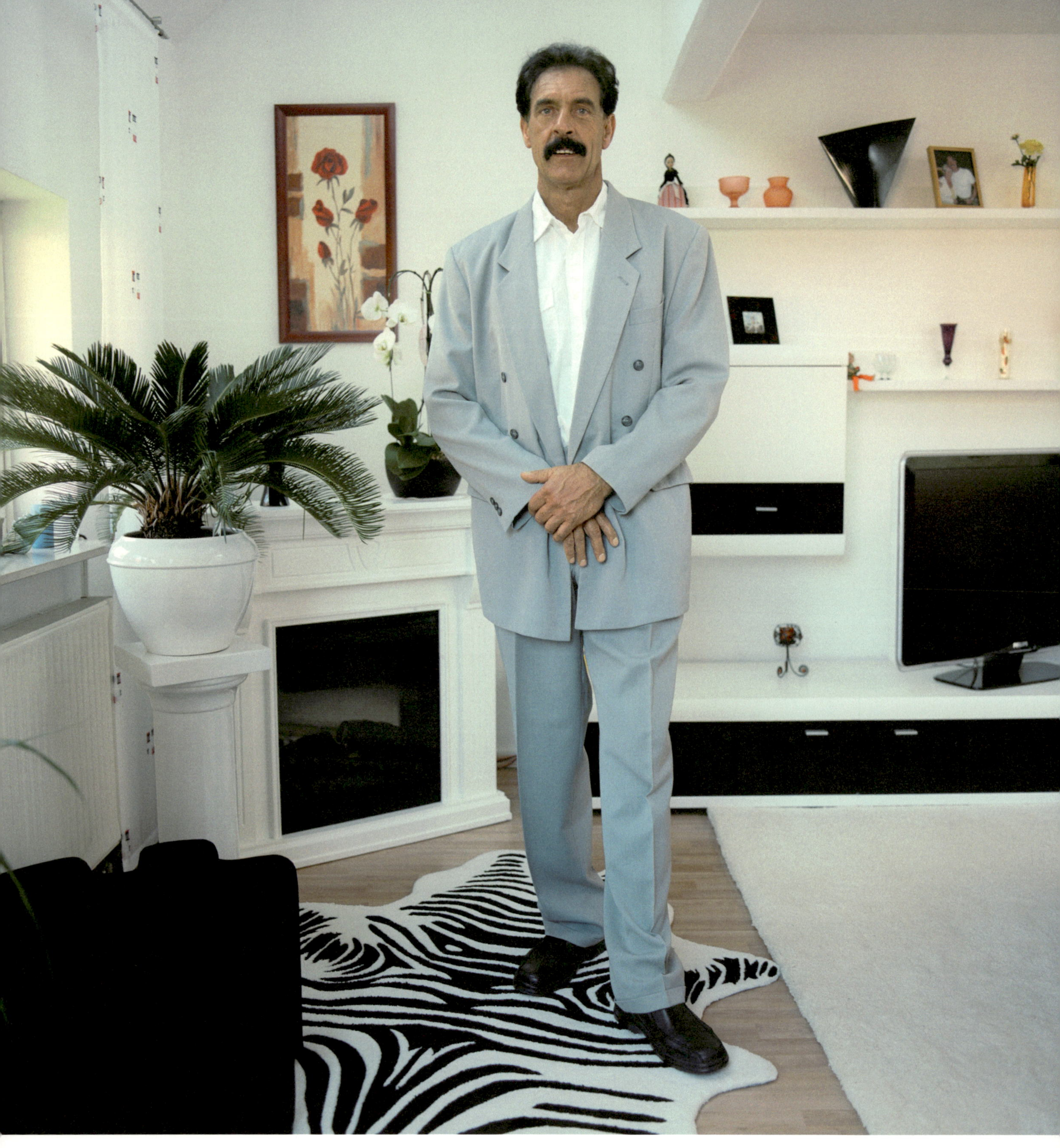

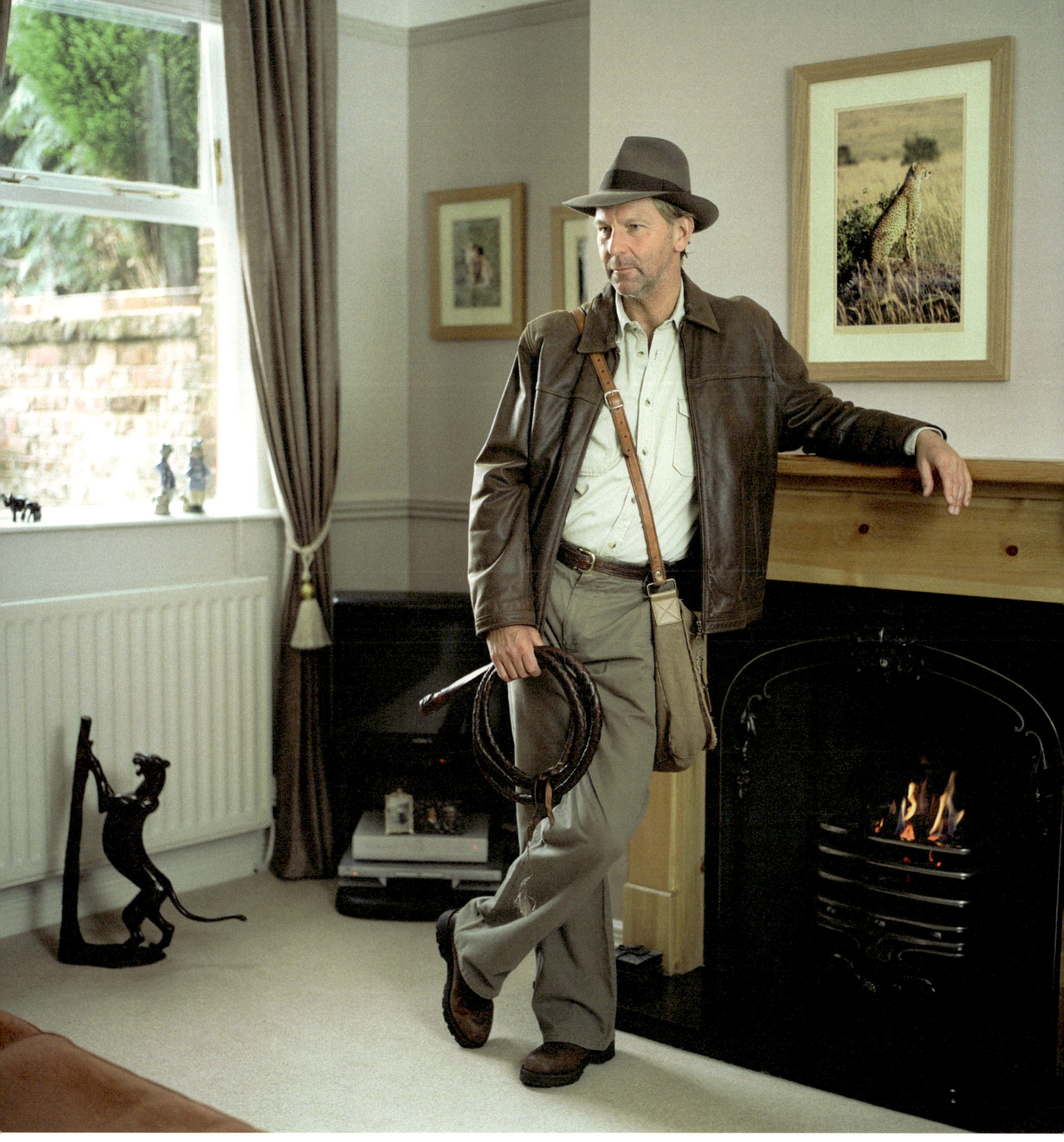

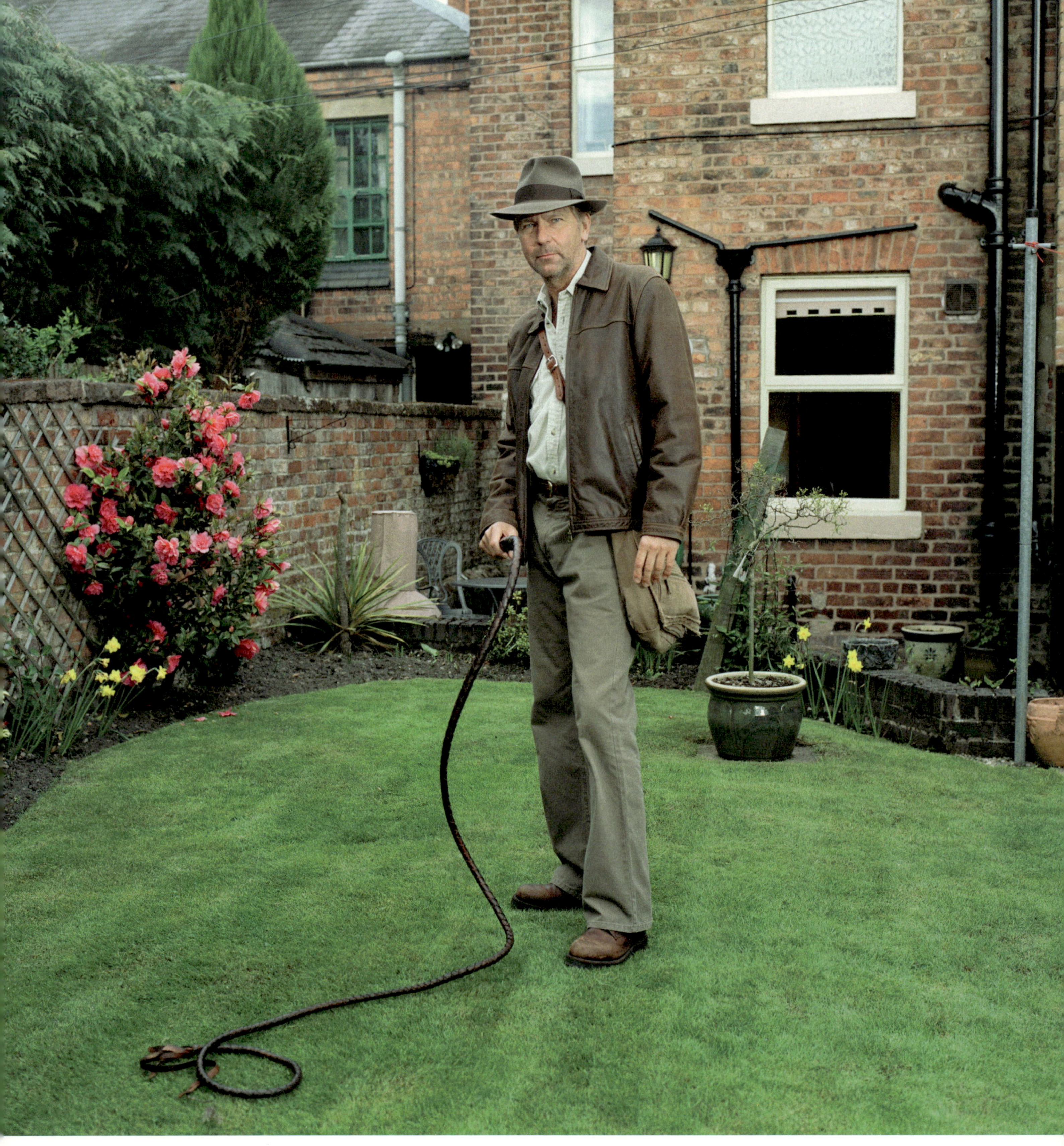

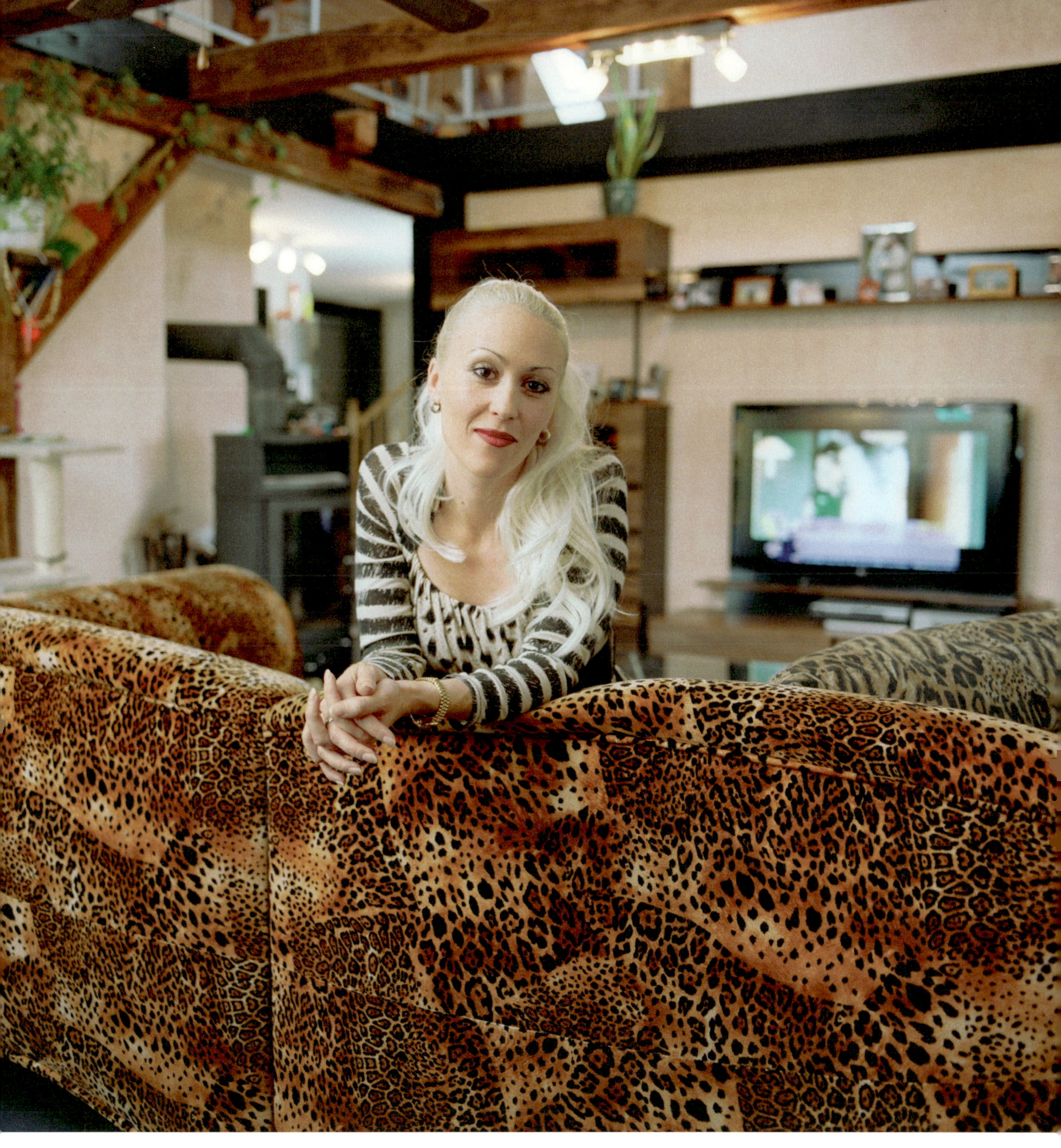

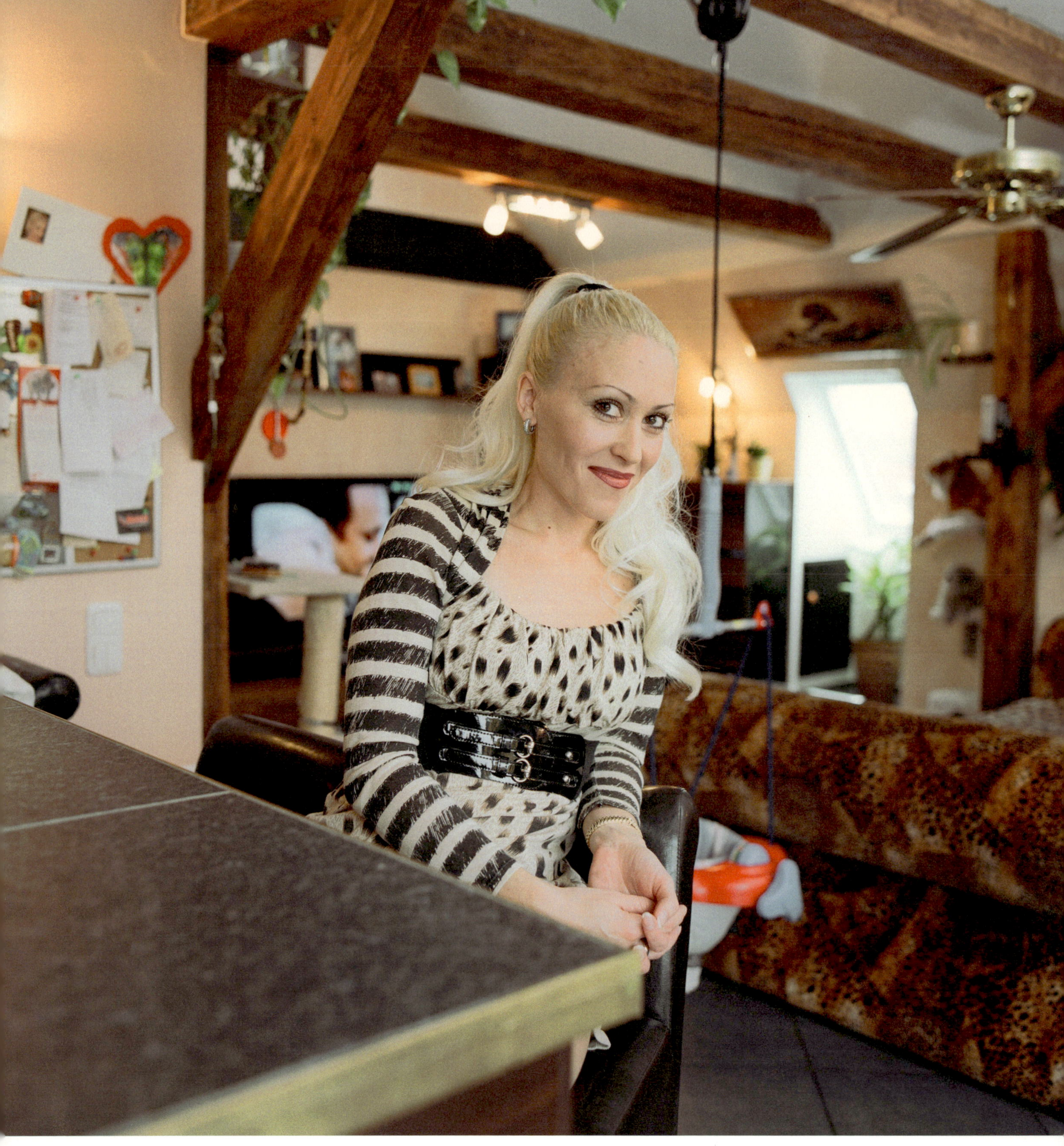

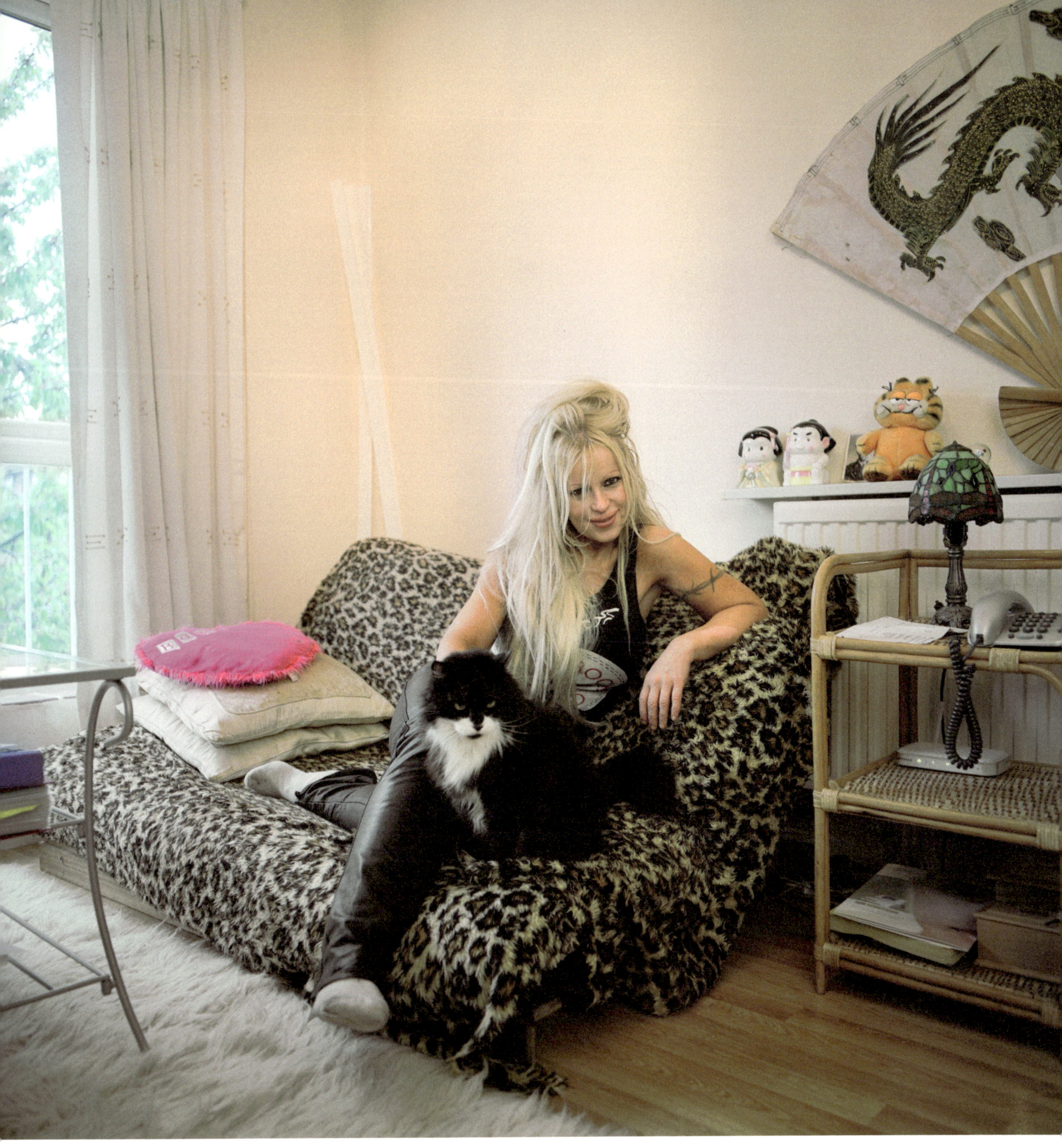

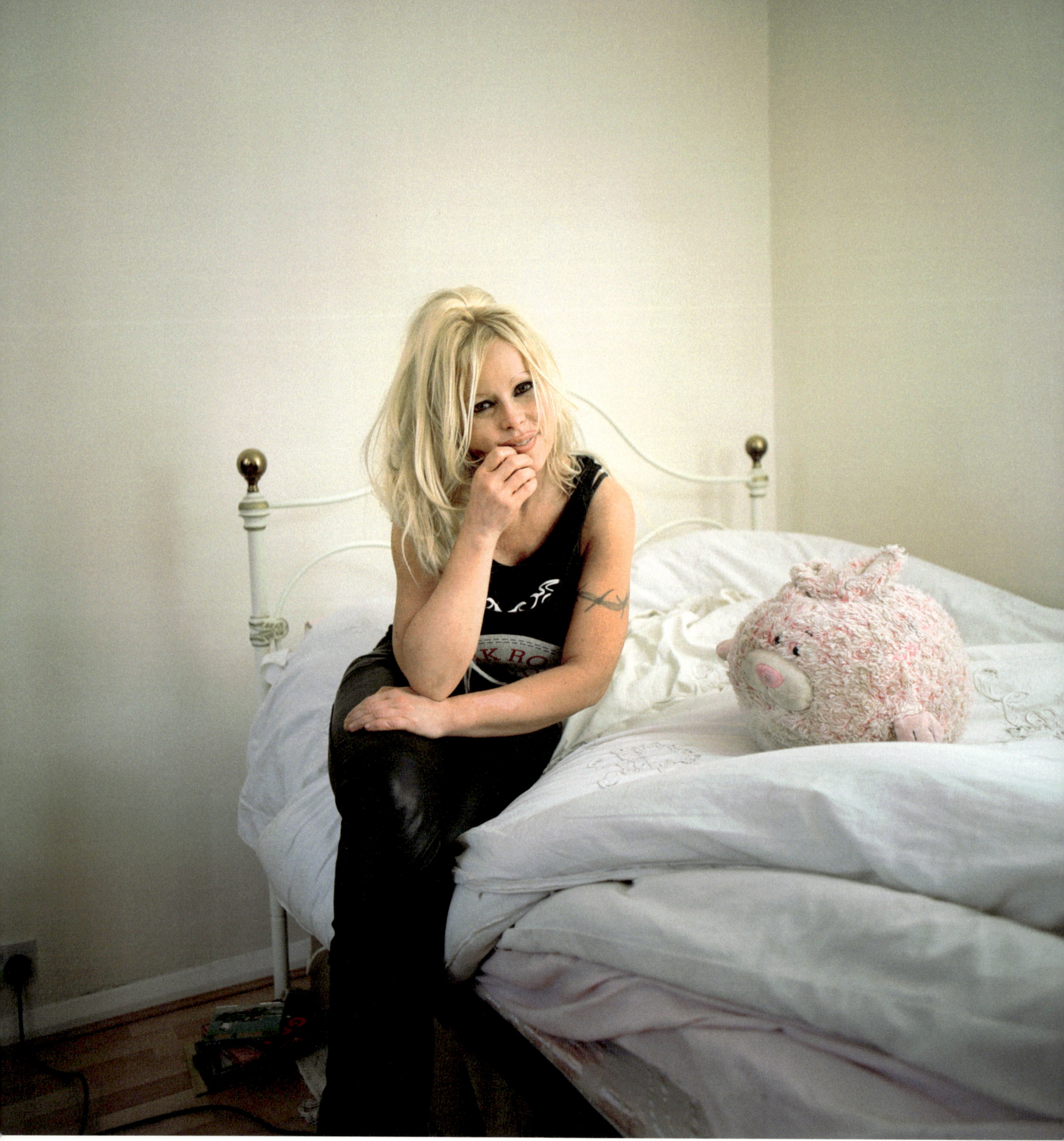

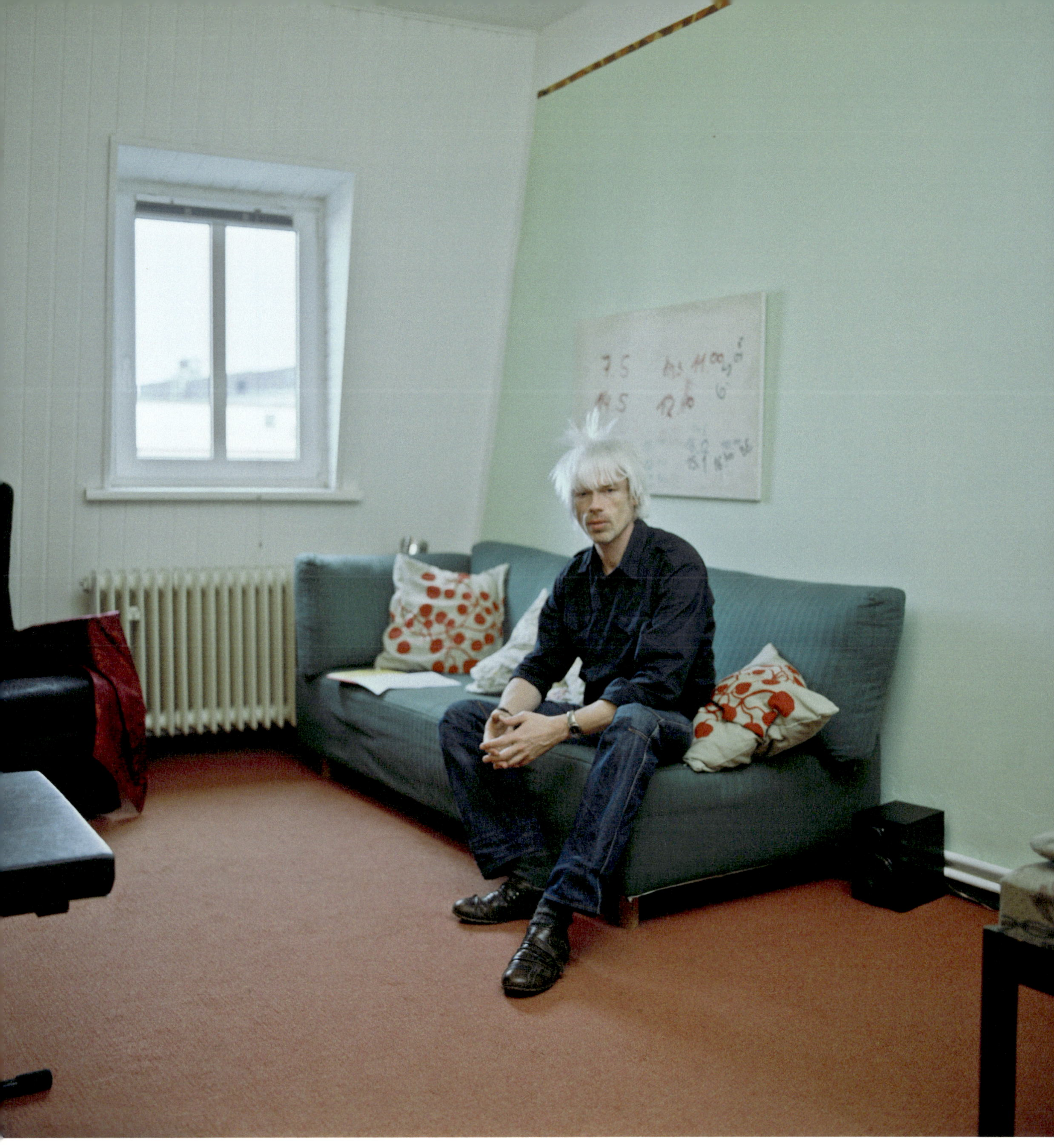

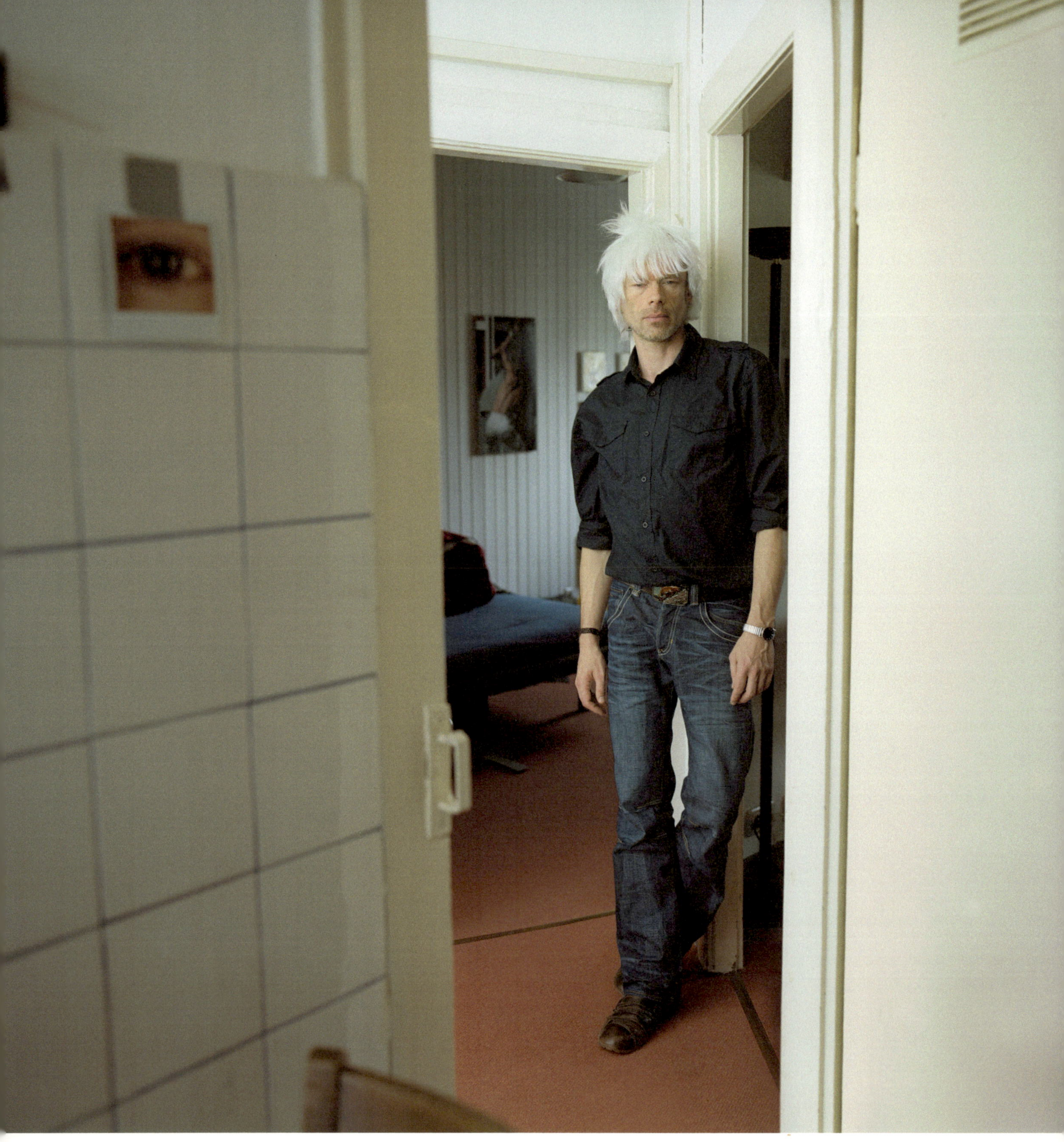

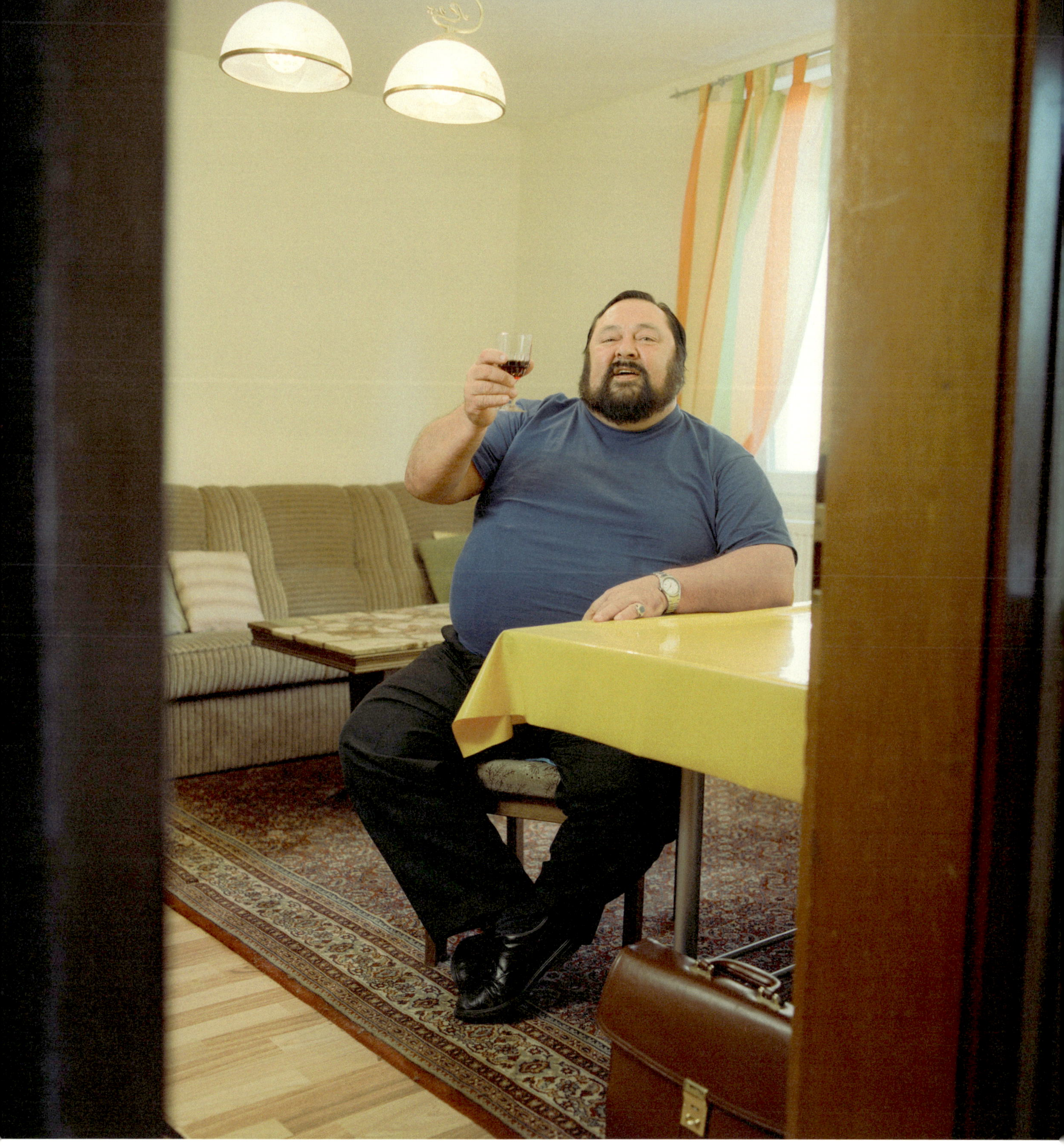

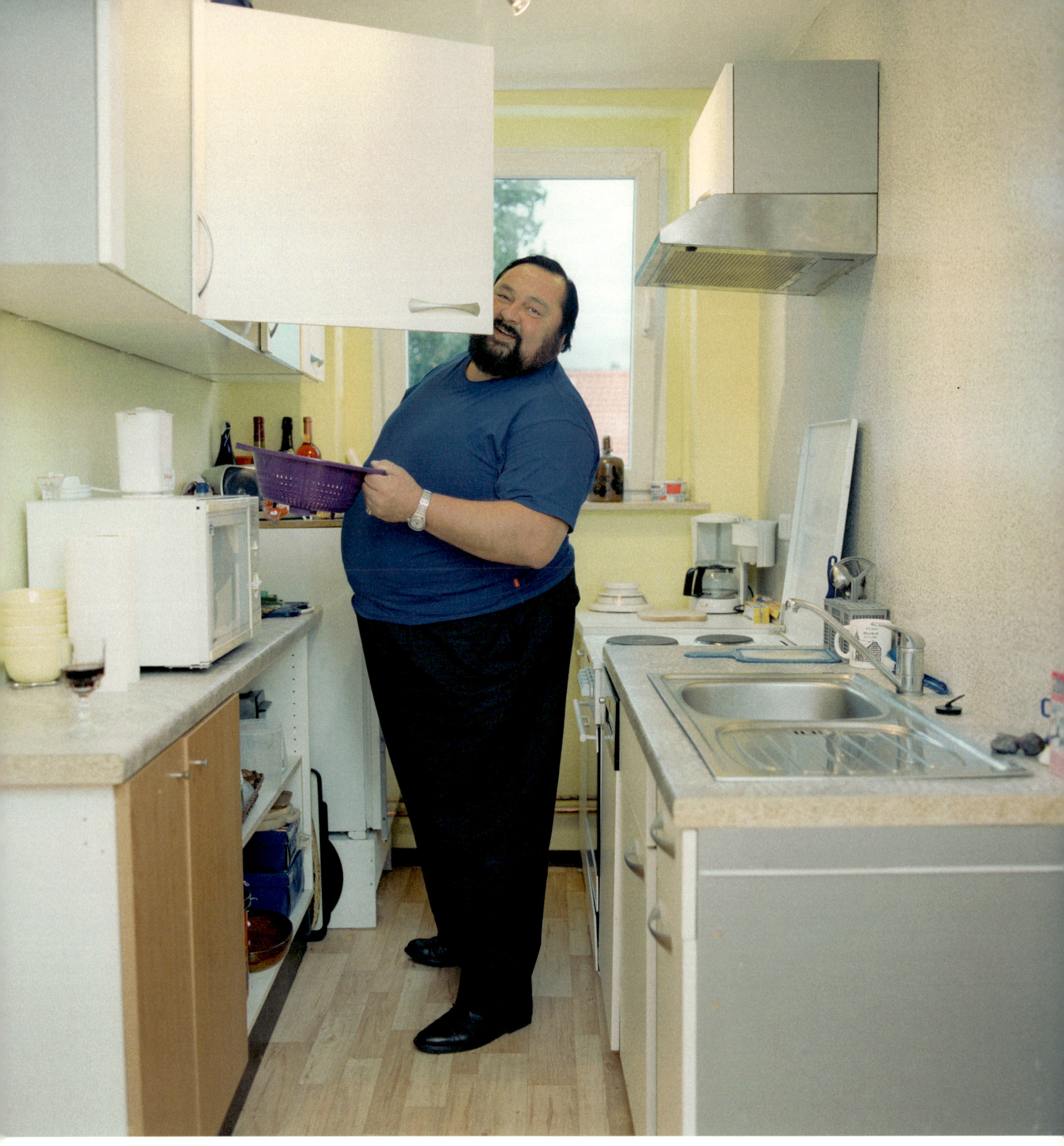

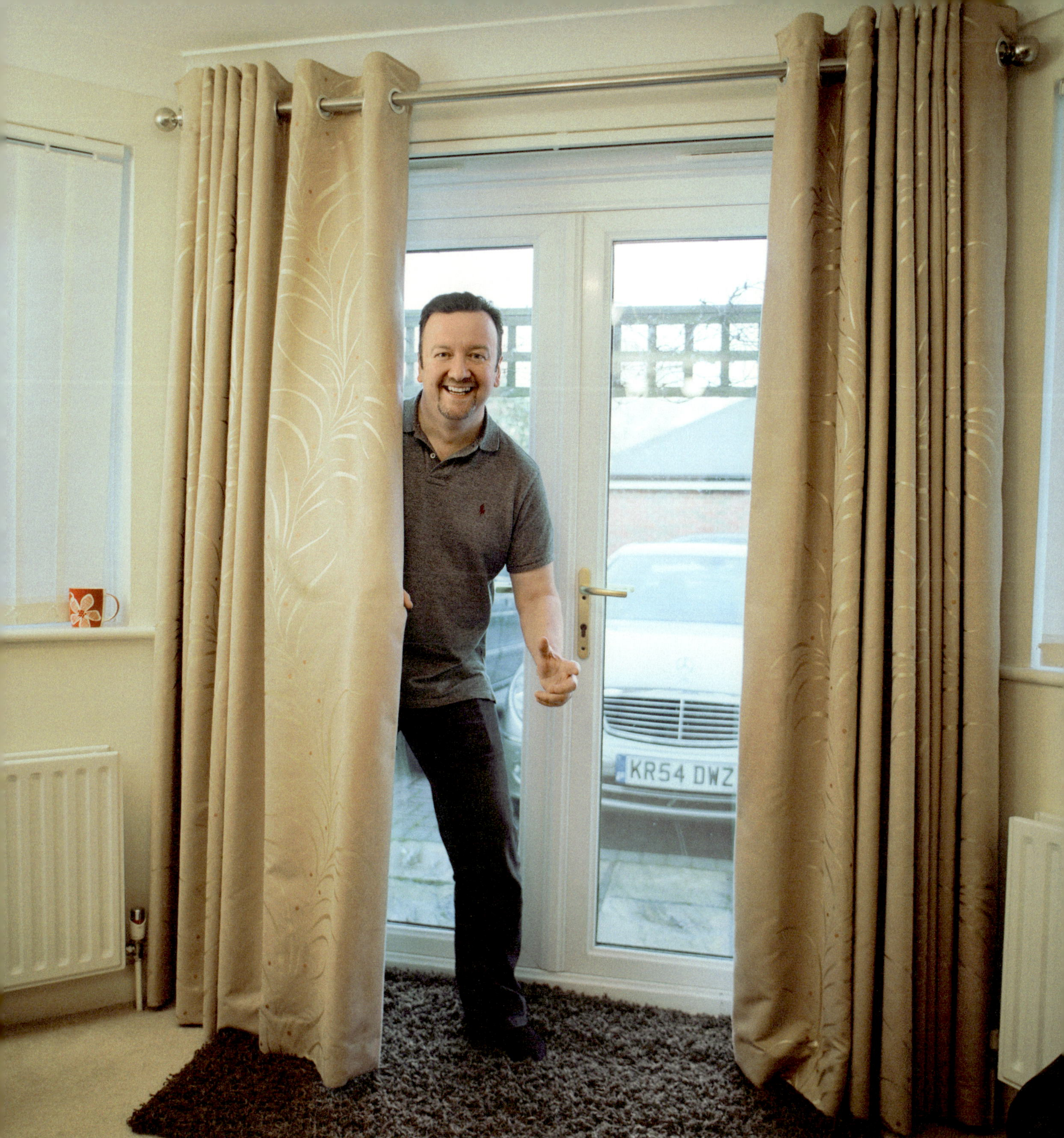

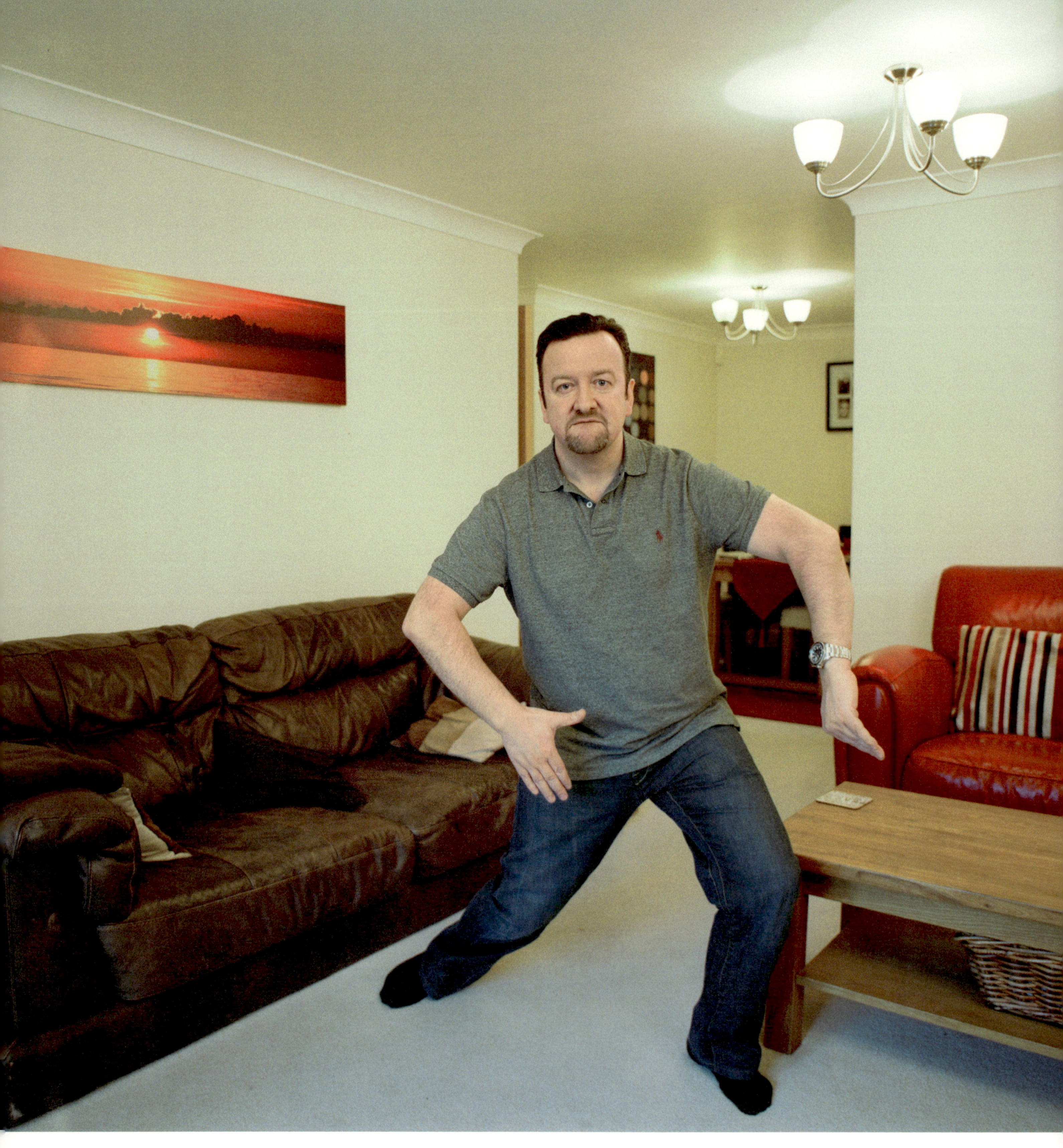

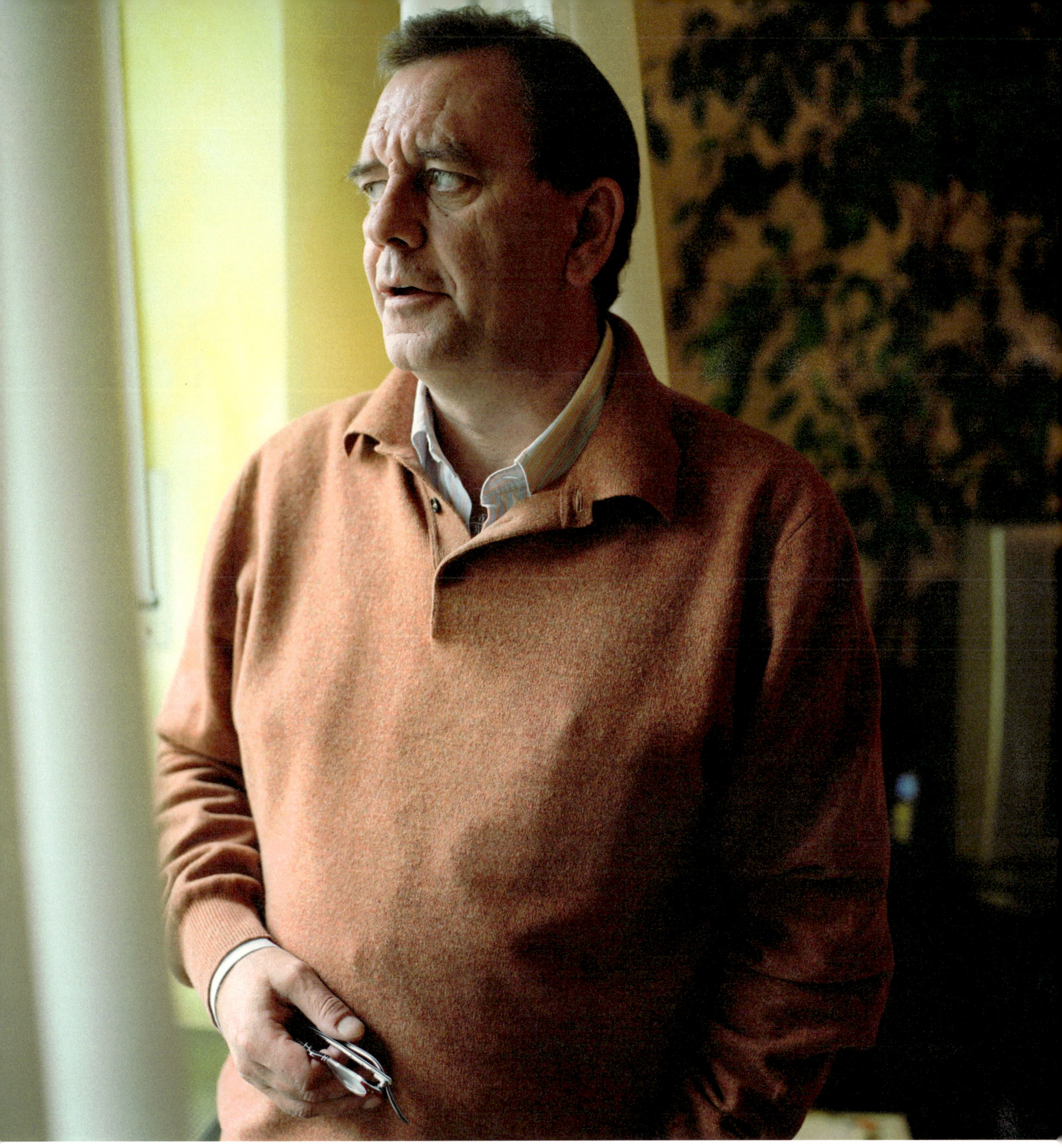

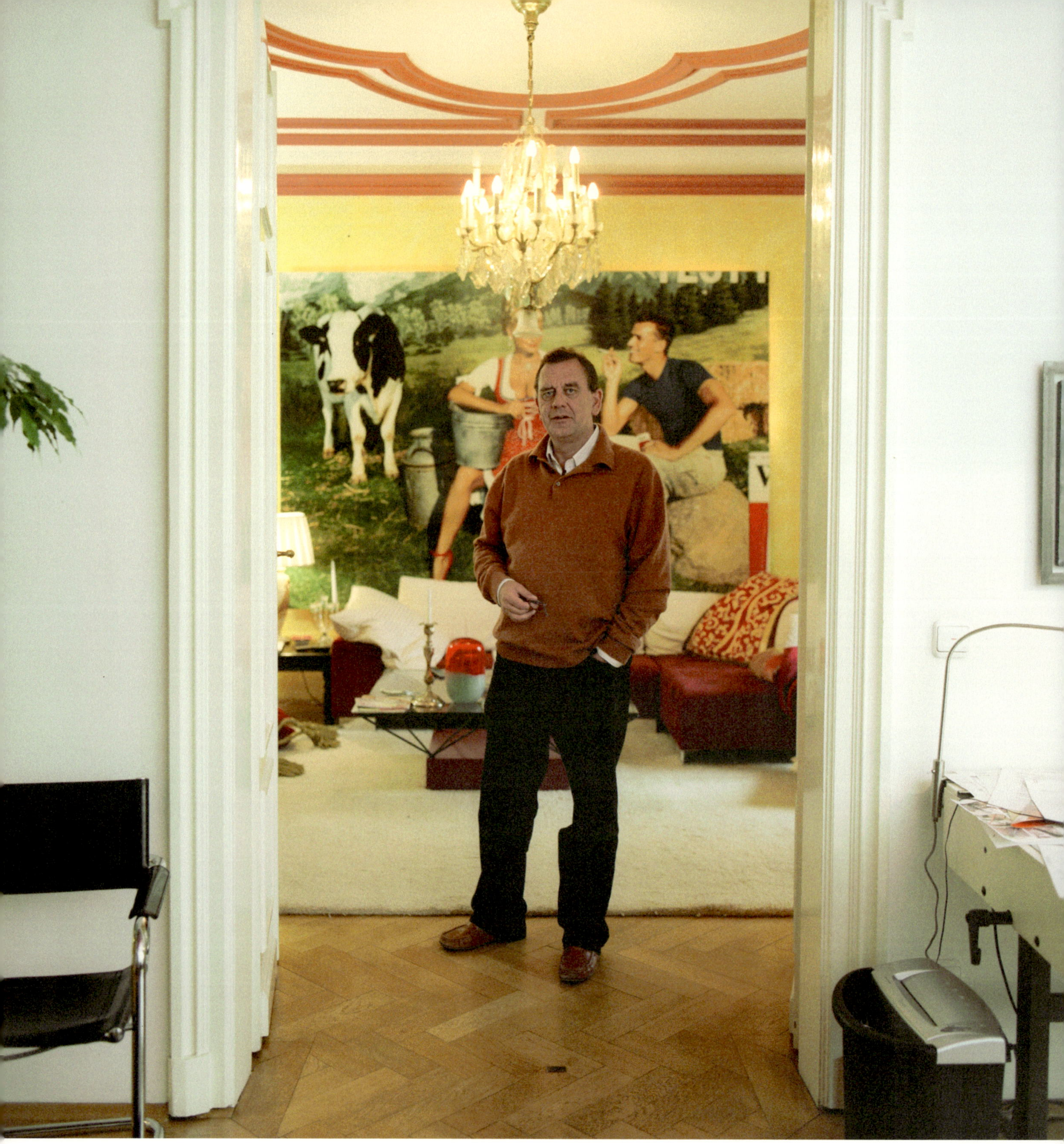

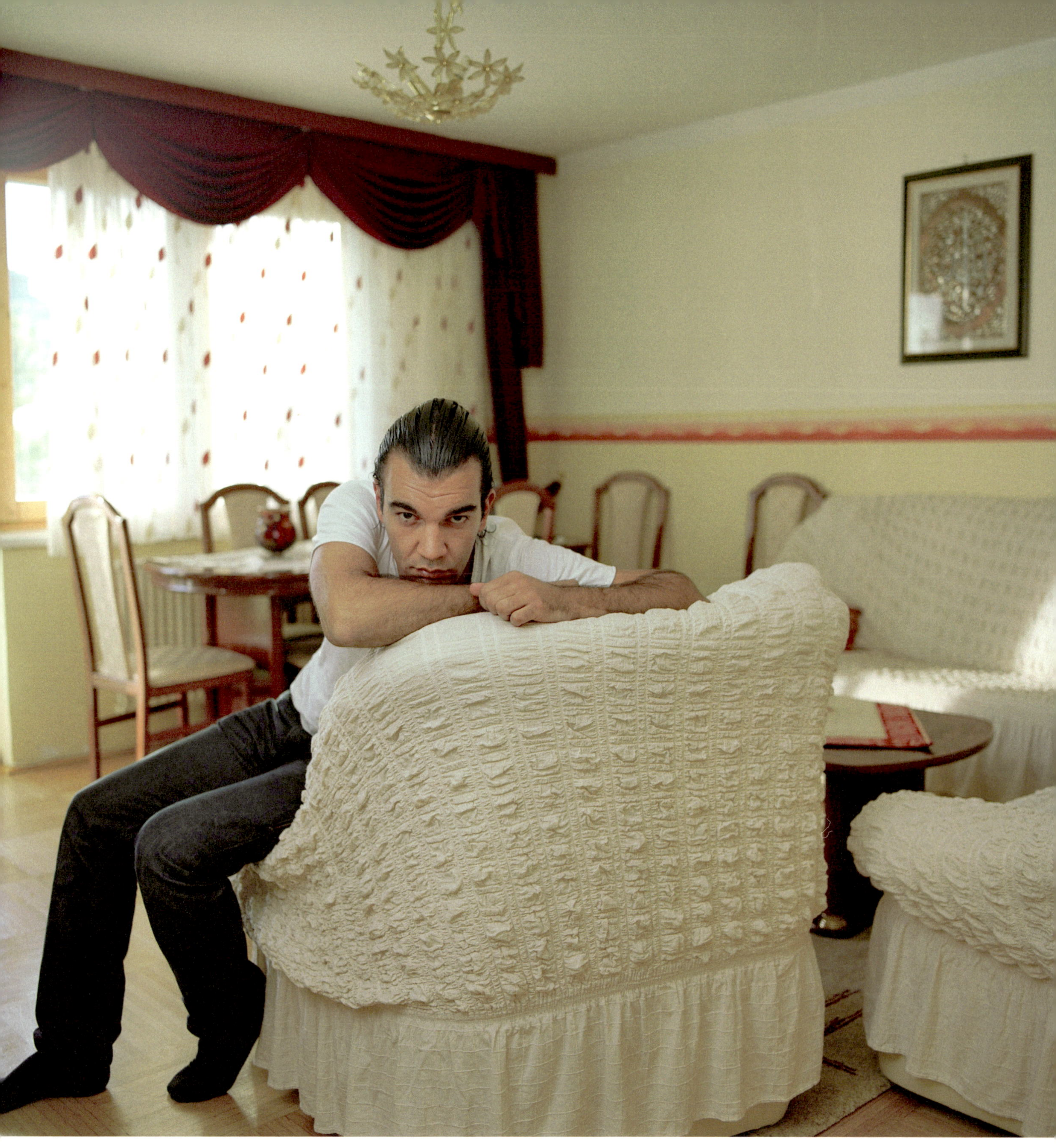

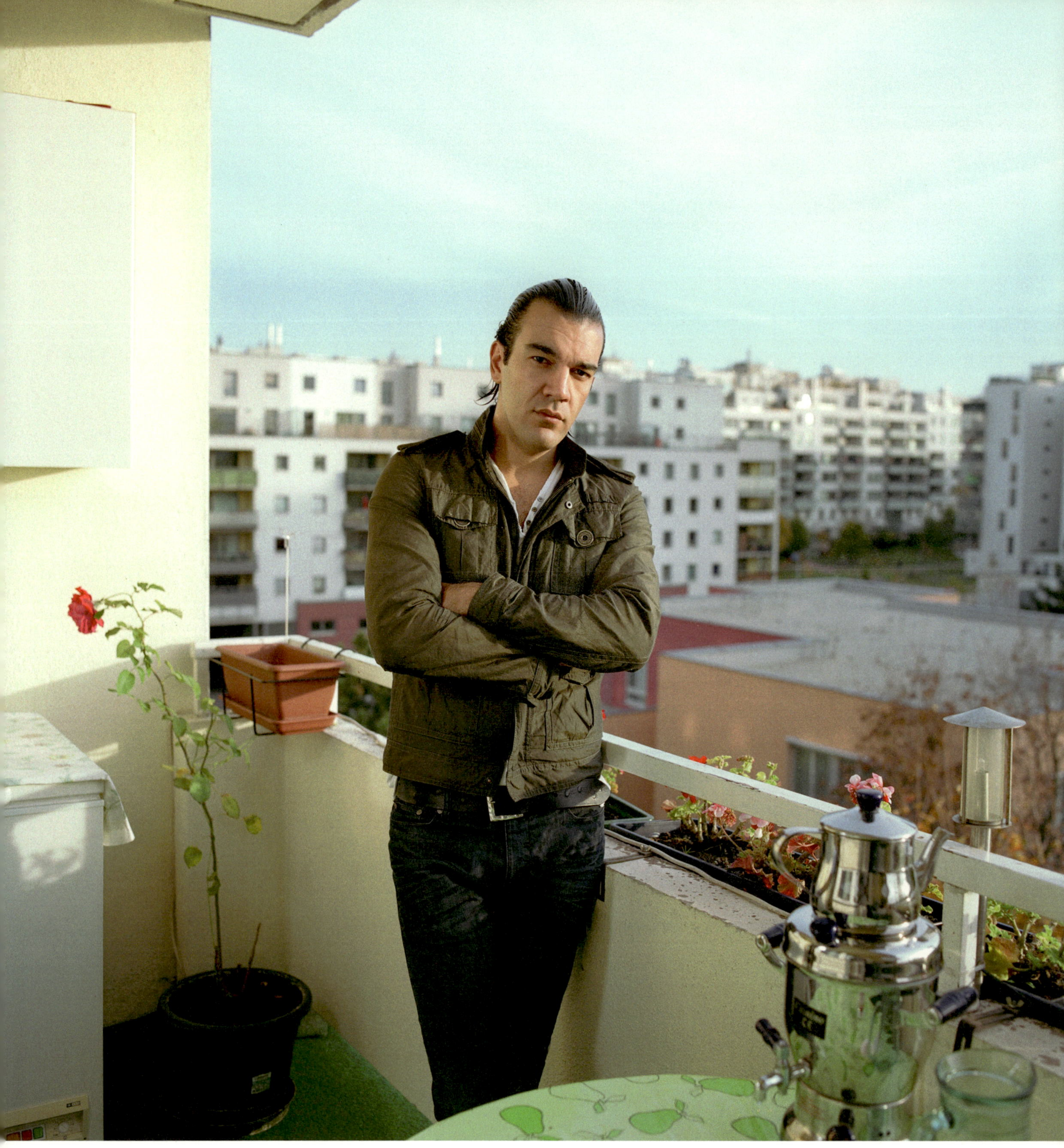

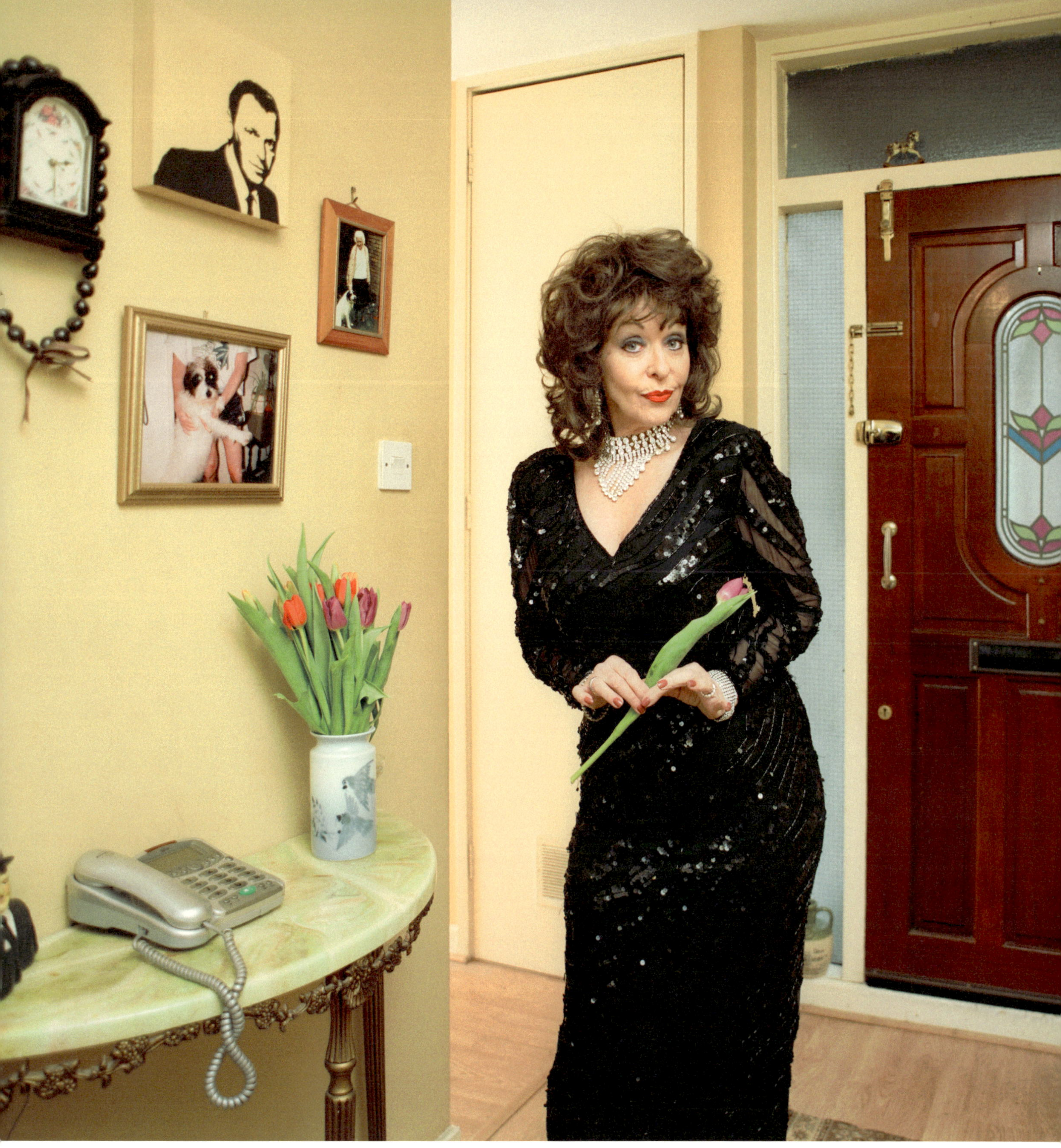

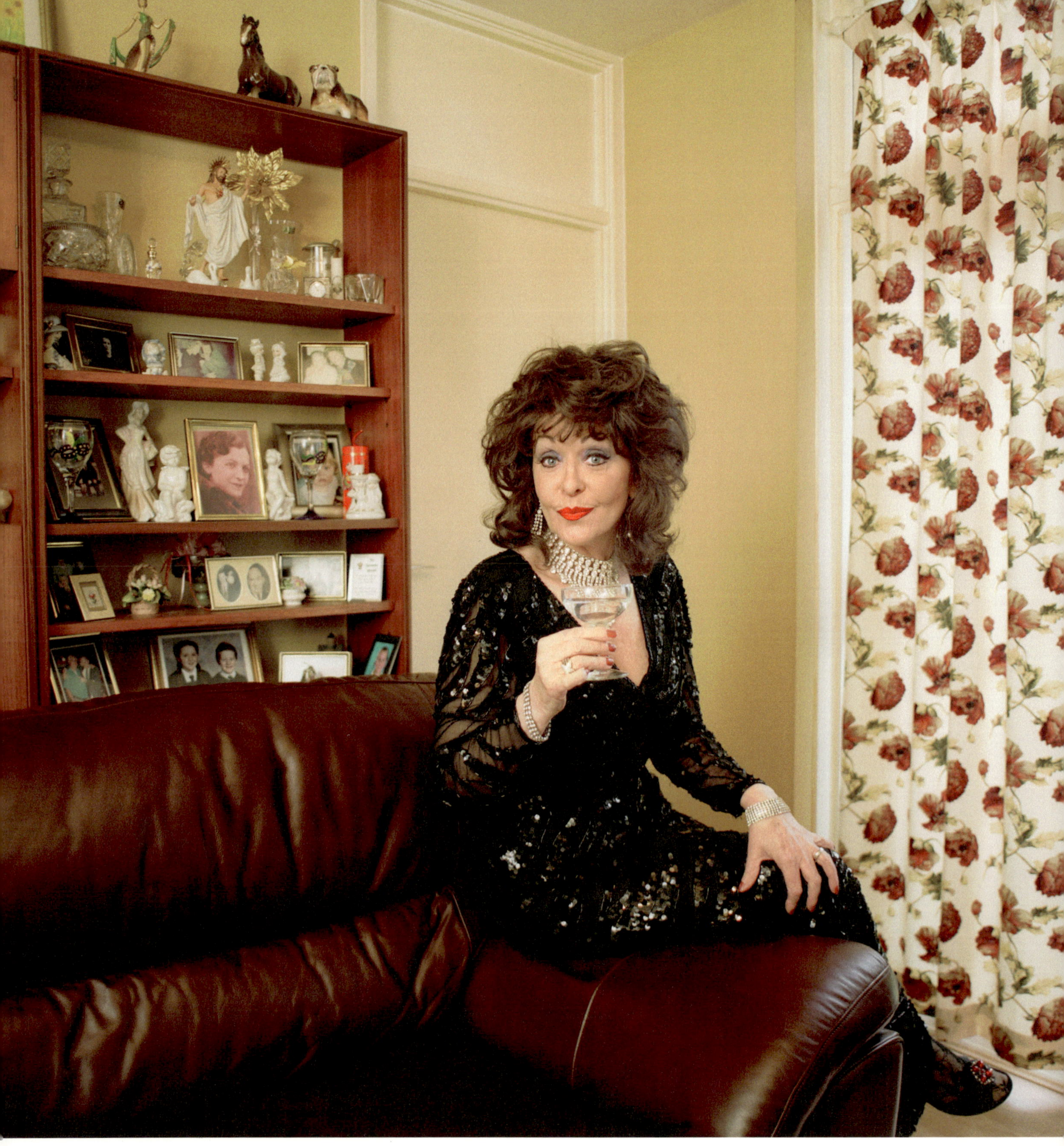

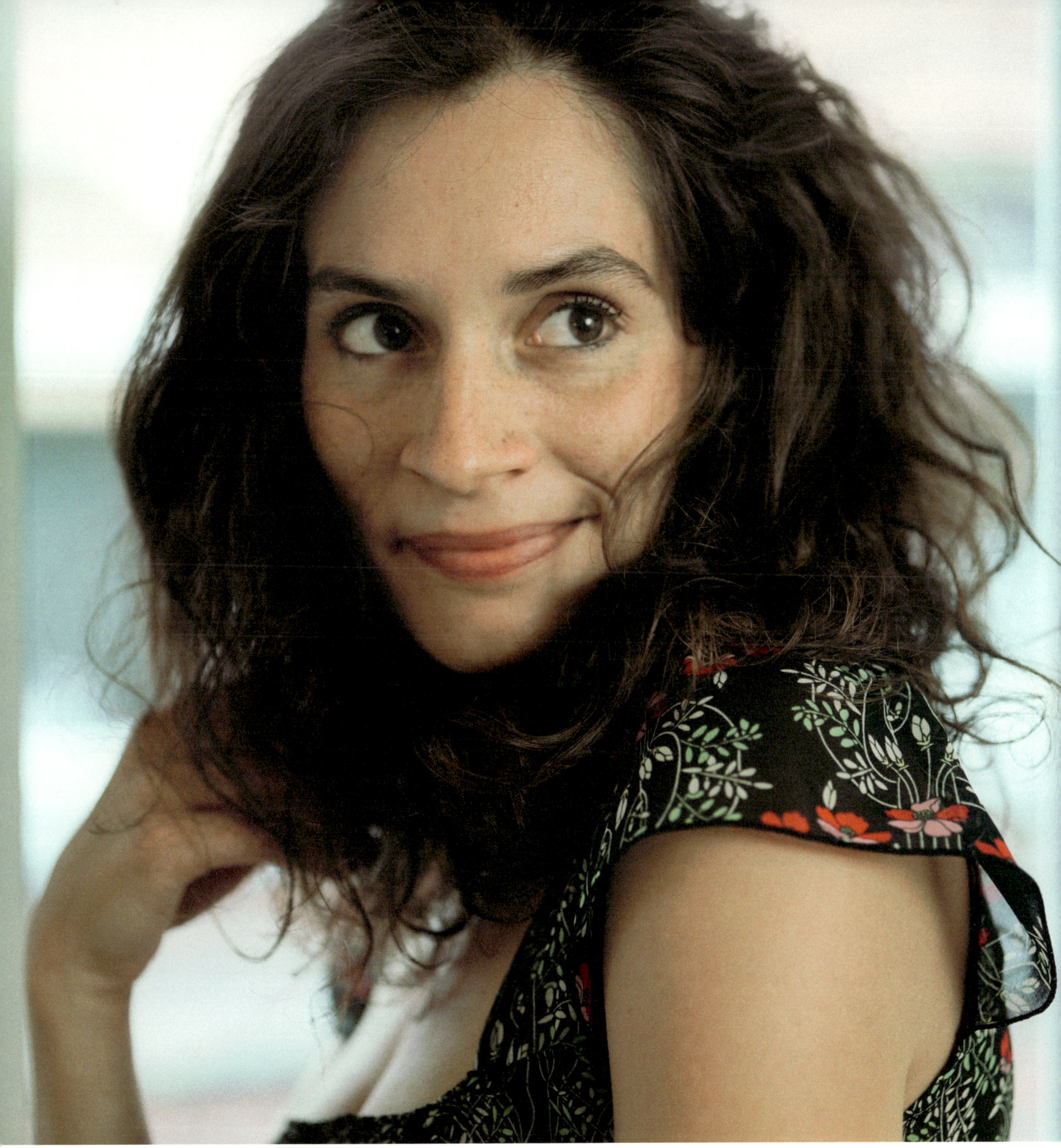

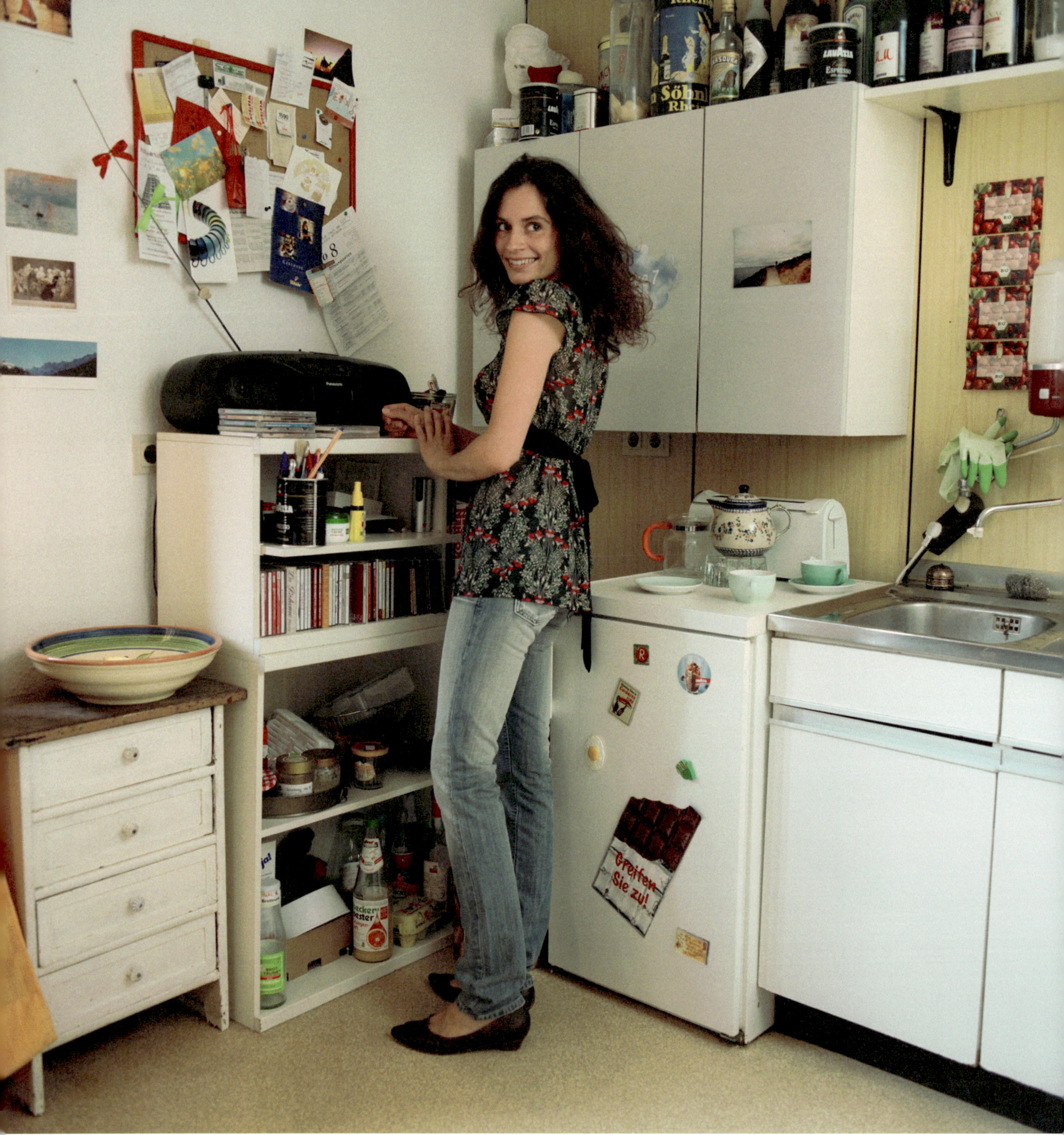

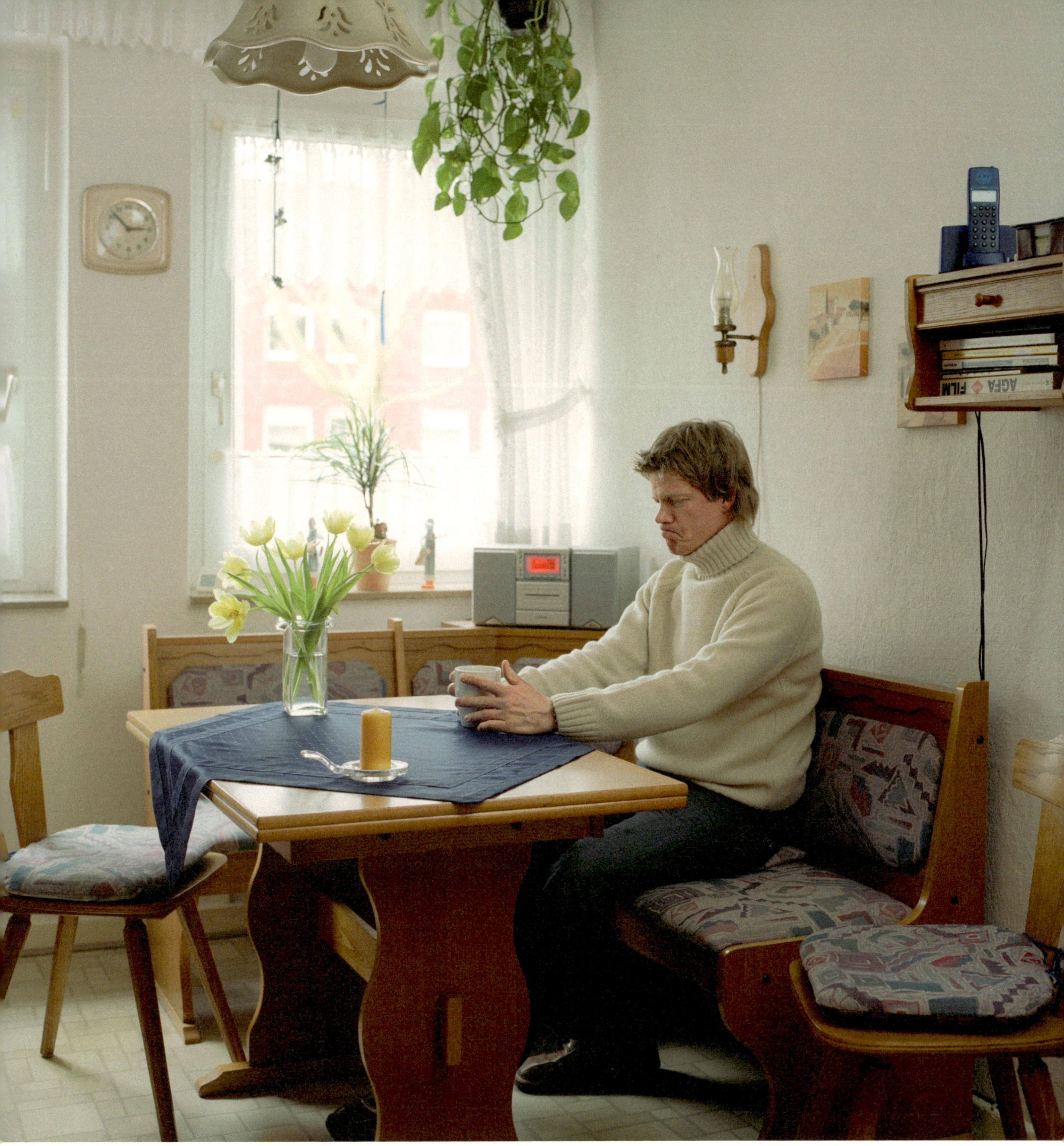

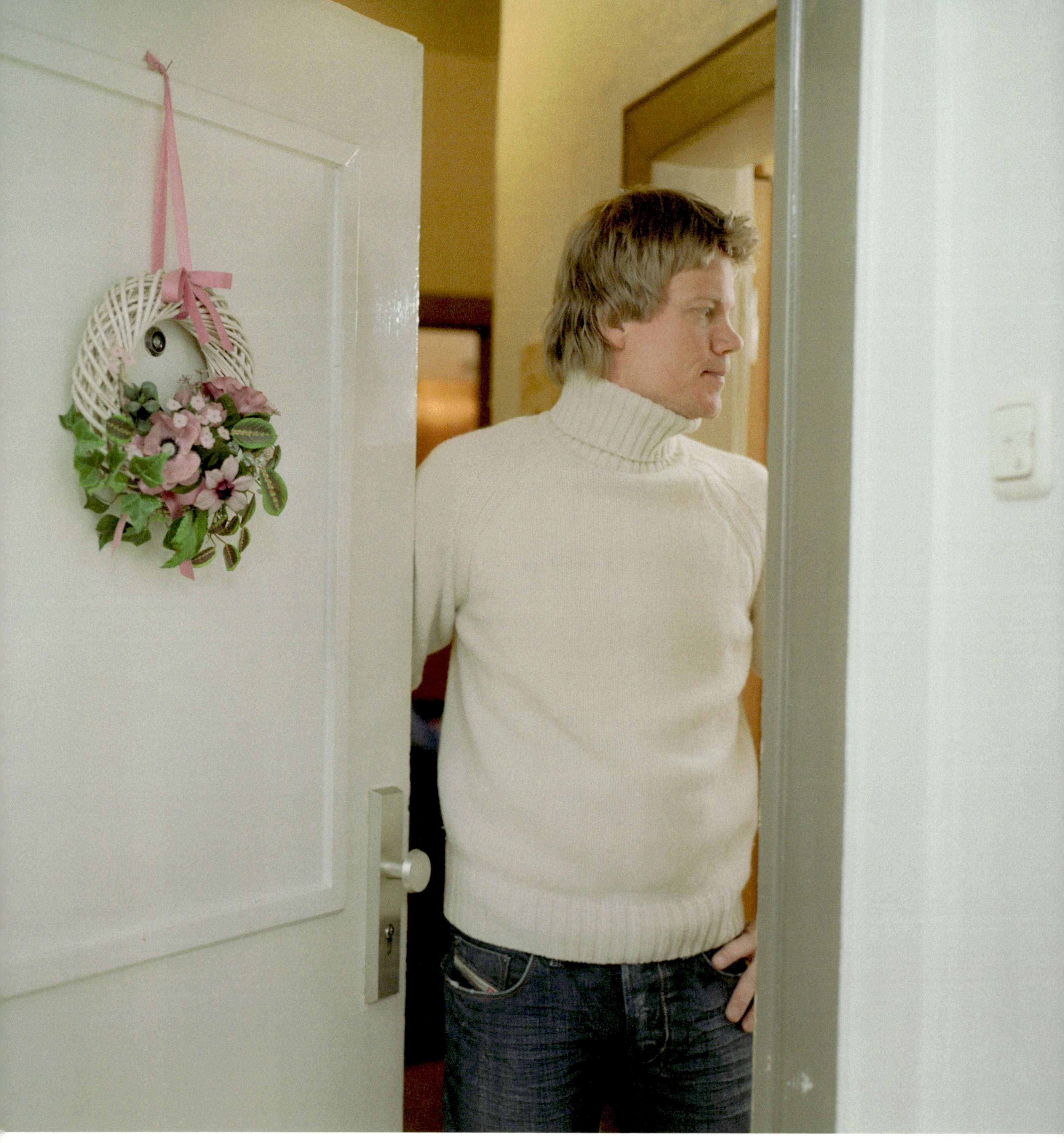

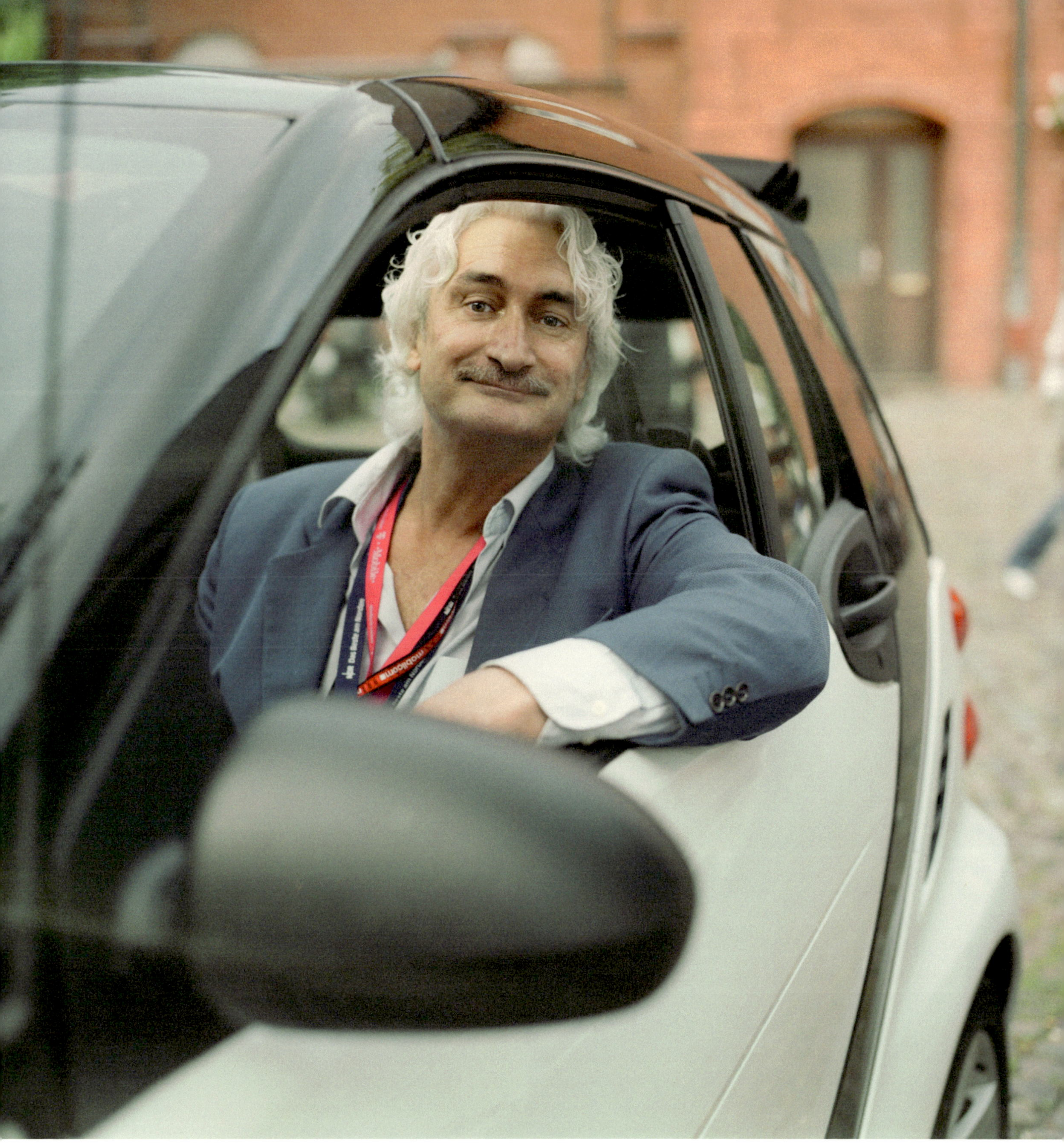

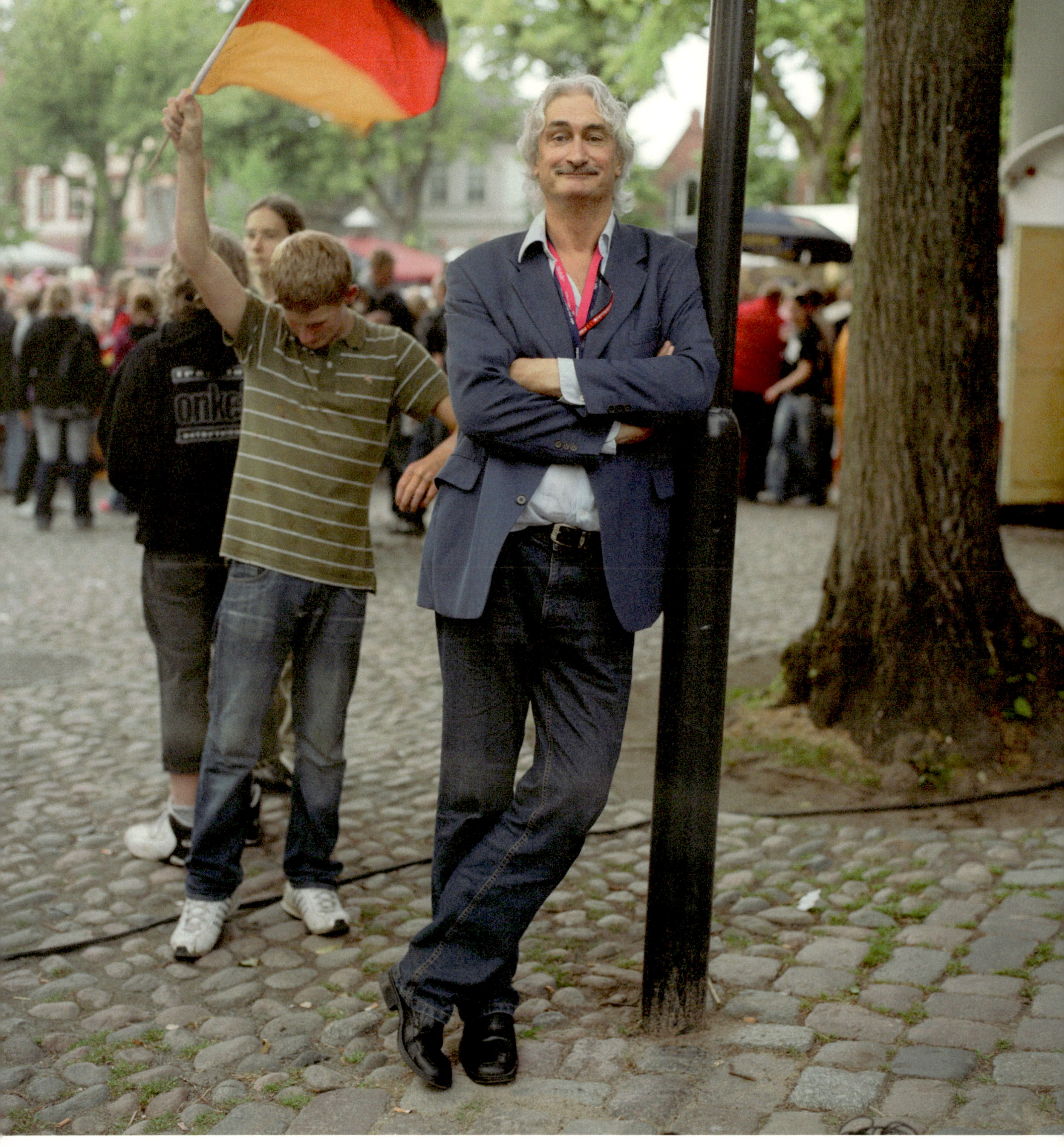

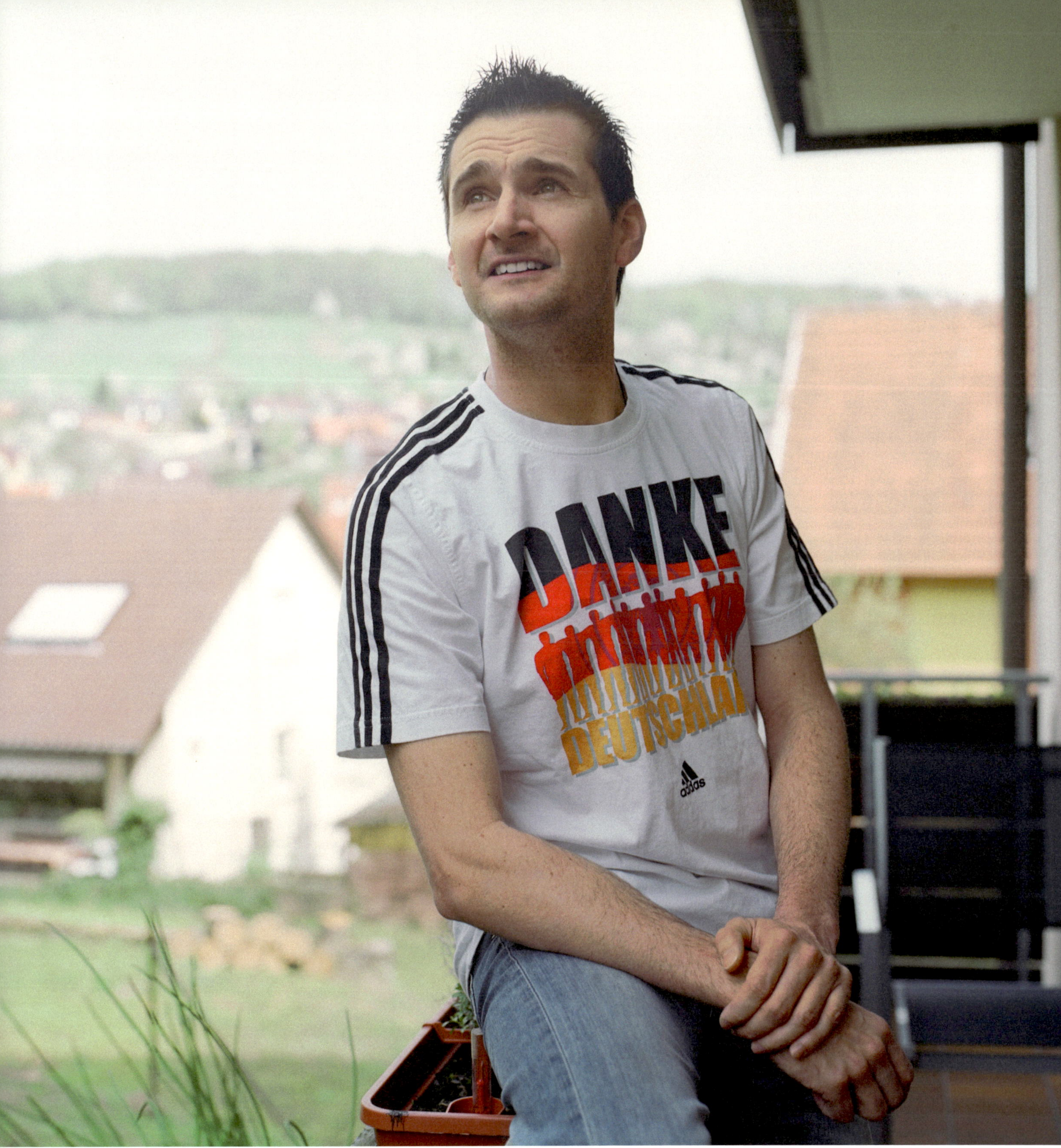

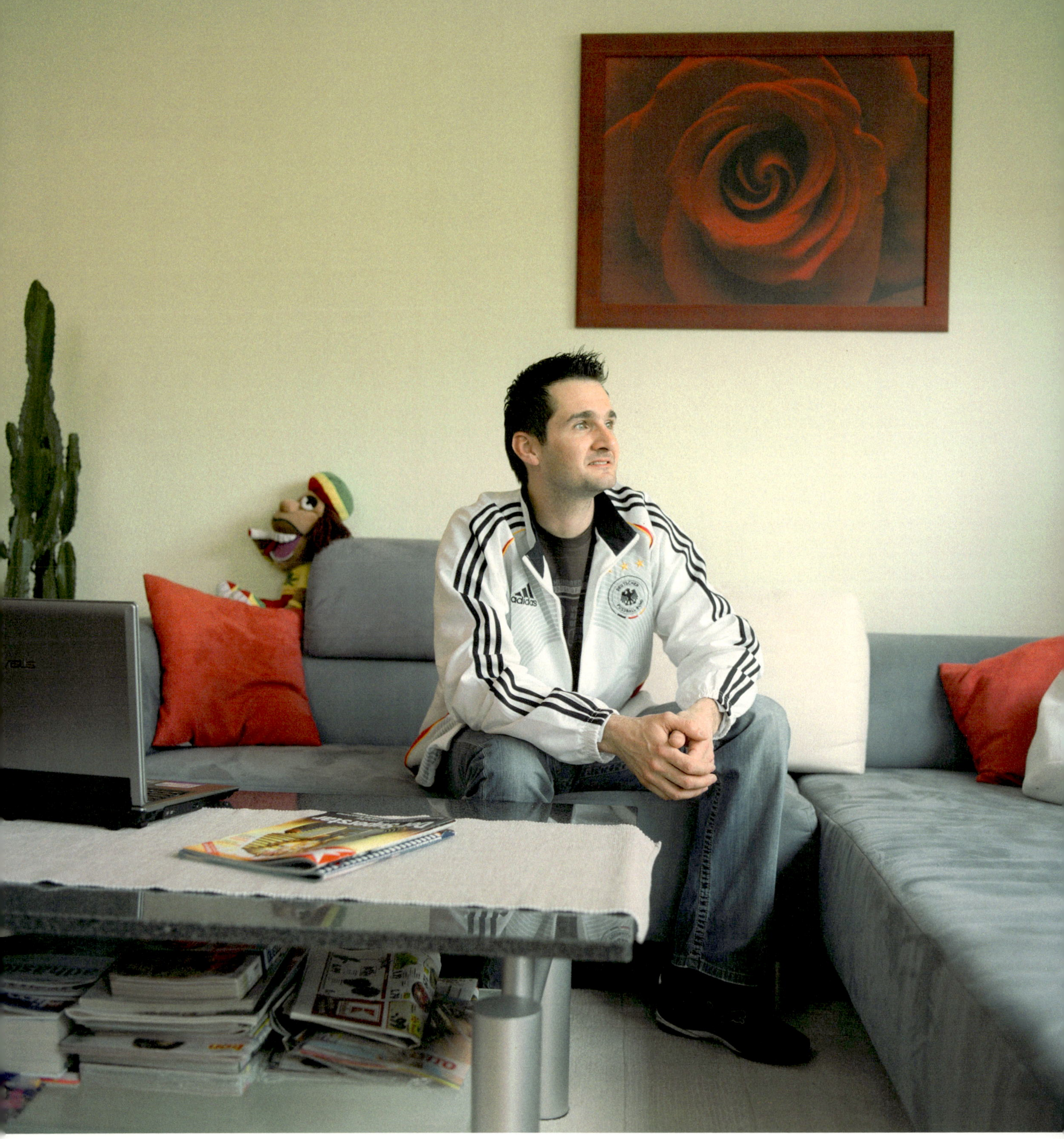

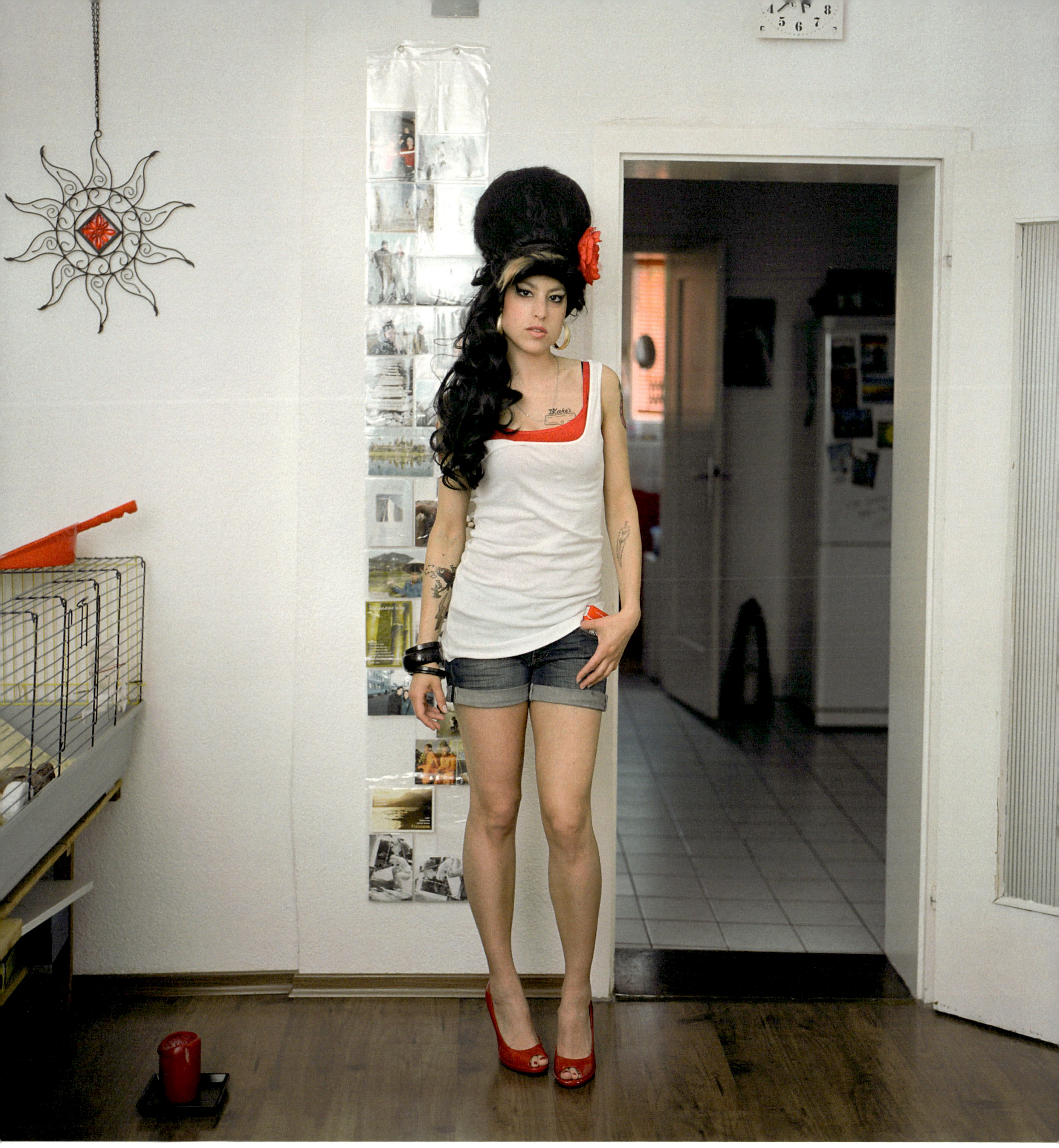

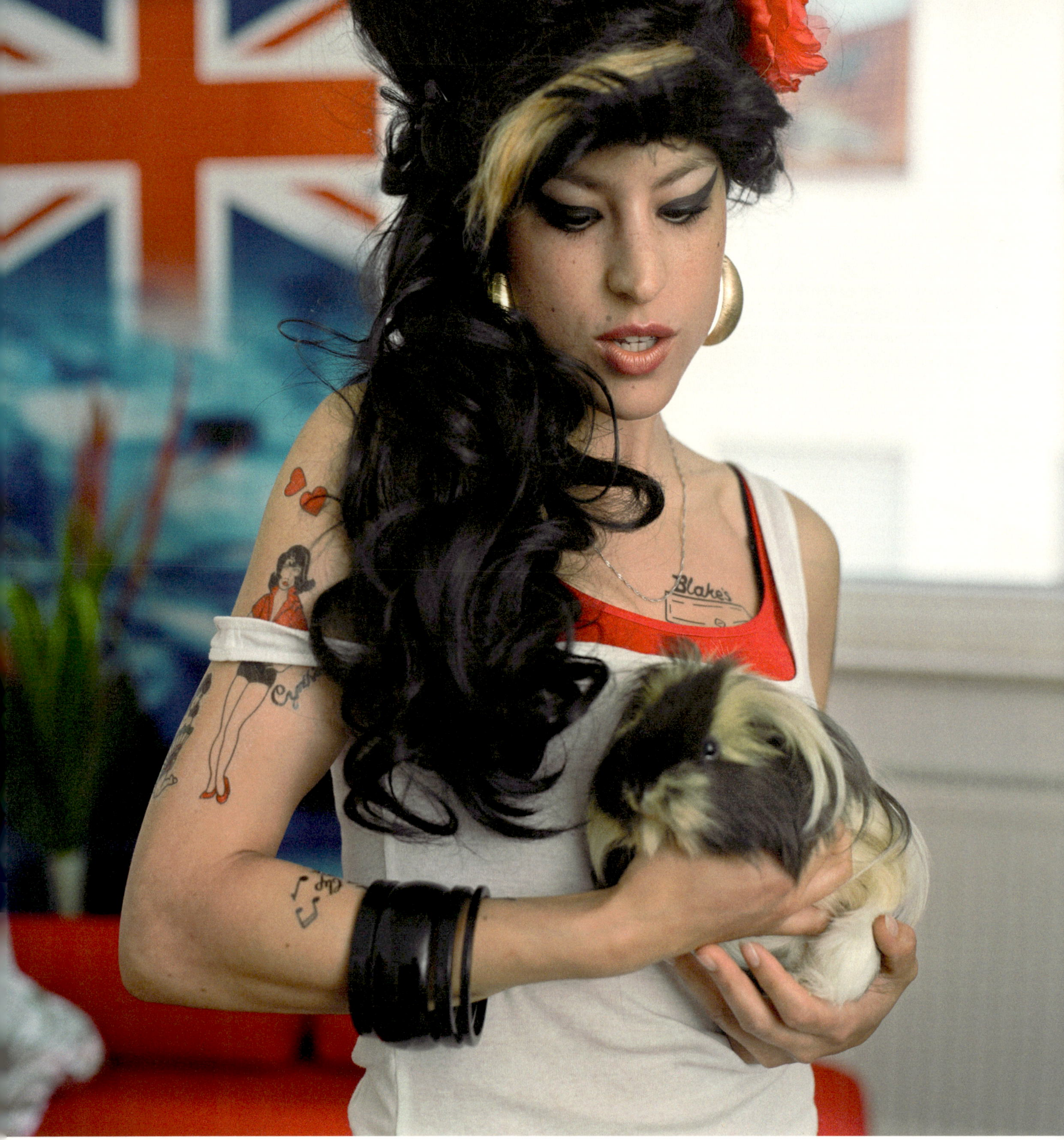

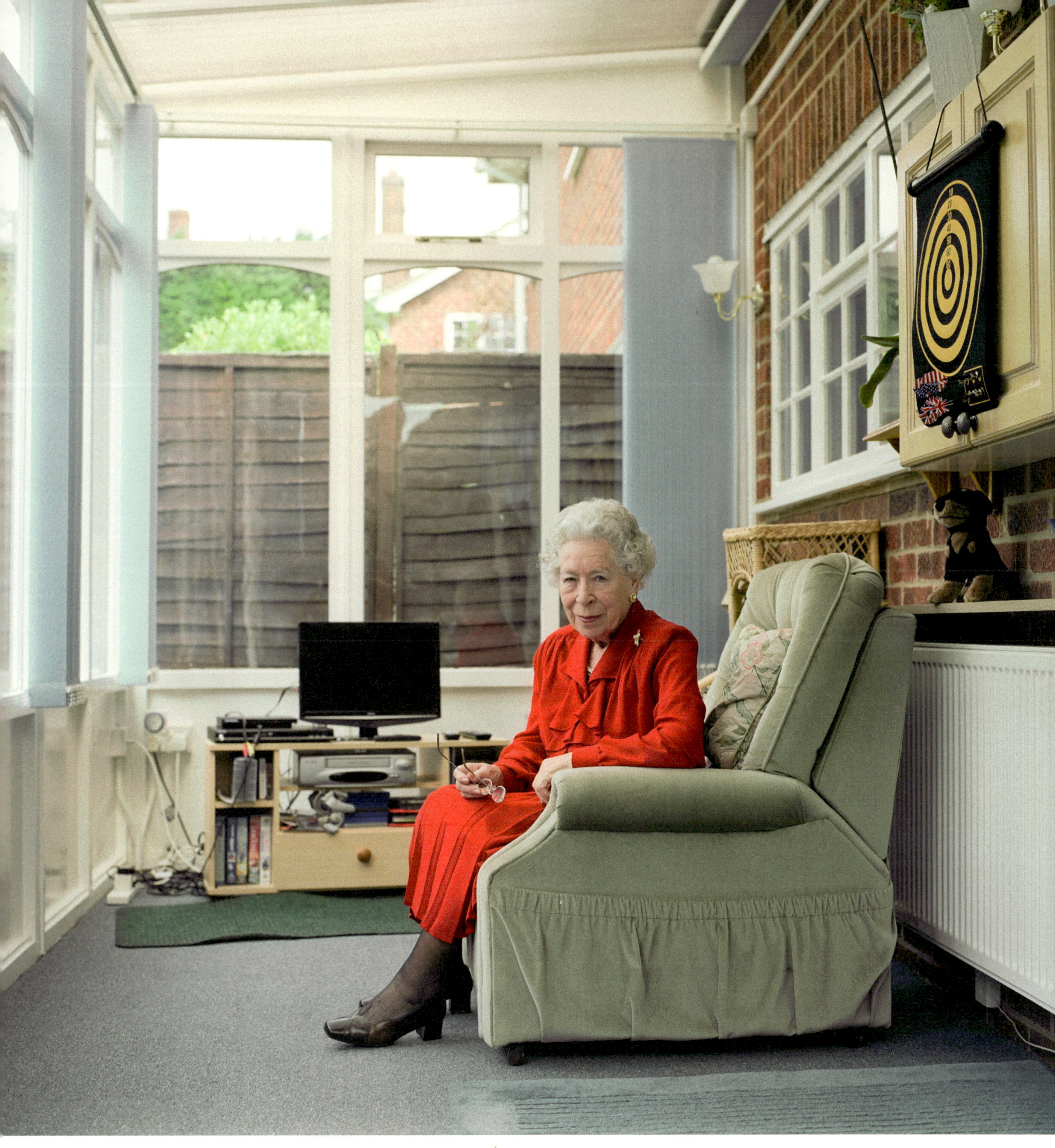

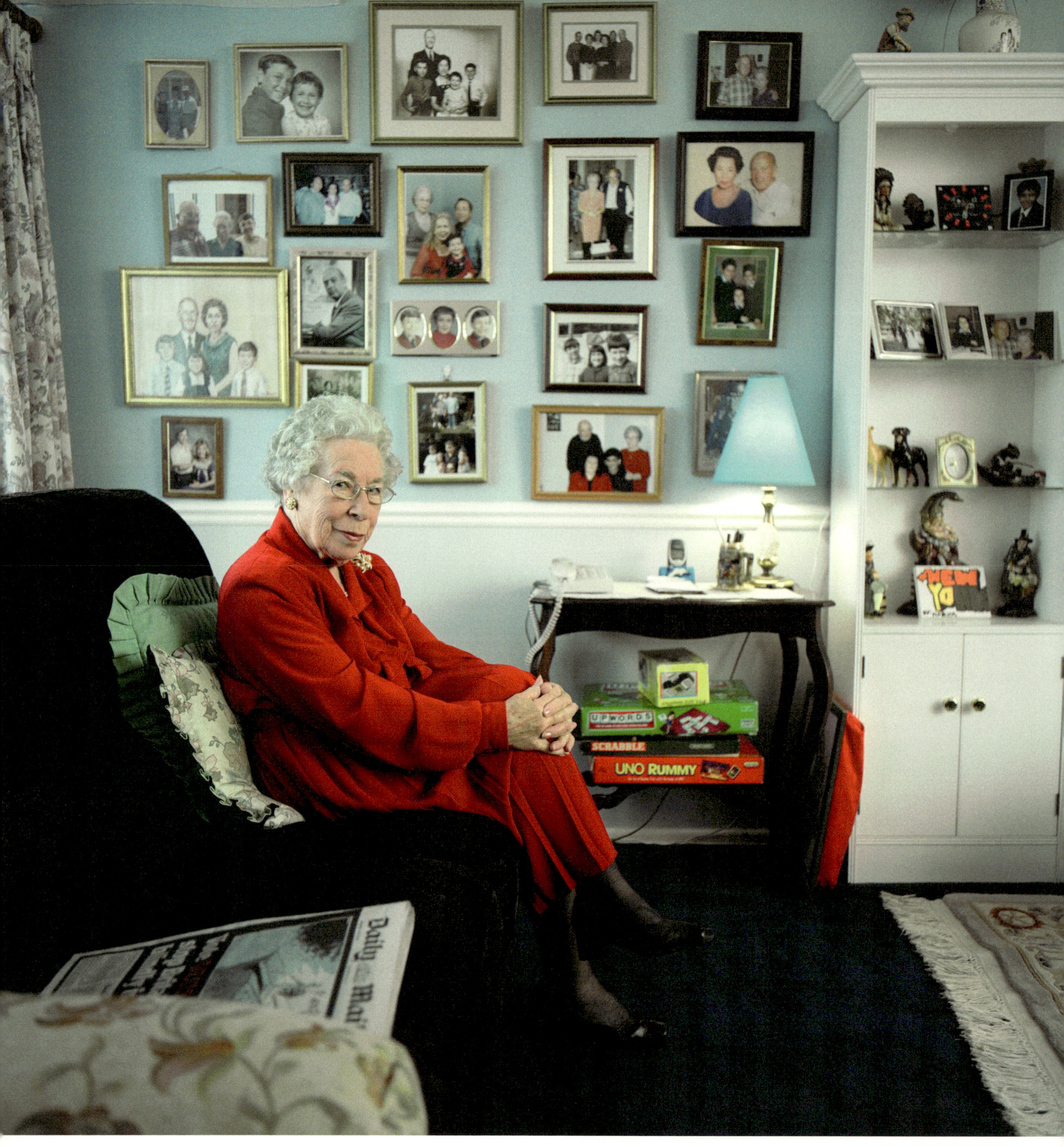
Daily Mail
UPWORDS
SCRABBLE
UNO RUMMY

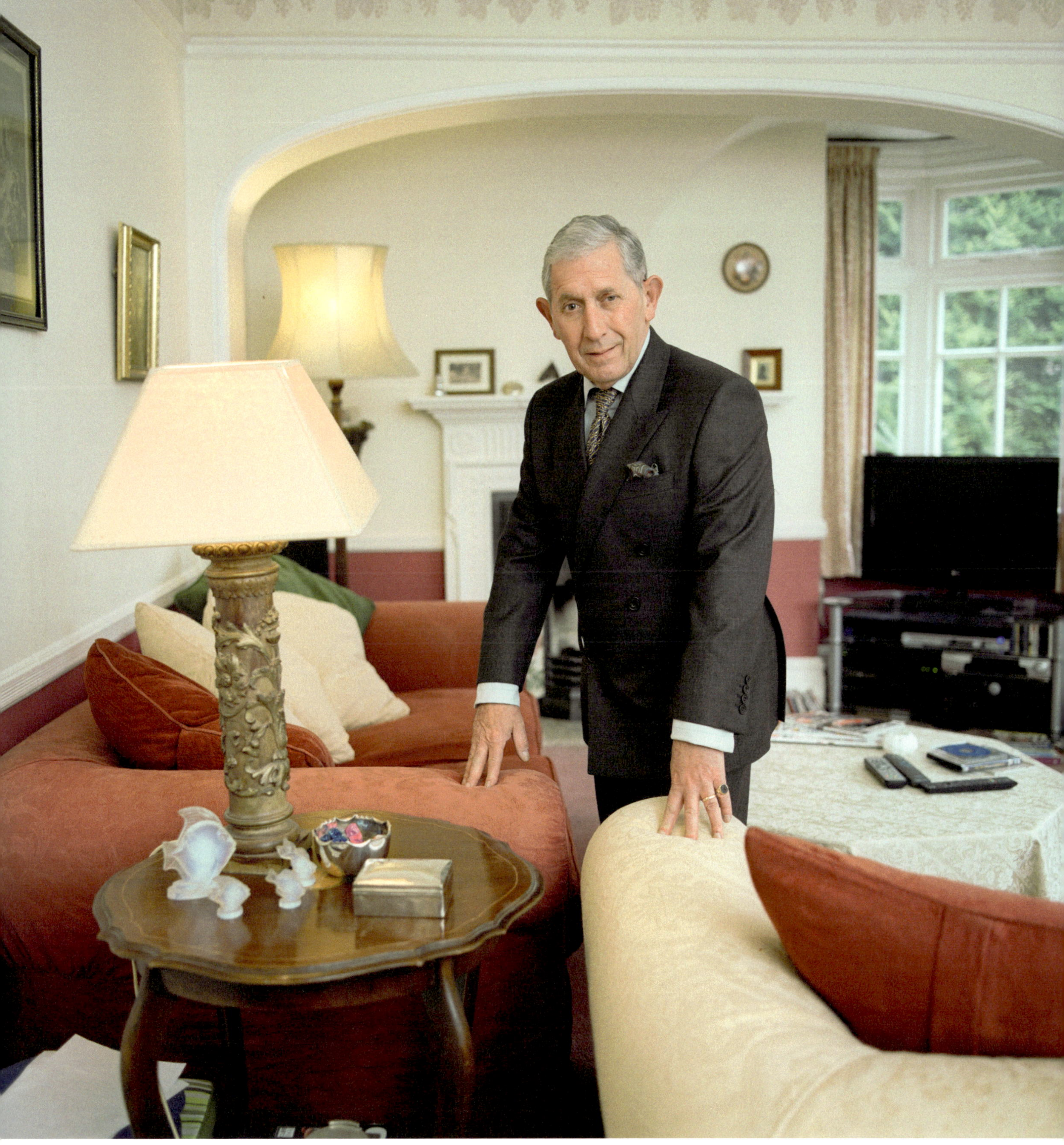

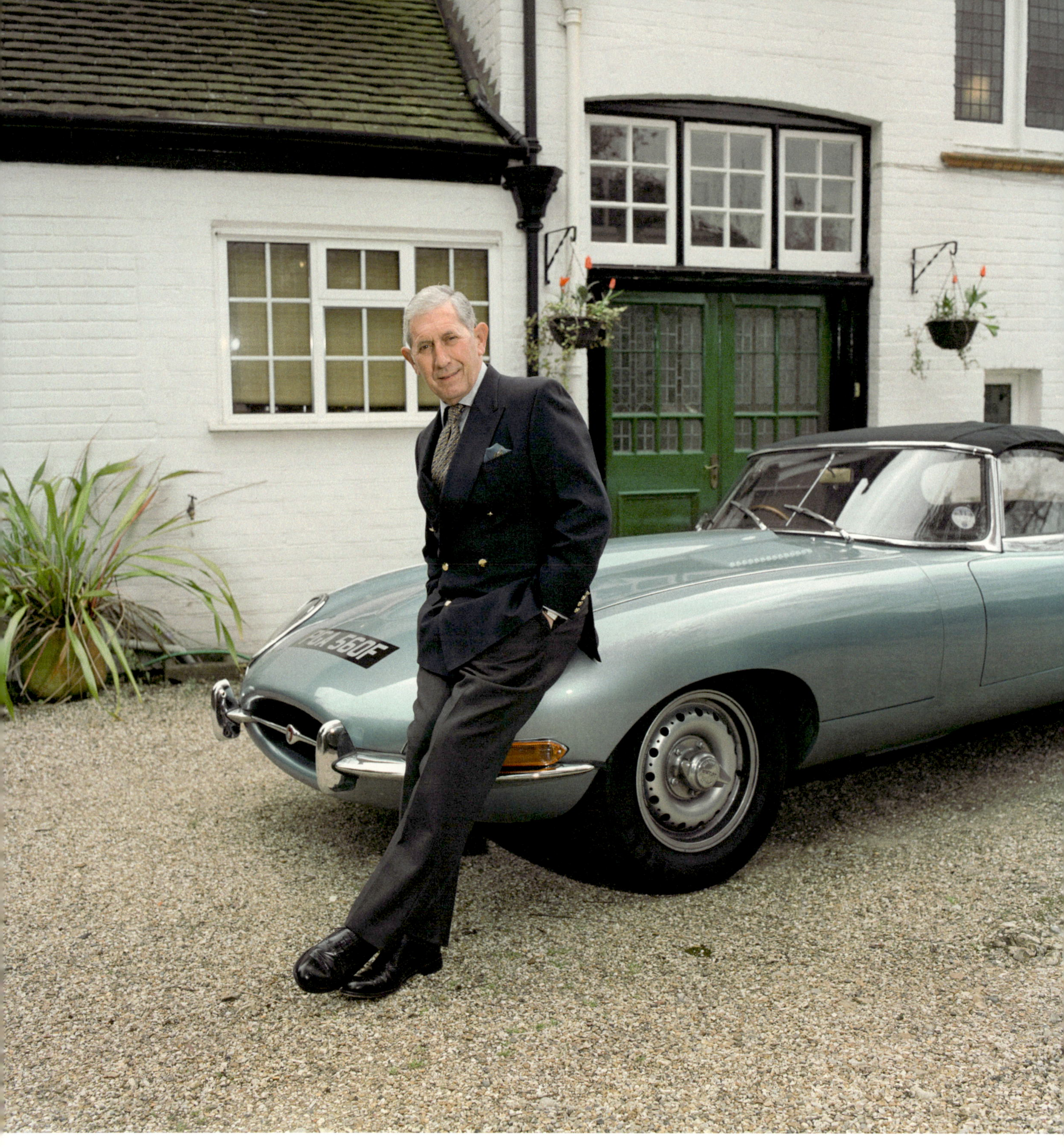

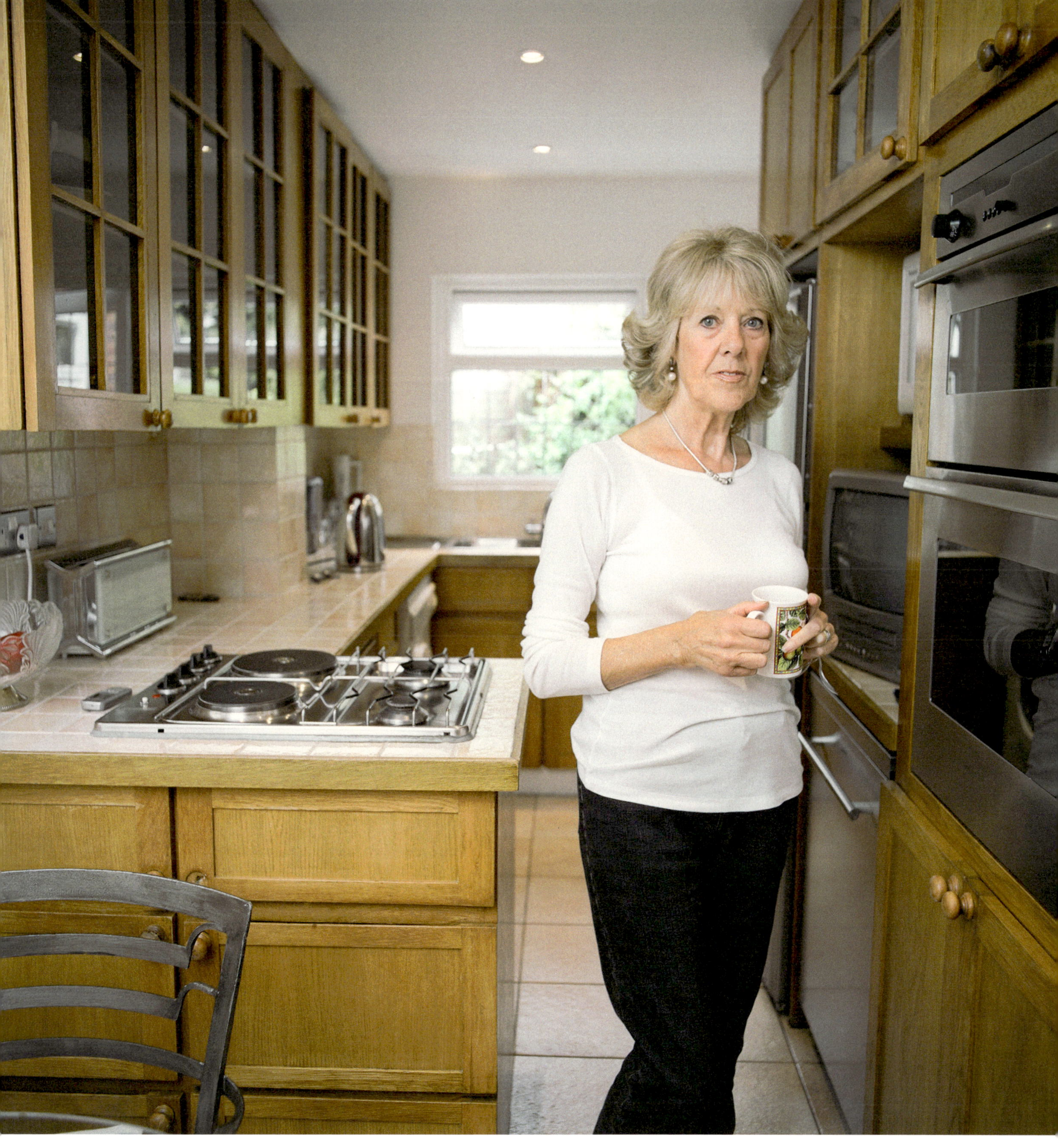

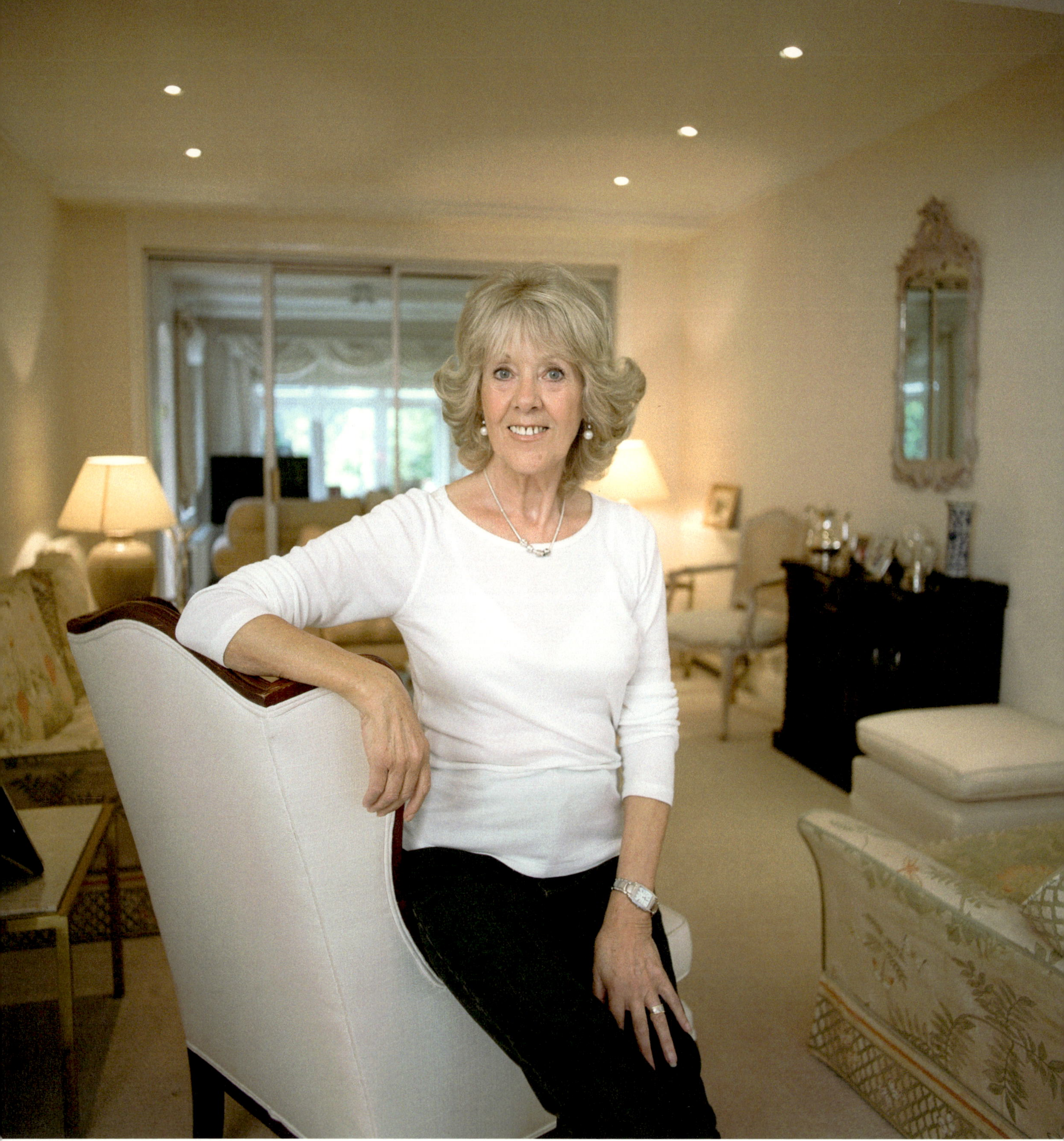

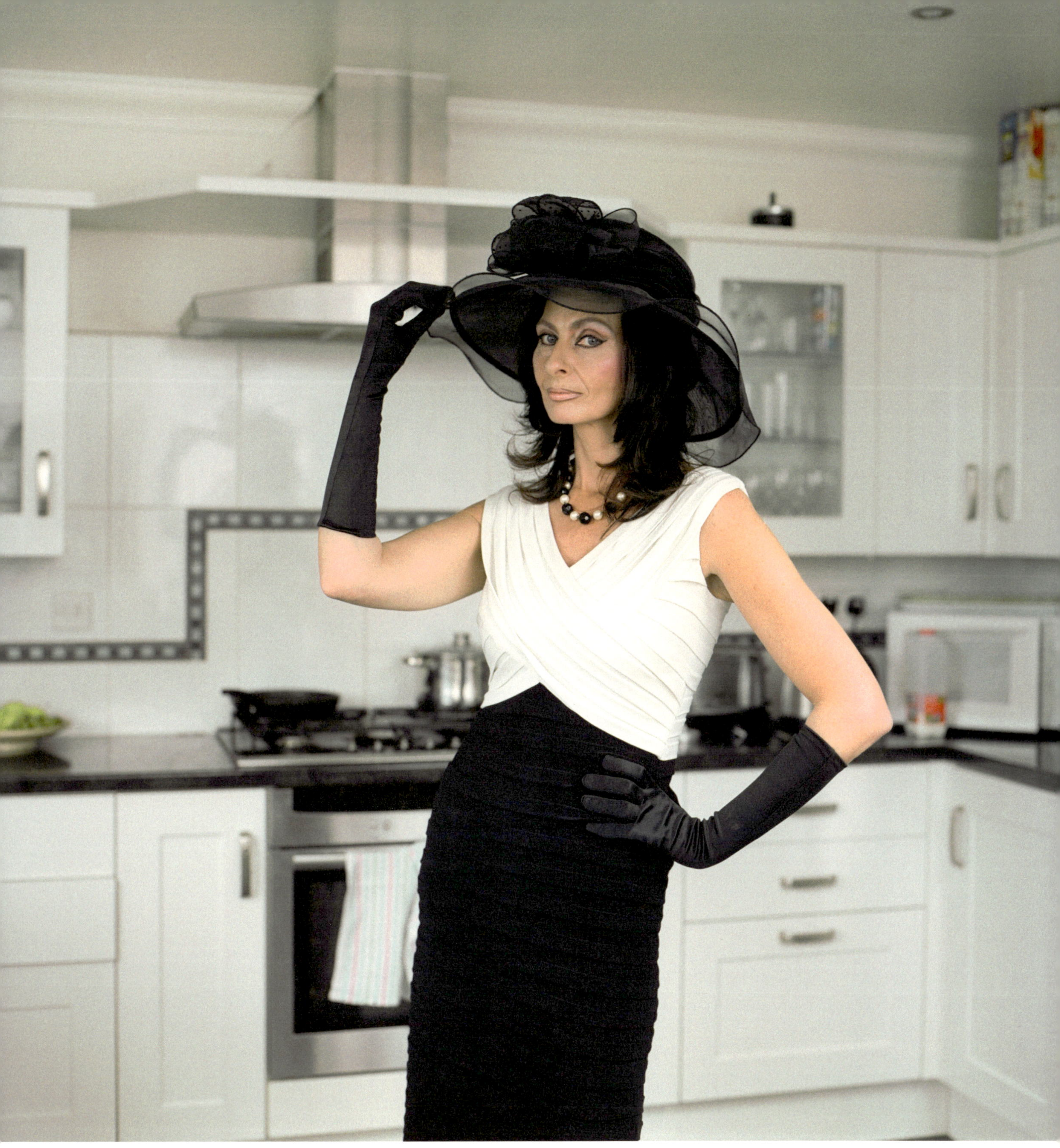

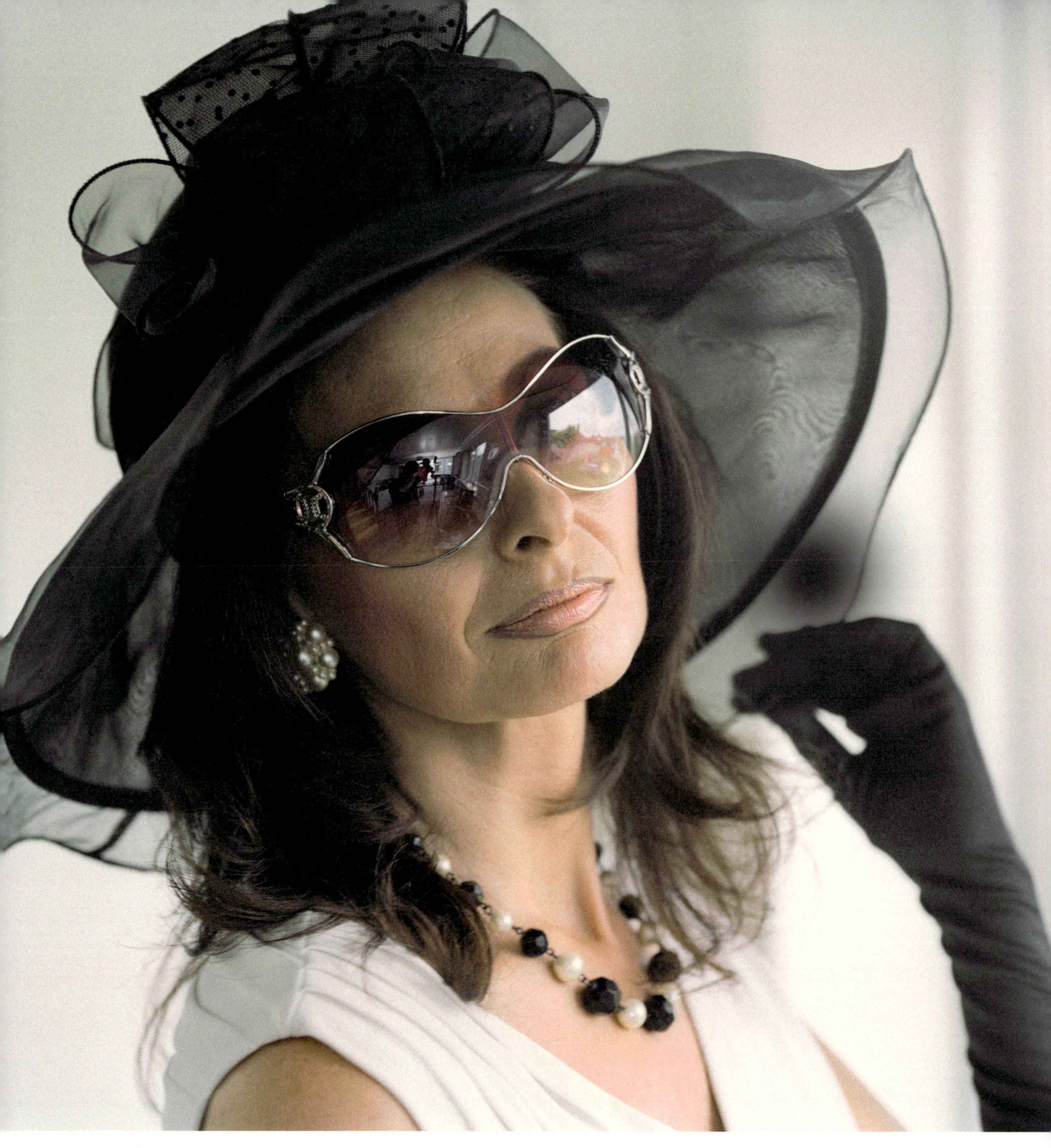

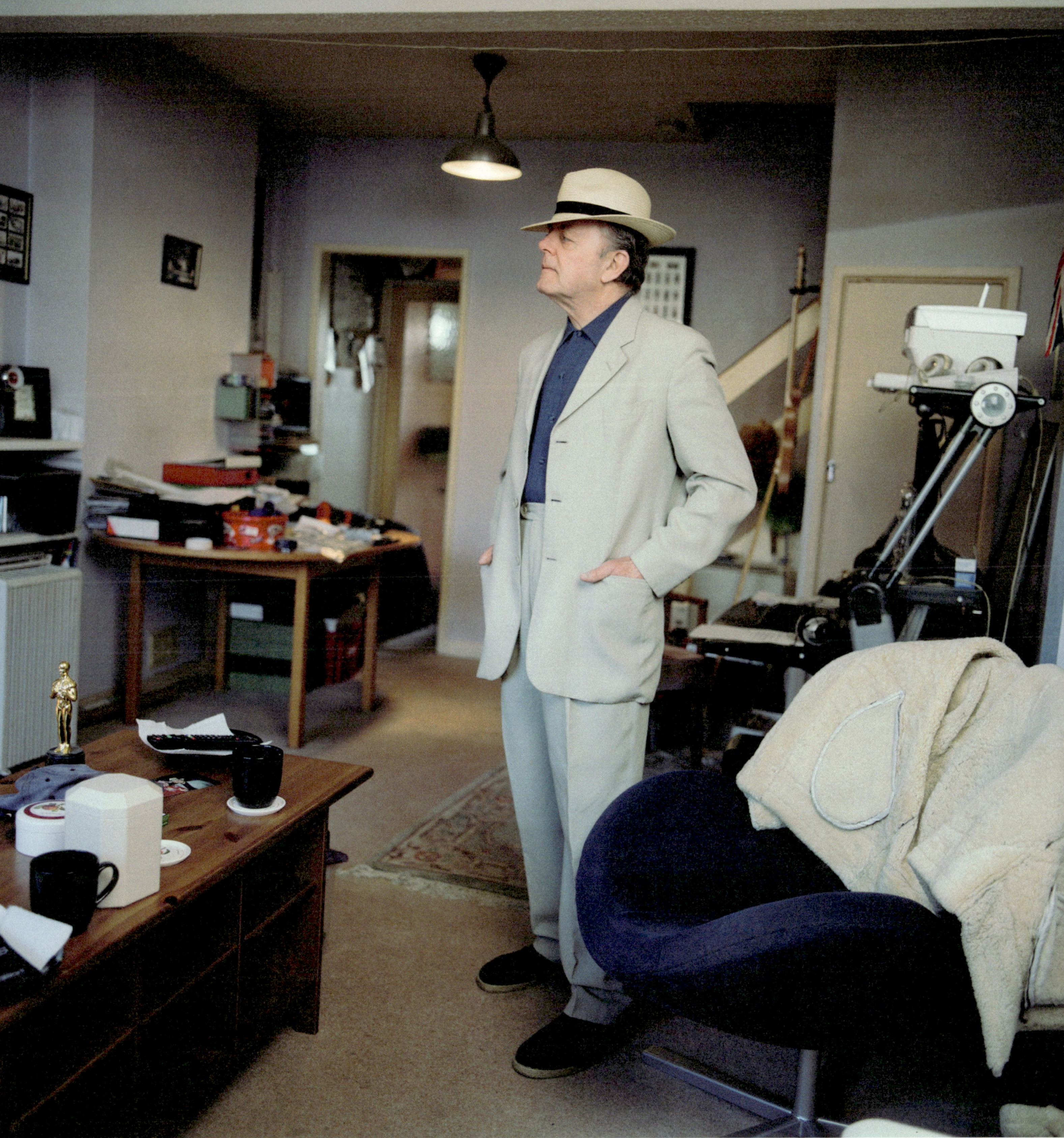

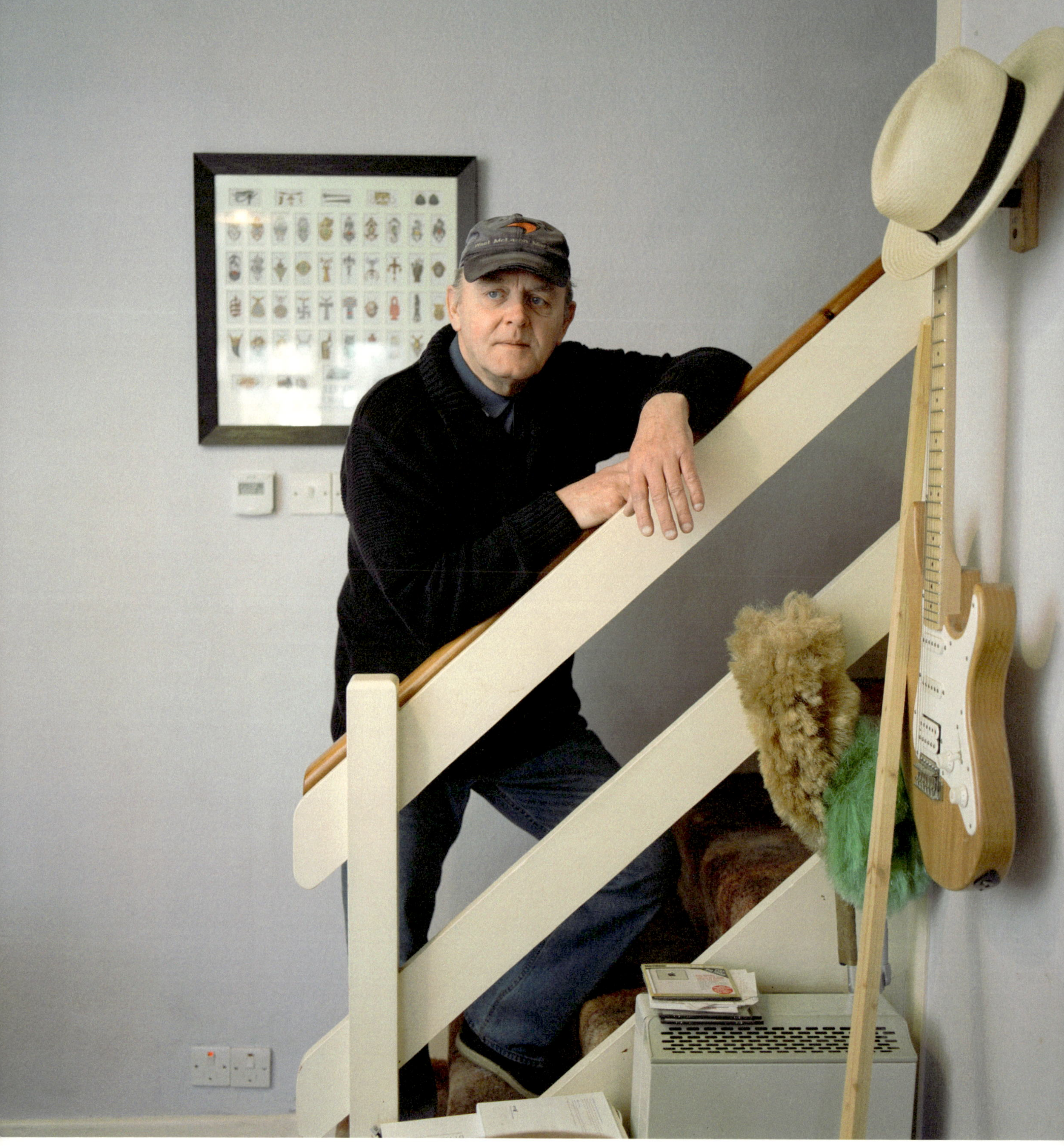

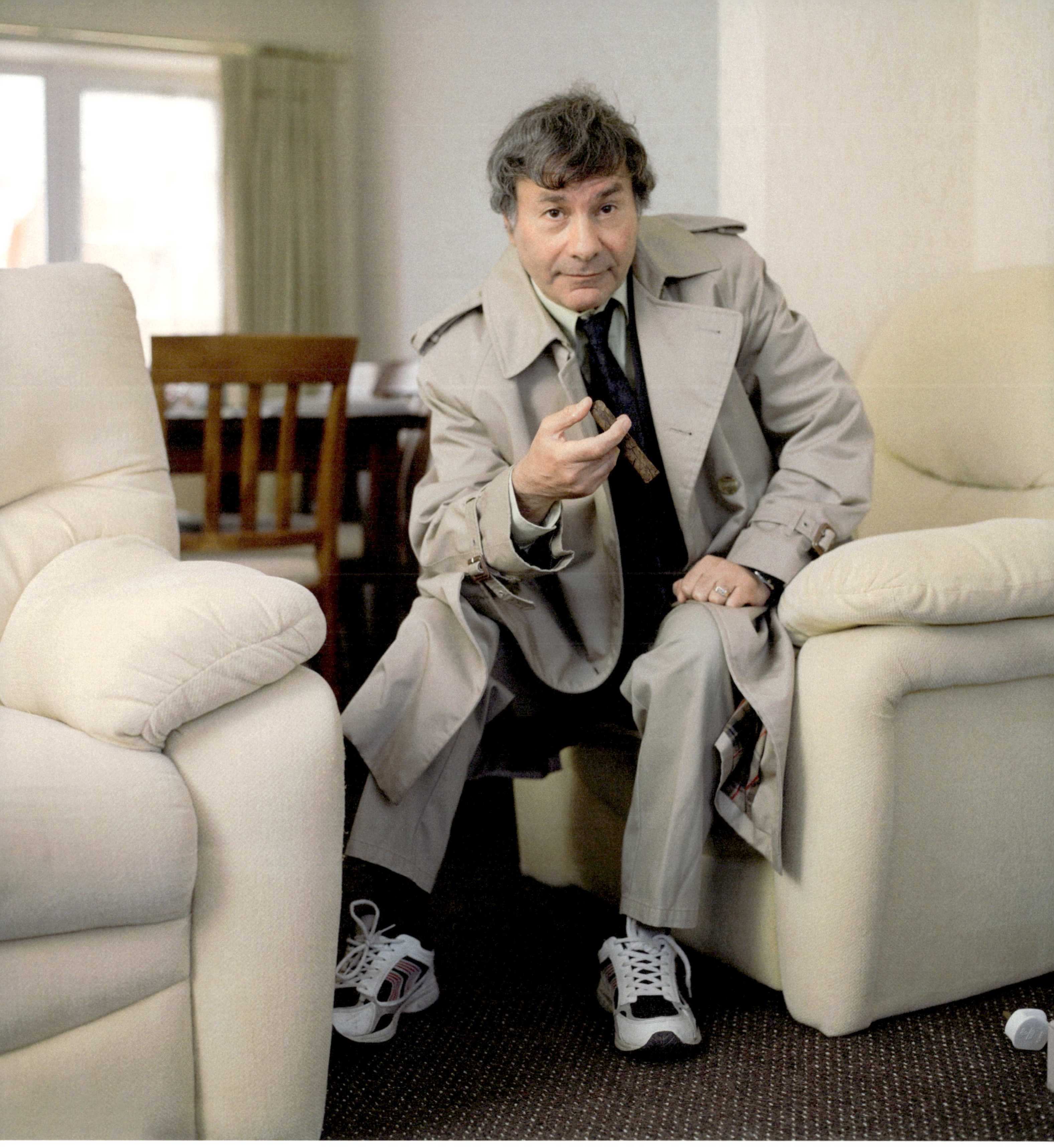

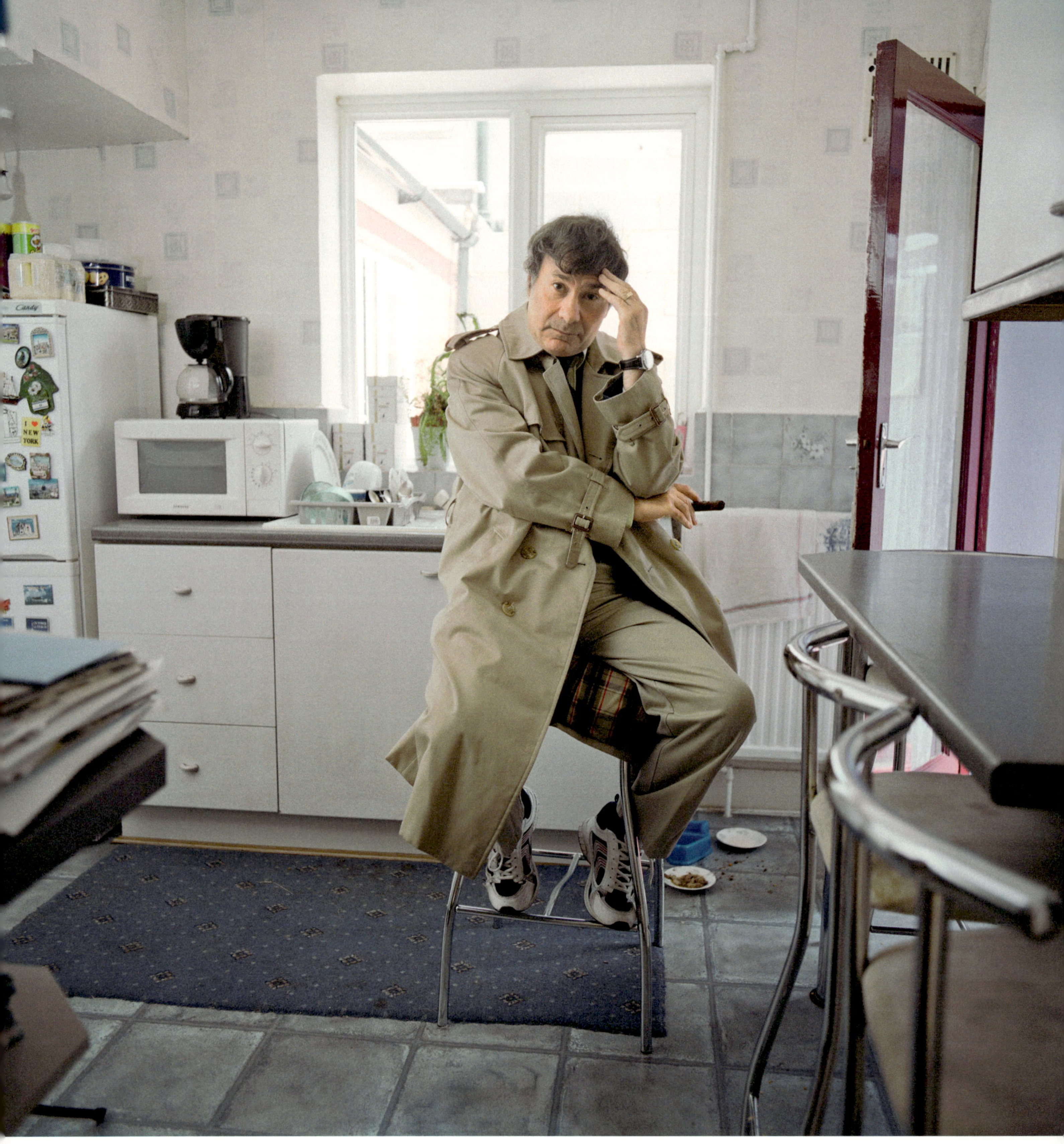

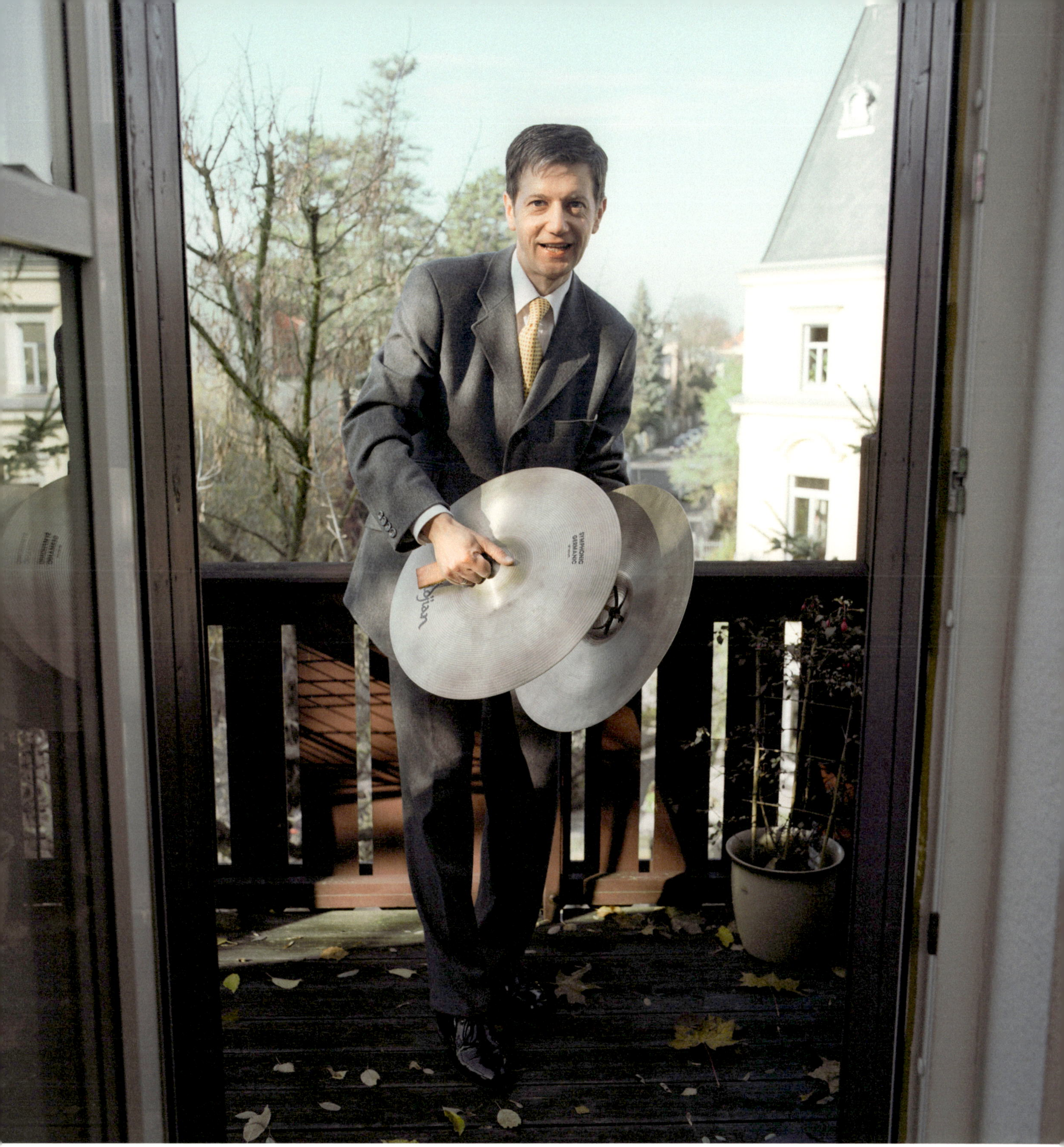

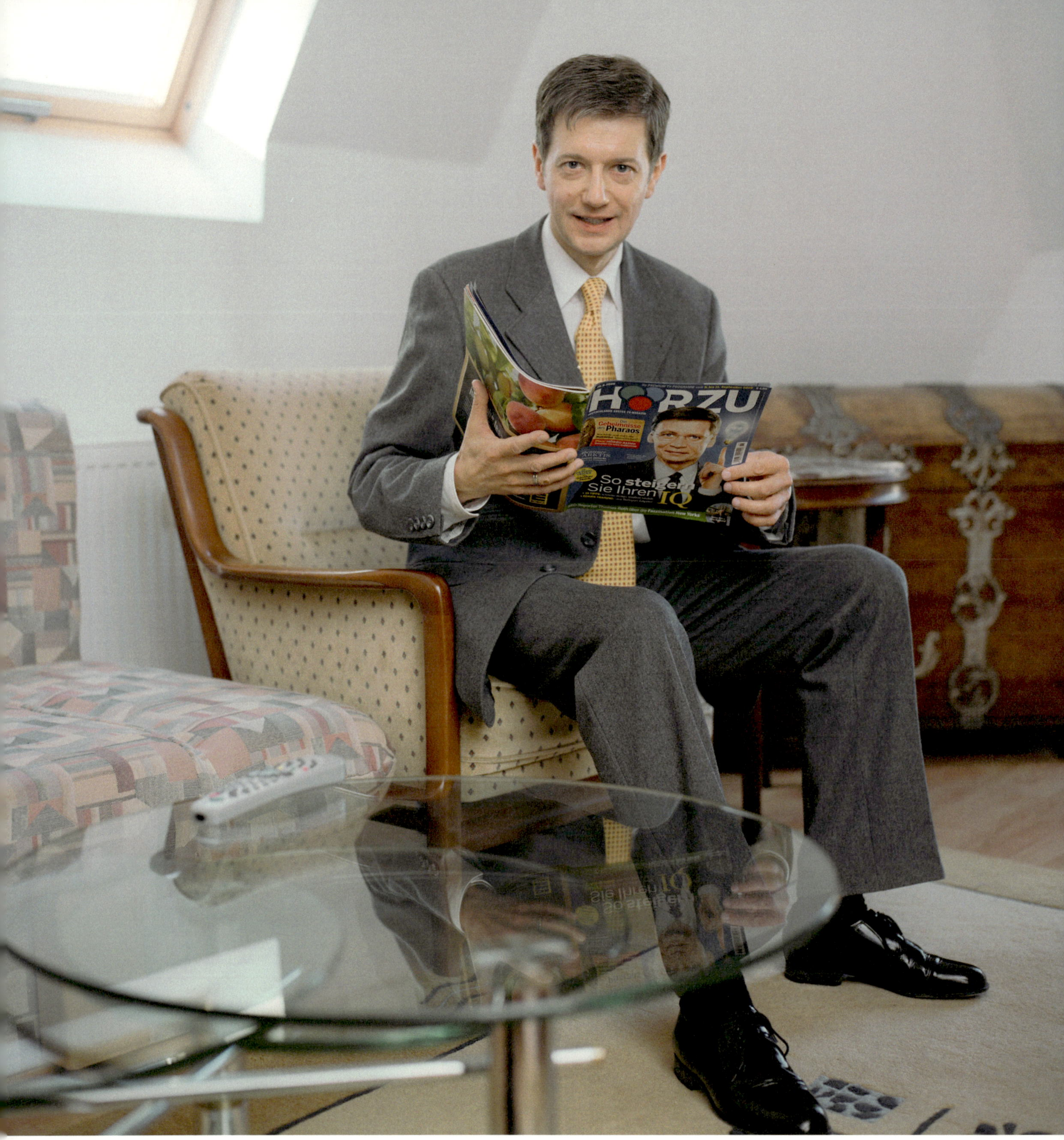

HÖRZU
Die Geheimnisse des Pharaos
So steigern Sie Ihren IQ

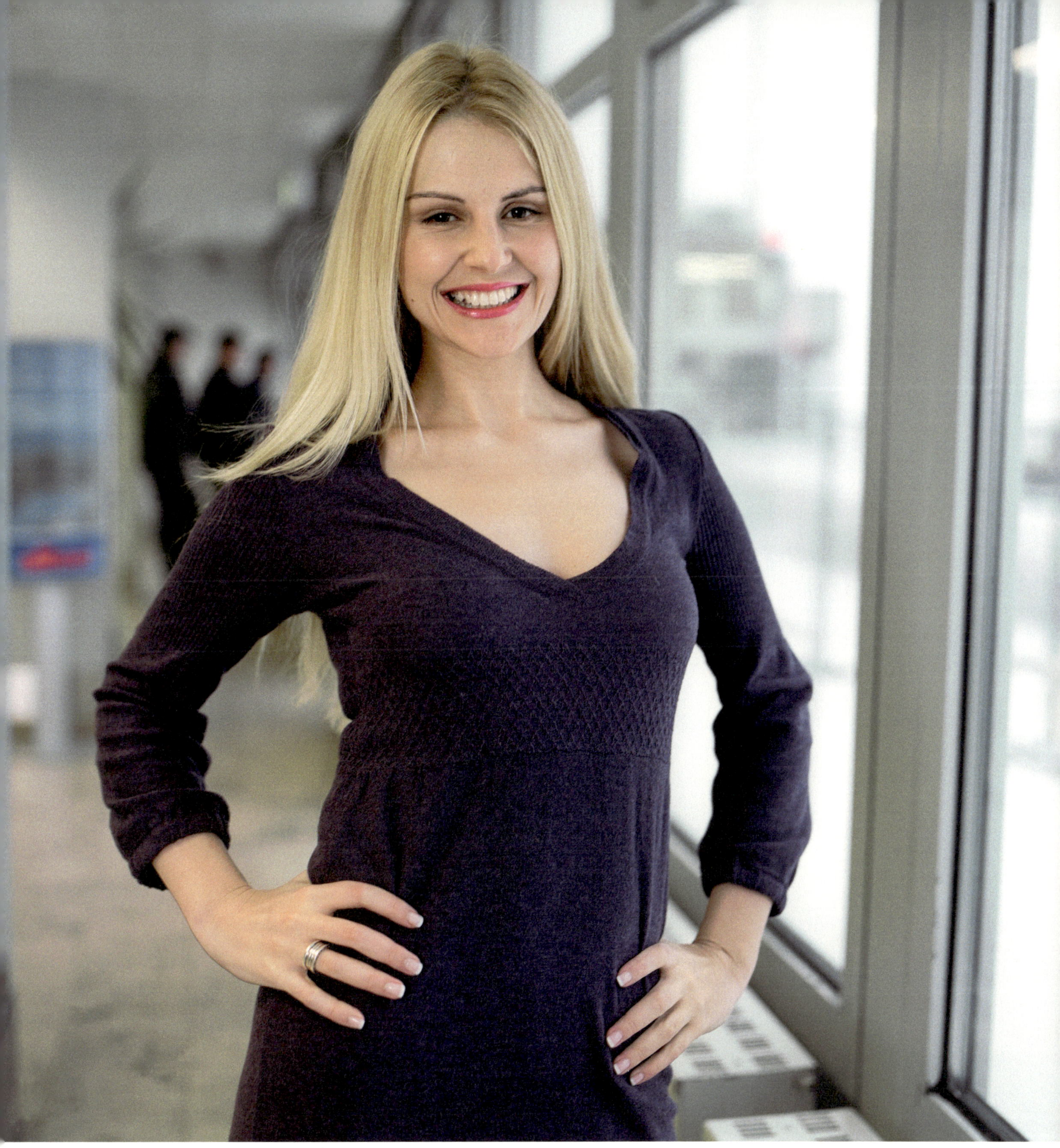

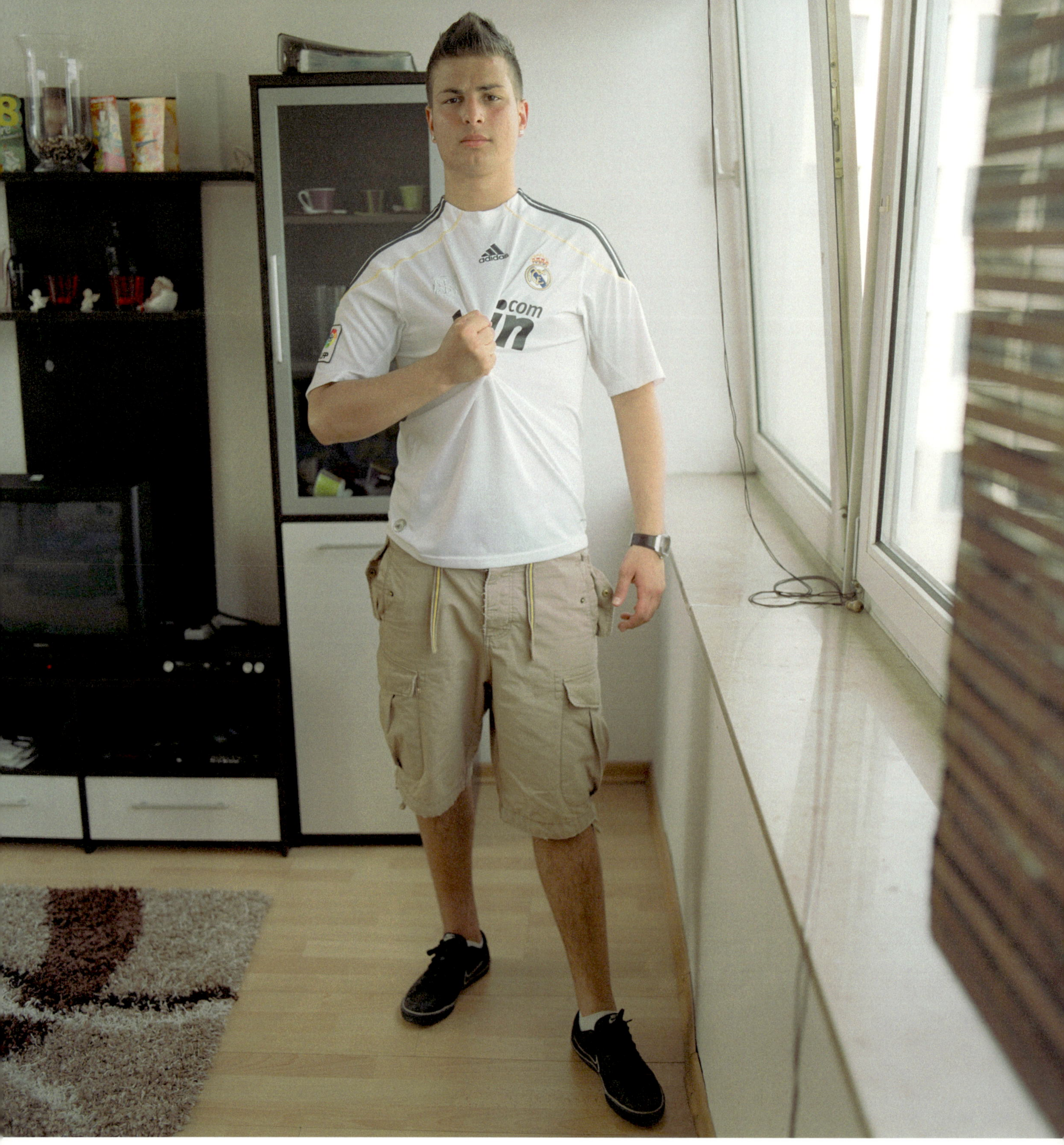

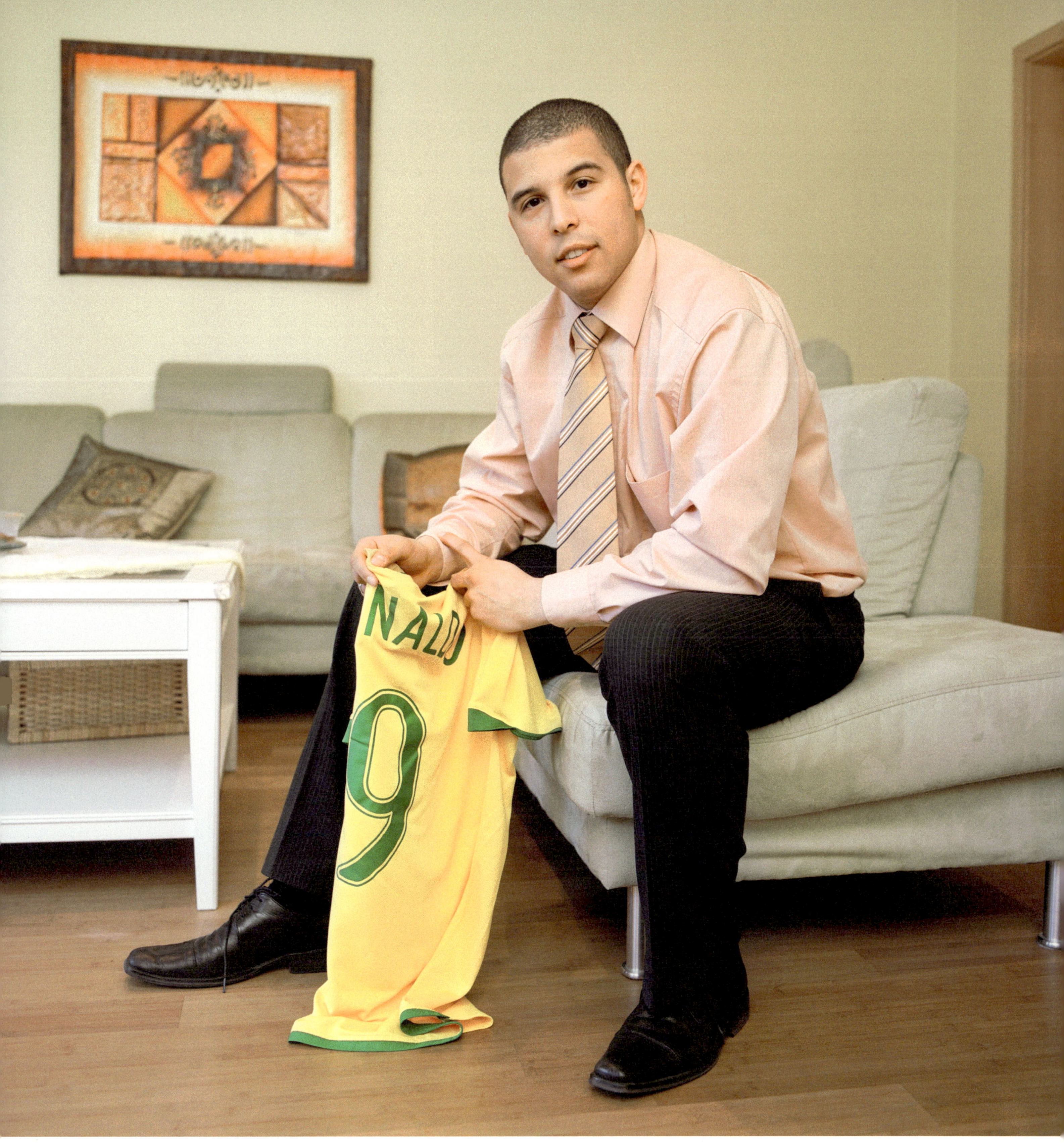
NALD O
9

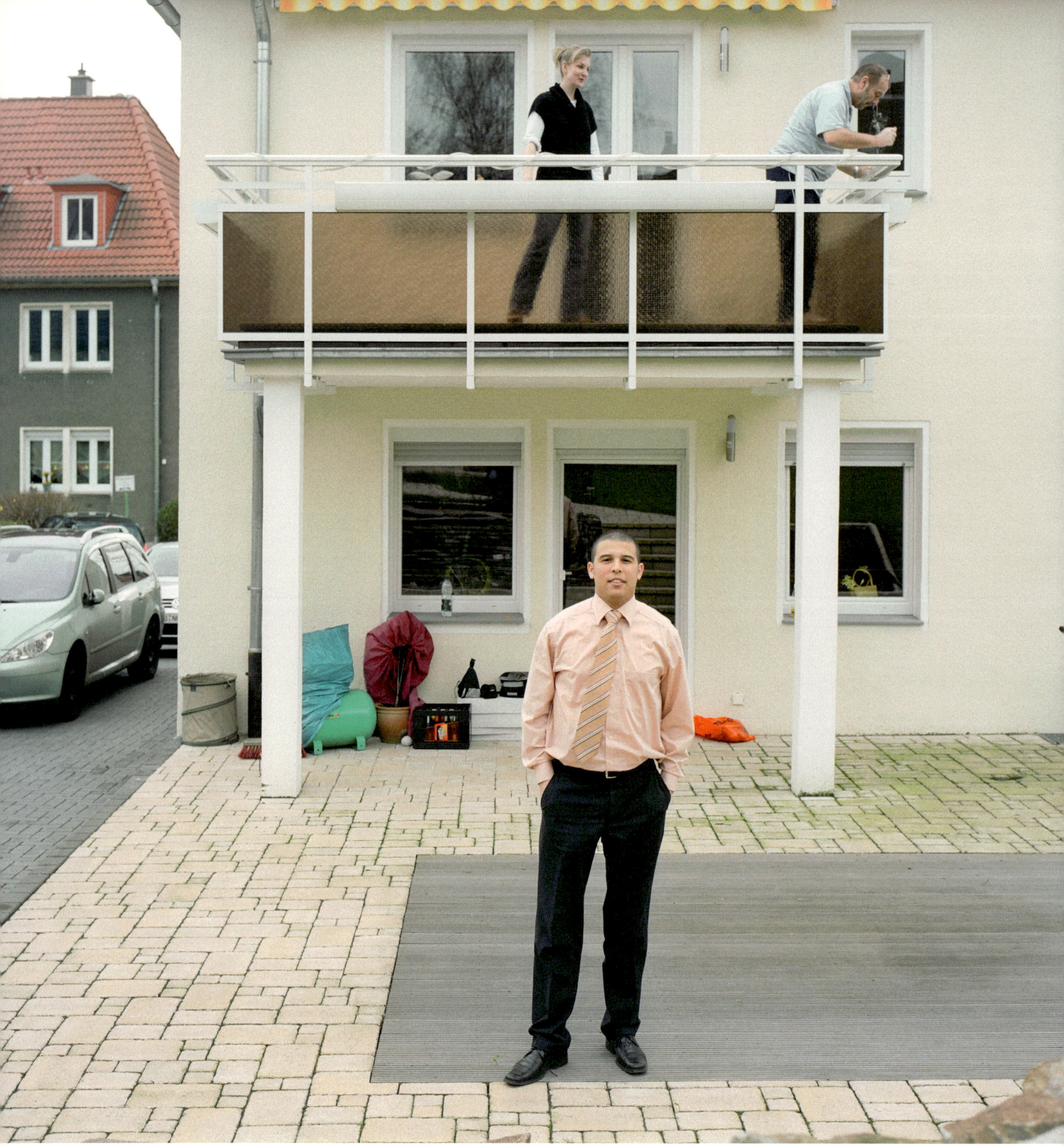

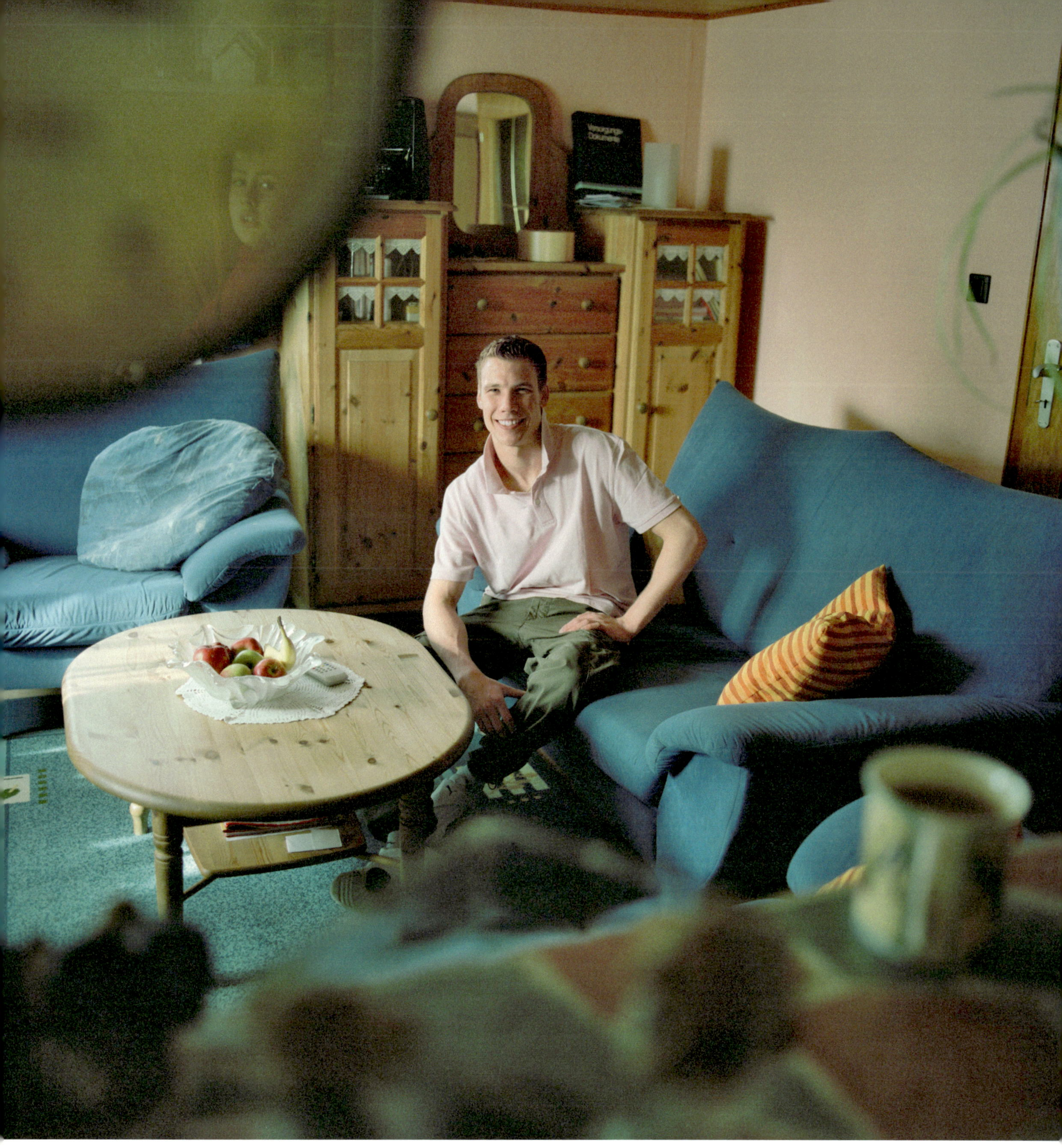

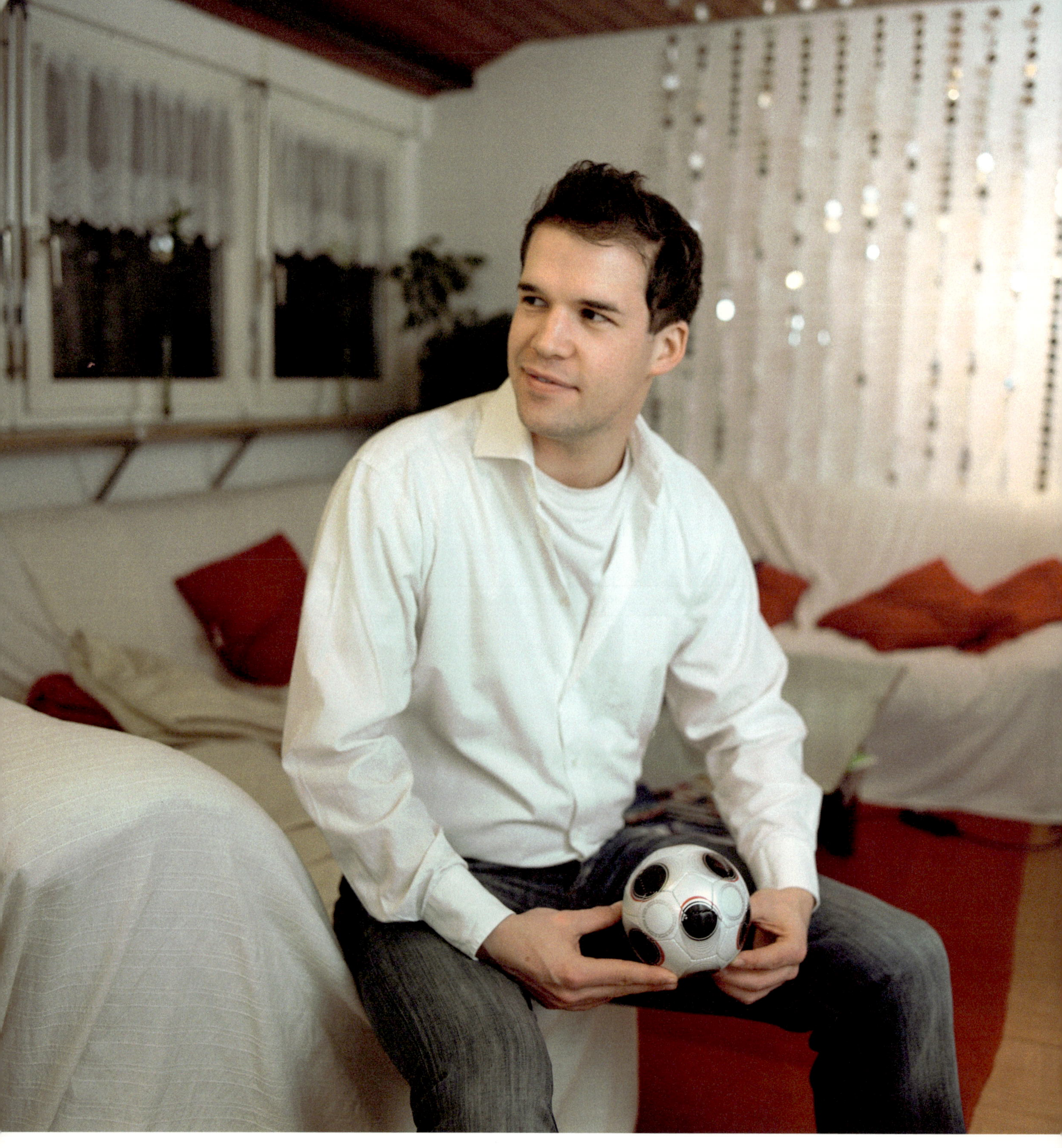

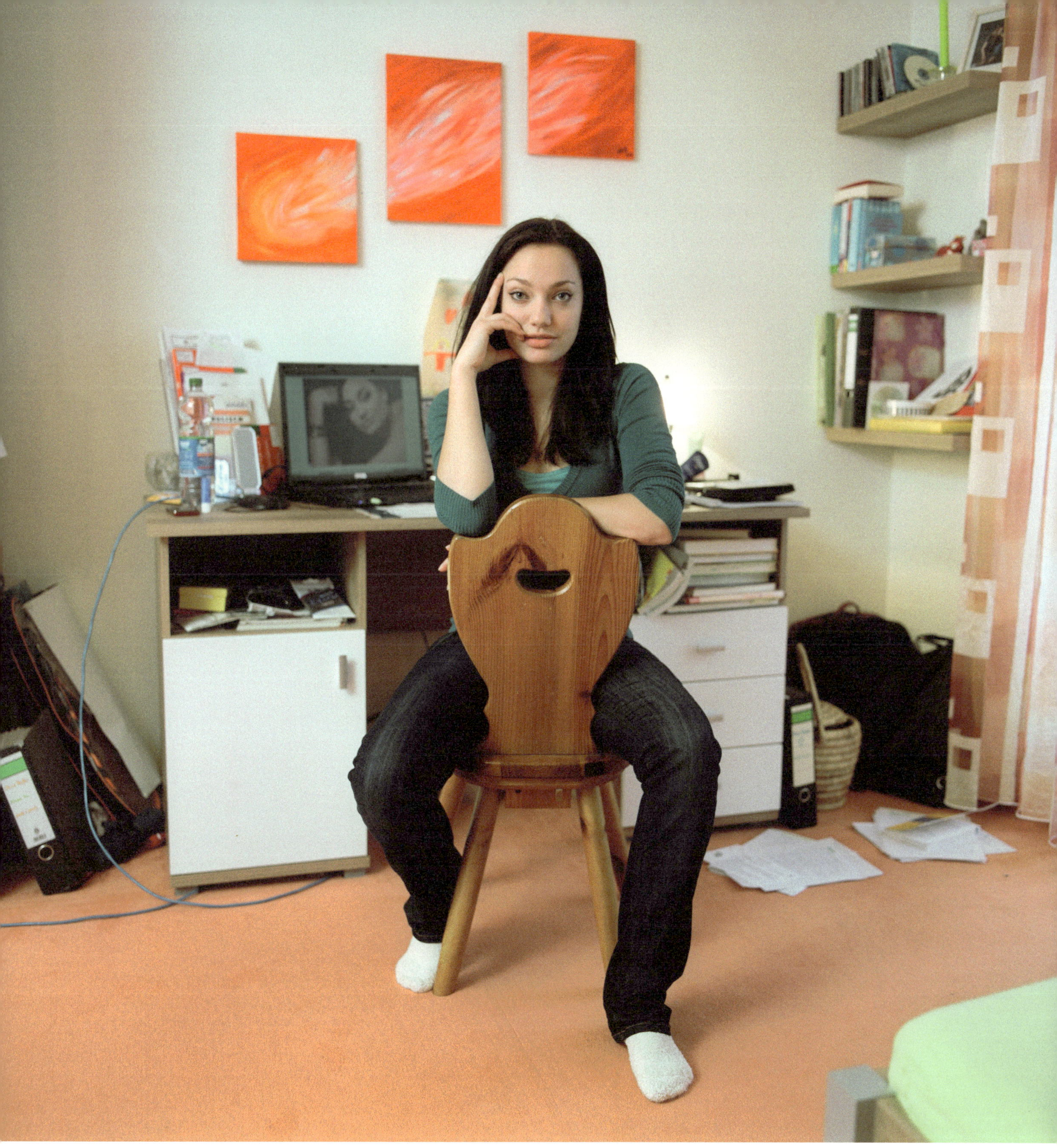

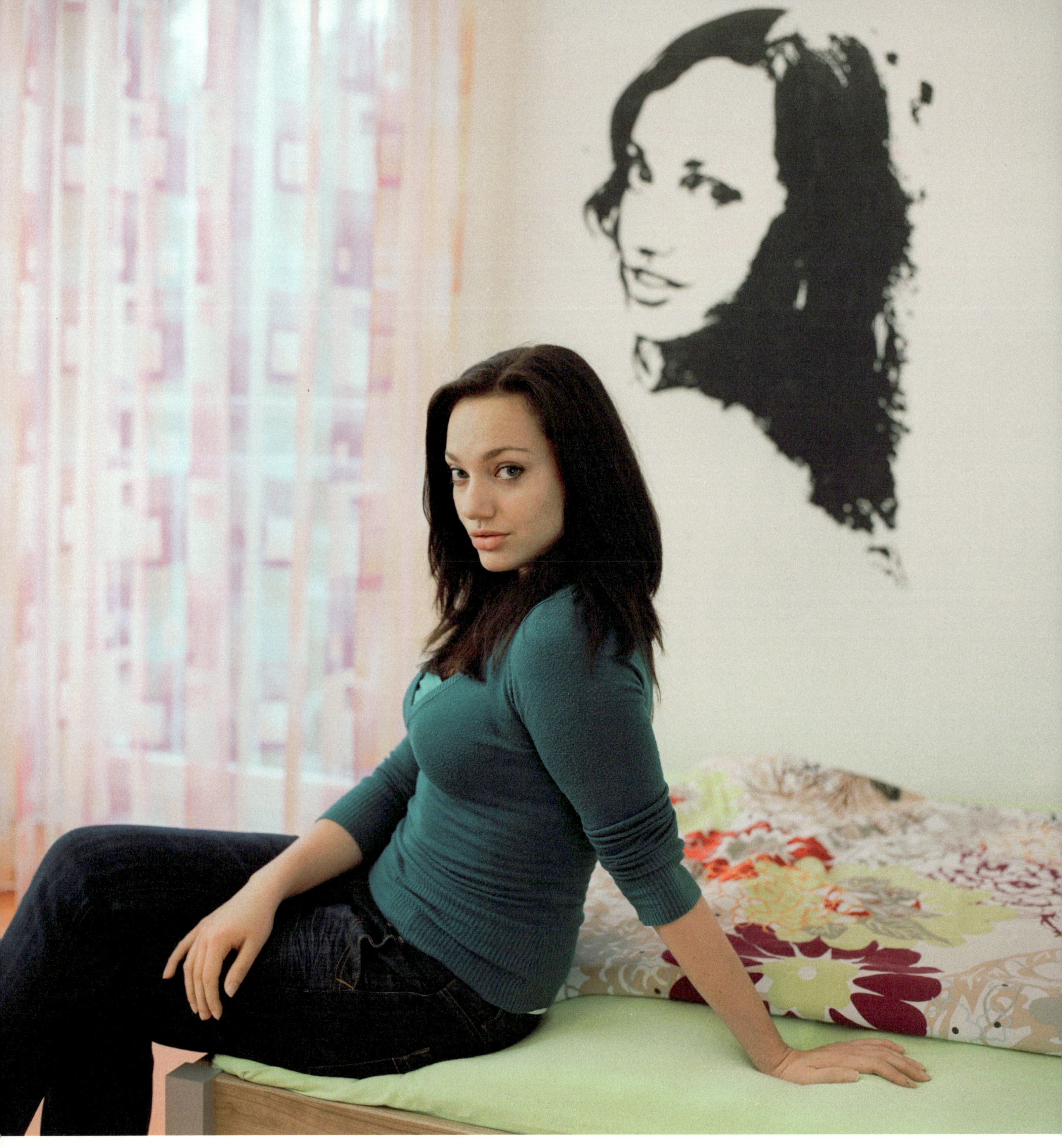

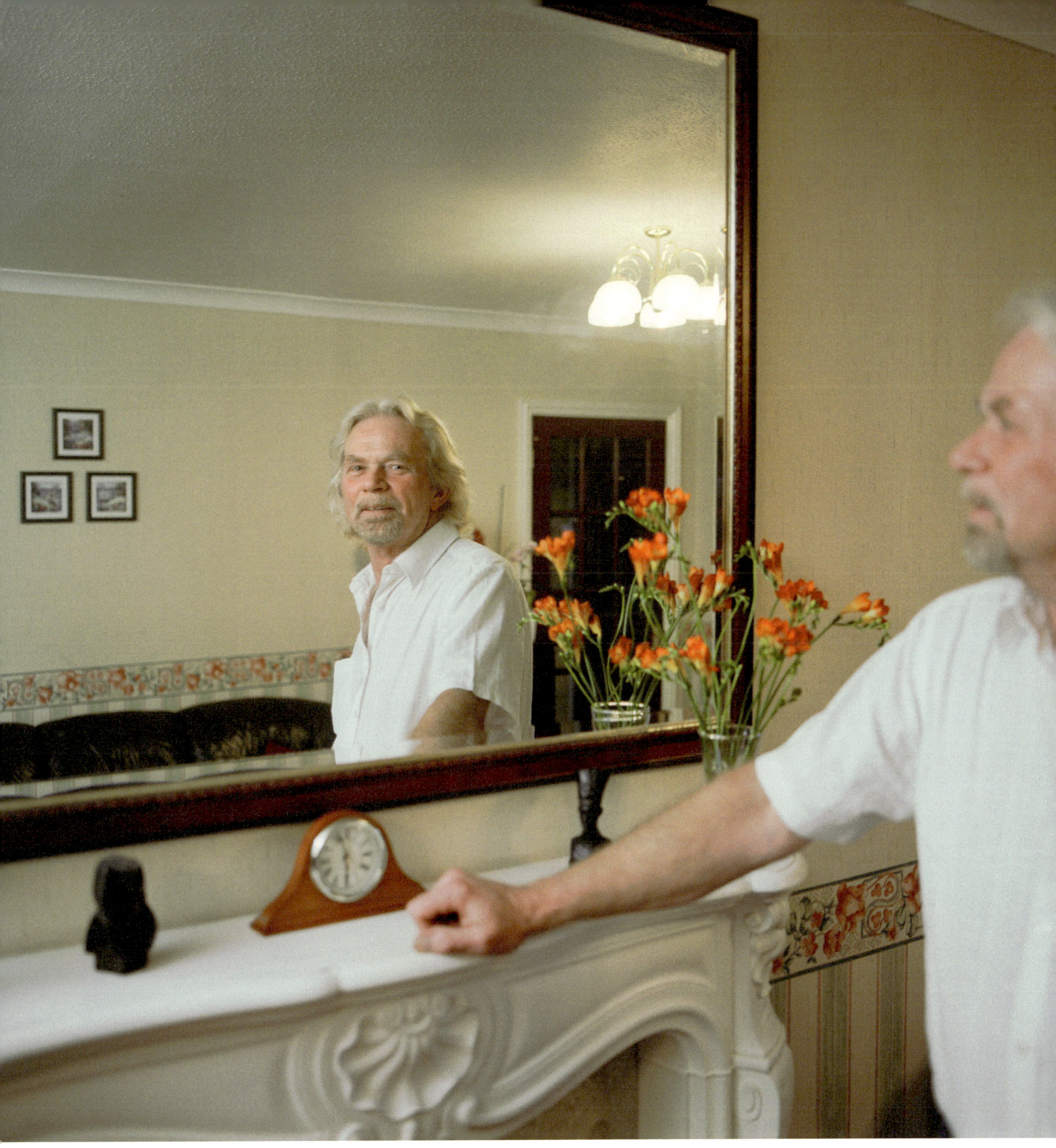

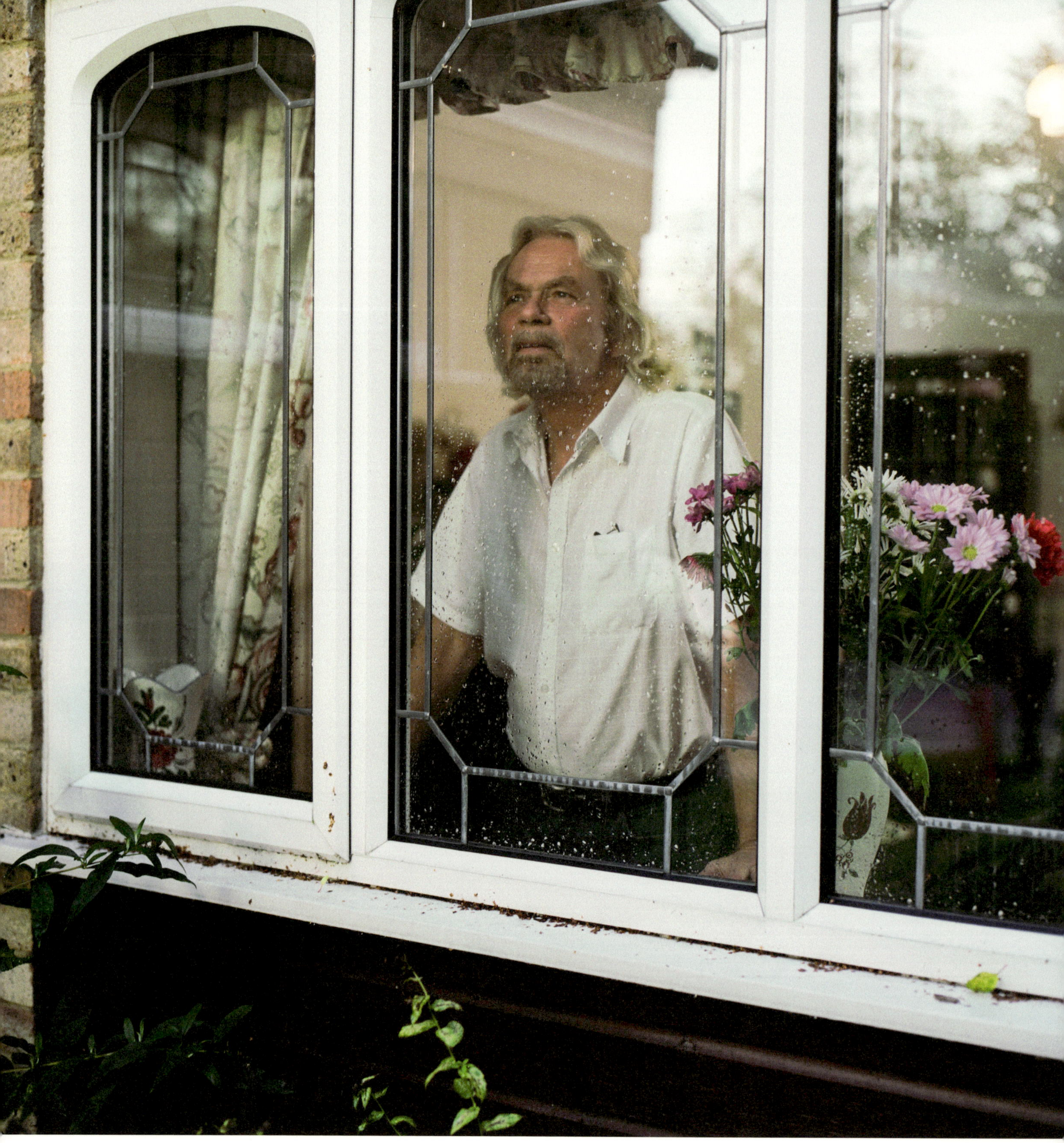

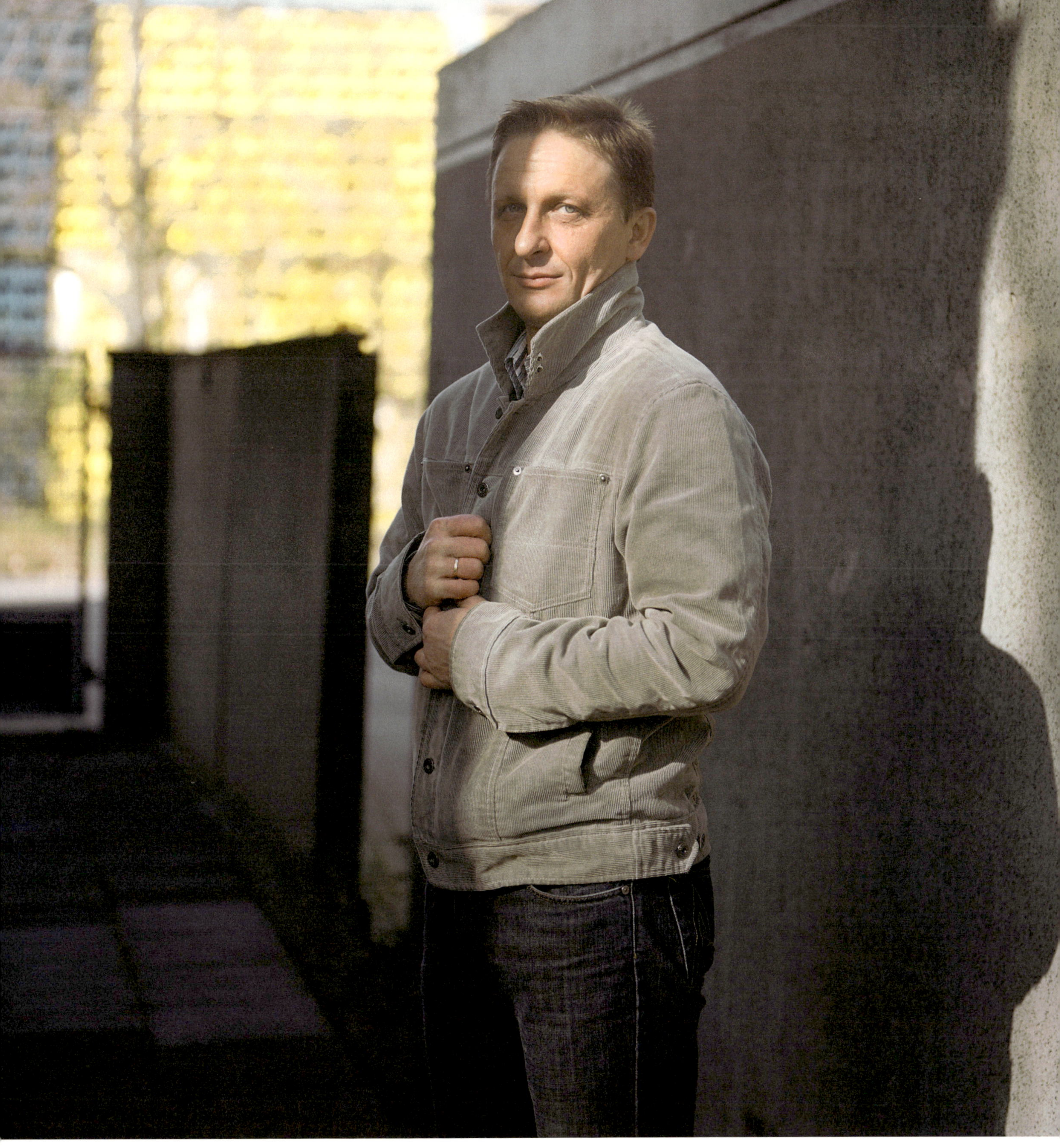

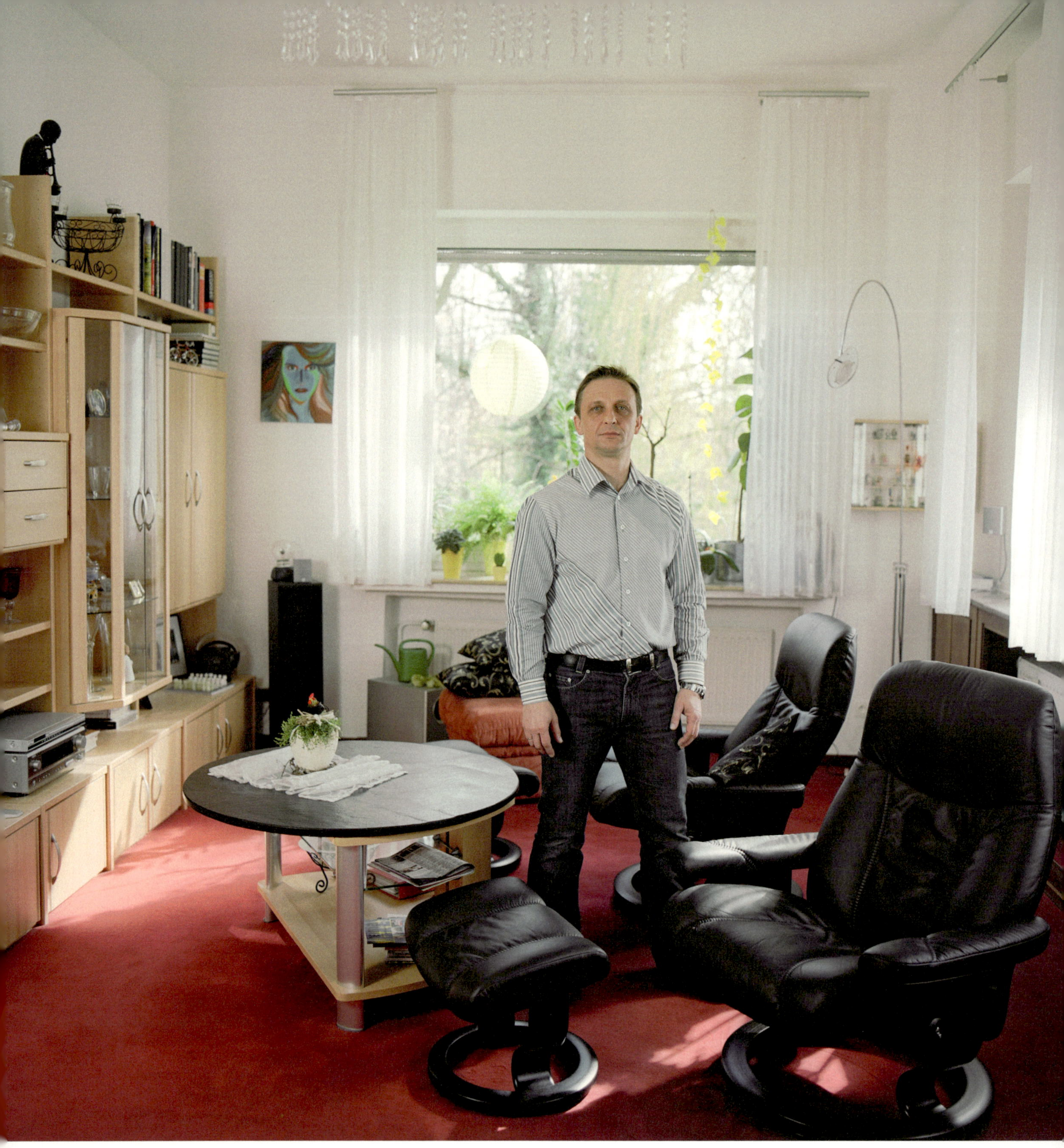

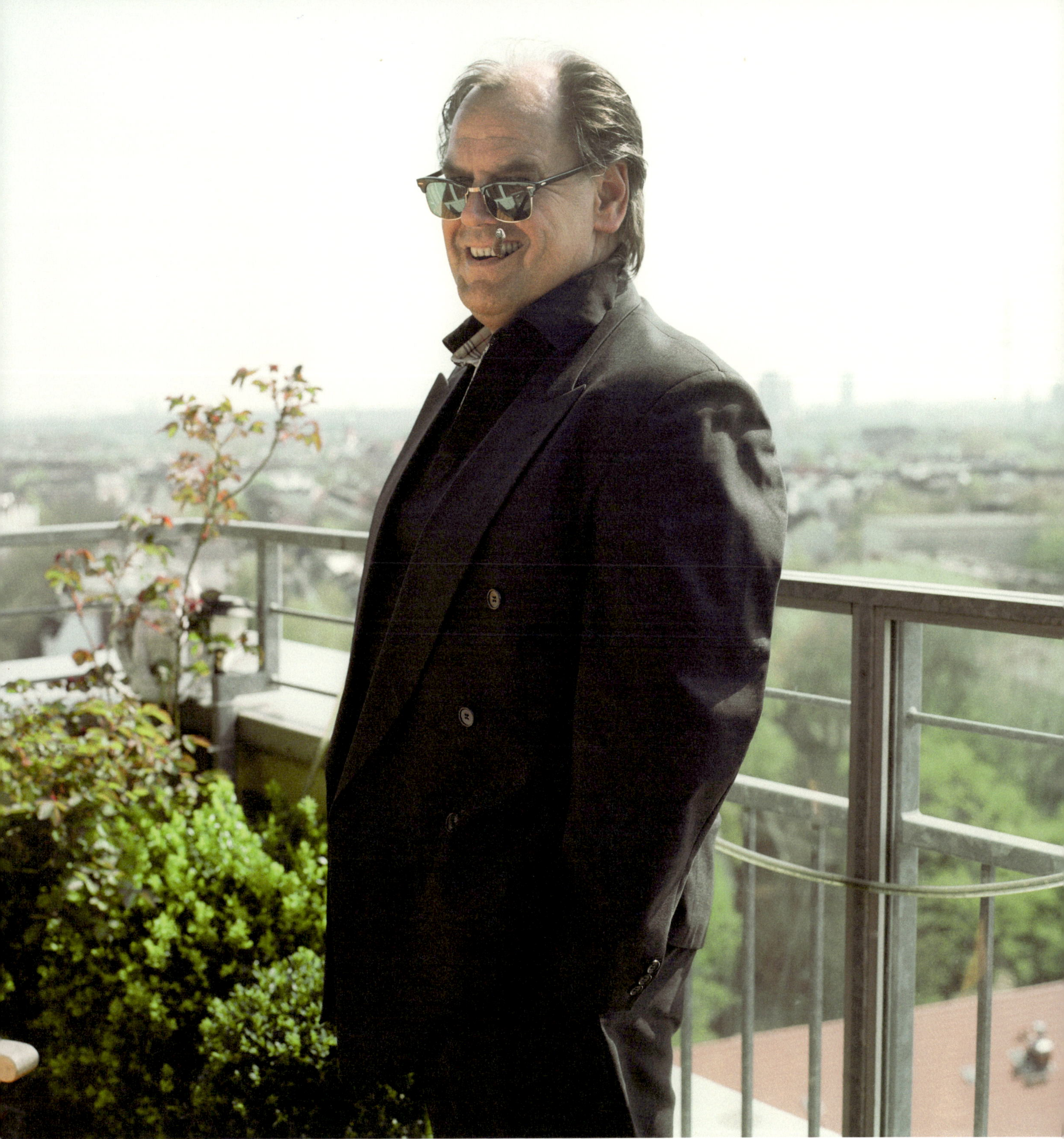

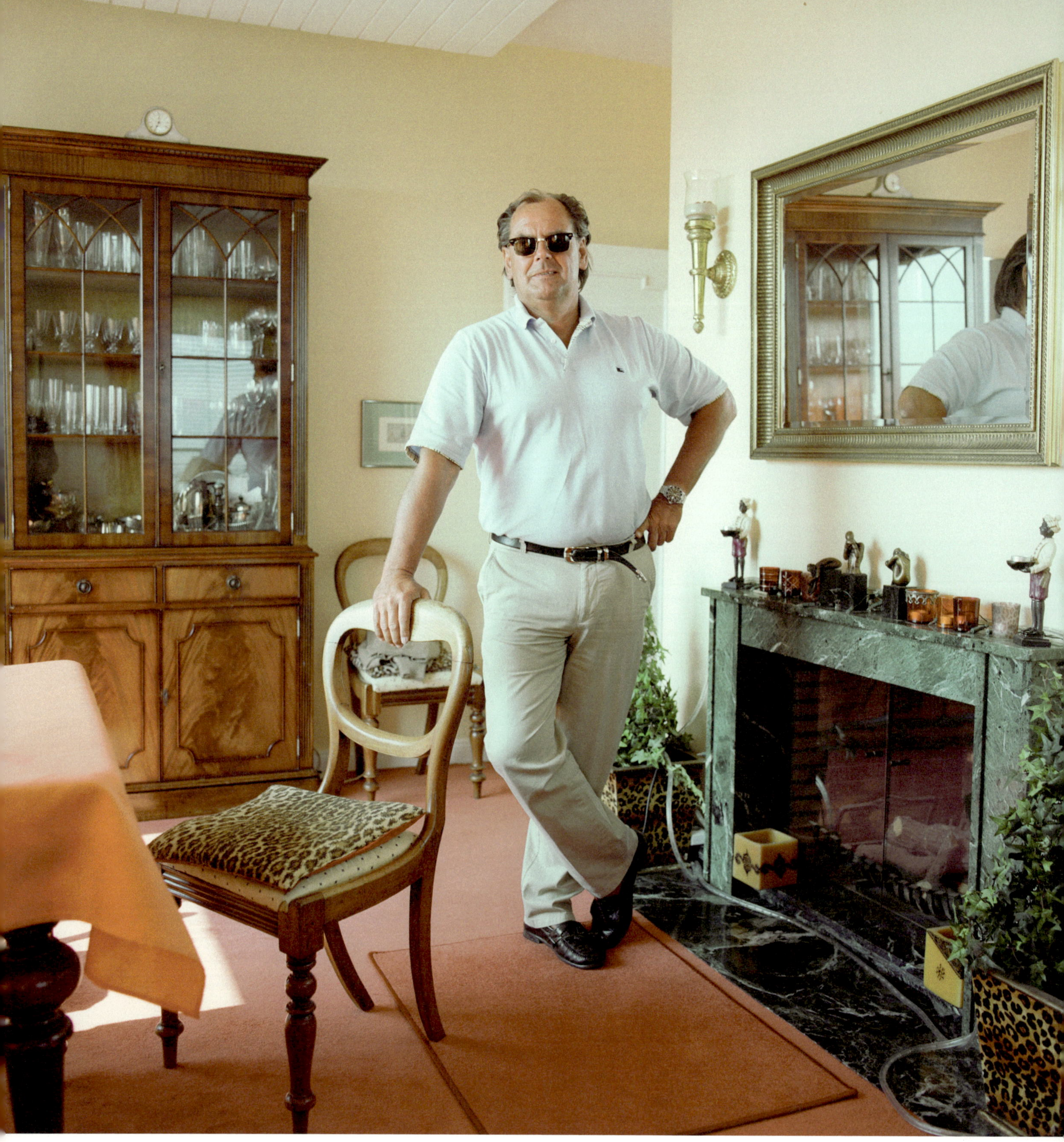

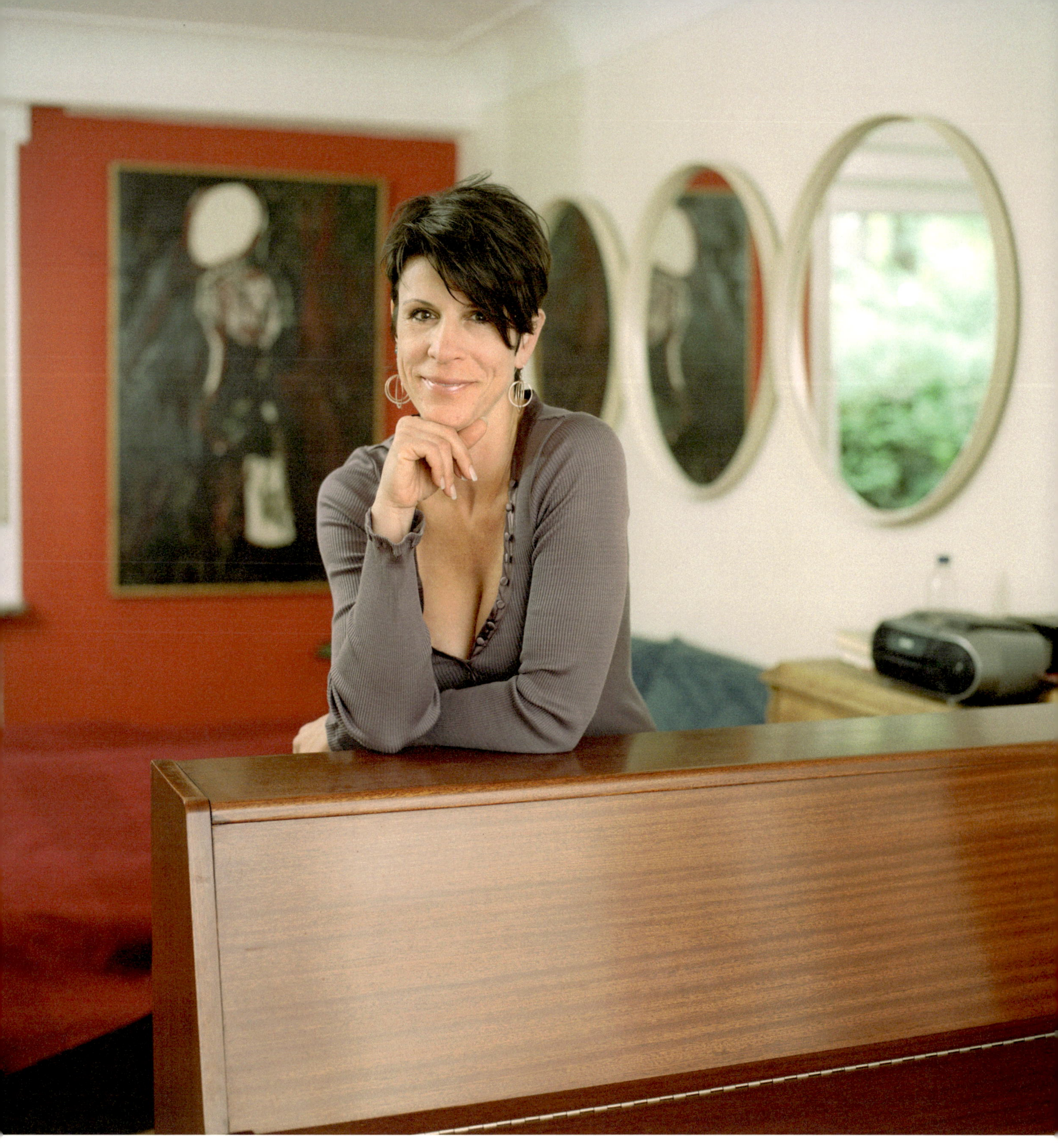

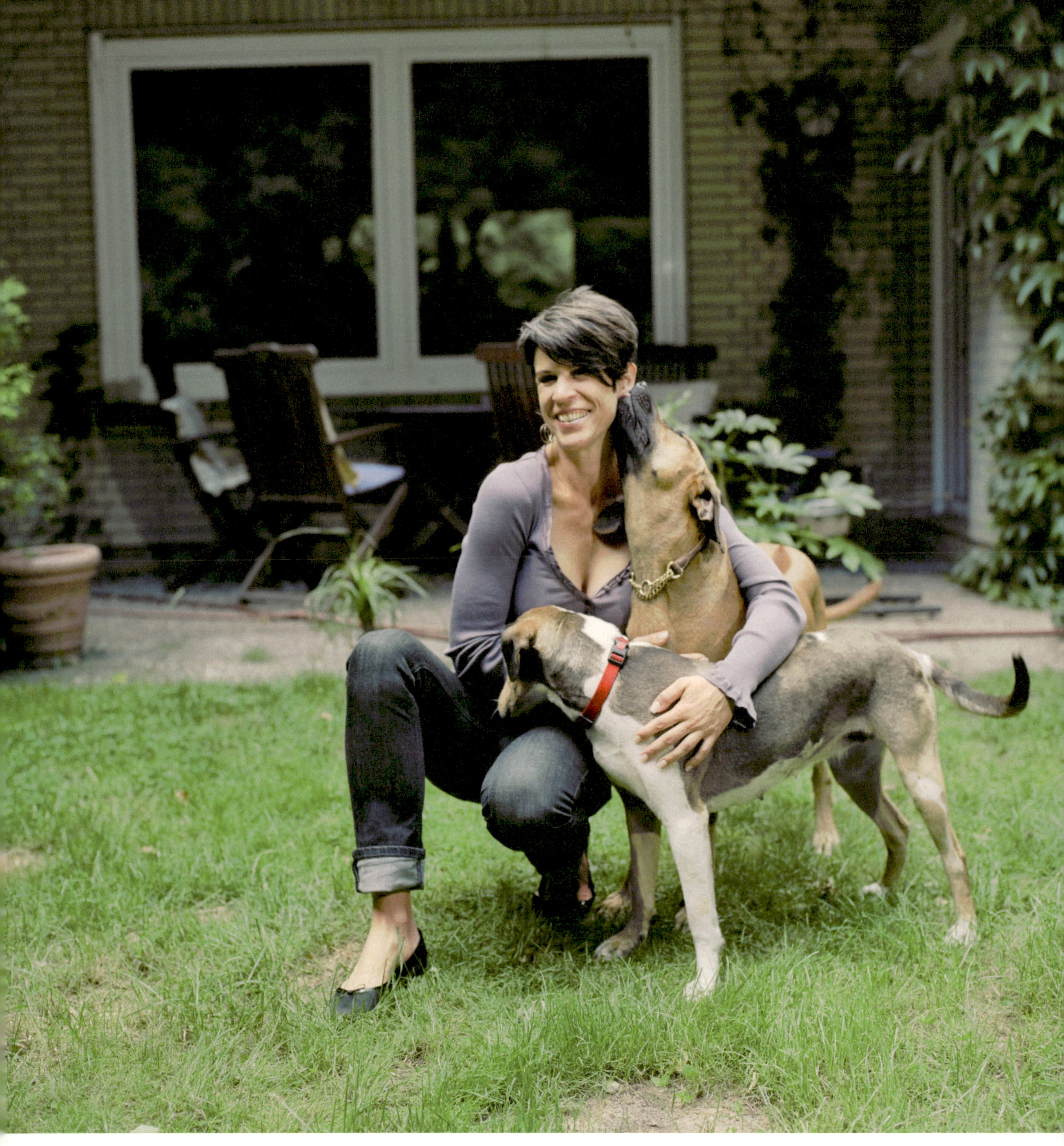

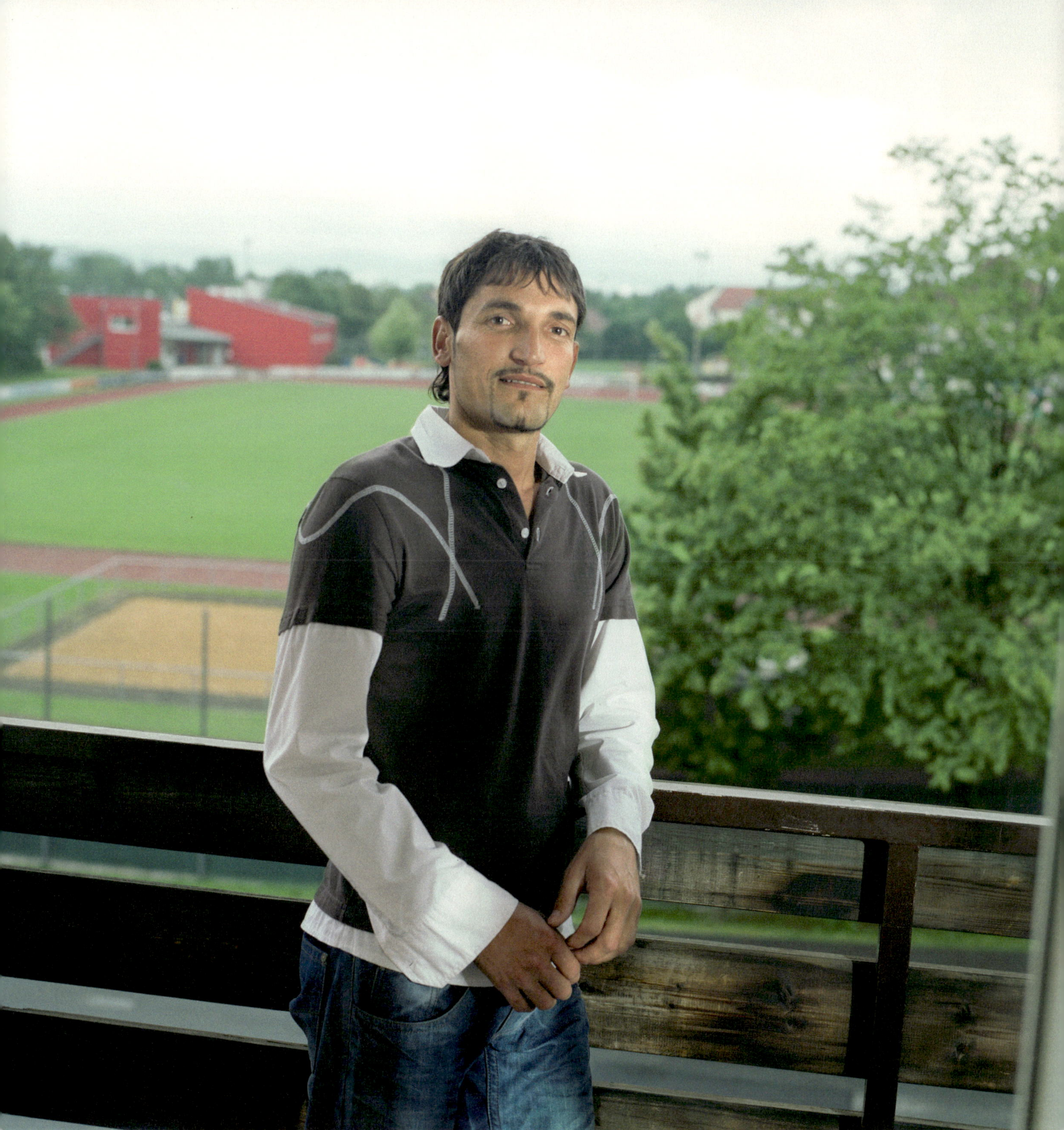

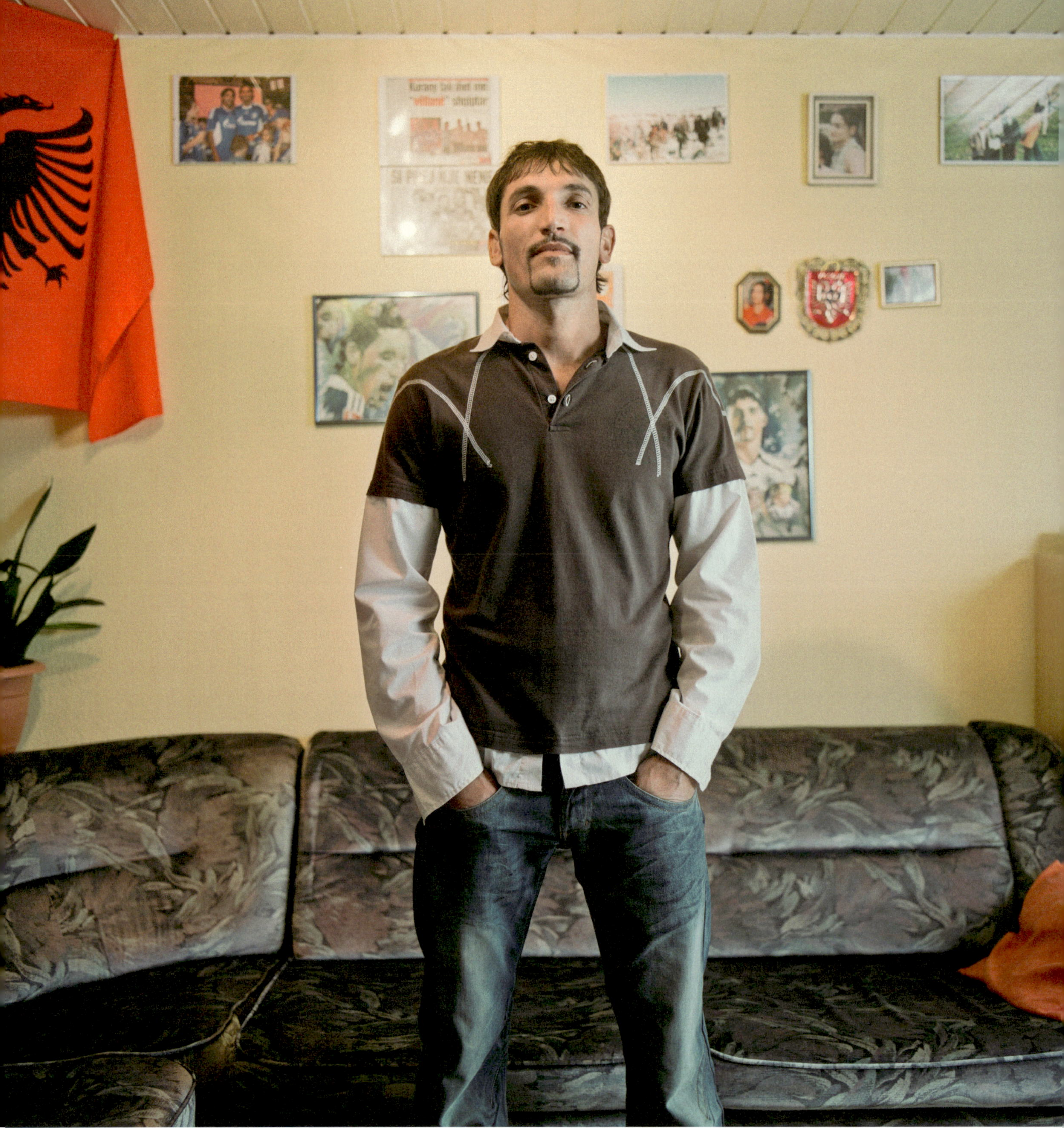

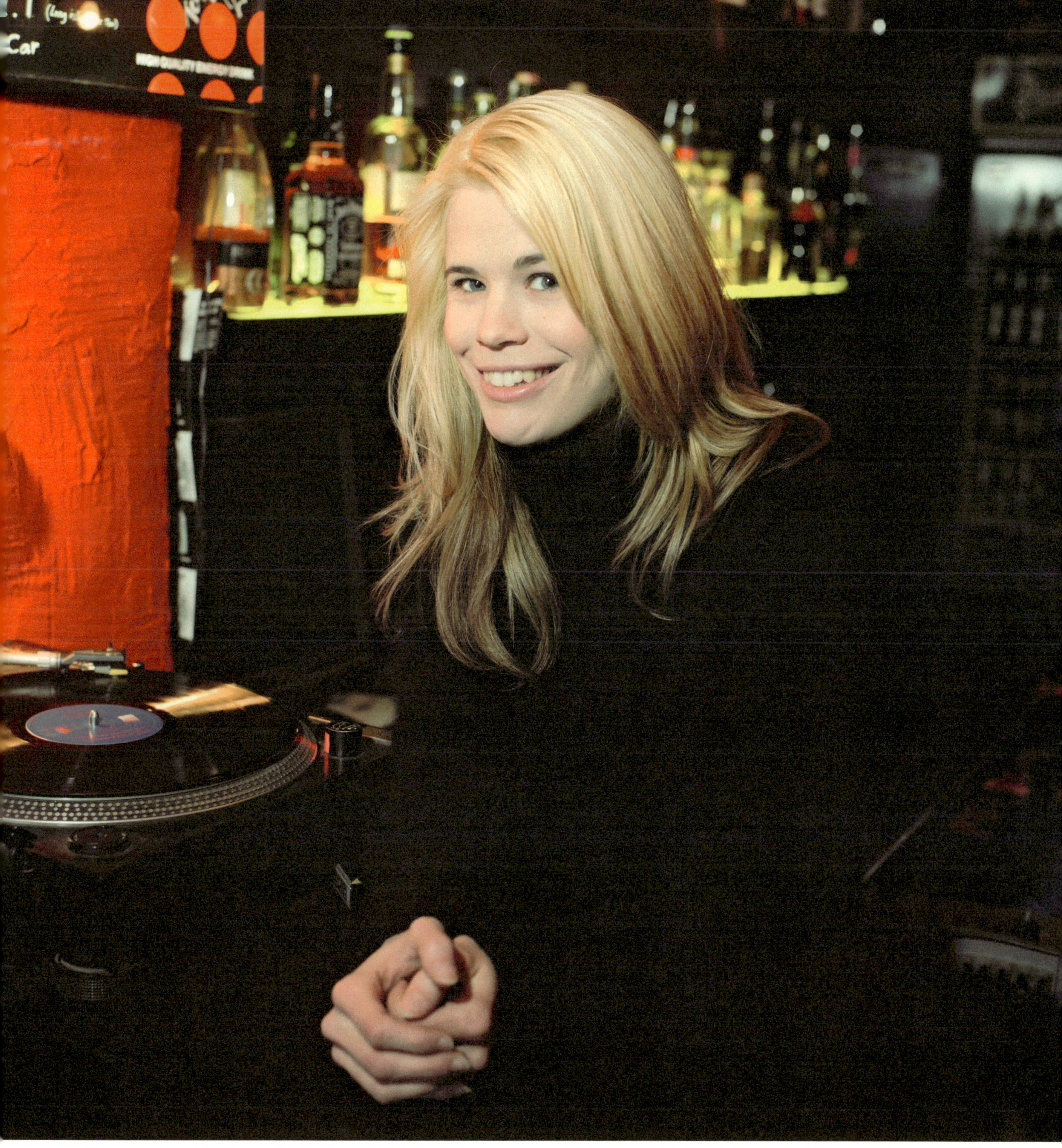

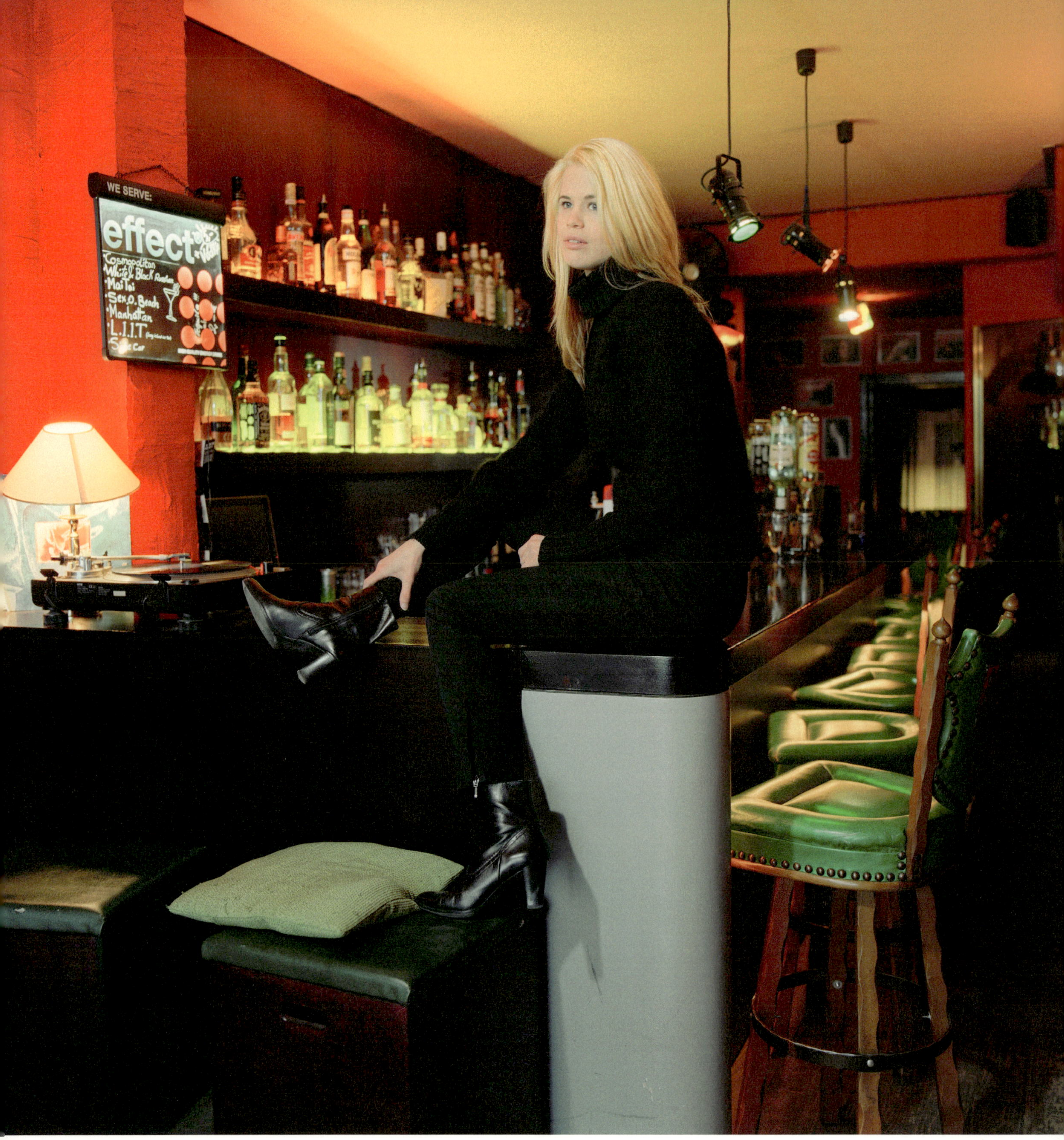

WE SERVE:
effect
Cosmopolitan
White & Black Russian
Mai Tai
Sex o. Beach
Manhattan
L.I.I.T

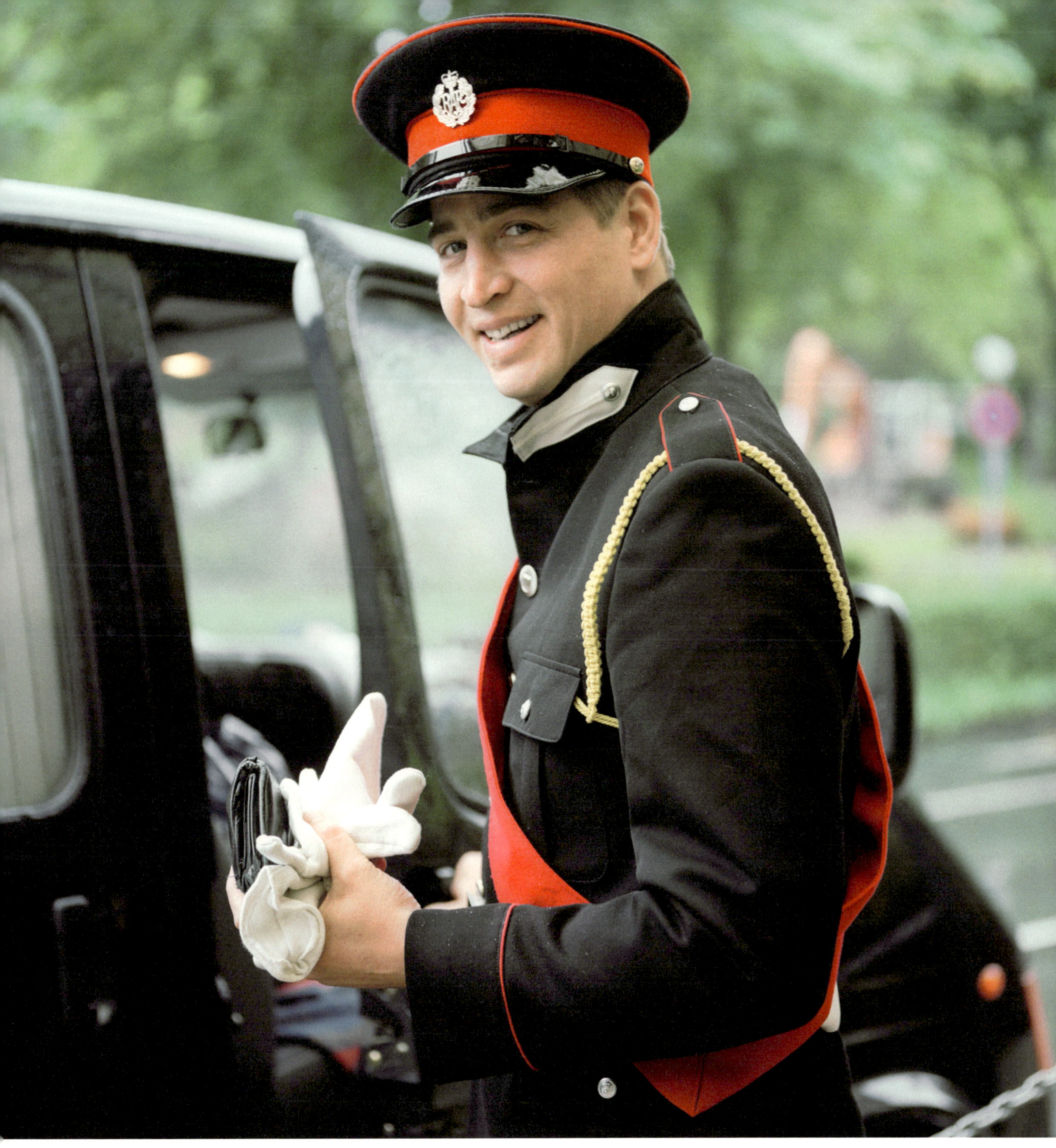

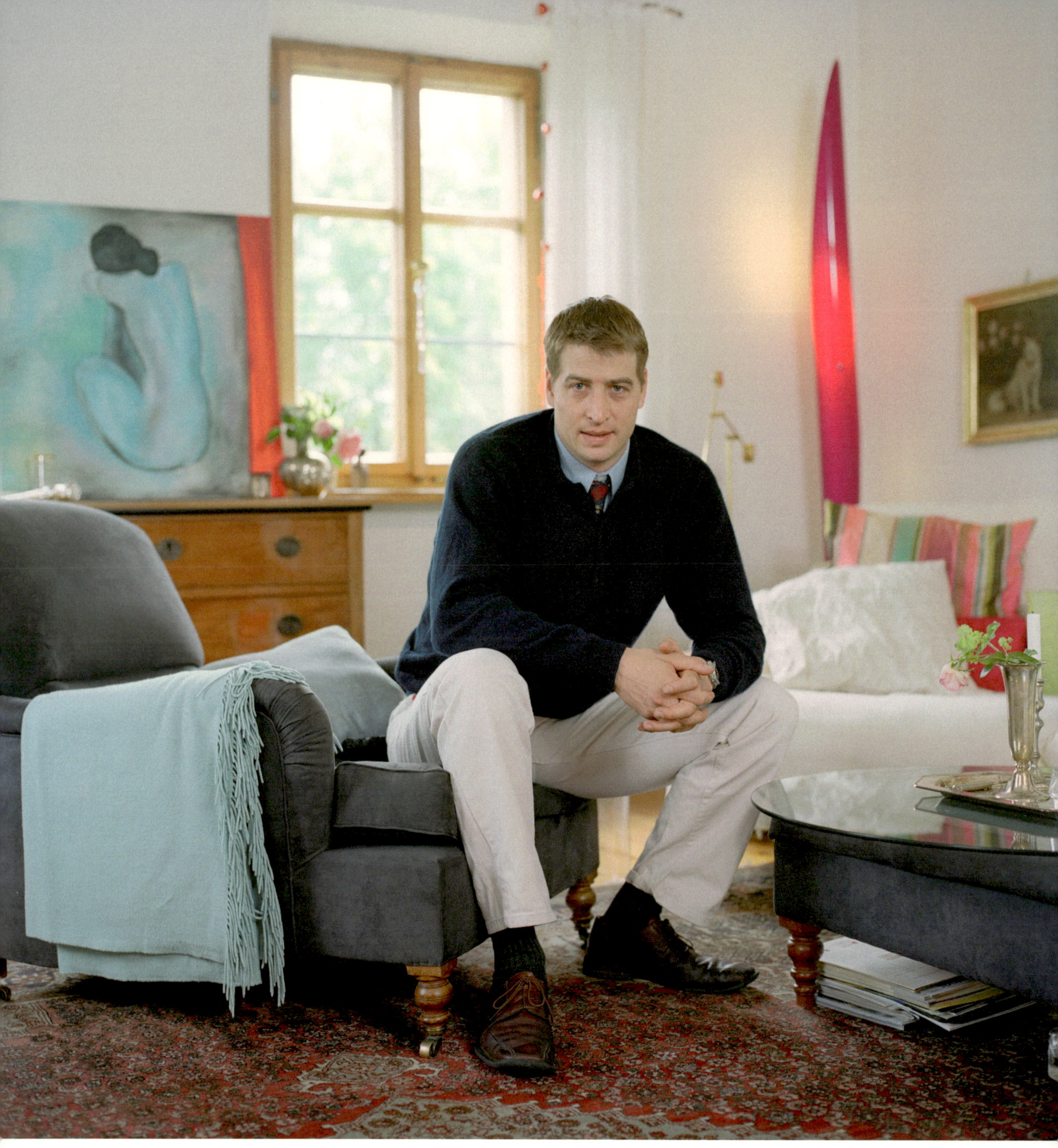

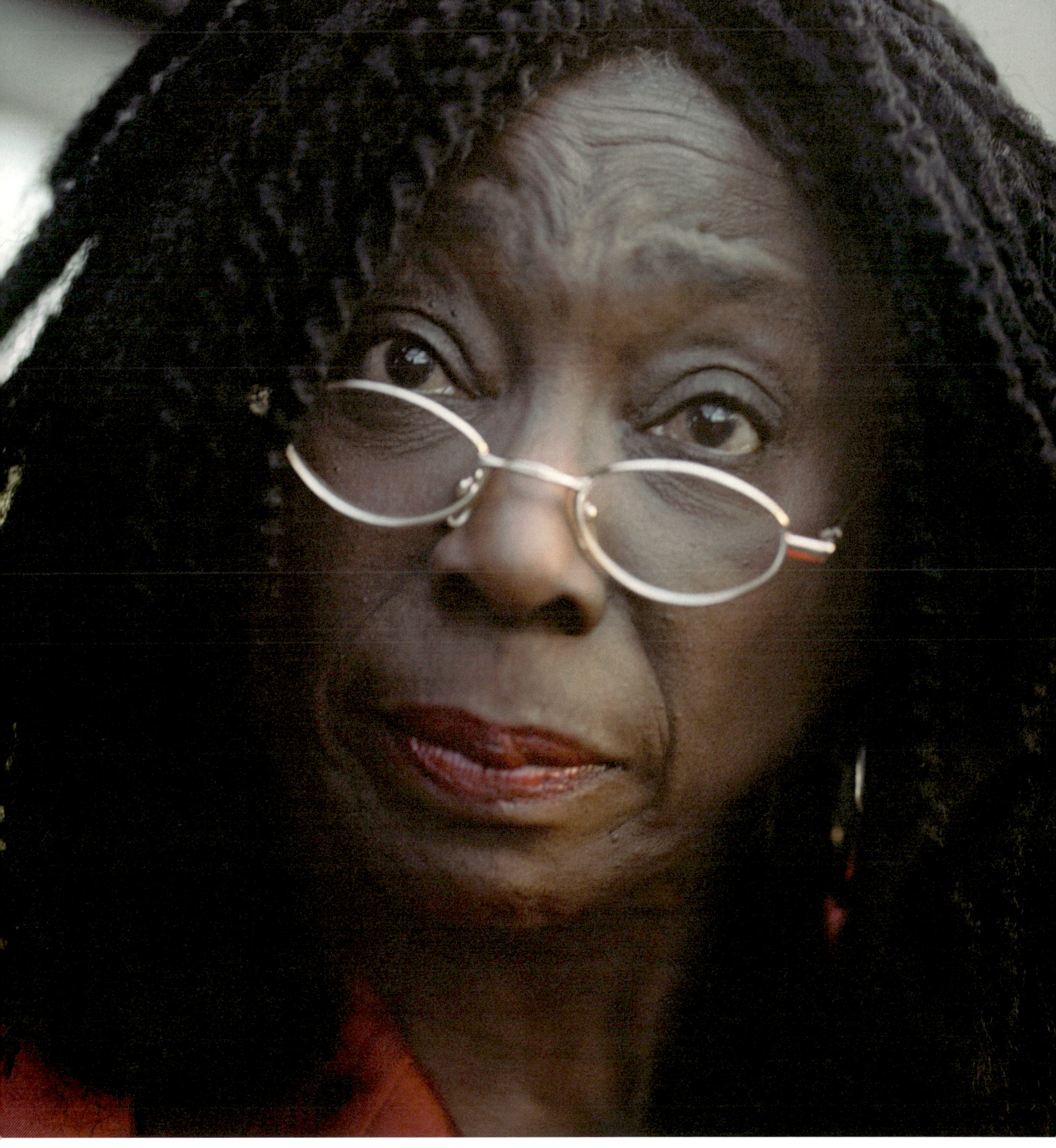

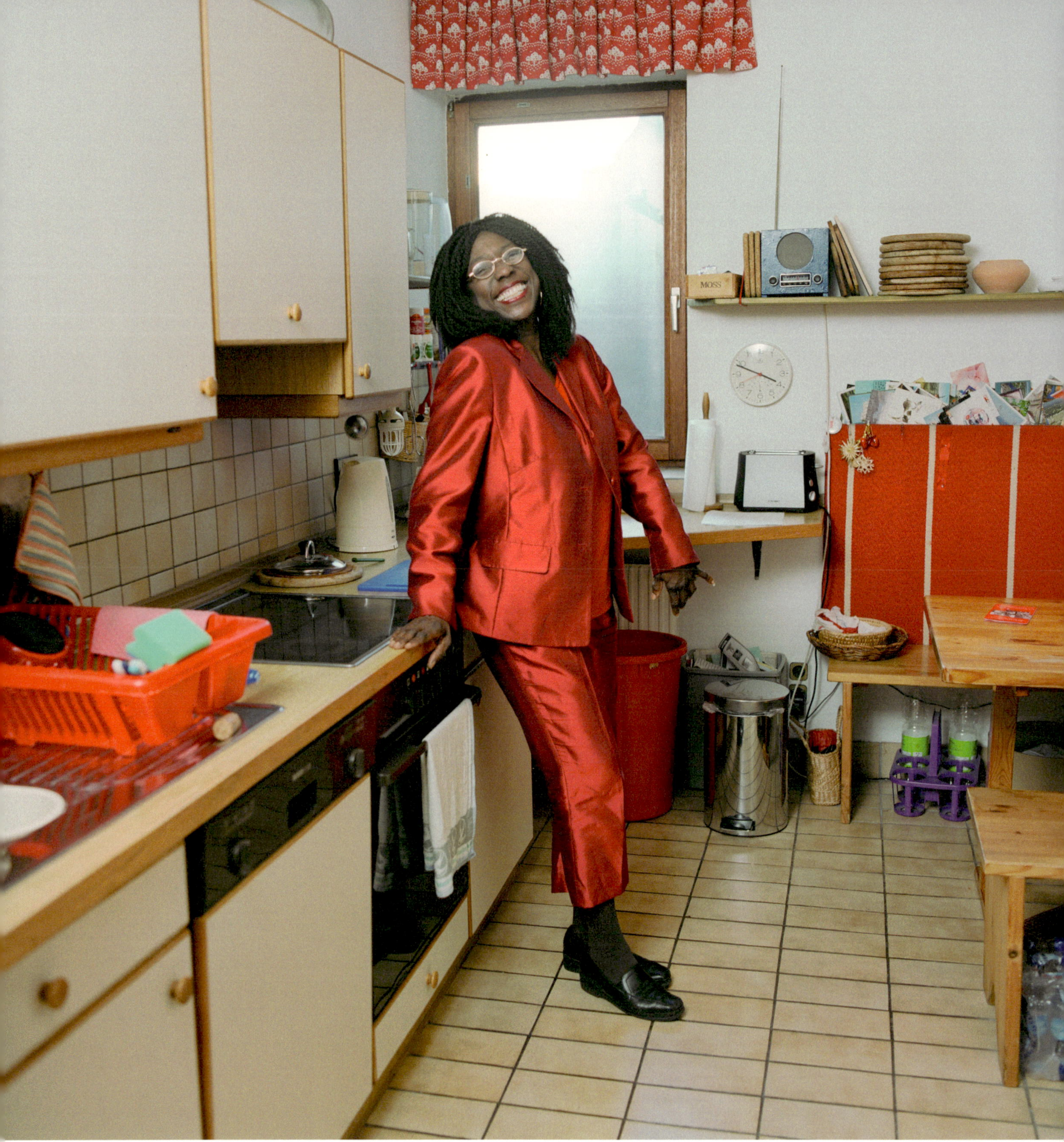

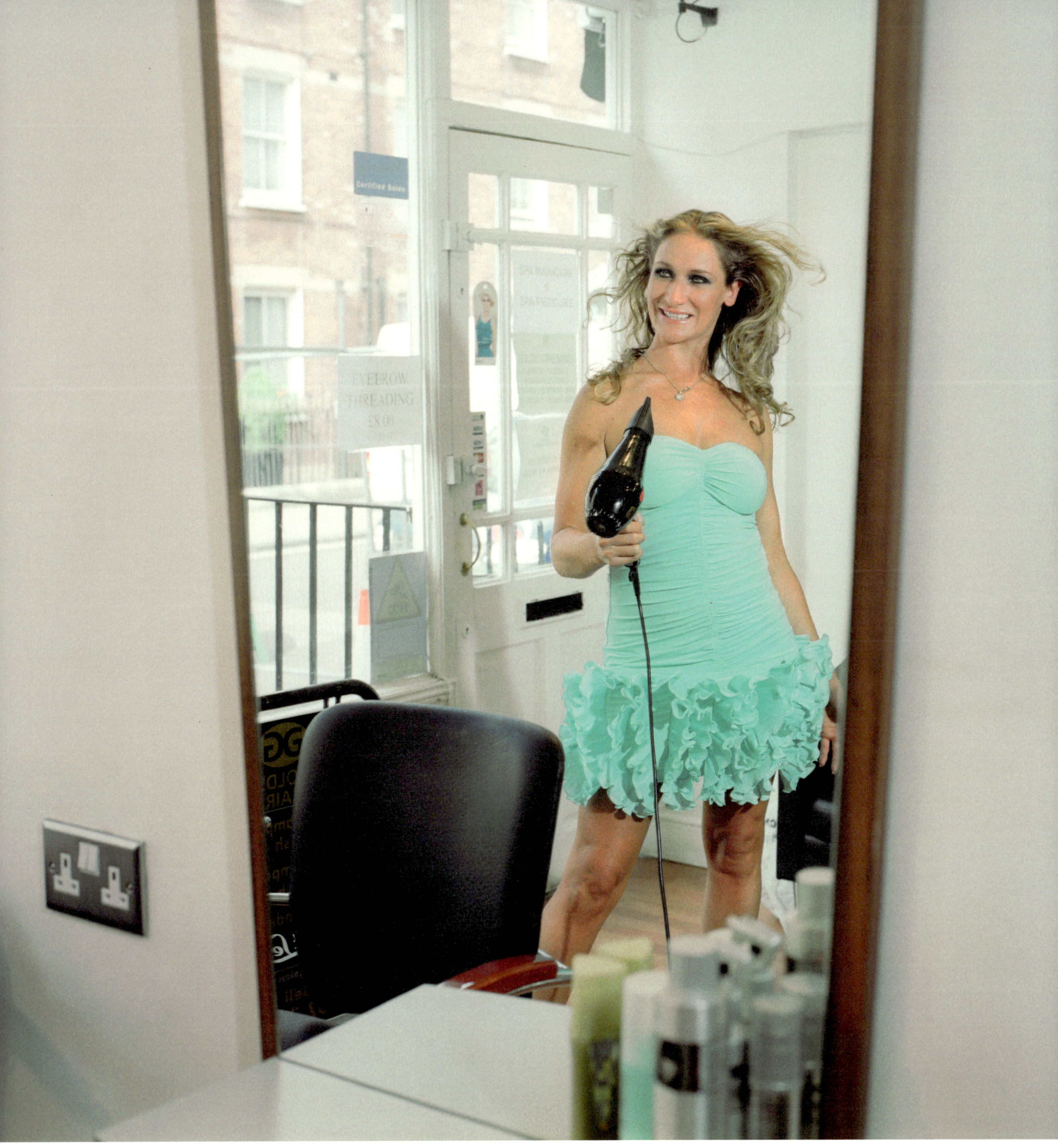

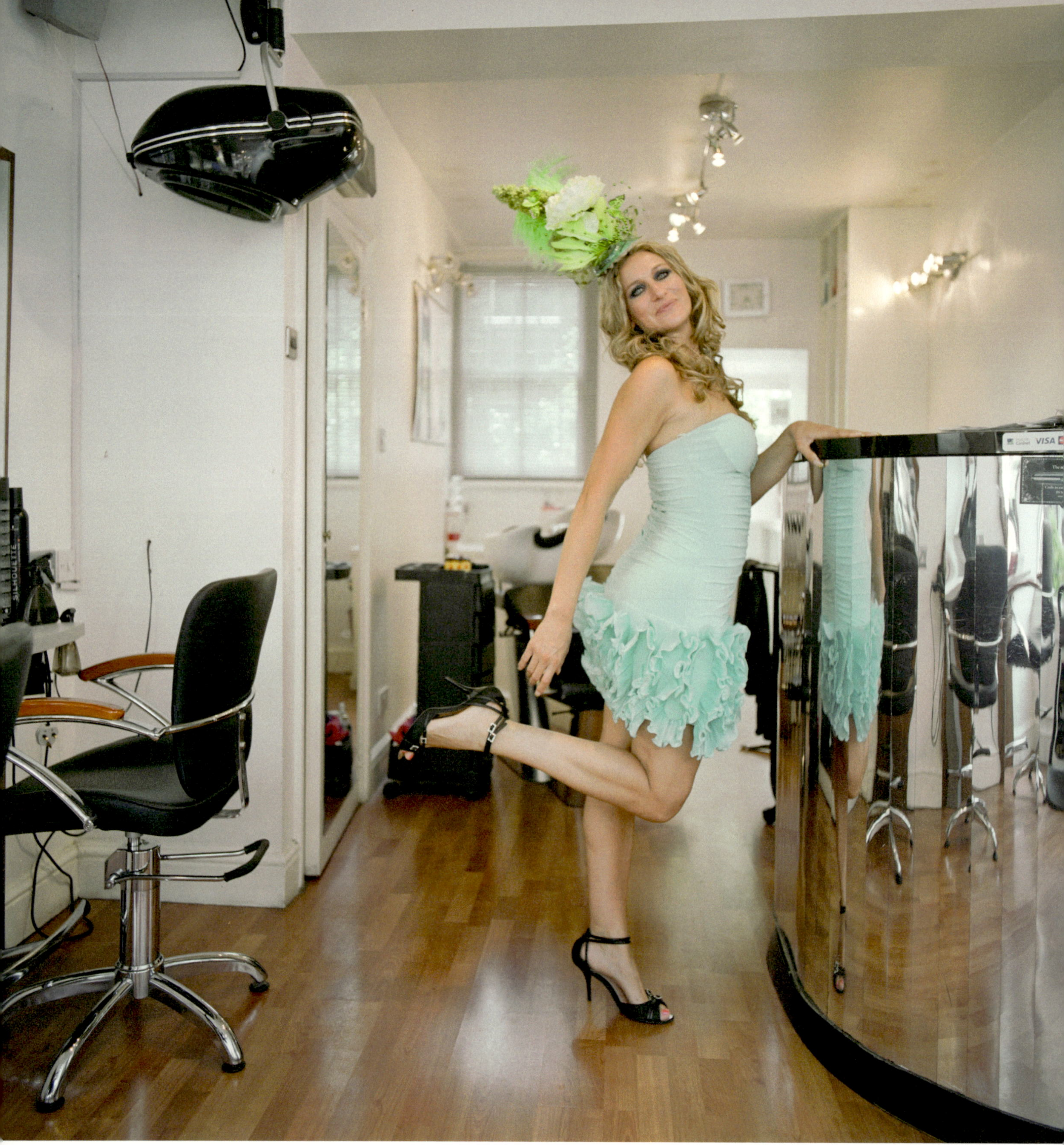

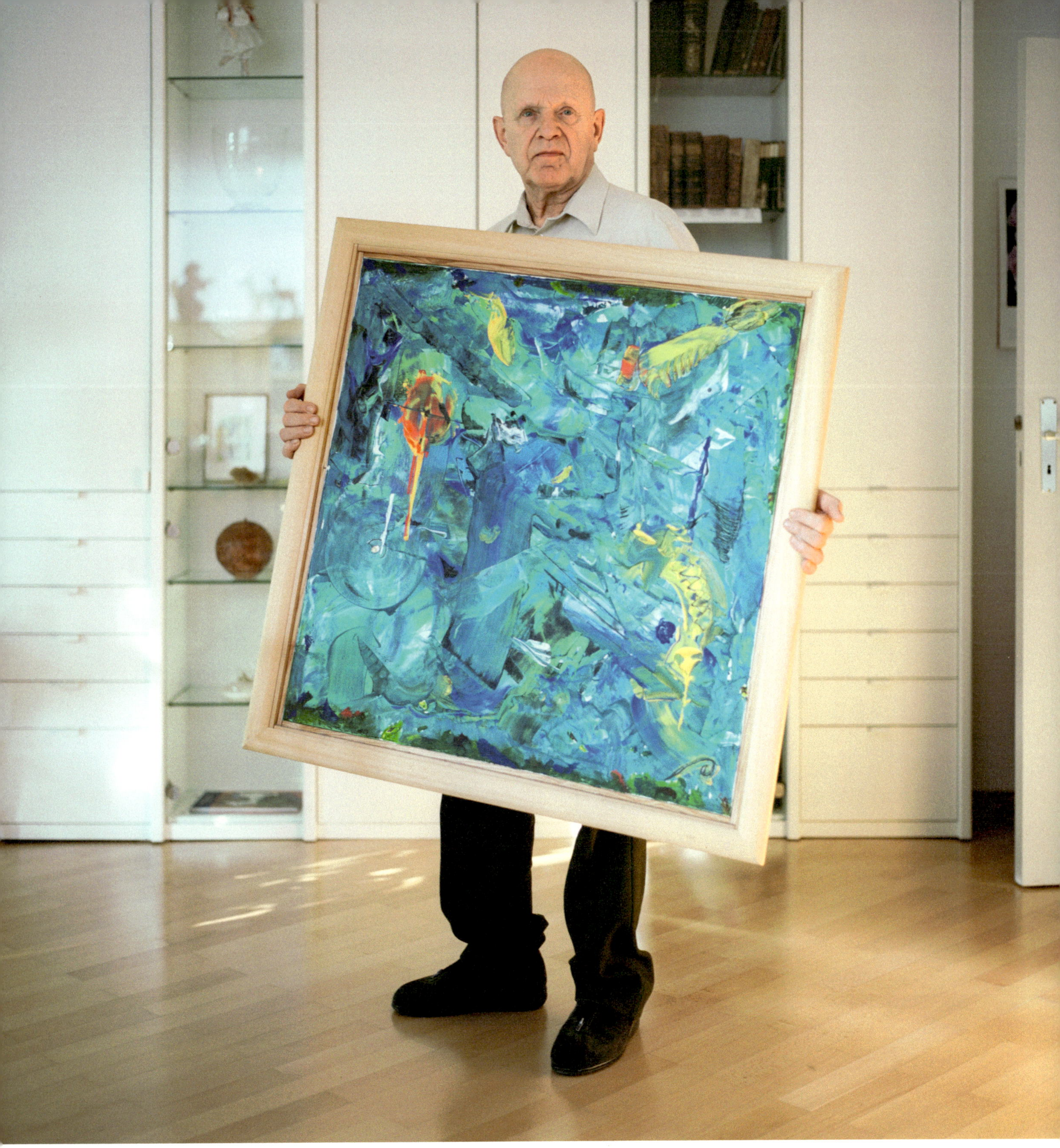

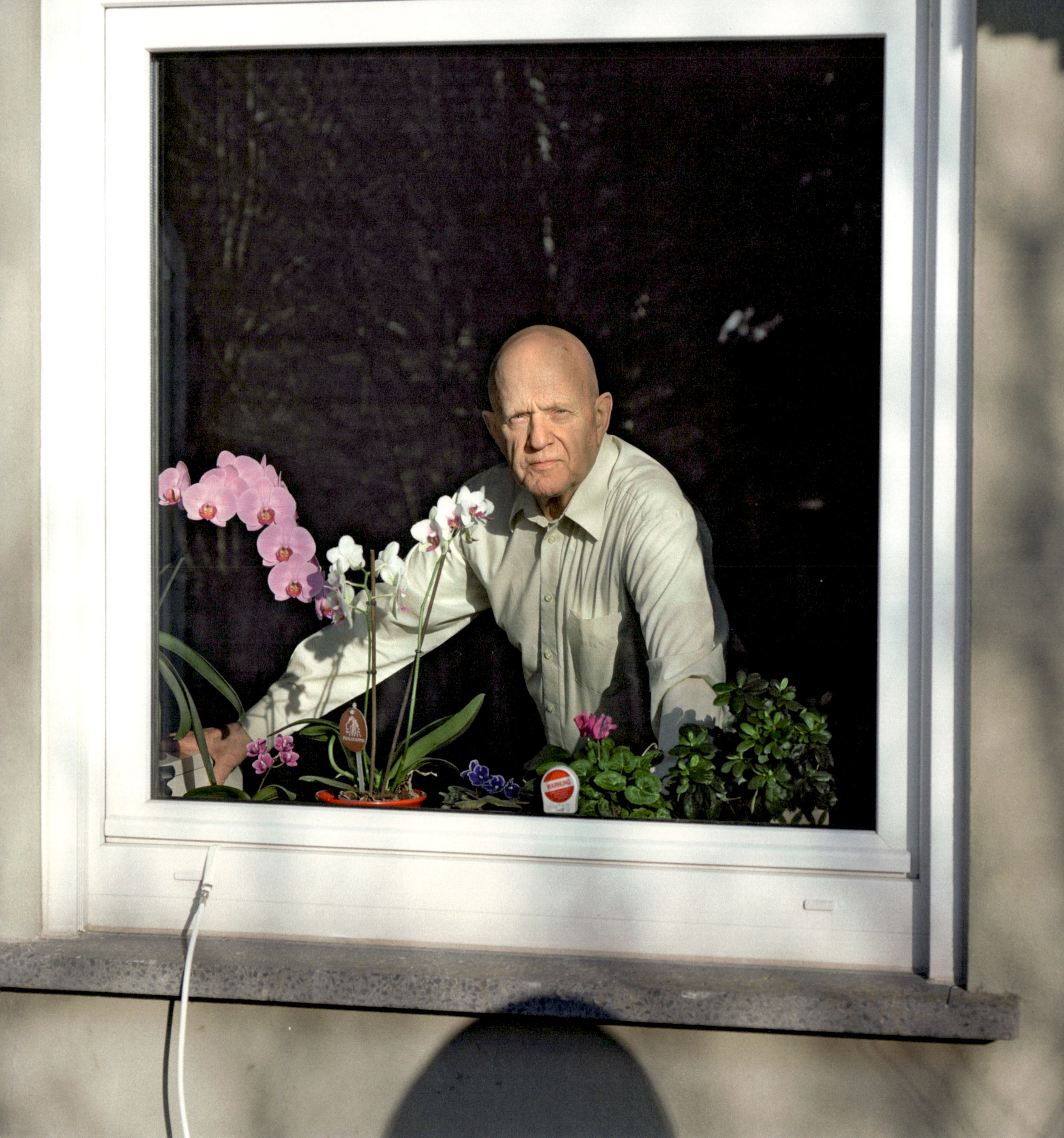

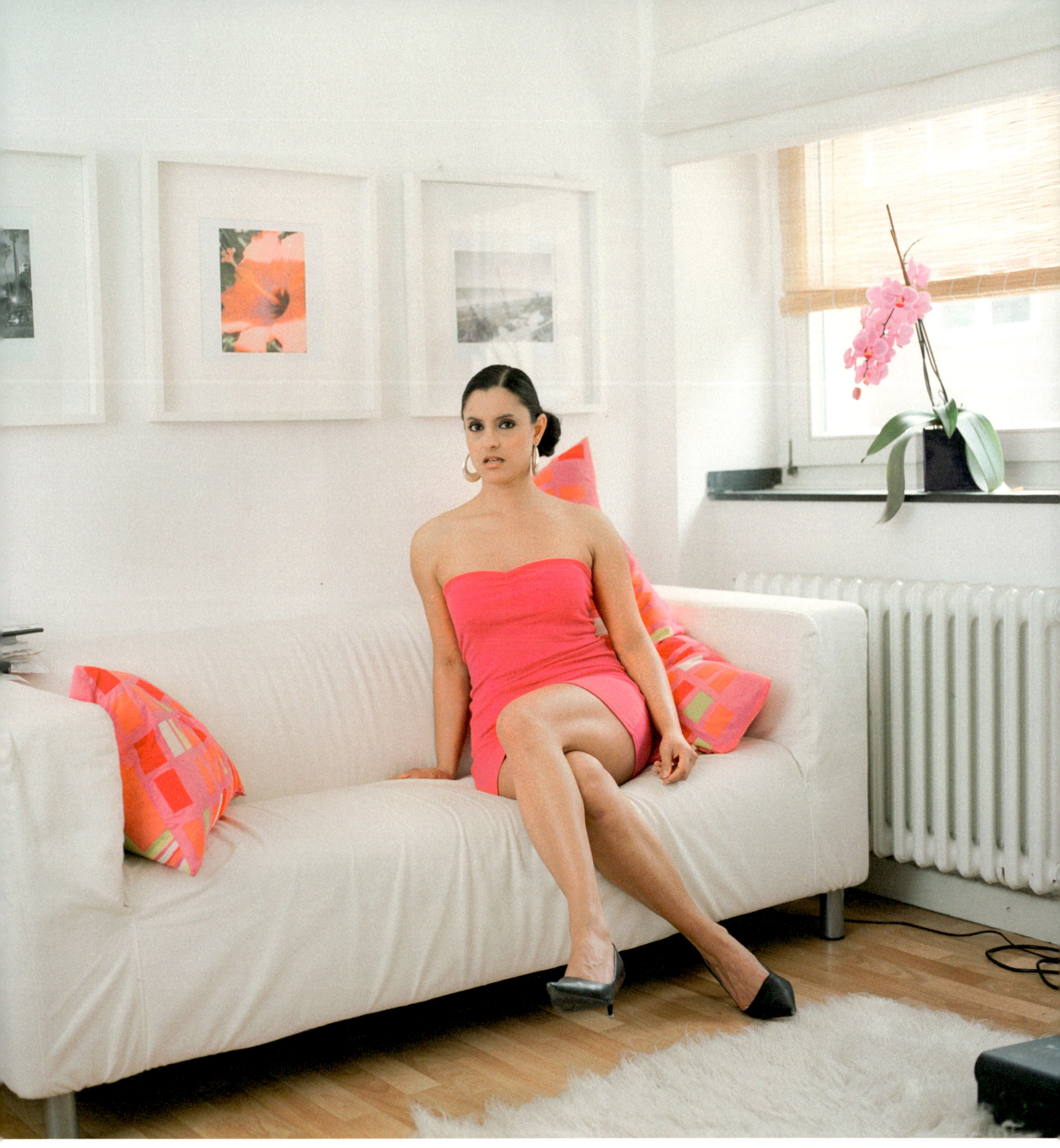

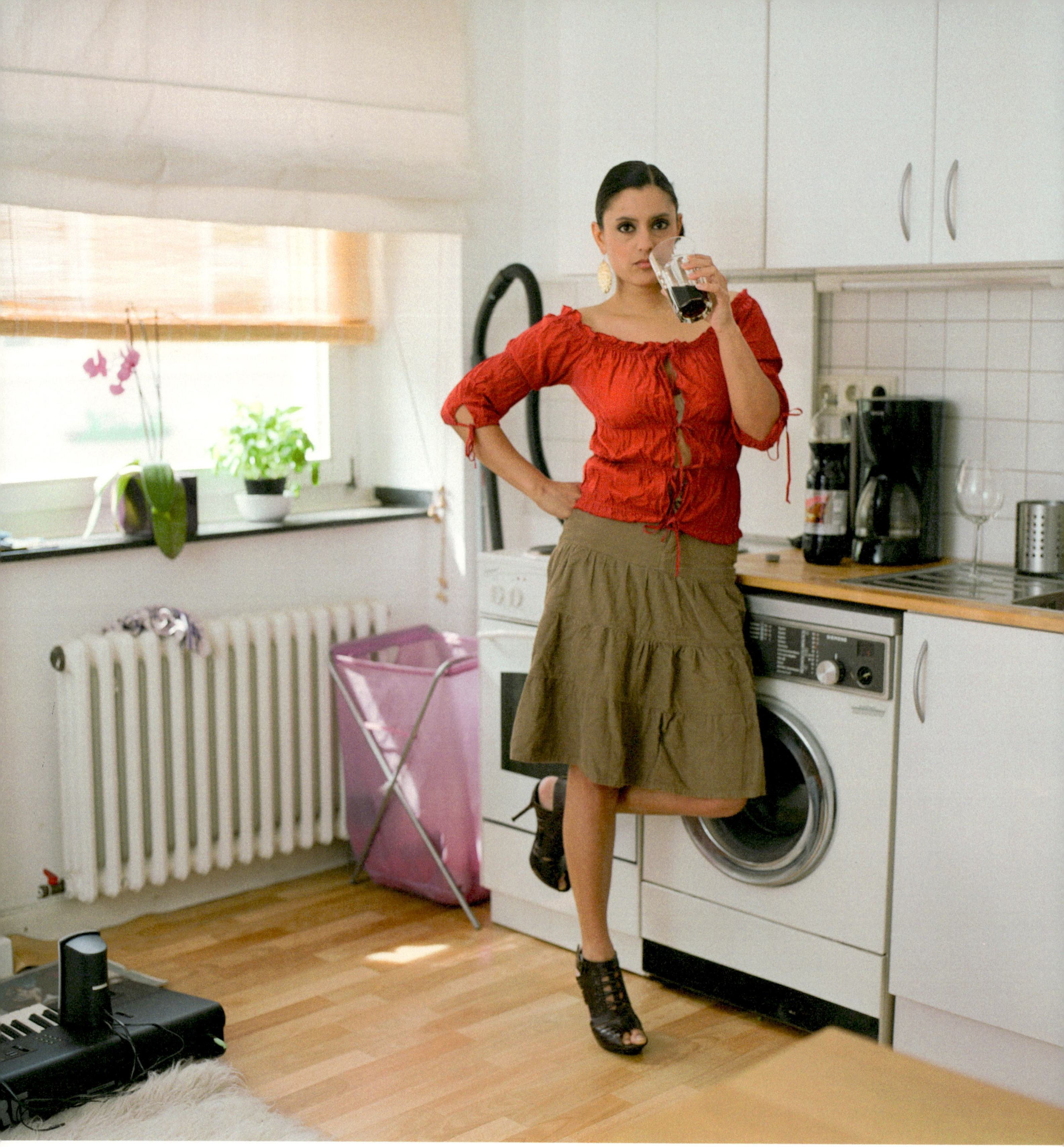

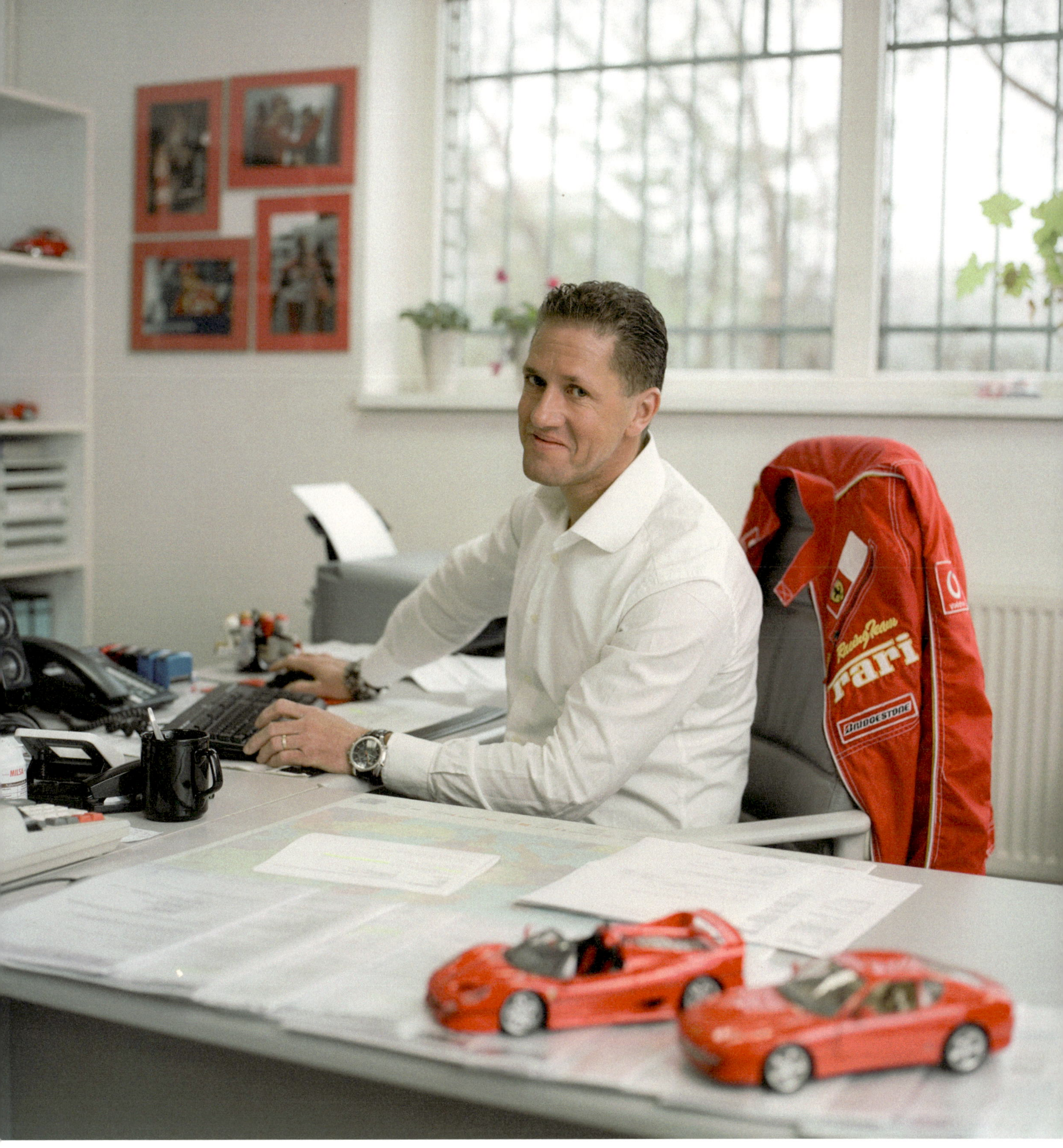

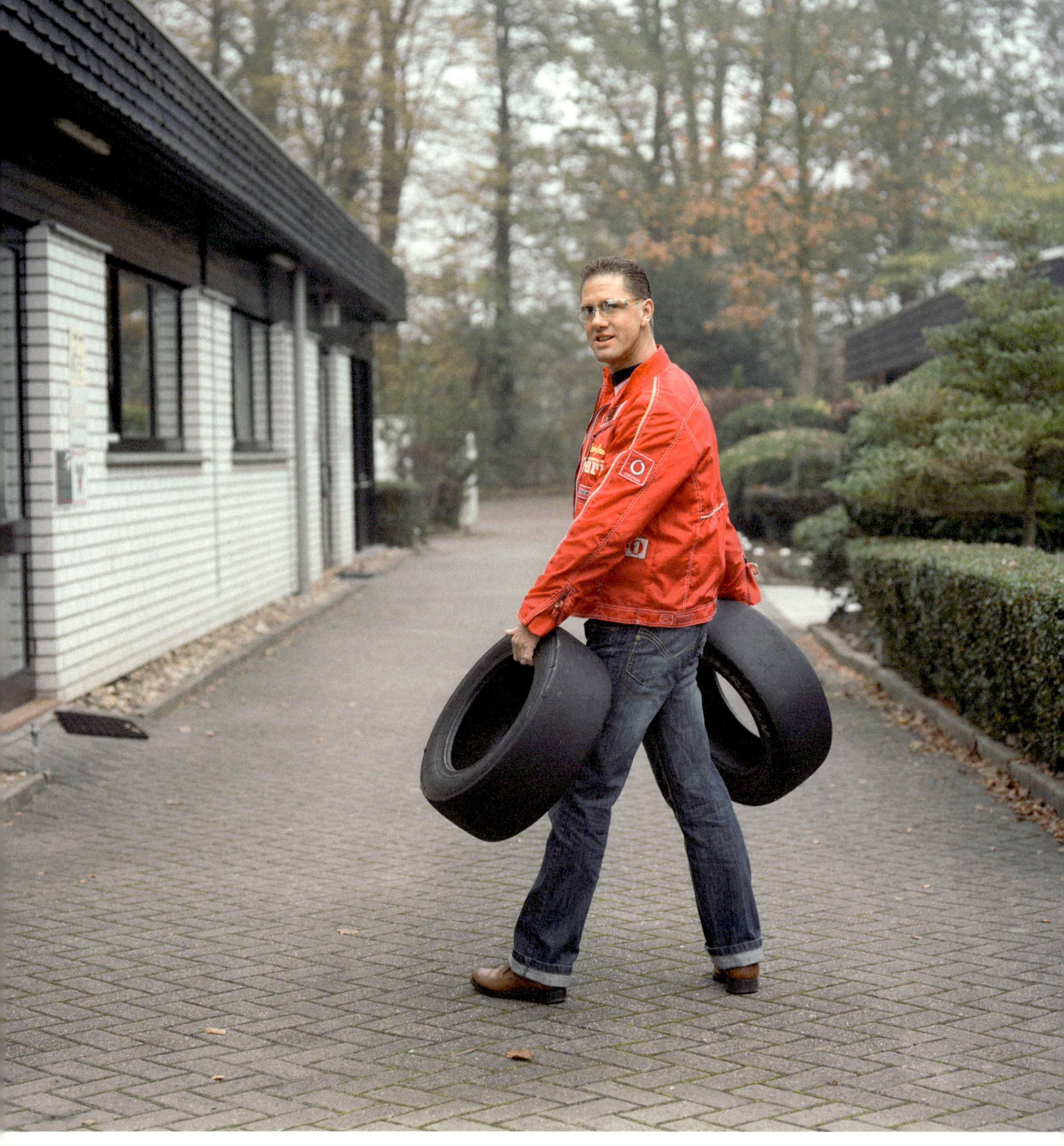

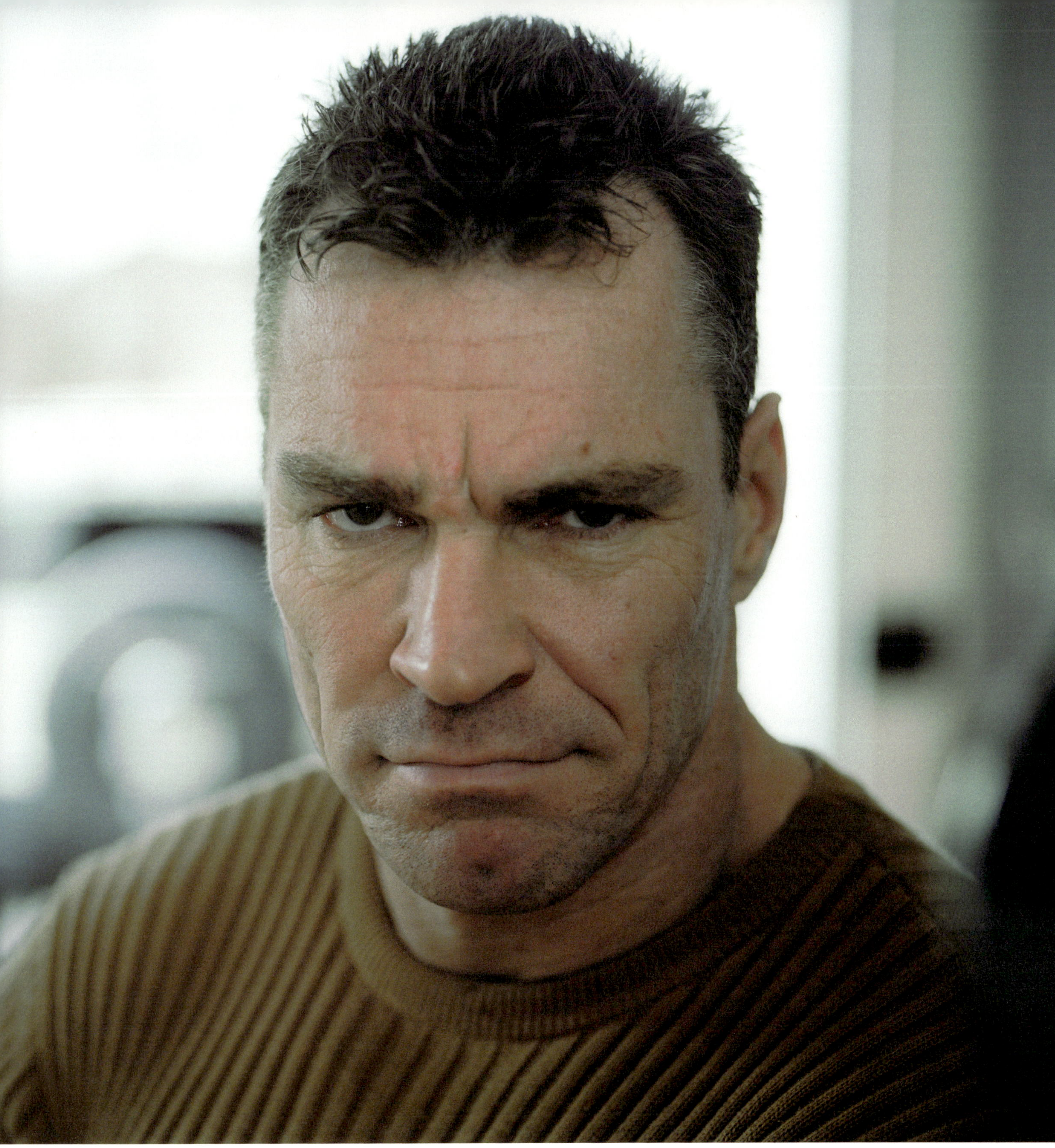

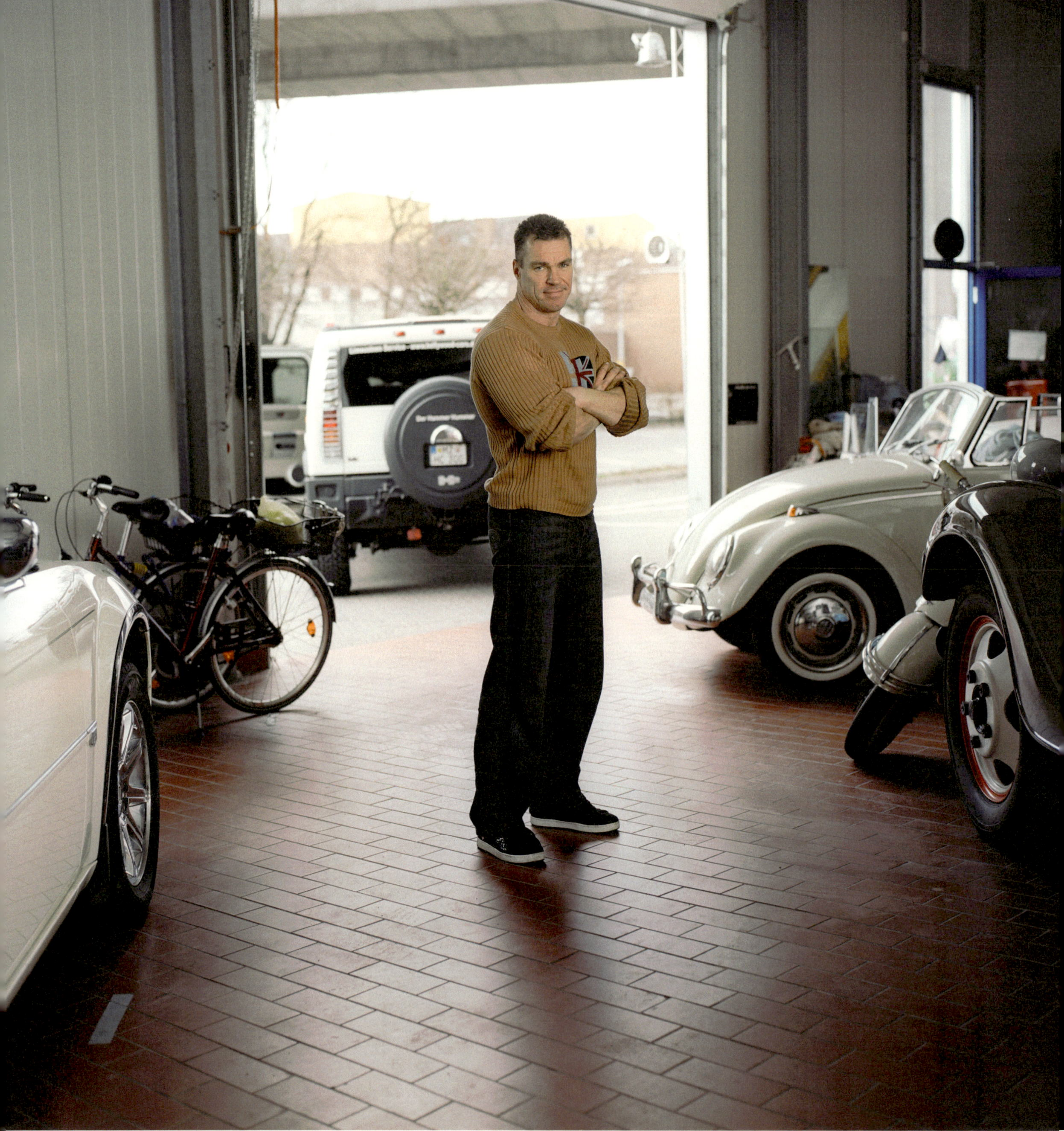

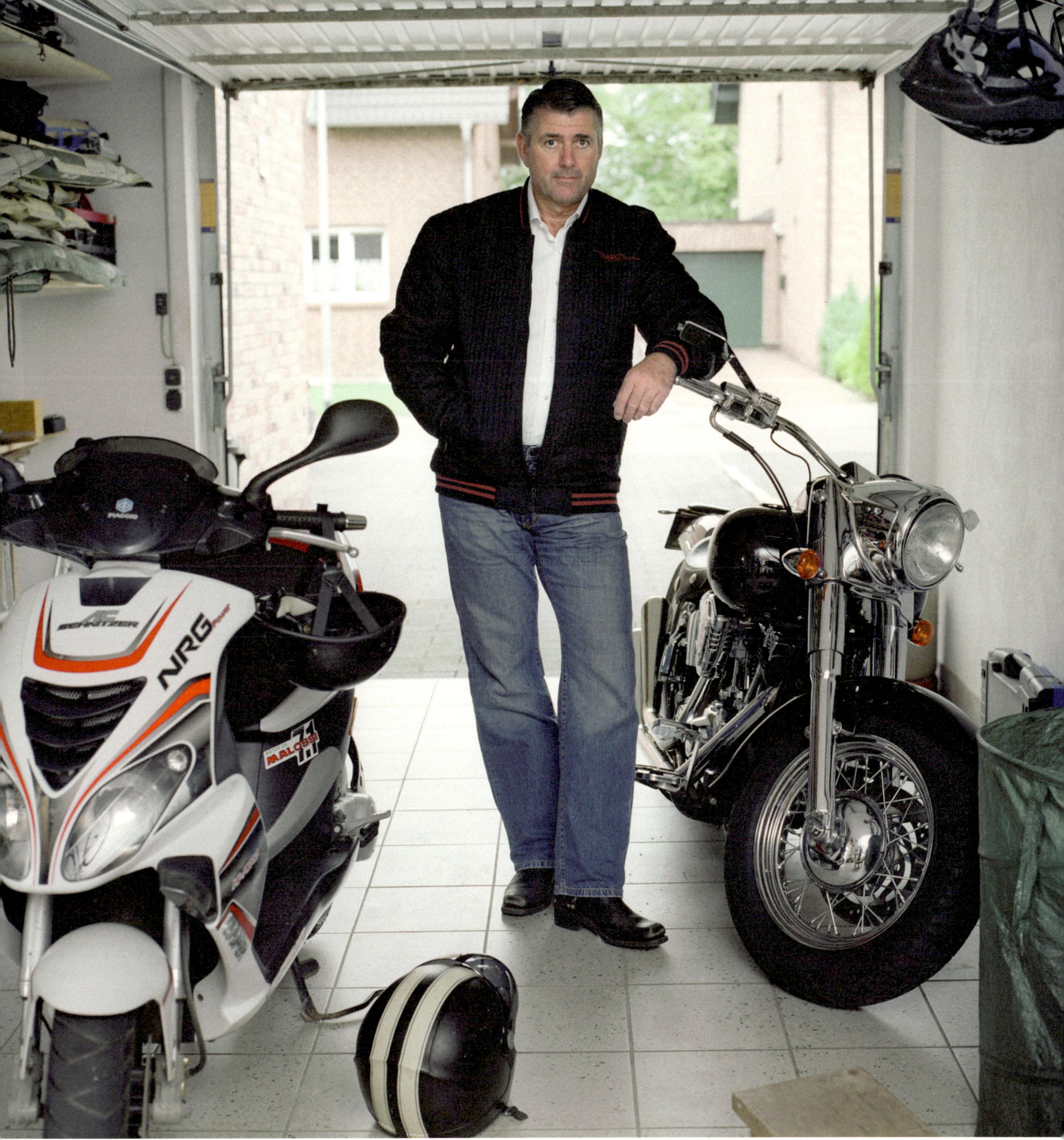

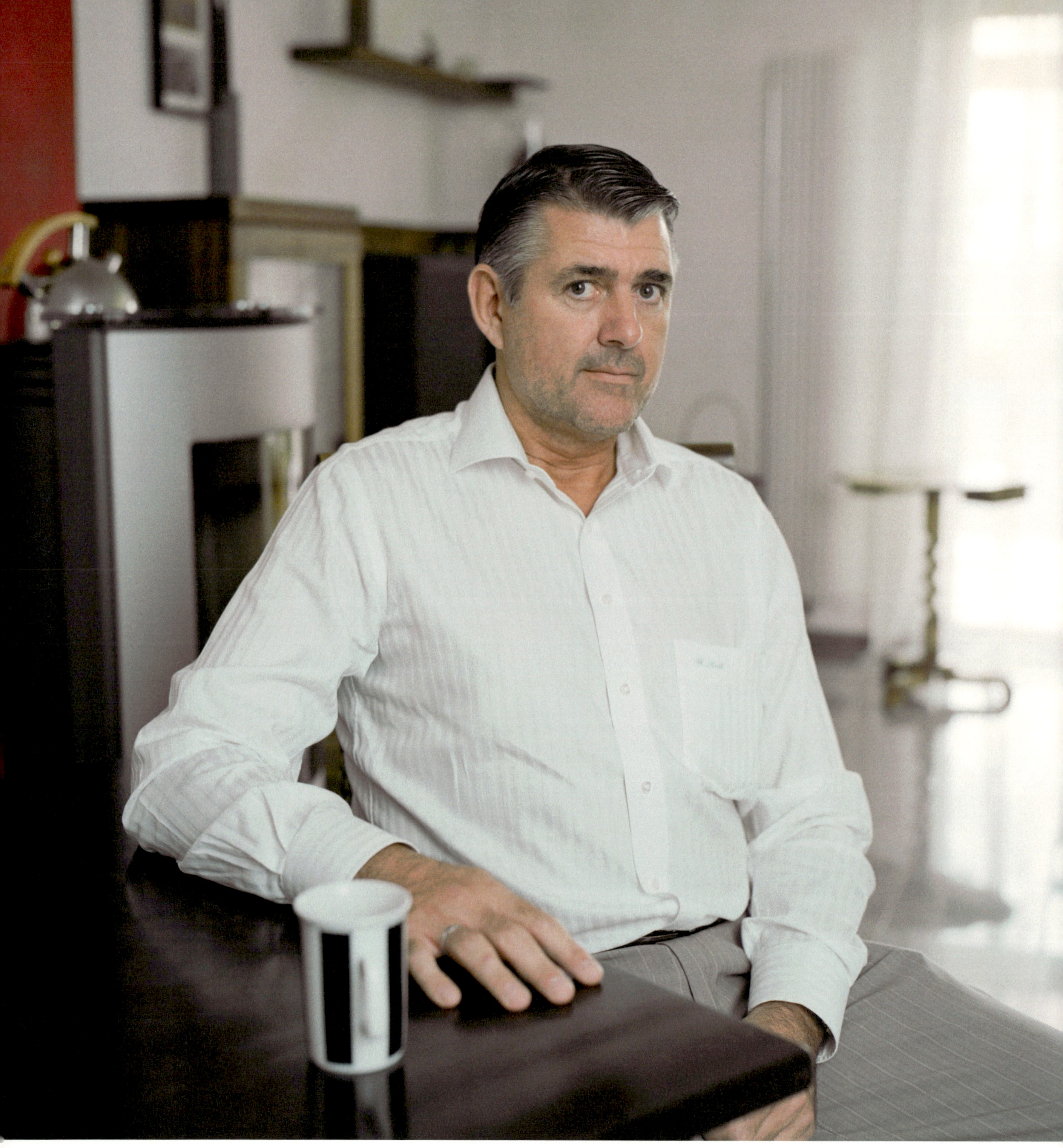

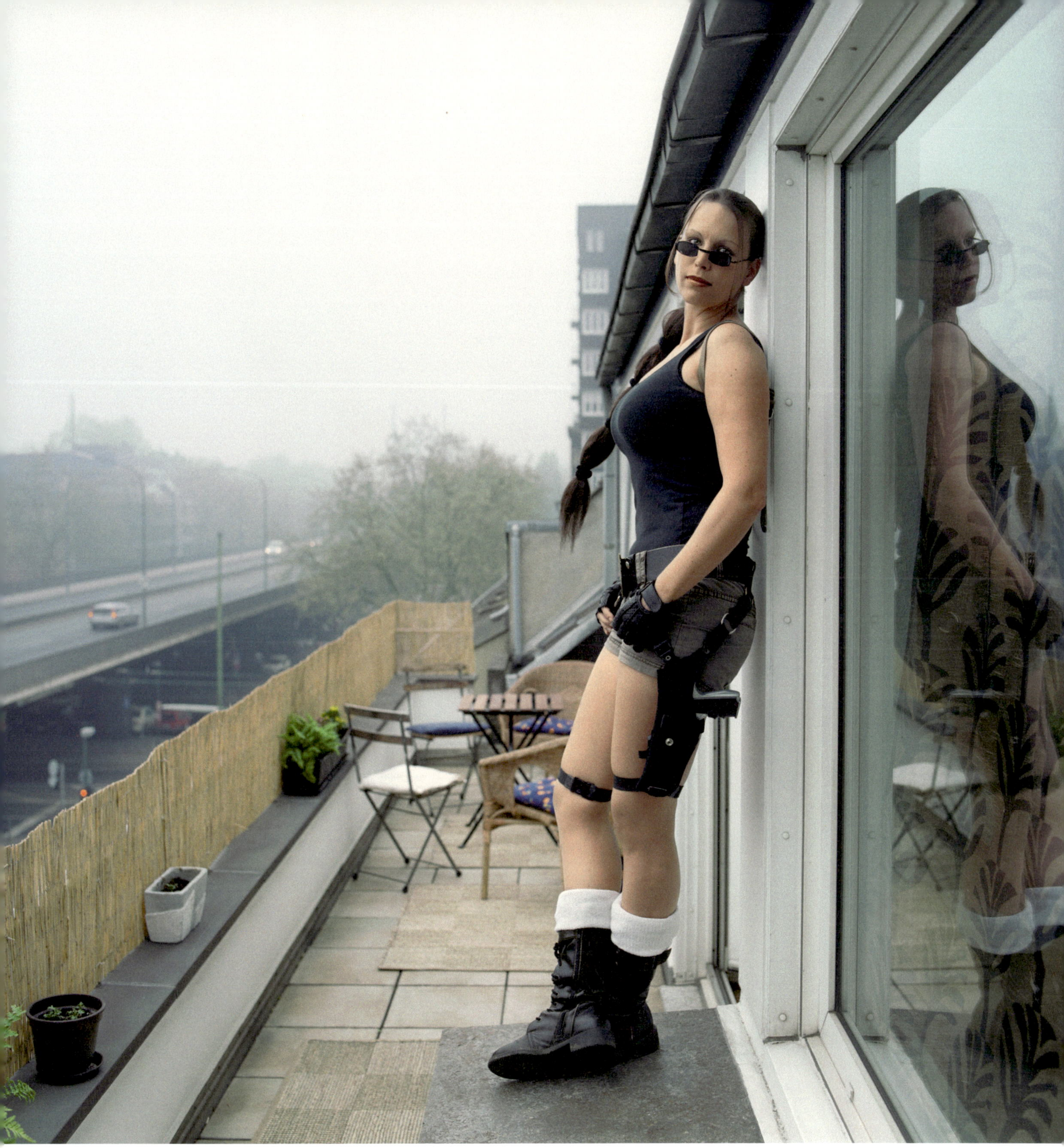

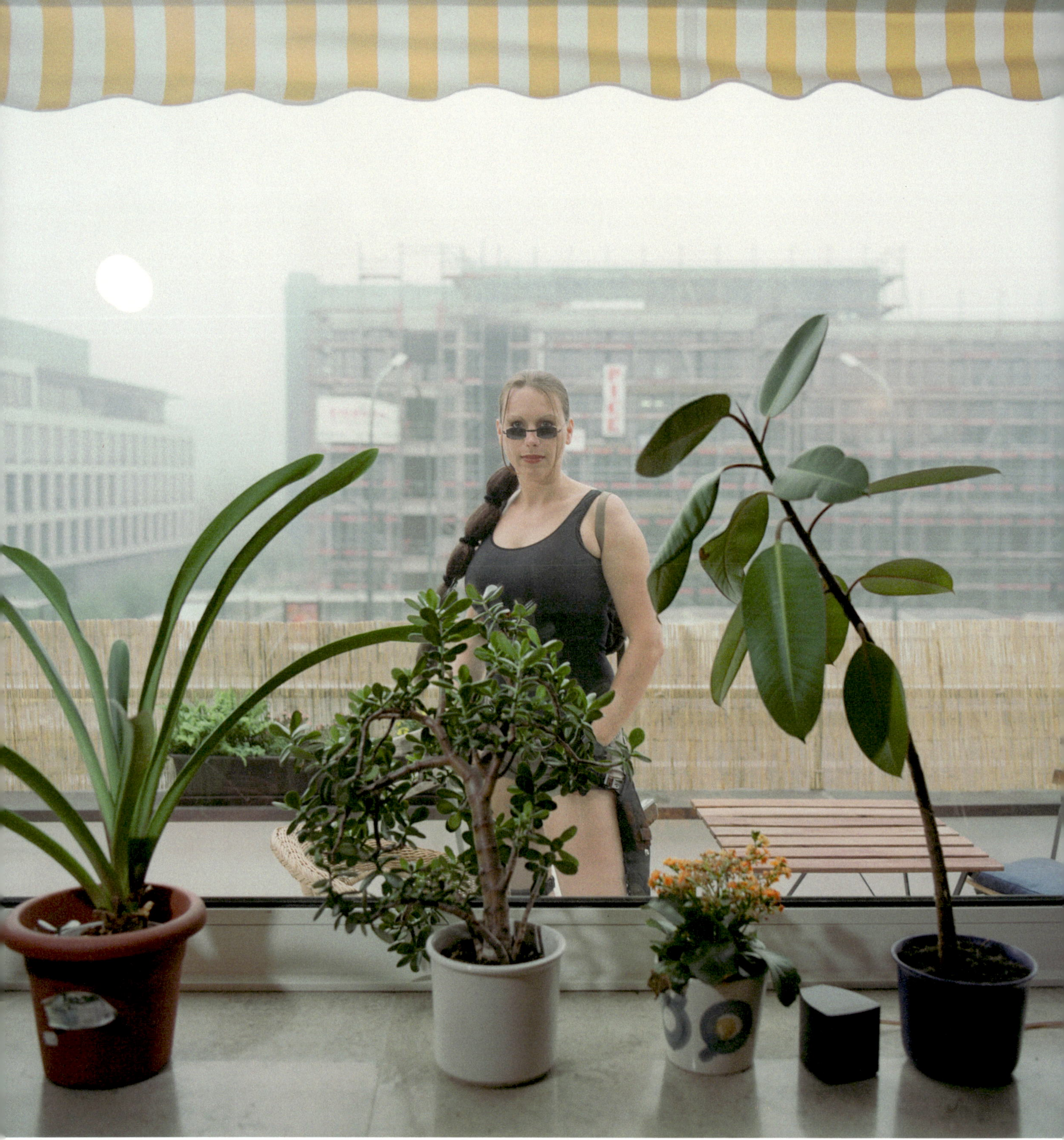

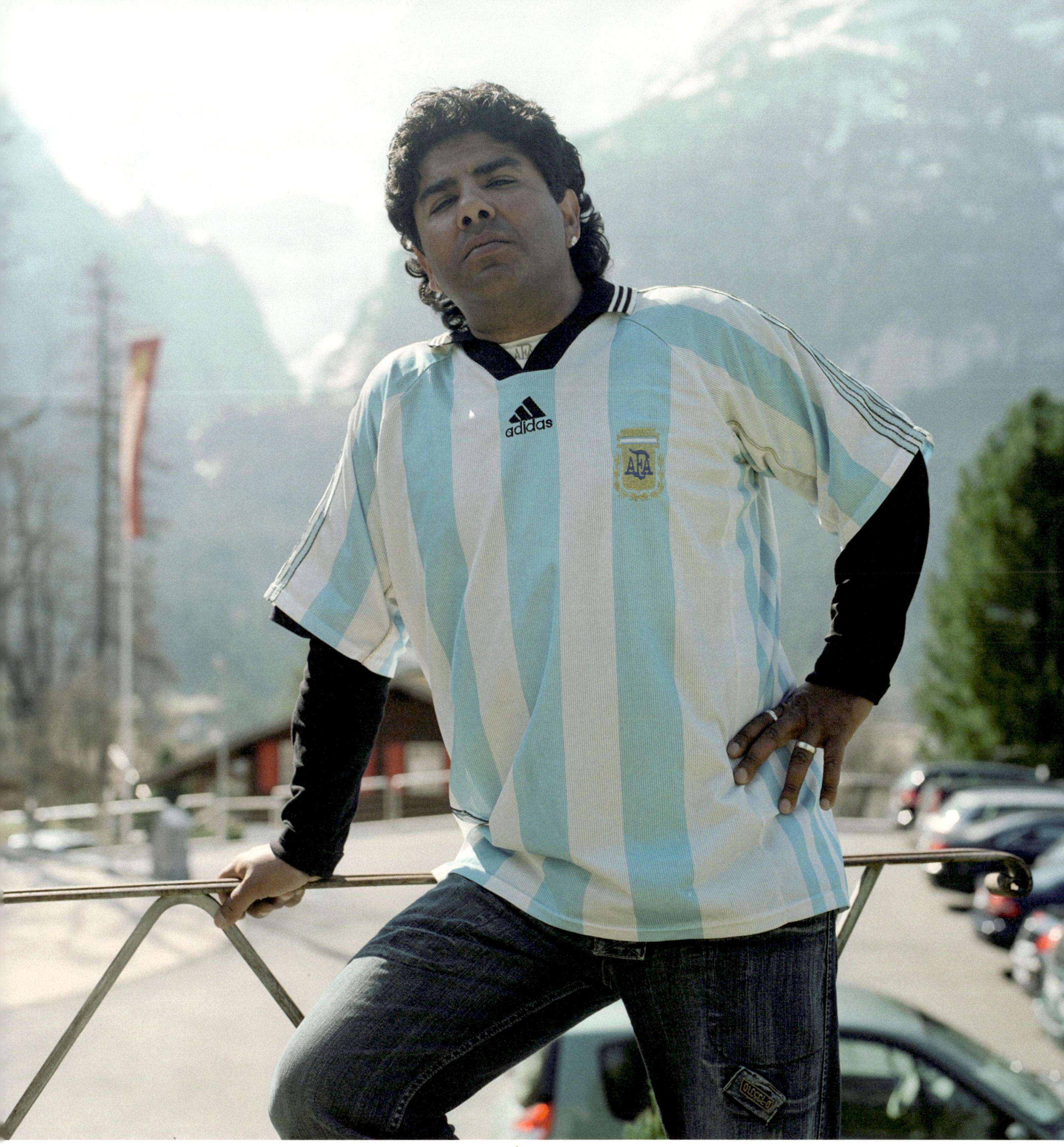

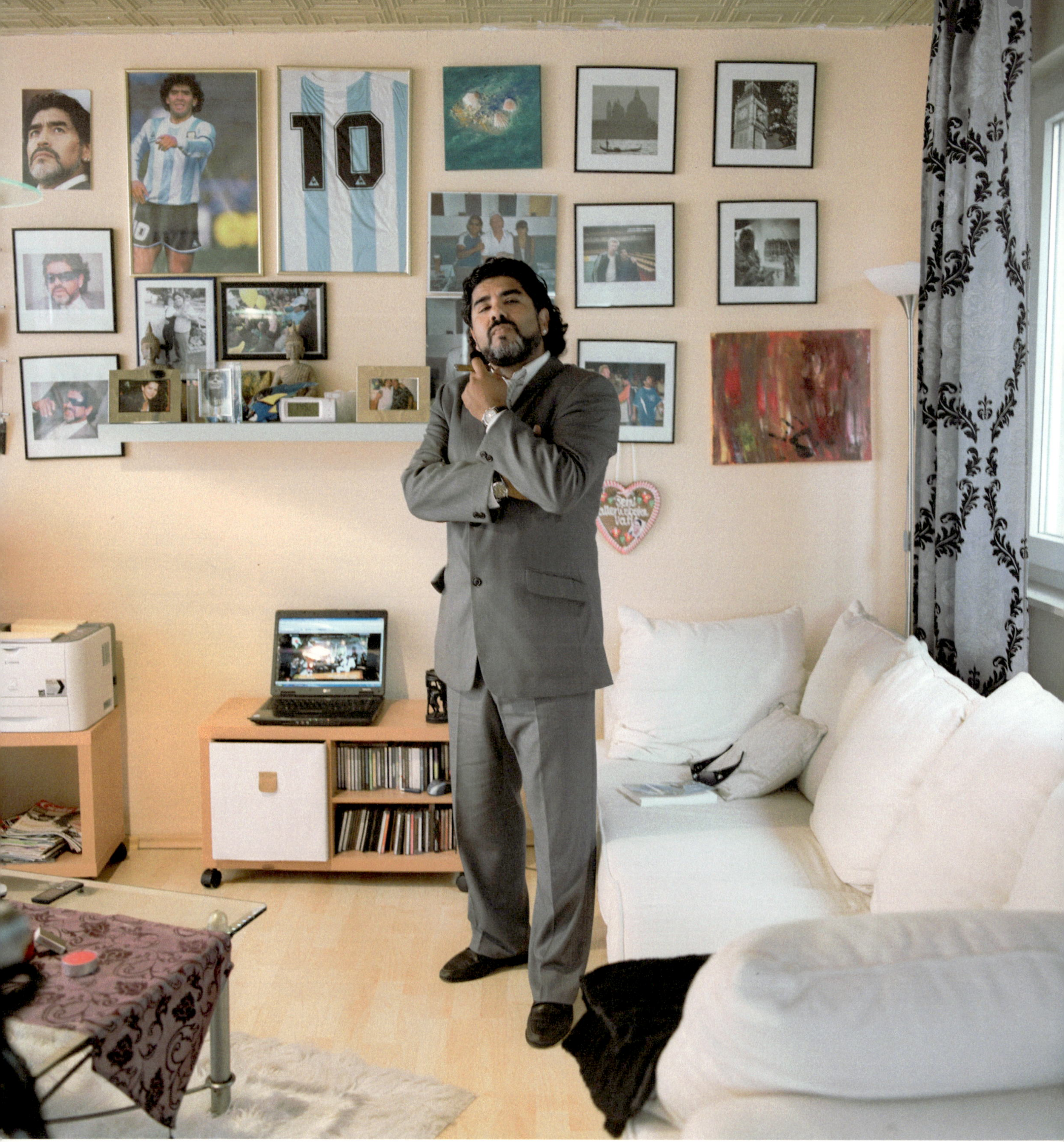

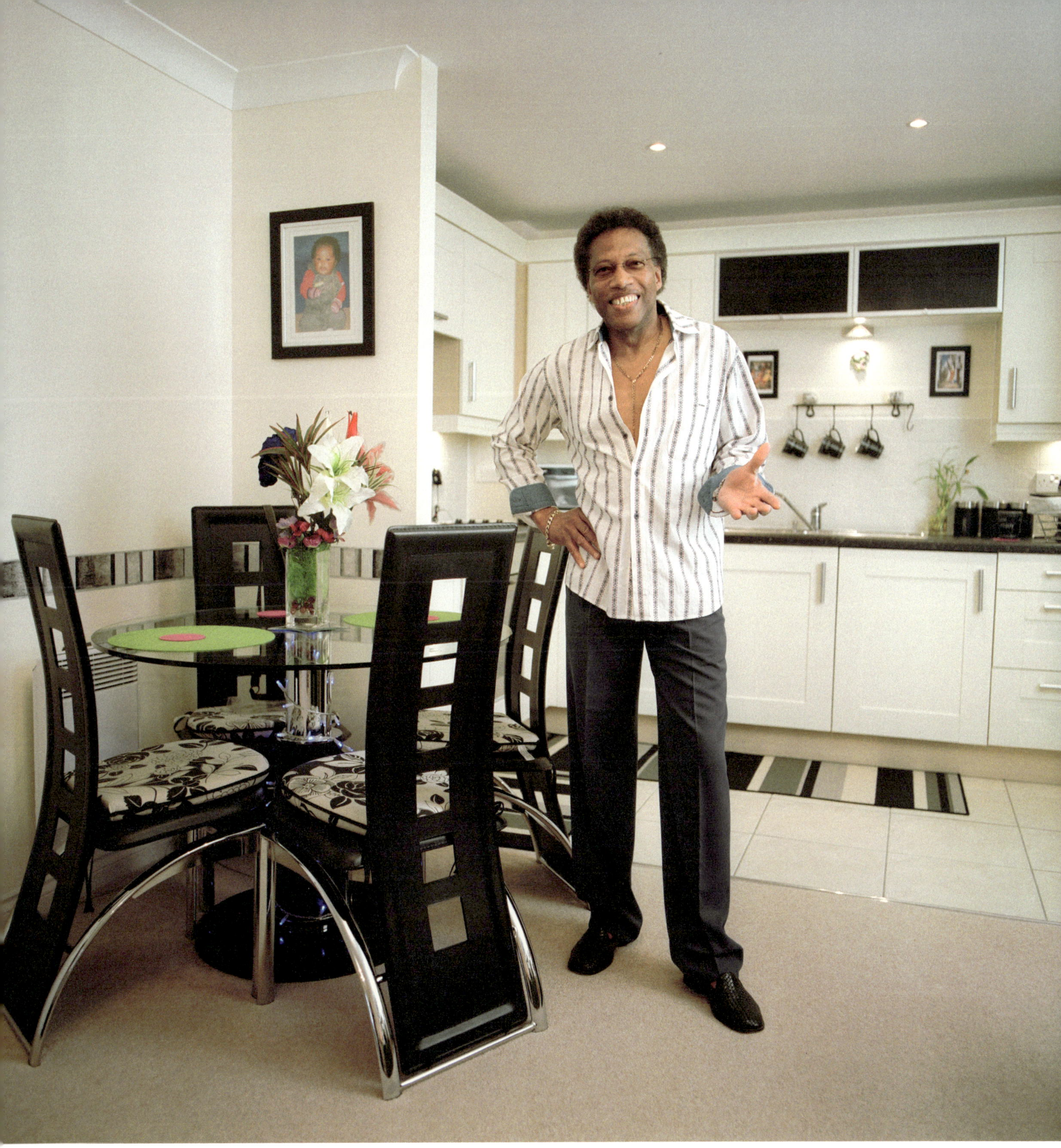

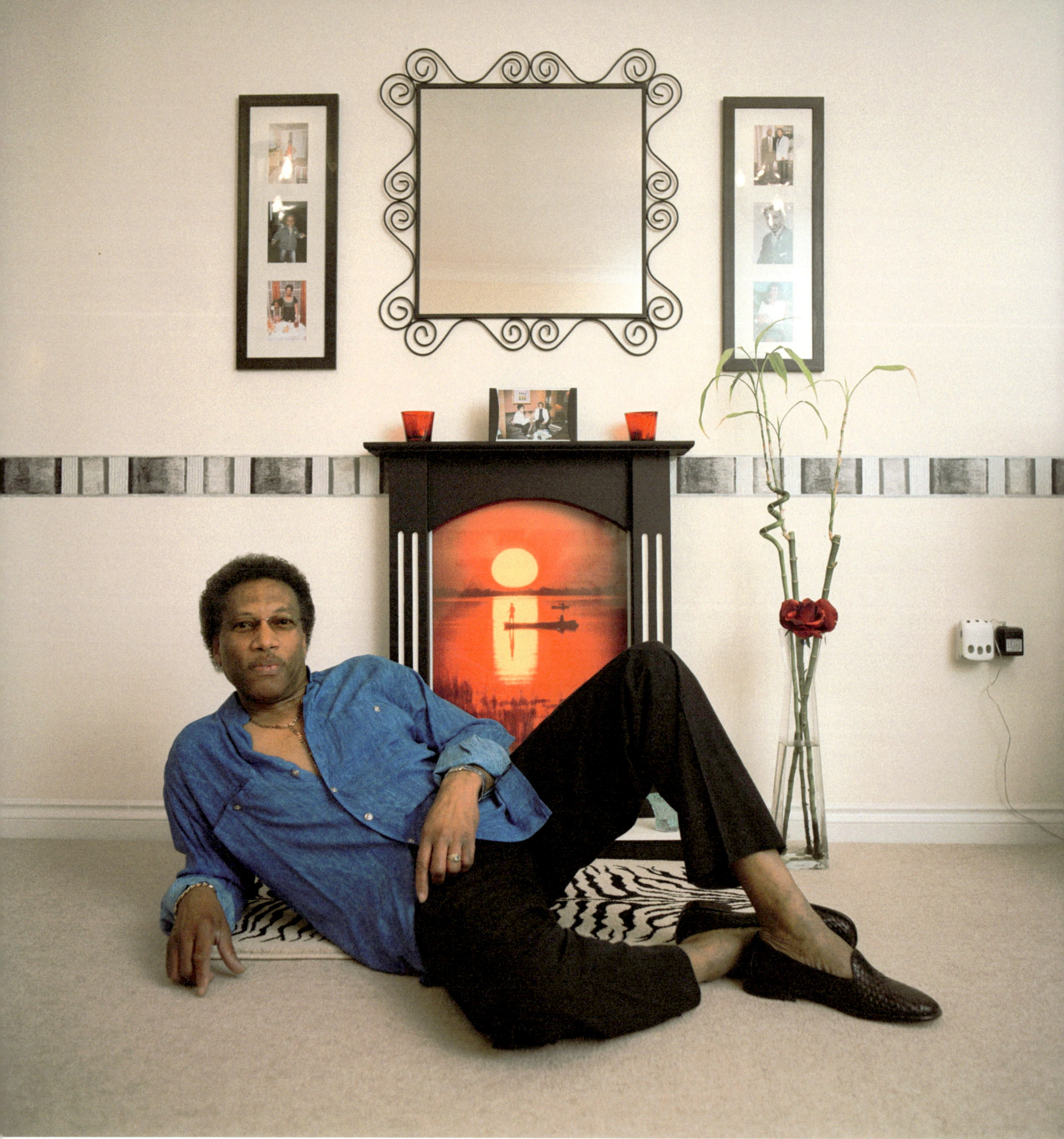

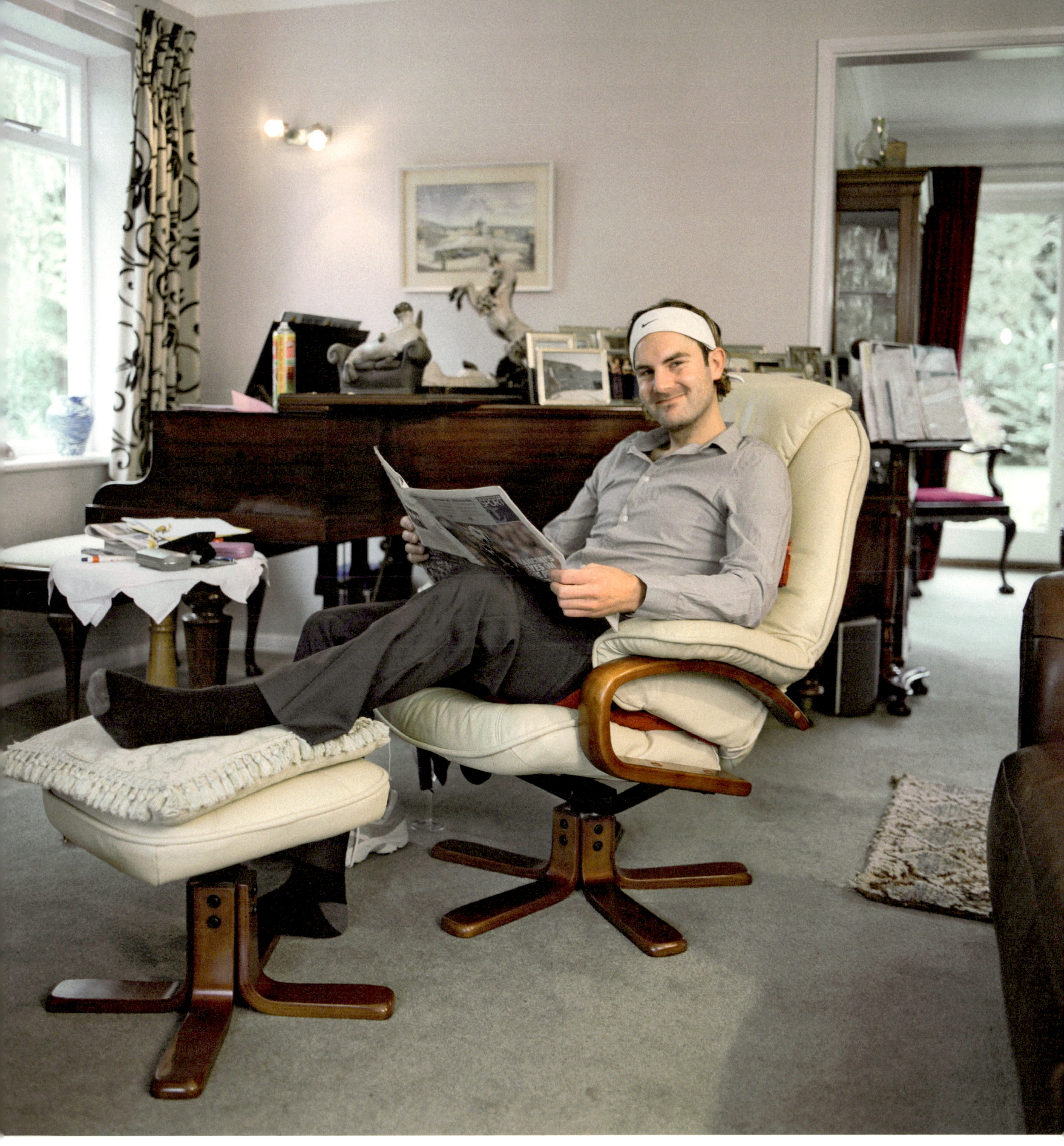

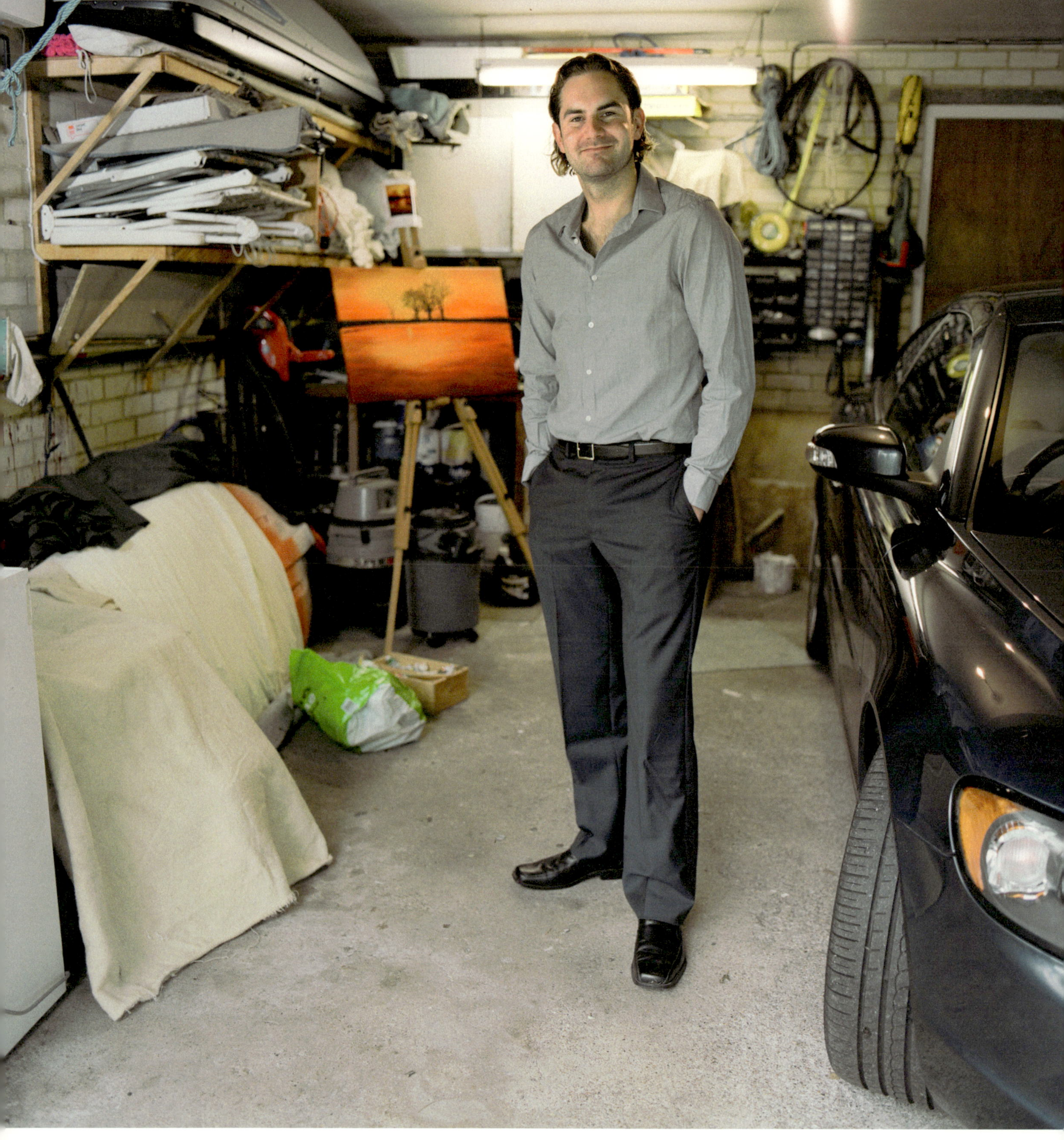

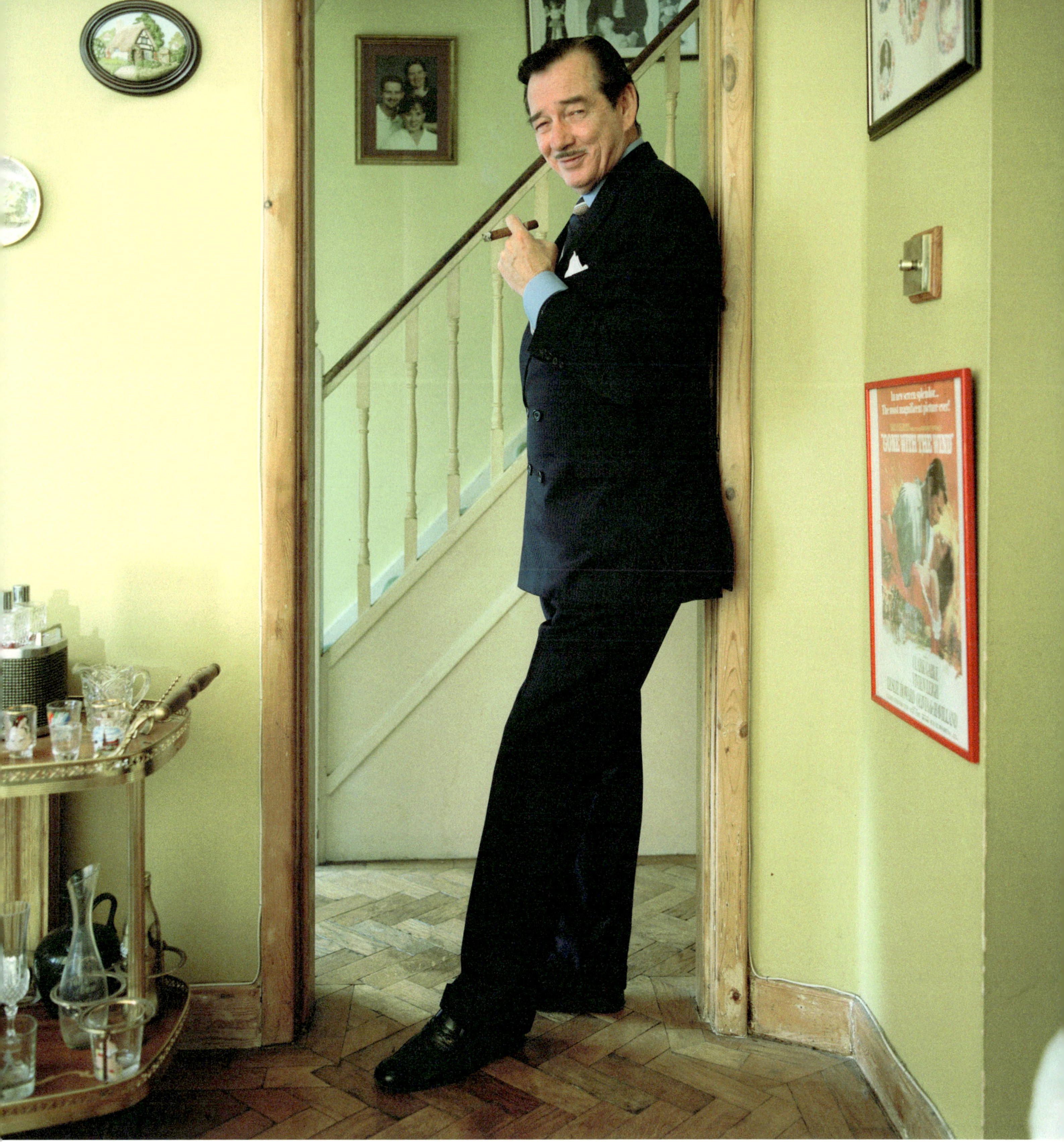

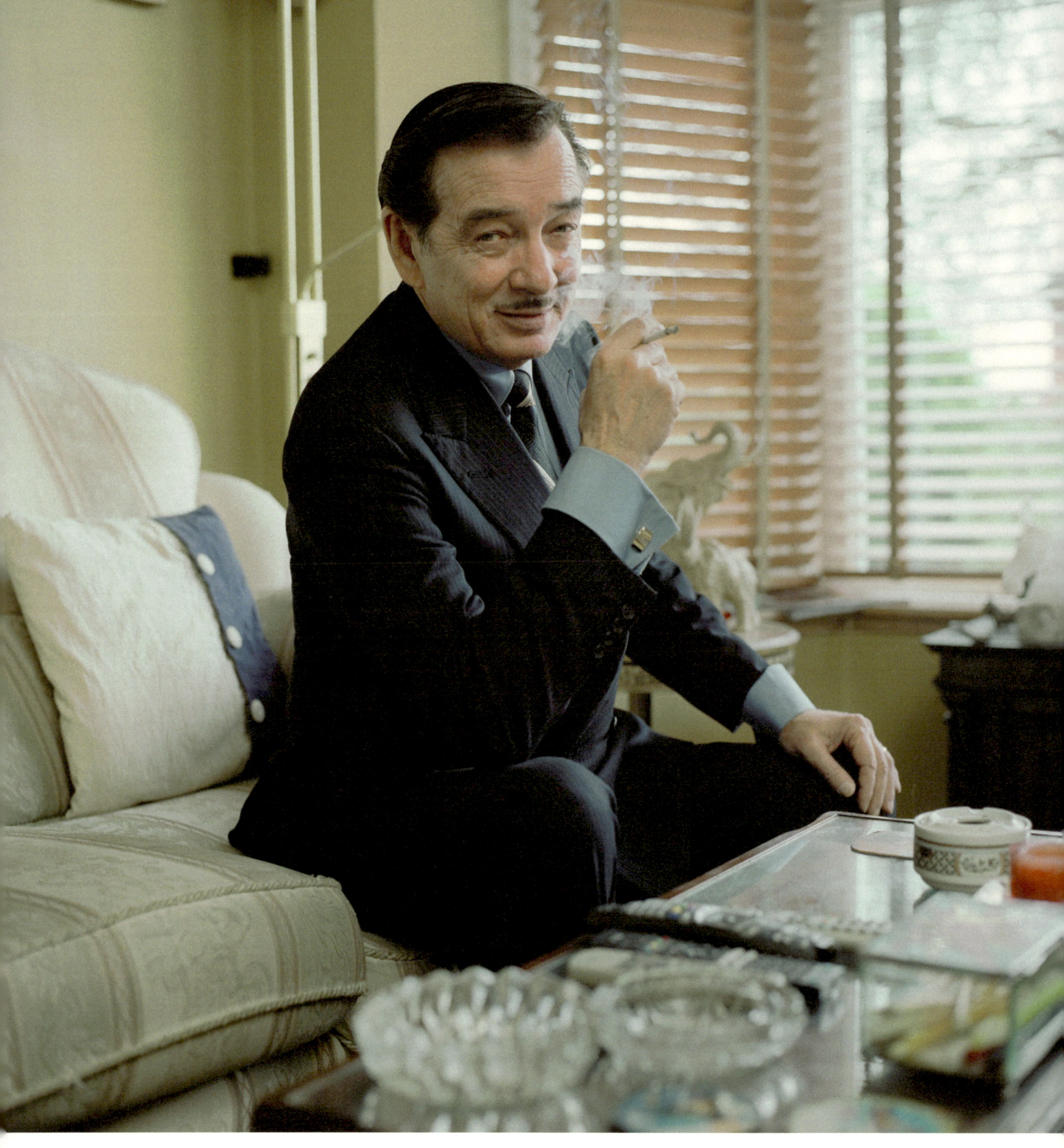

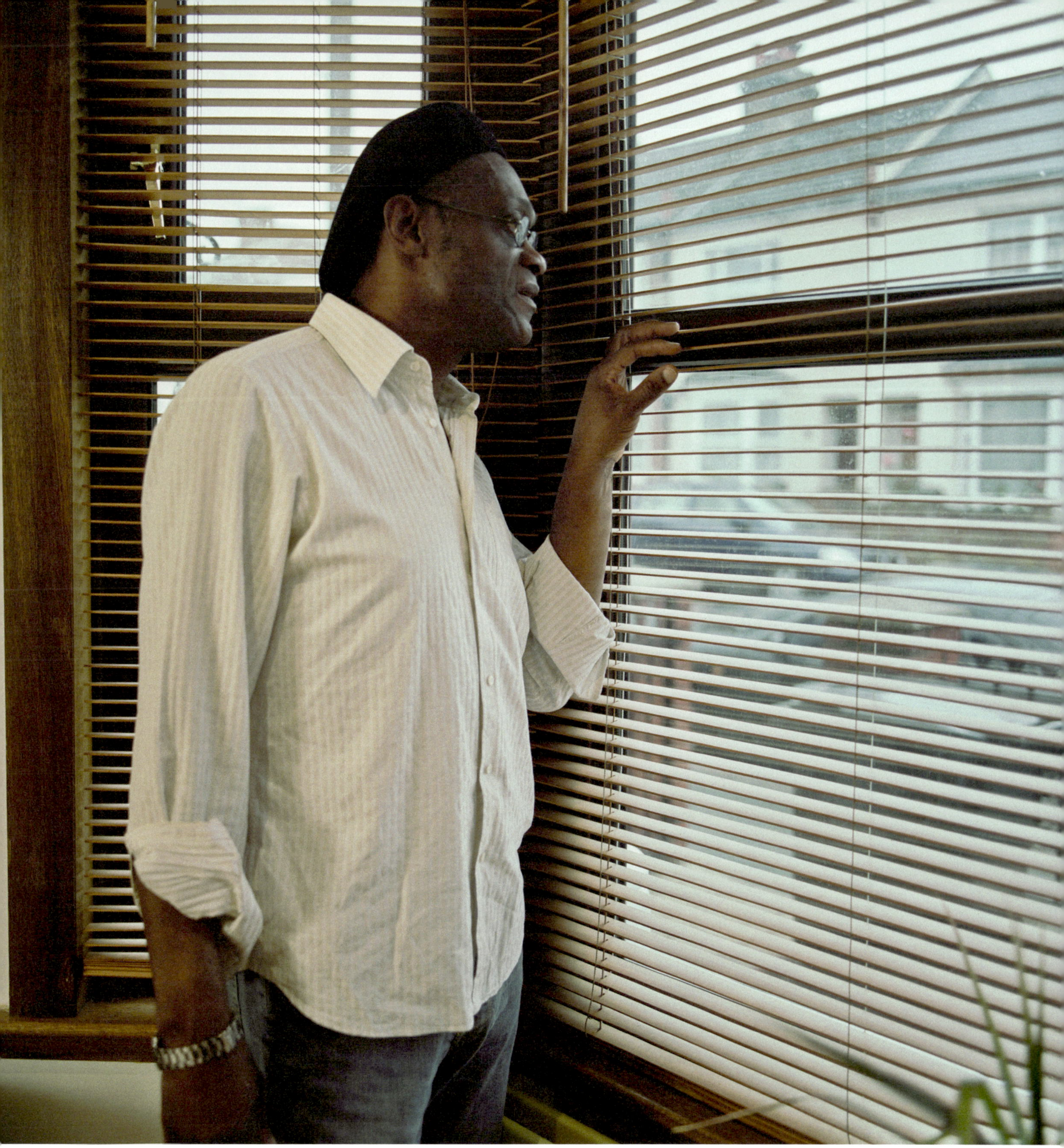

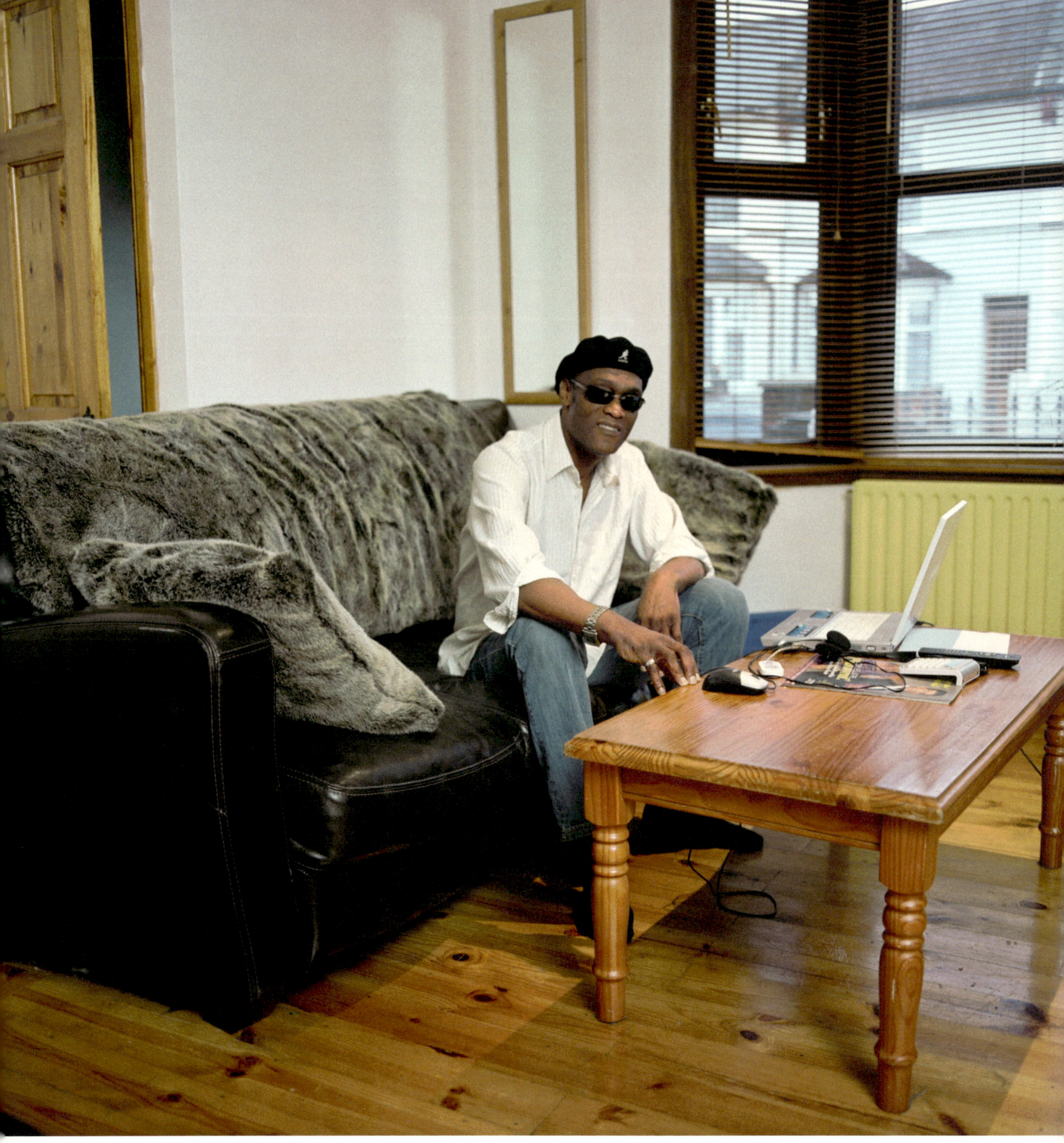

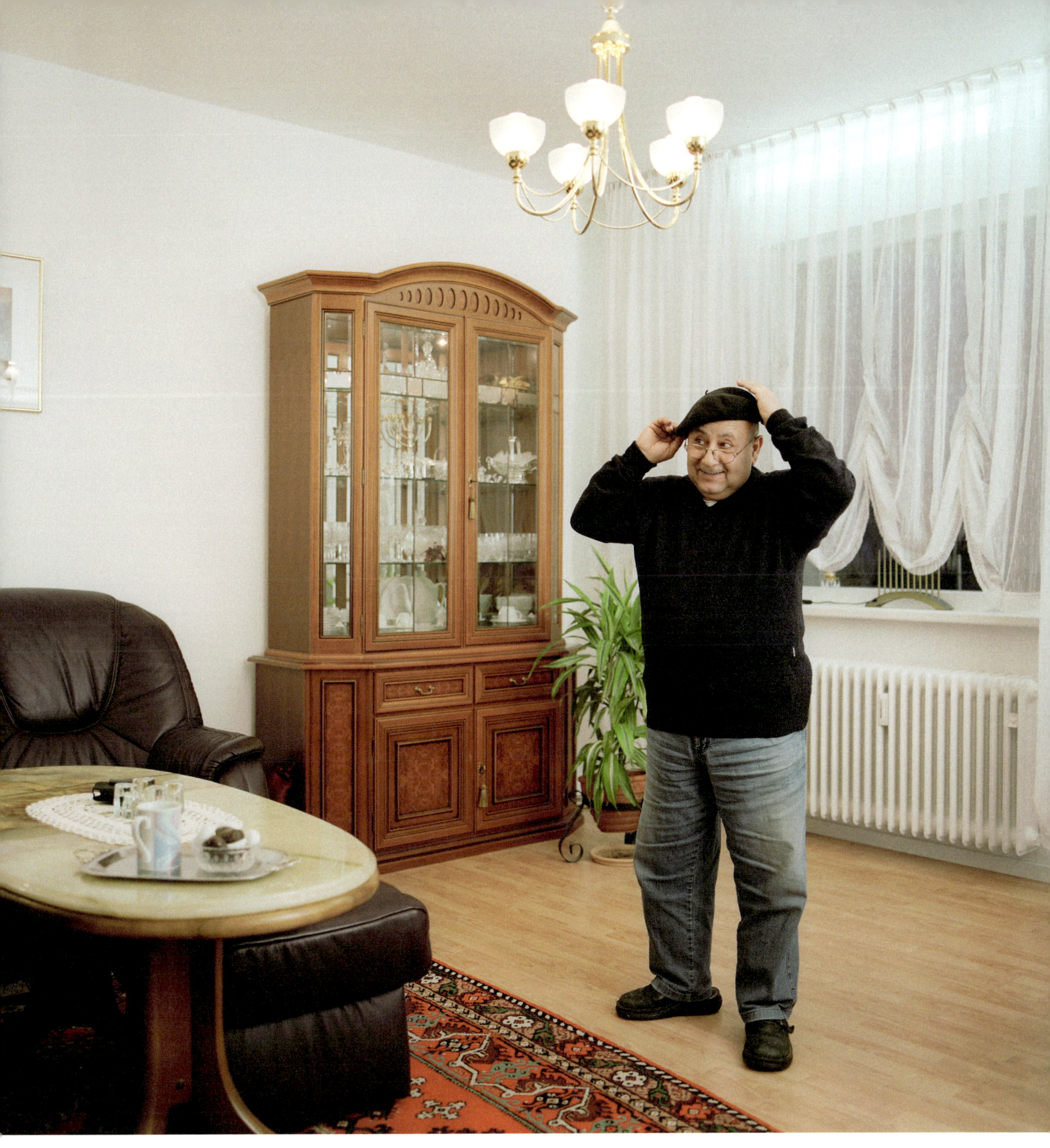

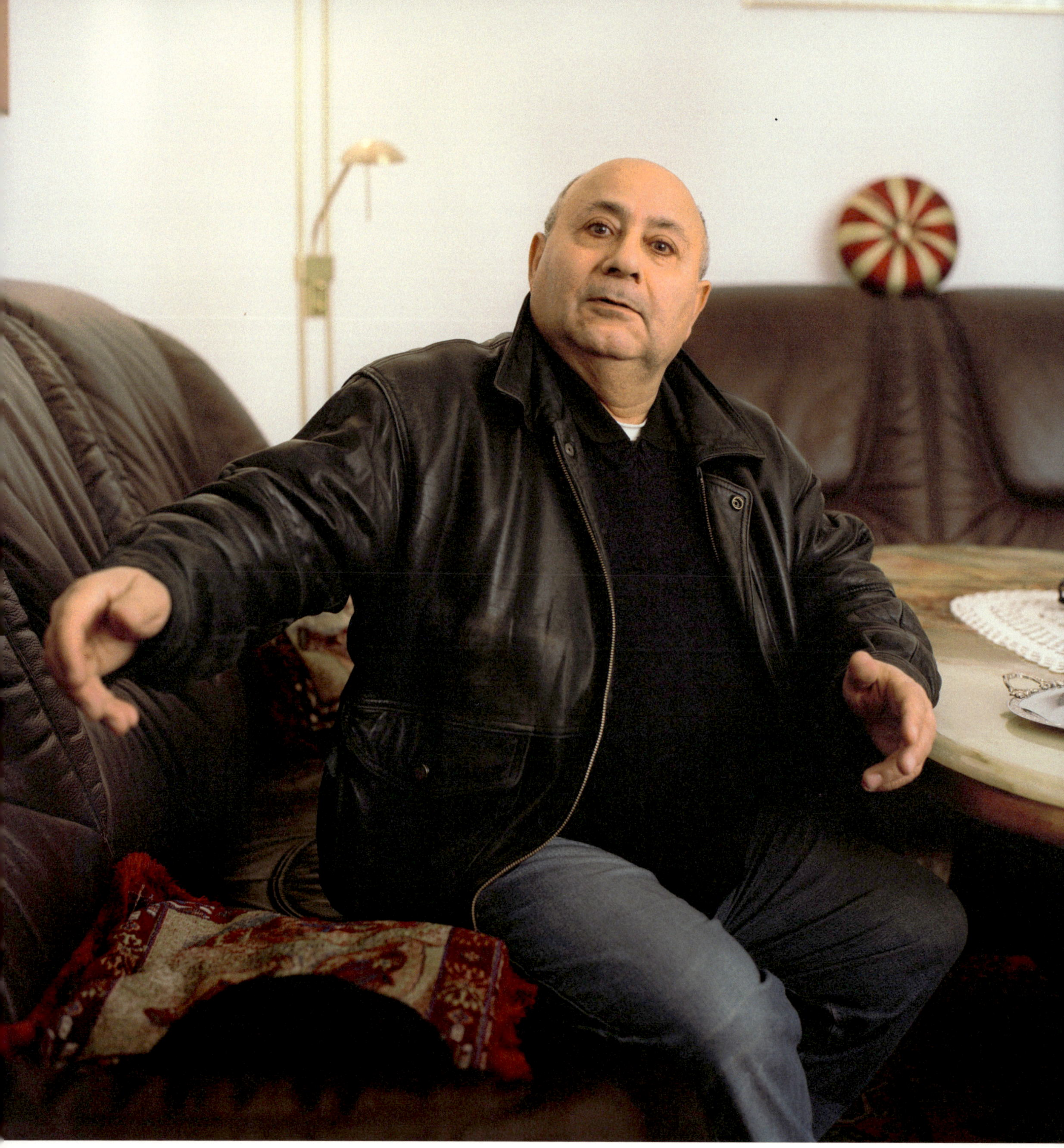

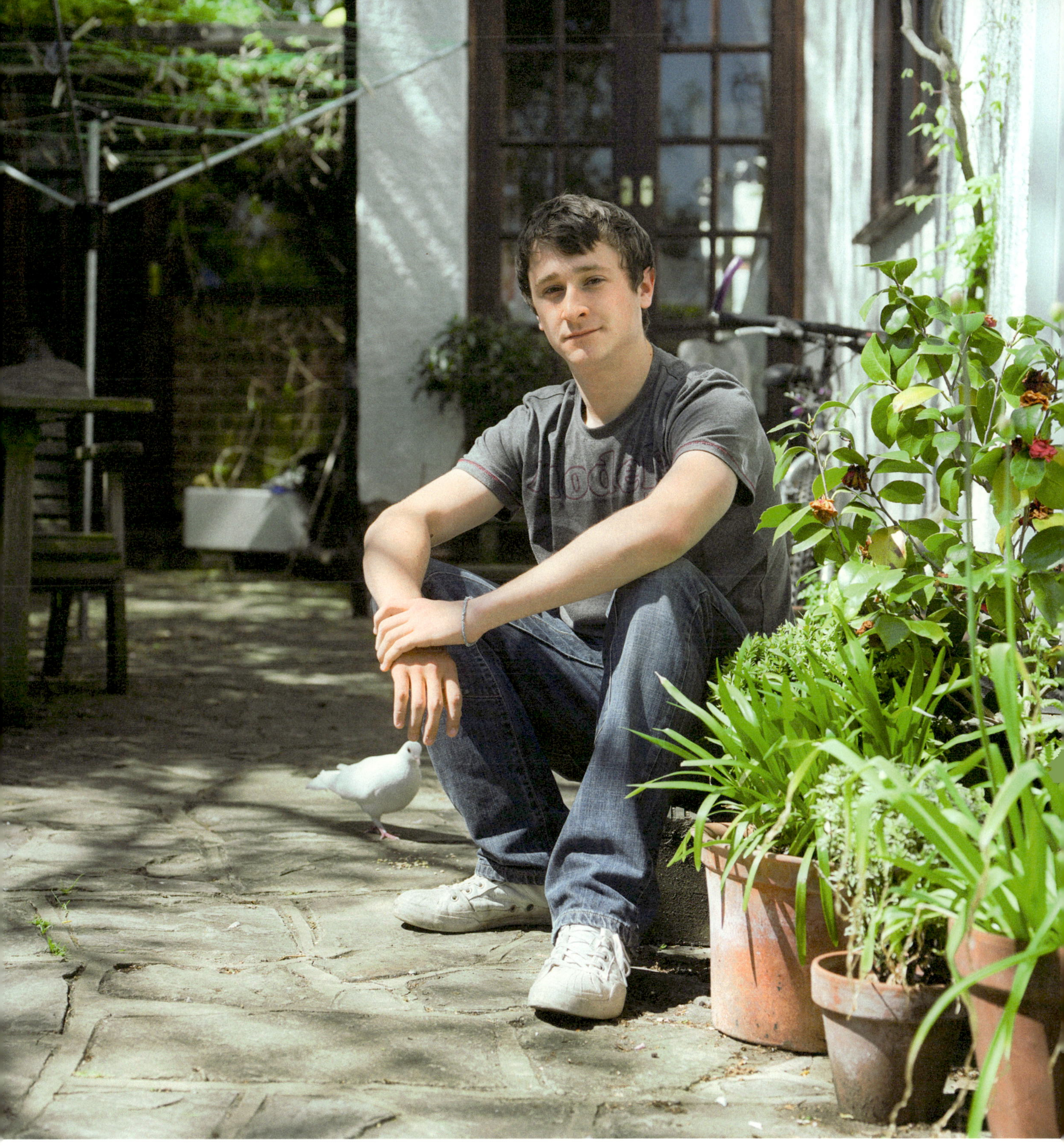

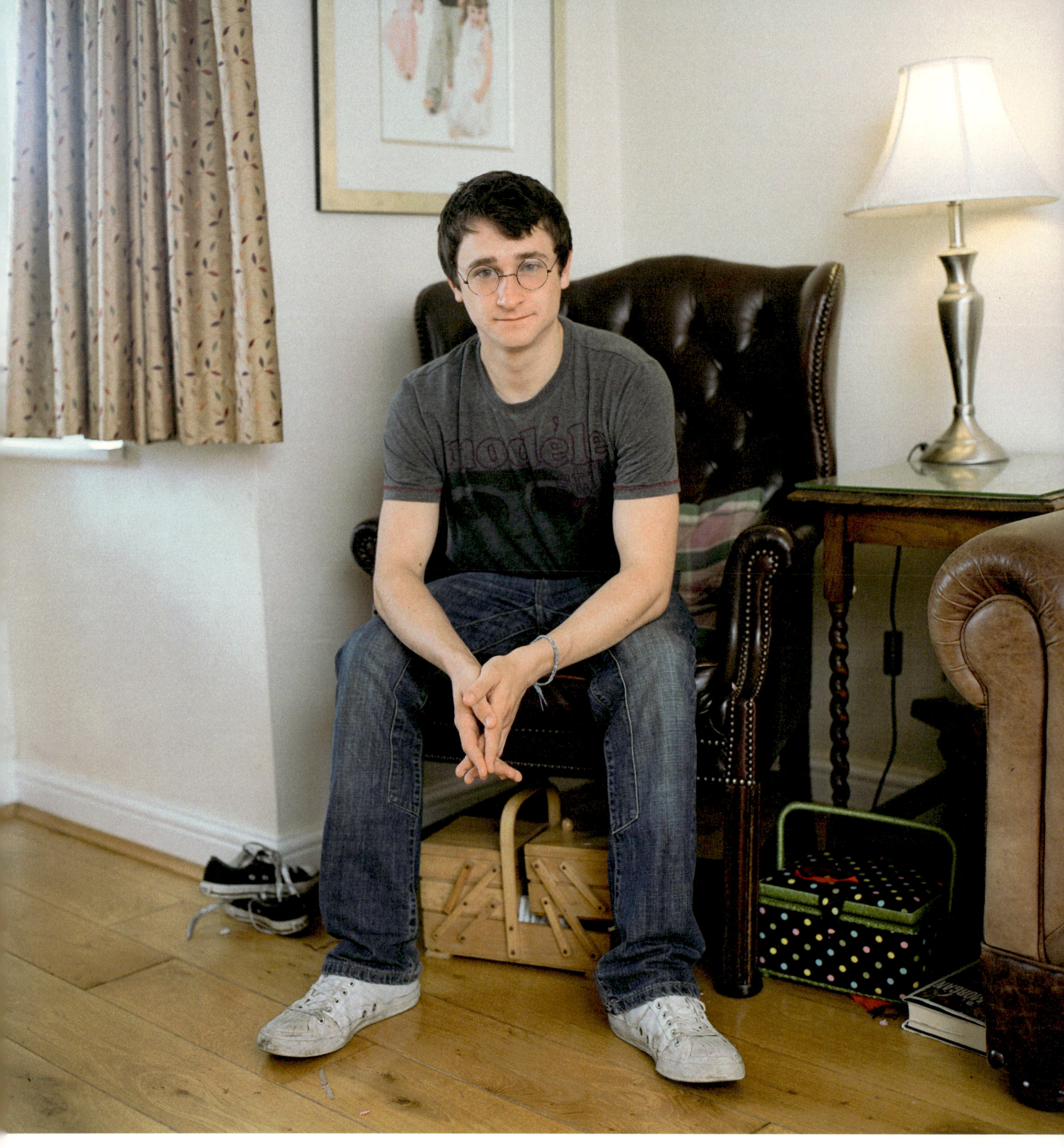

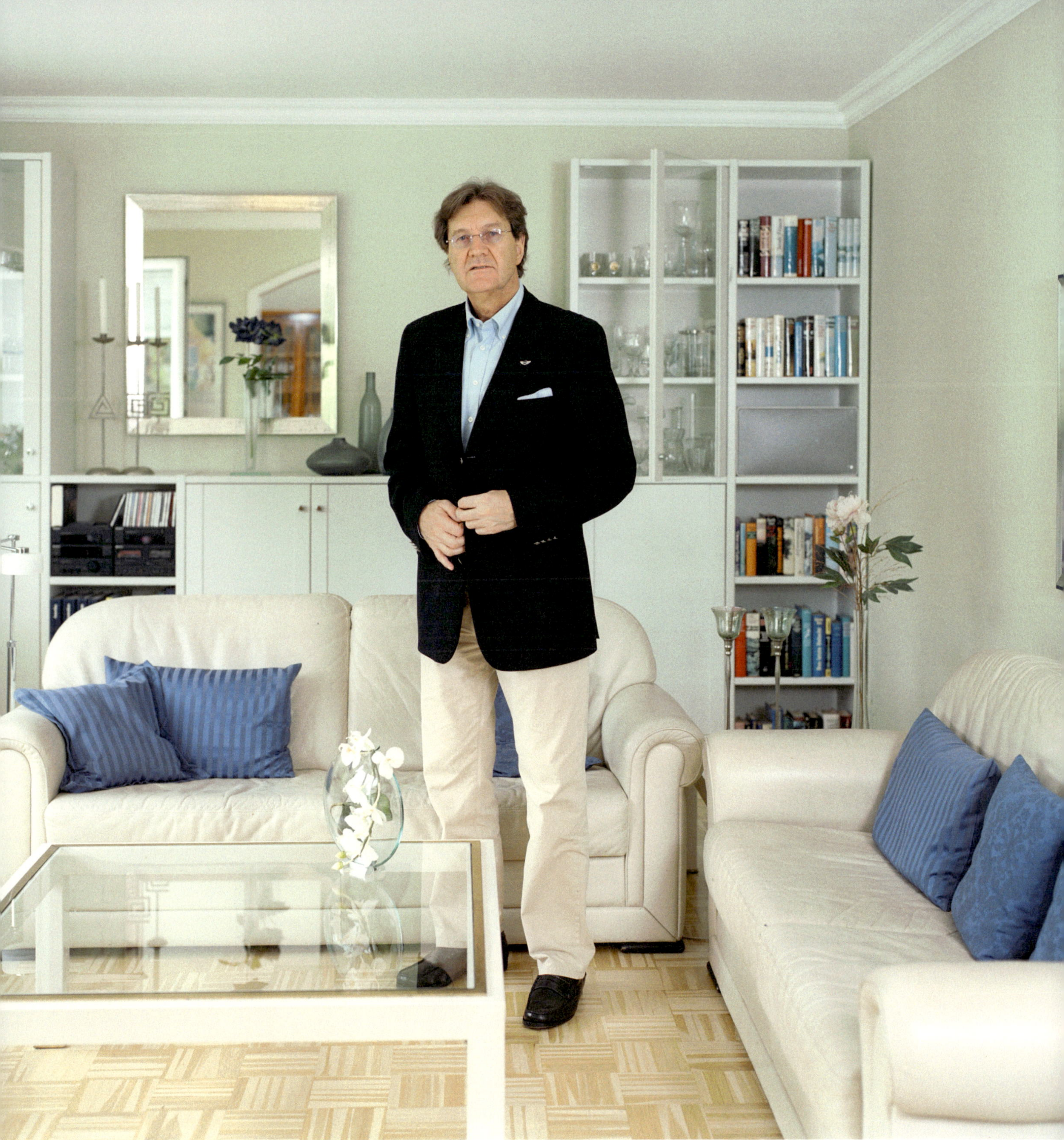

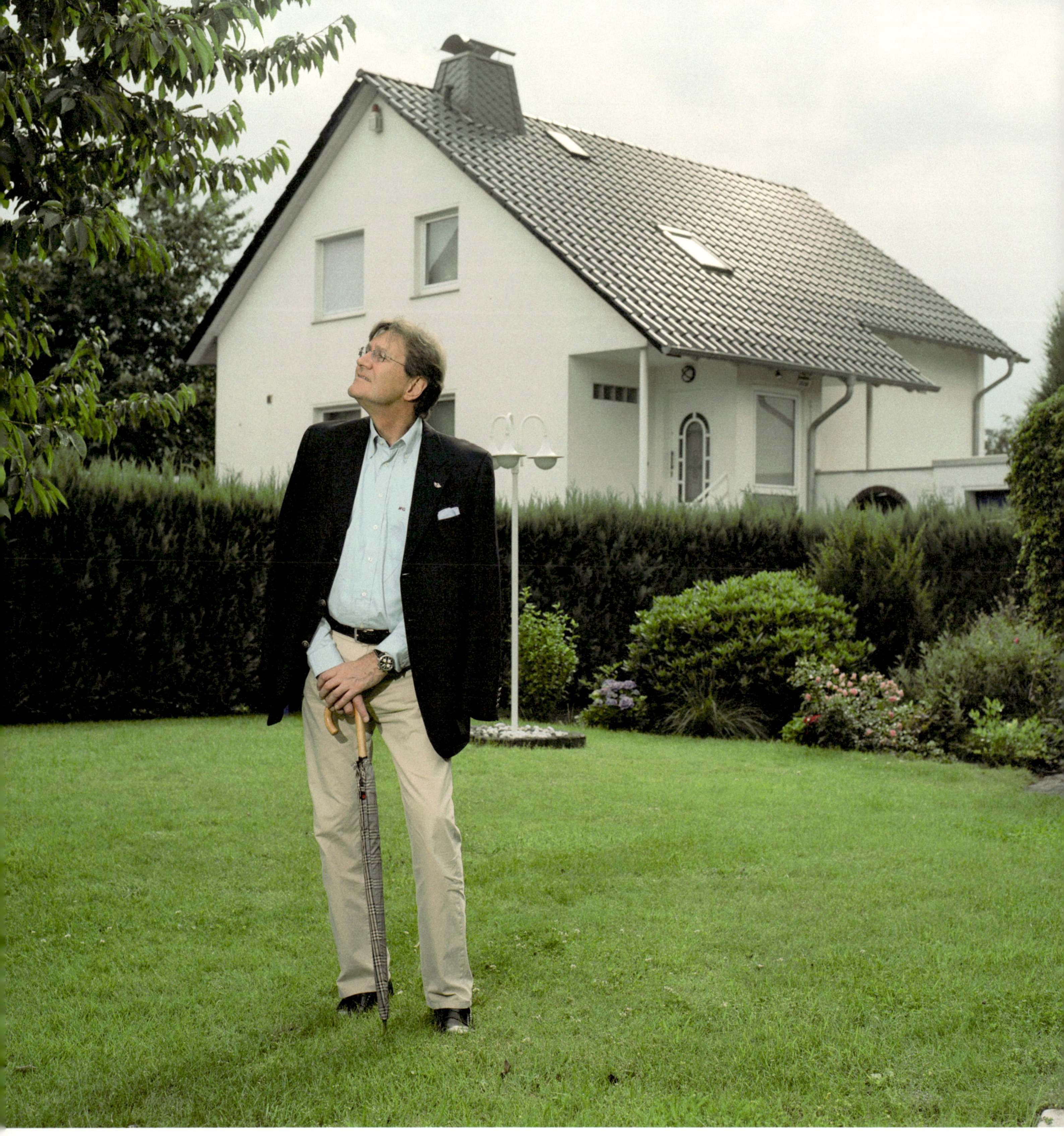

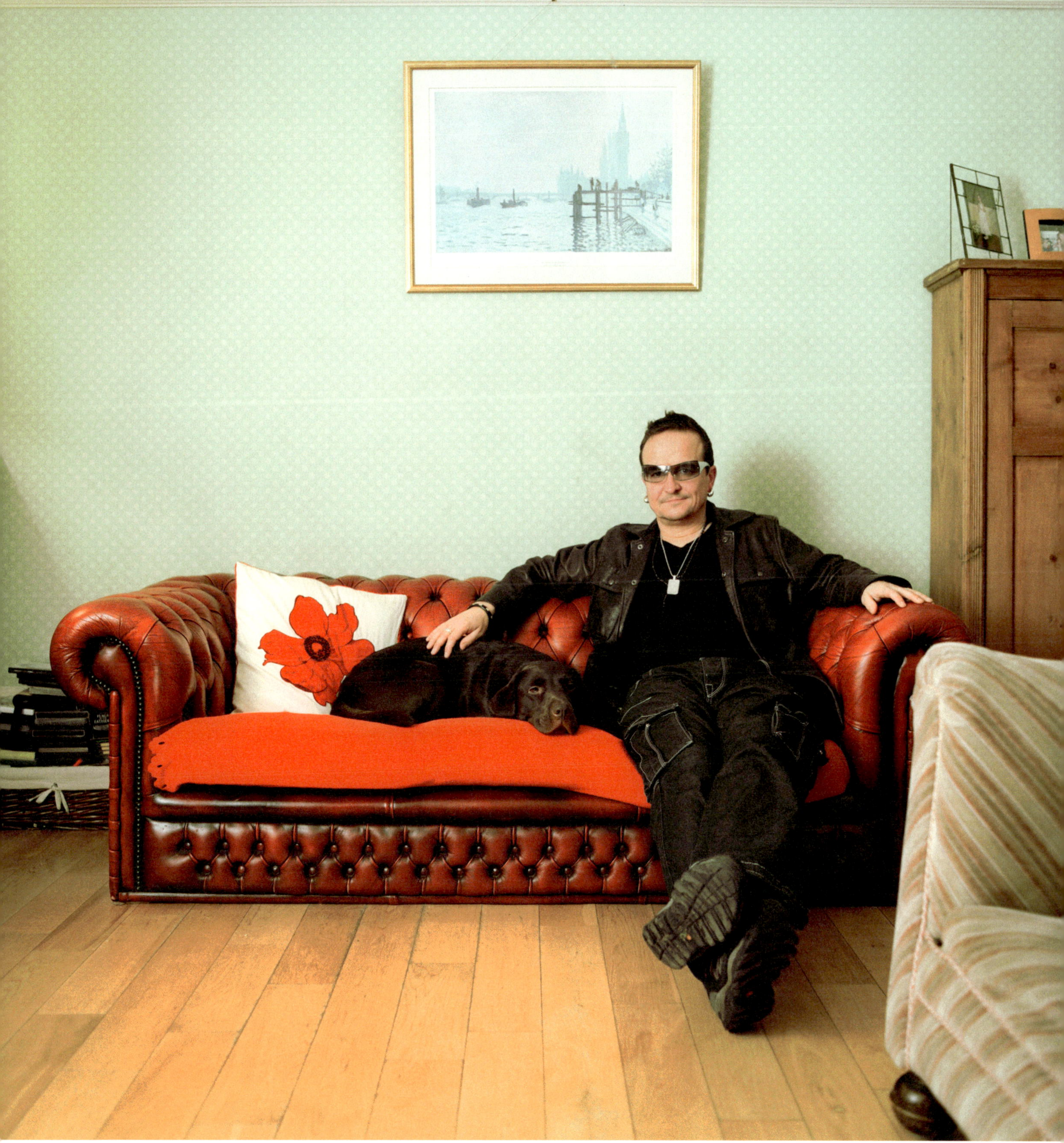

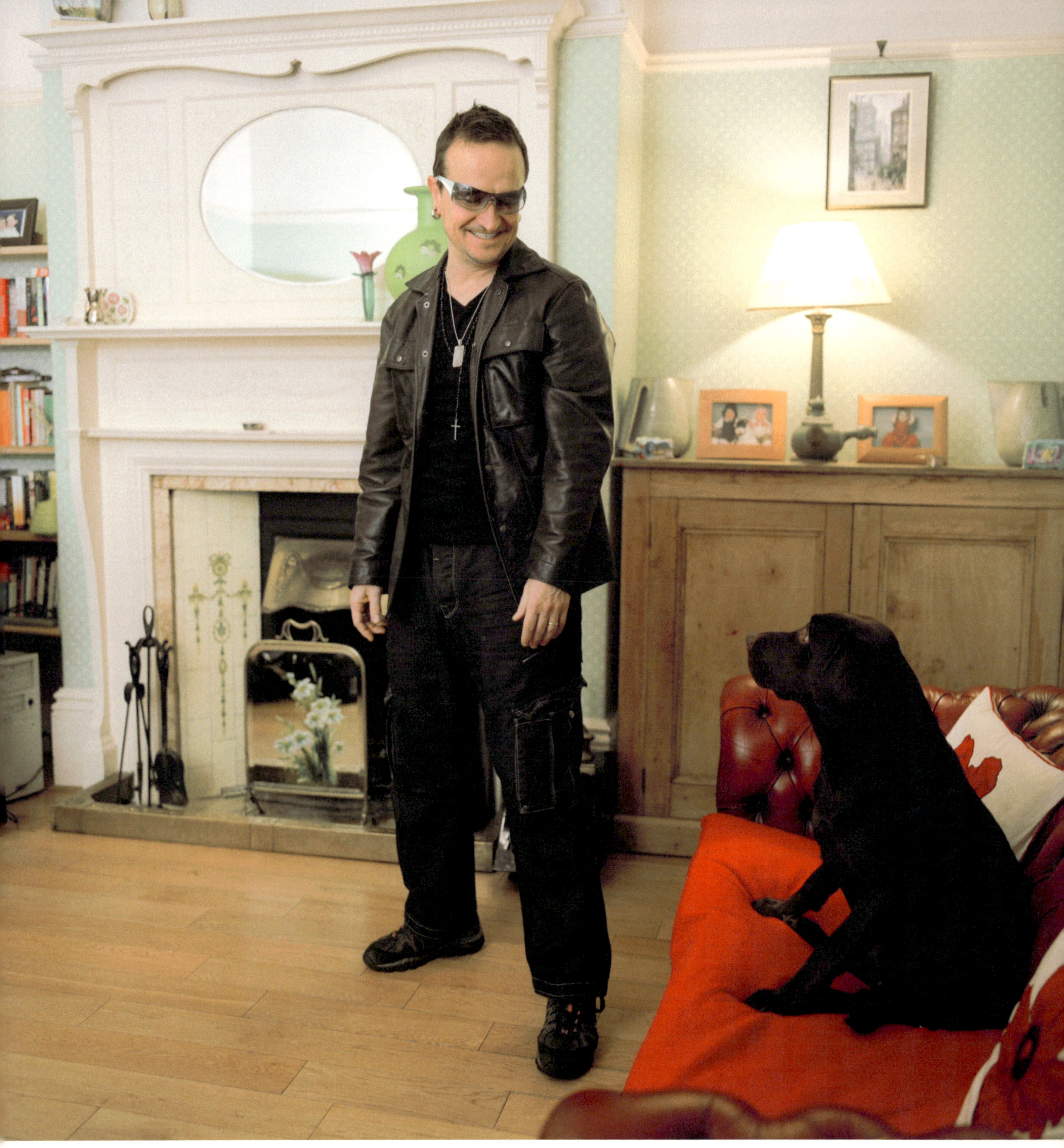

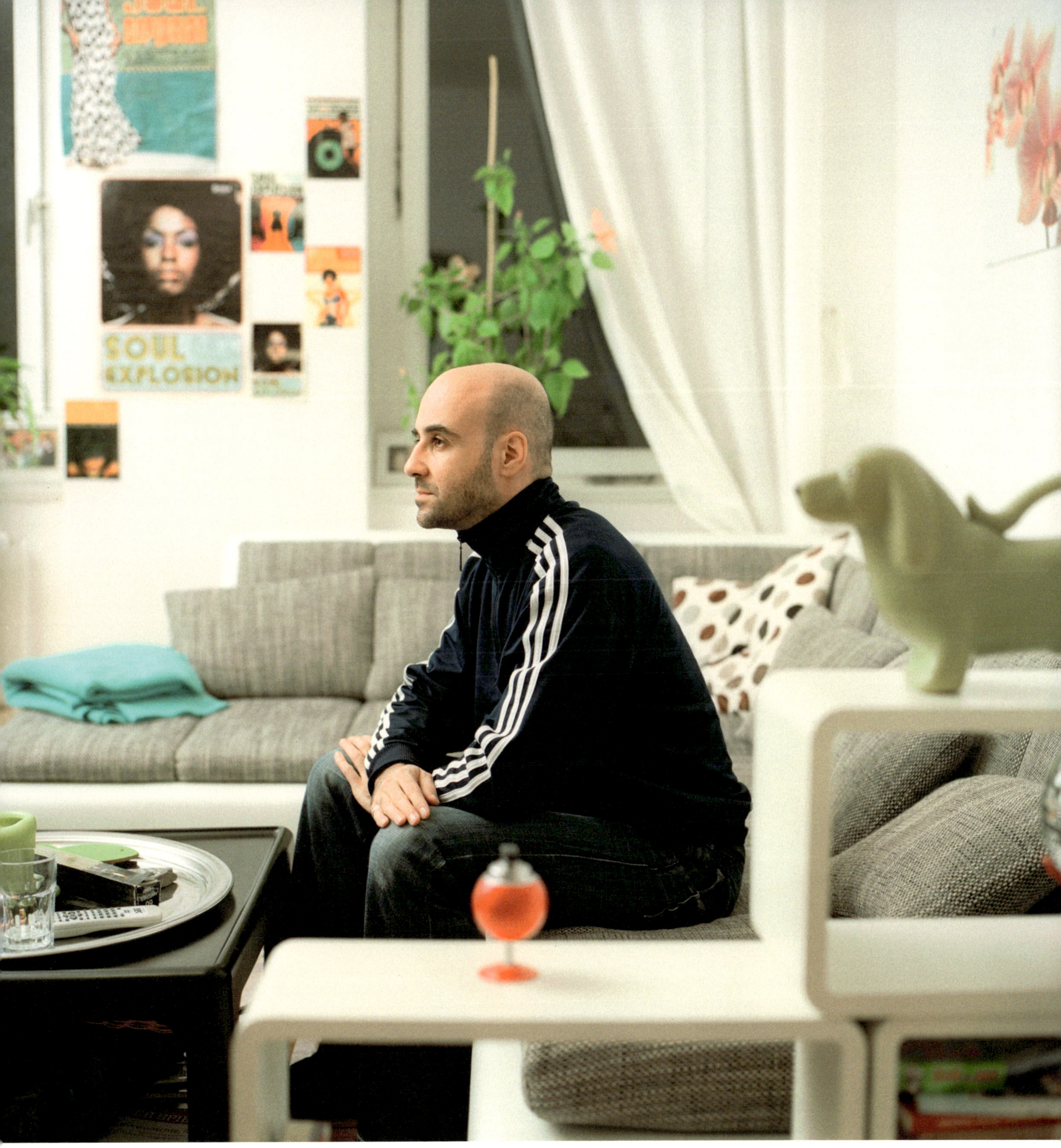

SOUL
EXPLOSION

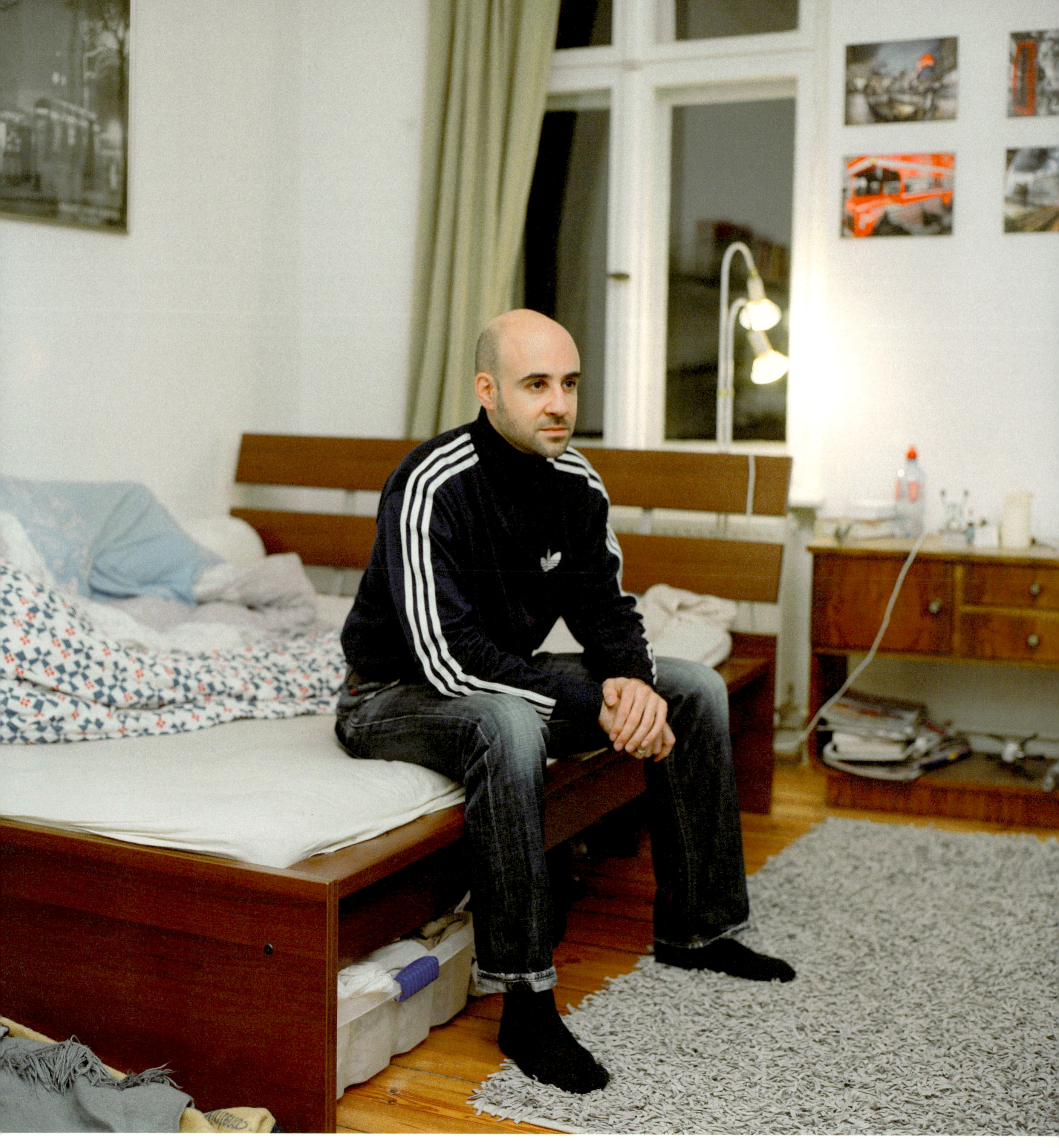

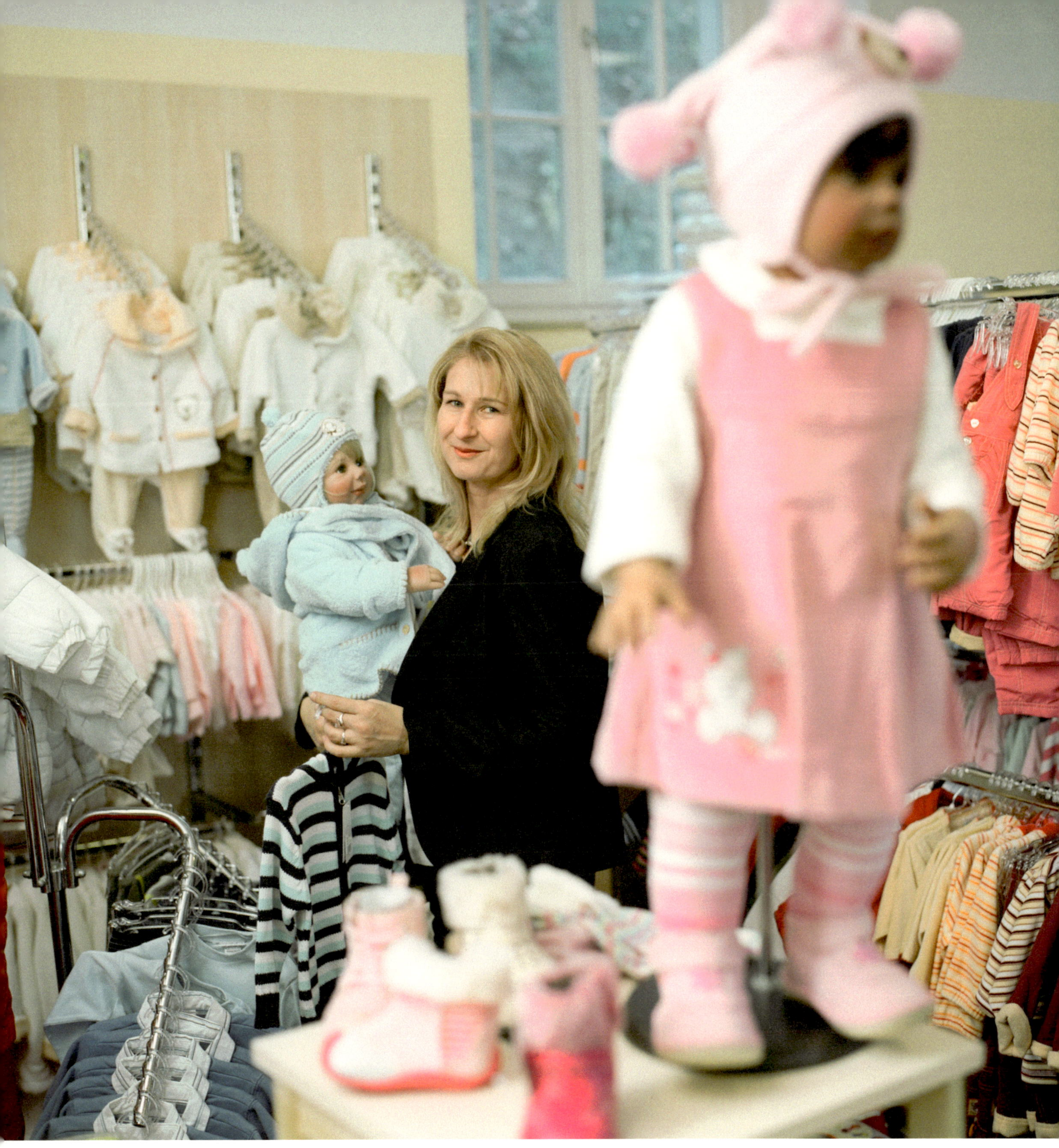

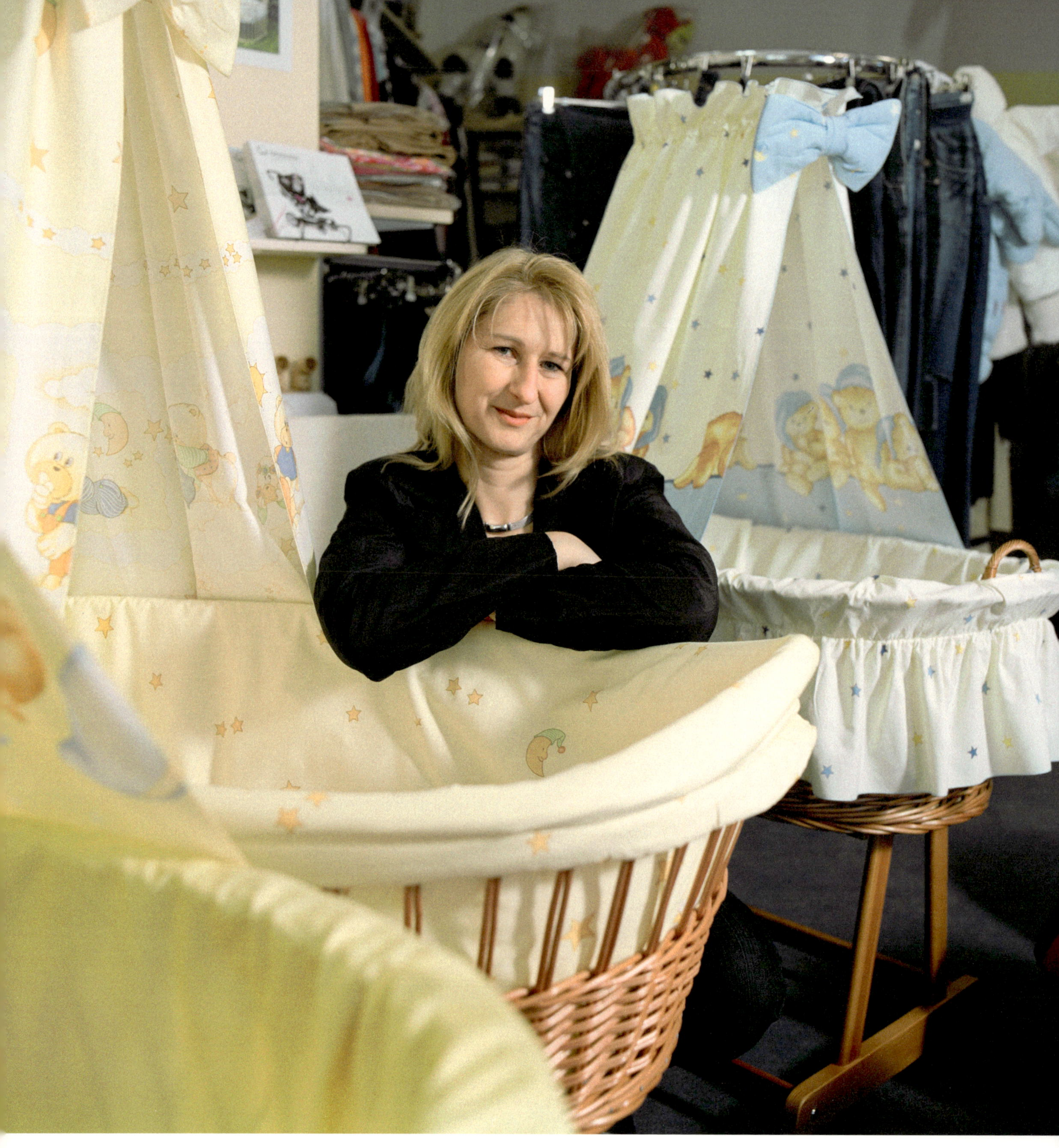

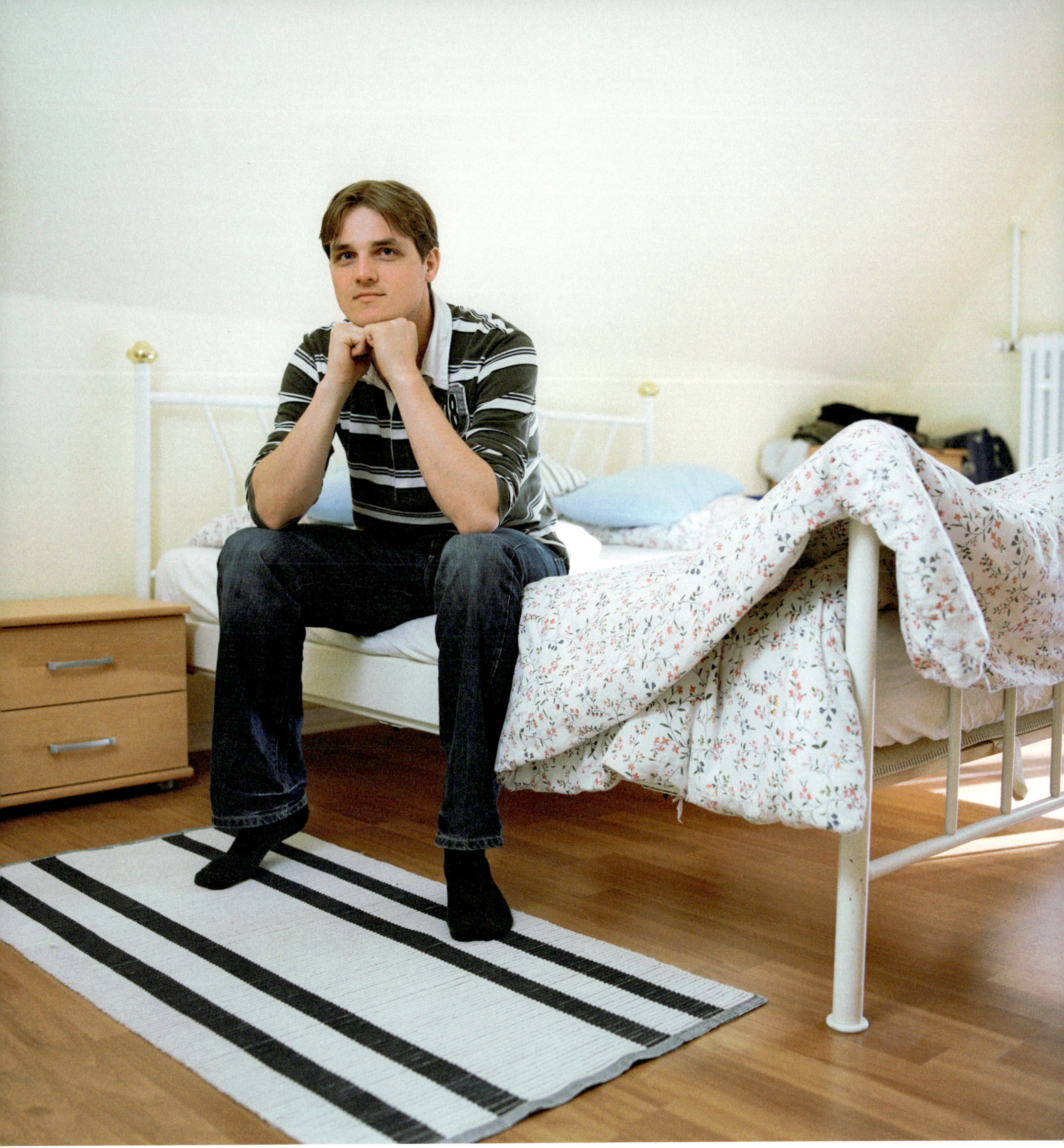

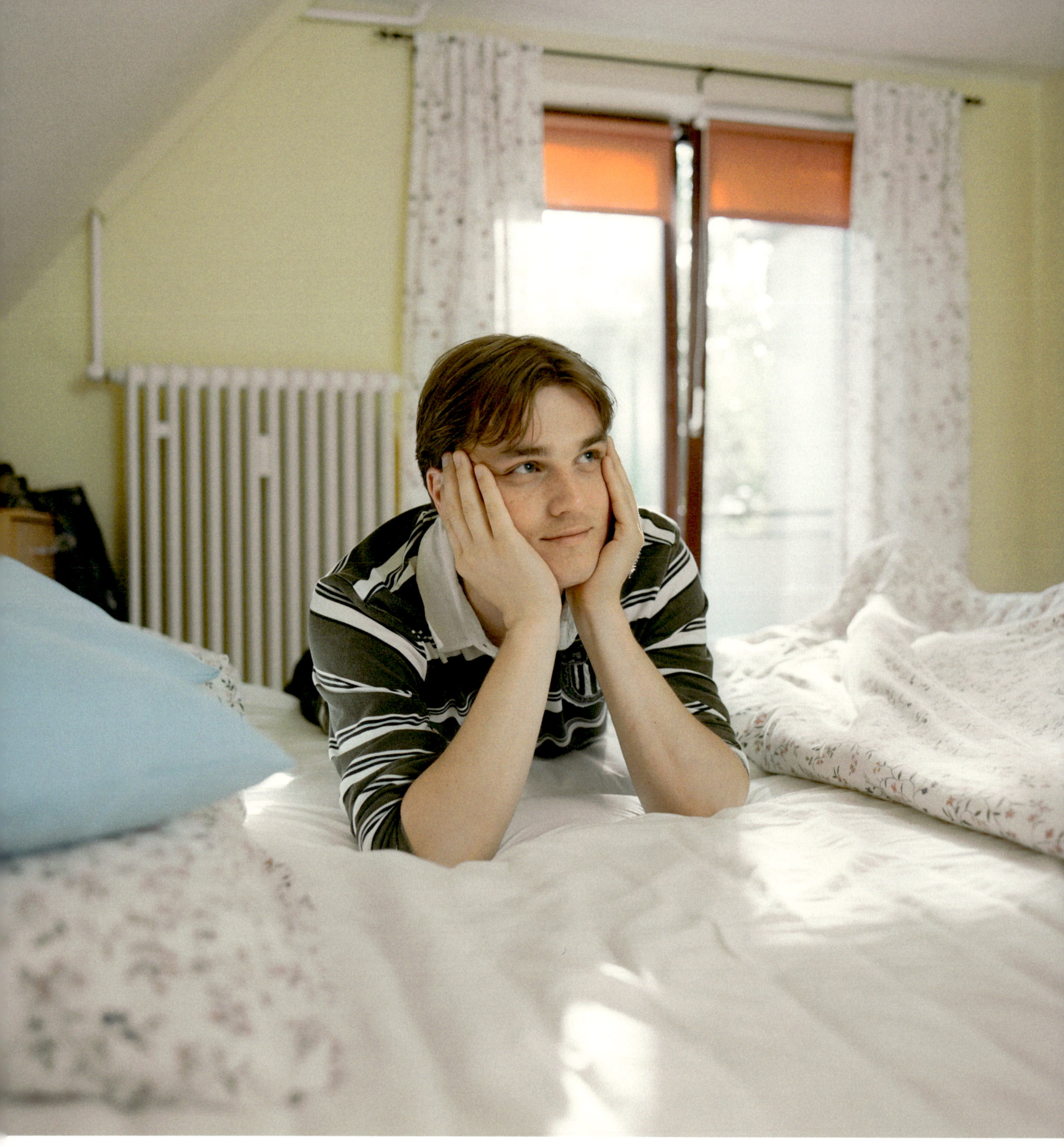

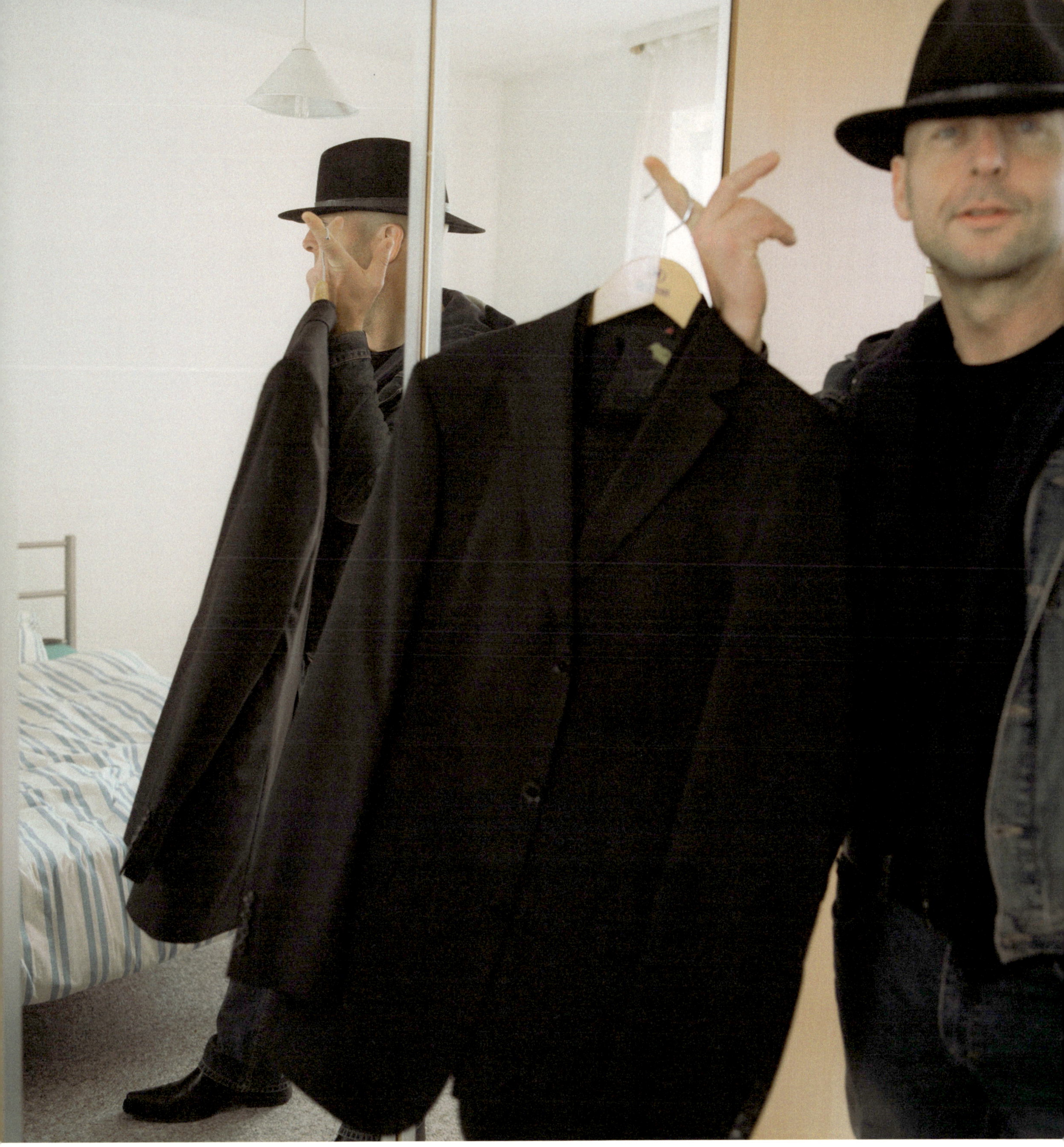

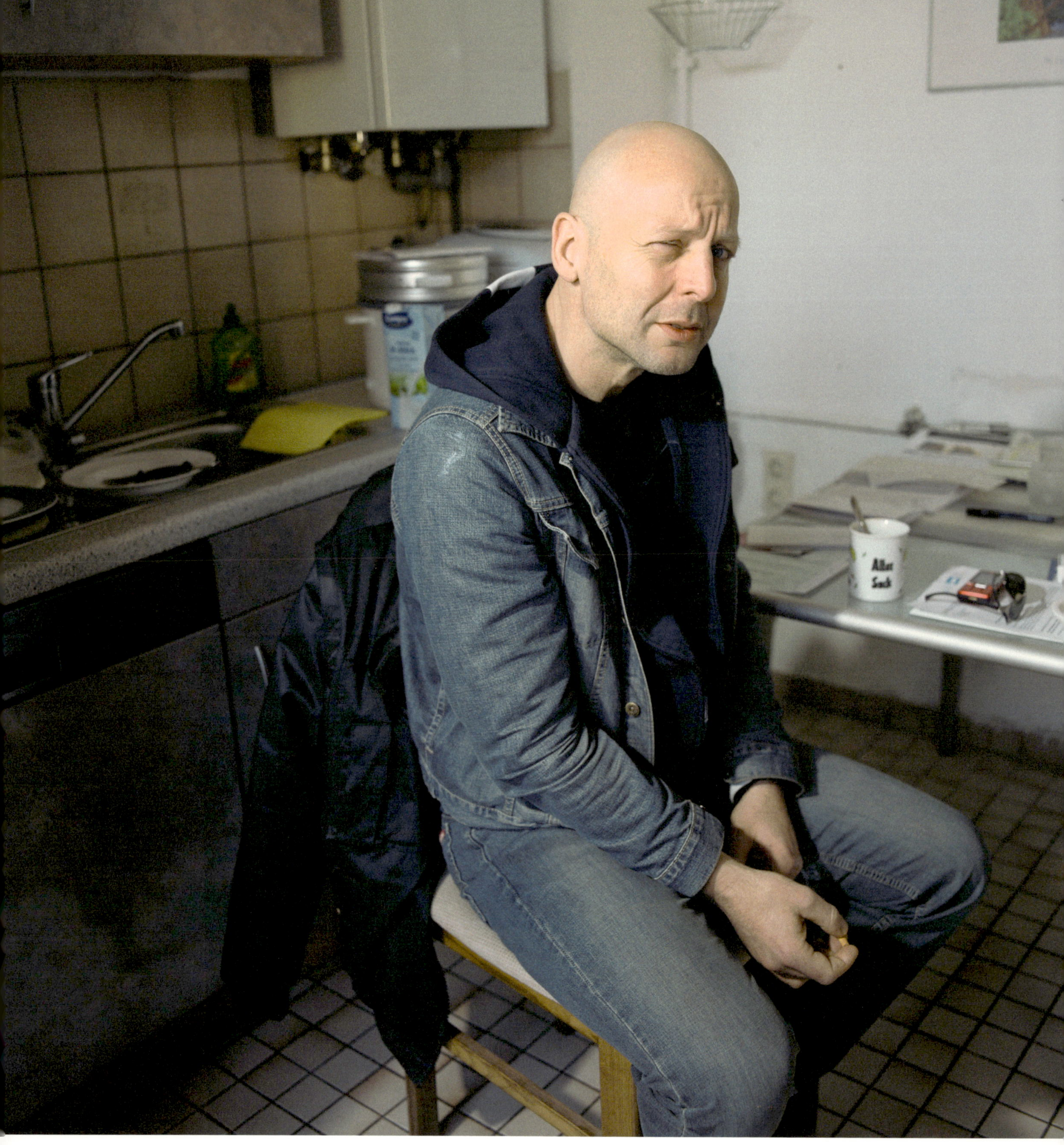

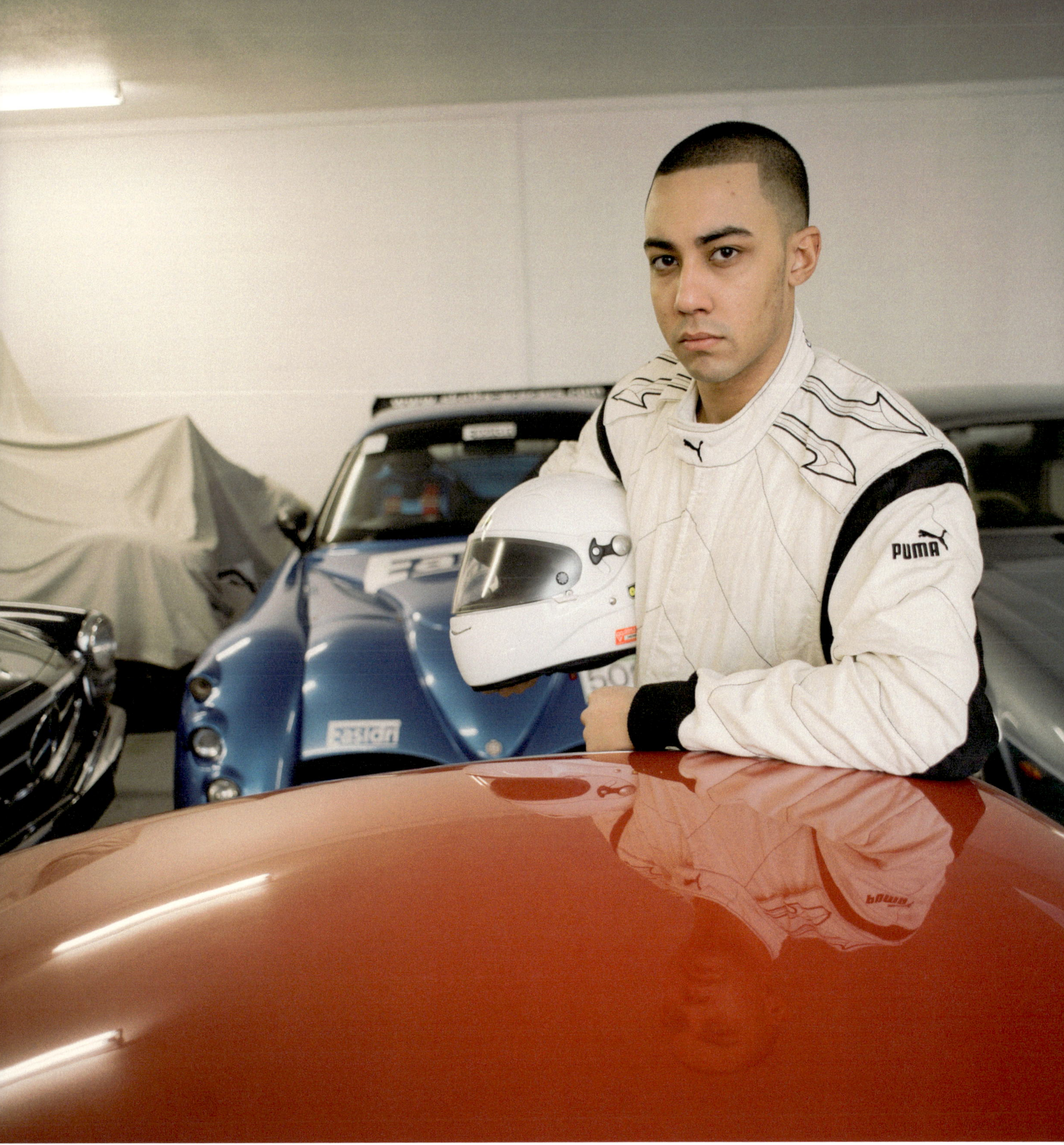

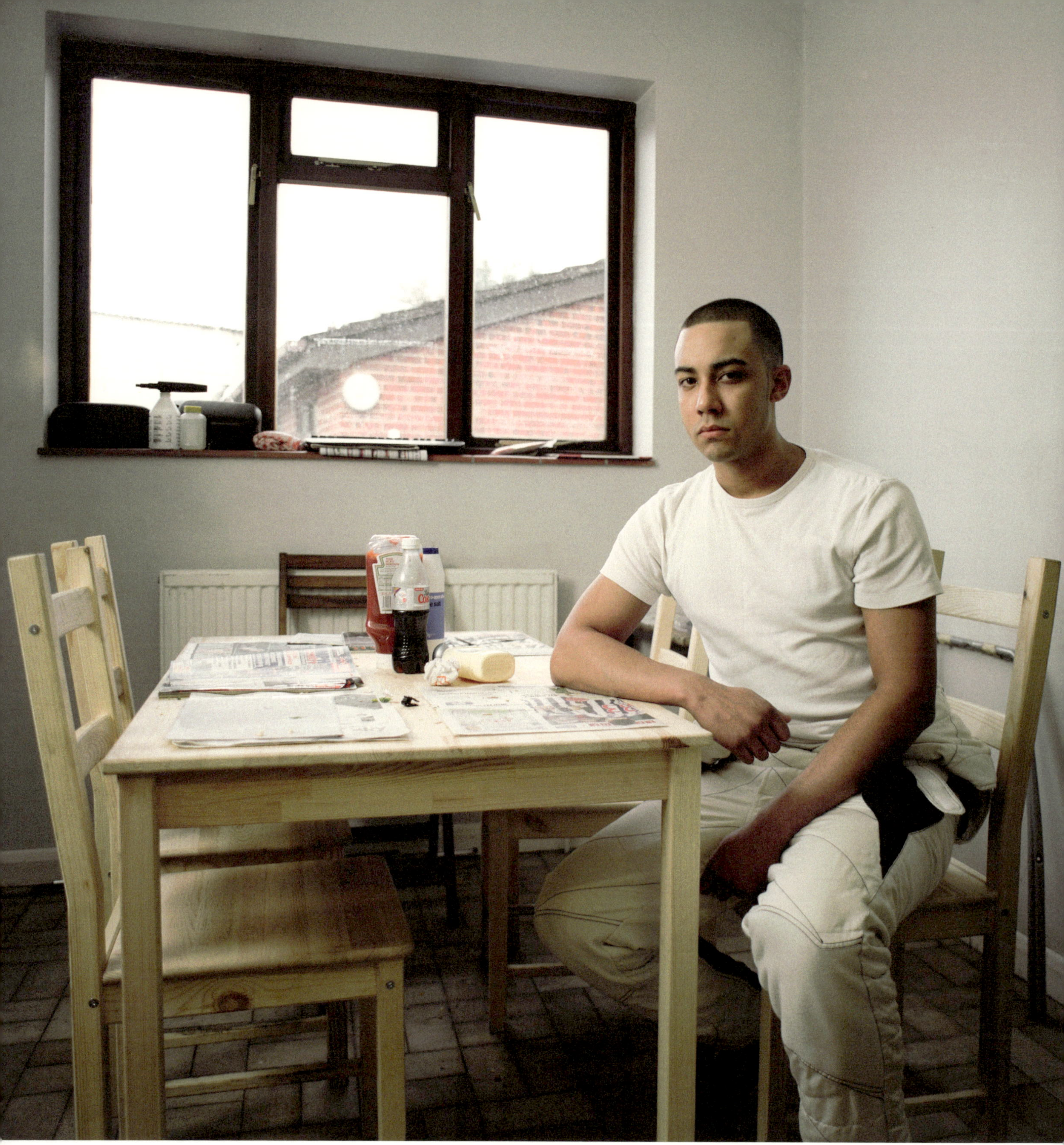

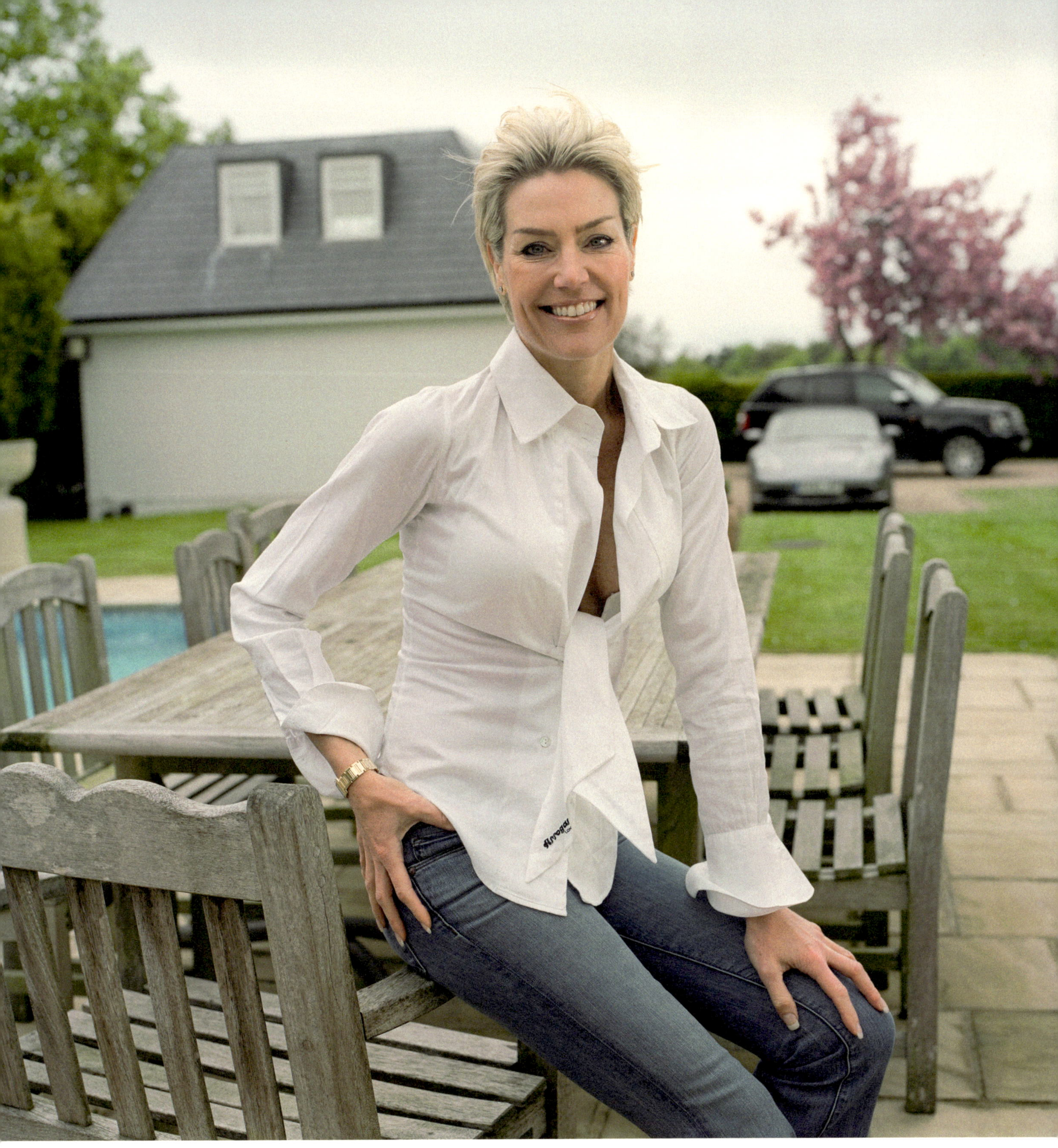

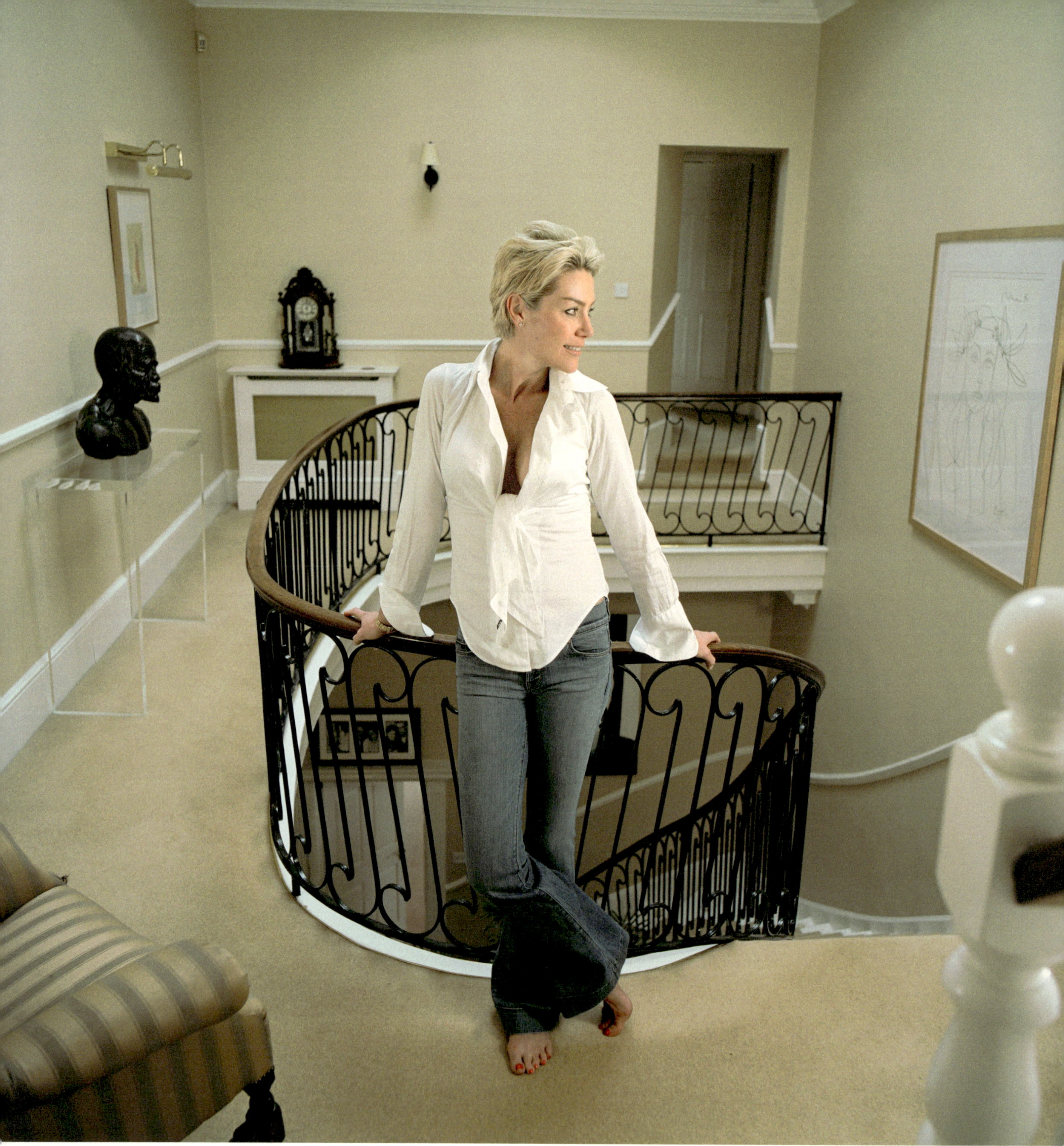

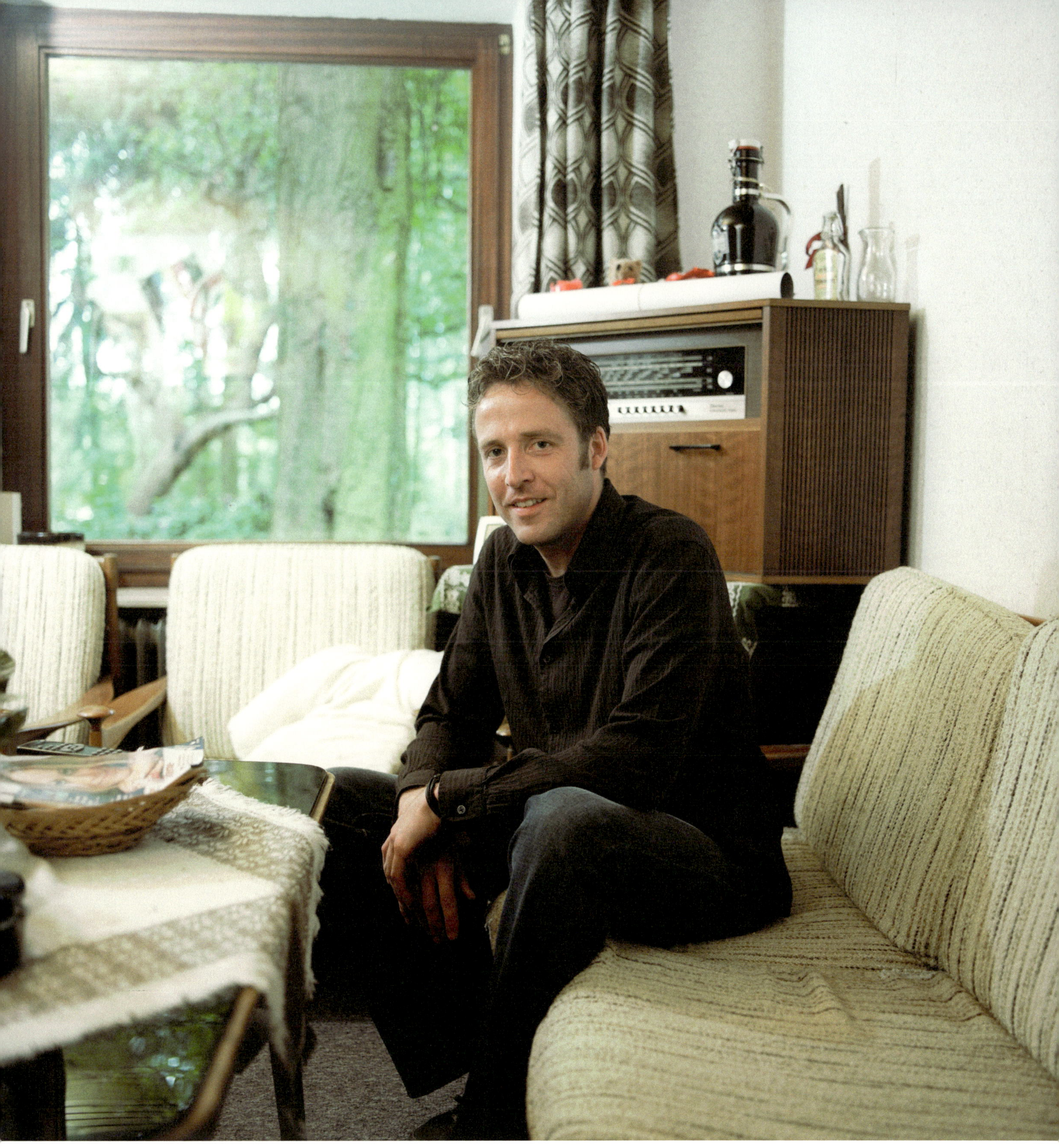

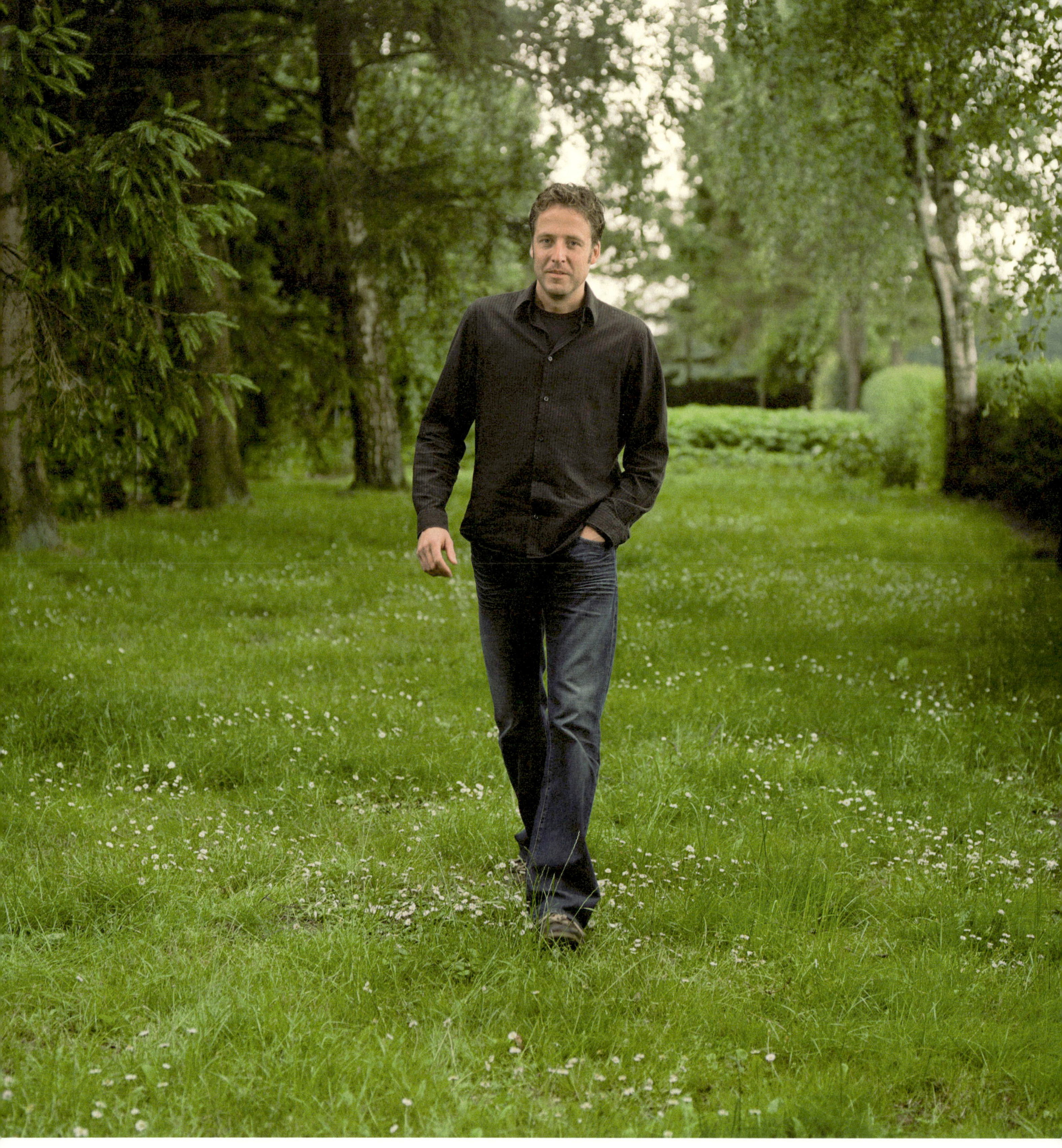

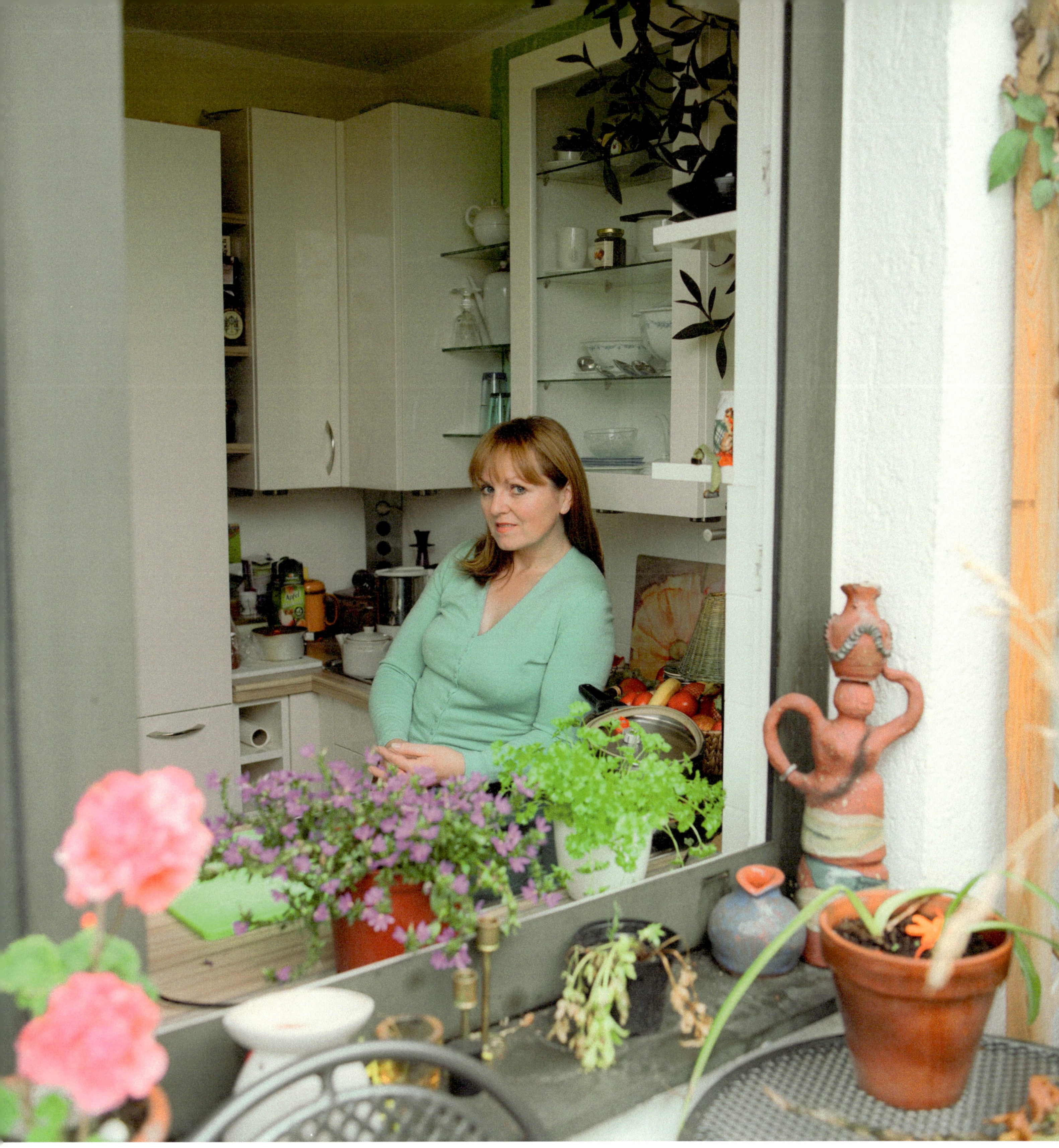

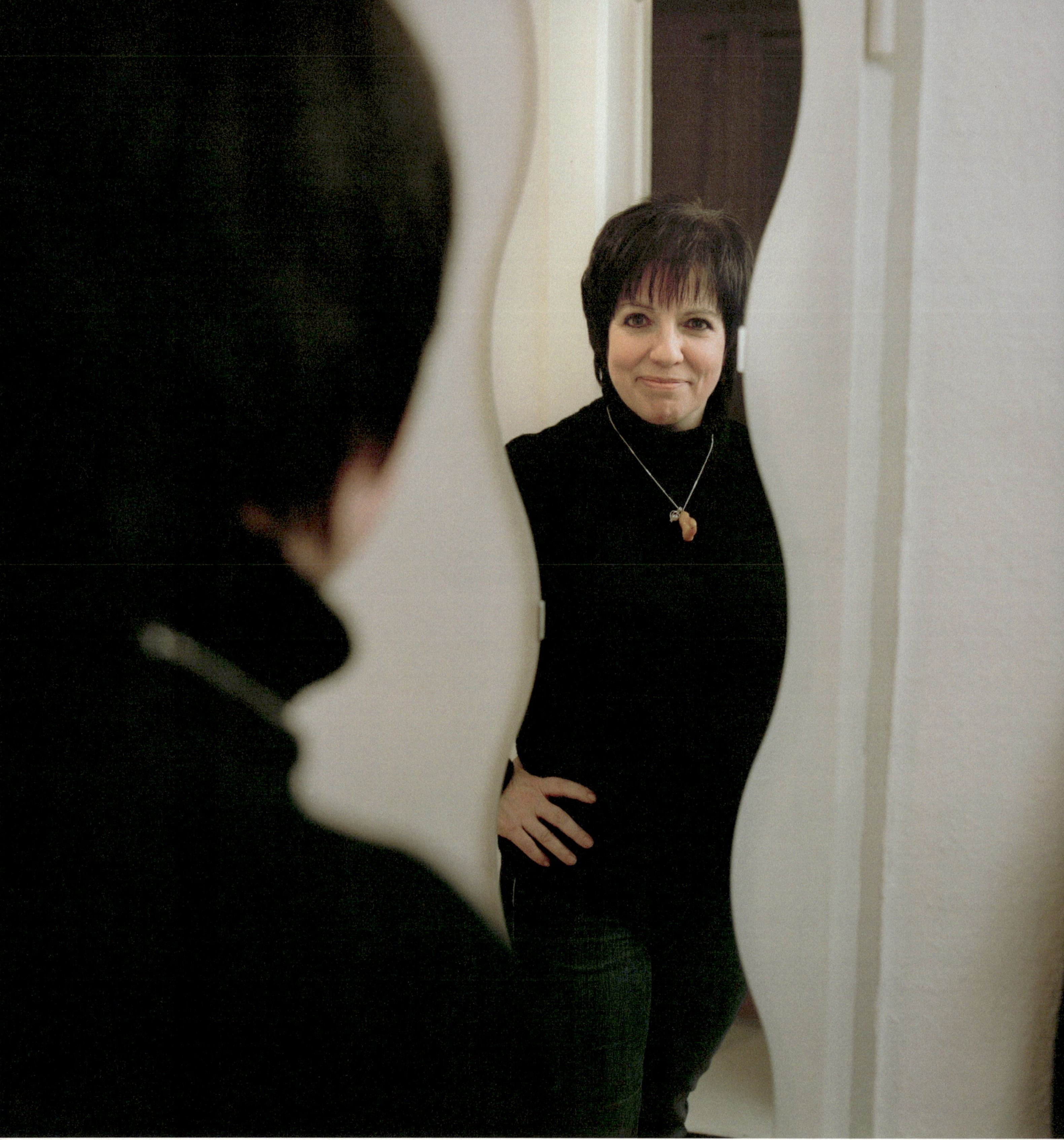

«In der Kluft zwischen Bild und Wahrnehmung ist die Wirklichkeit aufgehoben.»

"Reality becomes suspended over the chasm that opens up between image and perception."

Caroline Morpeth

Niklaus Spoerri
Who is Who?

Fotodokumentarisches Nachschlagewerk der
internationalen Double-Szene
**Documentary photo reference work on the international
doubles scene**

**Niklaus Spoerri
Irene Jost/Culture_Art_Communications
2. stock süd netthoevel & gaberthüel
Institut für moderne Kunst Nürnberg**

VERLAG *für* MODERNE KUNST

Inhalt/Contents

1   Niklaus Spoerri   **Dokumentarische Fotoporträts**
1   Documentary Portraits

158   Jimmy Wales   **Wessen Doppelgänger? Der echte Mensch und seine Rolle**
160   Whose Lookalike? The Real and the Character

162   Jean-Martin Büttner   **Sich aufgeben, um jemand zu sein**
164   Giving Oneself up to be Somebody

166   Caroline Morpeth   **Spiegelei**
169   Spitting in the Mirror

172   Markus Reich   **(Fast) wie ein Ei dem anderen**
174   (Almost) alike as two Peas in a Pod

176   Rudolf Scheutle   **Der Ruhm der anderen**
178   The Fame of the Others

180   Silvia Jaklitsch   **«You are either professional or not»**
182   "You are either professional or not"

184   Manfred Prisching   **Wenn die Menschen sich verdoppeln**
189   When People Duplicate themselves

194   Jens Groß   **Die theatrale Konsequenz des Doubles**
196   The theatrical Consequence of the Lookalike

198   **Index**
202   **Biografien/Biographies**
206   **Impressum/Imprint**
208   **Thank you**

Wessen Doppelgänger?
Der echte Mensch
und seine Rolle

von Jimmy Wales

1915 wurden die Vereinigten Staaten von einer Hysterie namens «Chaplinitis» überrollt. Charlie Chaplin betrat die Bühne. 1914, in *Kid Auto Races in Venice* aus dem legendären Keystone Pictures Studio, hatte er erstmals die Rolle des «Tramp», des Vagabunden gegeben, die rasch zu seinem Markenzeichen werden sollte. Innerhalb kürzester Zeit war er überall berühmt und beliebt.

Zu dieser Hysterie gehörte auch ein Charlie-Chaplin-Doppelgängerwettbewerb. Leute verkleideten sich samt Spazierstock und Schnauzbart als Vagabund und ahmten Chaplins klassischen Gang nach. Aus Jux nahm Chaplin selbst in einem Theater in San Francisco an einem dieser Wettbewerbe teil. Es ist zwar nicht überliefert, wie gut er sich im Detail geschlagen hat, aber wir wissen mit Sicherheit, dass er es nicht ins Finale geschafft hat oder gar als Sieger daraus hervorging.

Witzige Anekdote, ja, aber noch amüsanter wird es, wenn wir sie ein wenig genauer betrachten. Beim Wettbewerb ging es nicht darum, wer dem Schauspieler Charlie Chaplin am ähnlichsten sah, schliesslich wurde dieser ohne sein Vagabundenkostüm und ohne den typischen Gang kaum erkannt. Nein, es ging darum, wer die Rolle des Vagabunden am besten verkörperte. Würde der Schöpfer der Figur selbst seiner Schöpfung am ähnlichsten schauen? Wenn Gott den Menschen nach seinem Ebenbild erschaffen hat, würde es Gott mit Adam ins Finale seines eigenen Doppelgängerwettbewerbs schaffen?

Imitatoren von Prominenten ahmen die Verhaltensmuster, Gesten und Mimik nach, die uns so vertraut sind. Diese Eigenschaften gehören jedoch meist zur Rolle, zum Image, das dessen Schöpfer zu gestalten versucht, nicht zur wahren Persönlichkeit desselben. Wir betrachten die Fotos in diesem Buch mit gemischten Gefühlen. Die Bilder lösen unterschiedliche Reaktionen aus, je nachdem wie wahrheitsgetreu die Kopie wirkt, oder wie interessant uns eine eventuelle Abweichung von ihr erscheint.

Da ist Sylvester Stallone in einem Fitnessstudio. Das Bild wirkt auf den ersten Blick ganz

Grossartig, Olivia sieht
genau wie Angelina Jolie
aus! Indes dürfen wir nicht
vergessen, dass Angelina
Jolie auch genau wie Olivia
aussieht!

selbstverständlich und schlüssig. Aber warum ist das so? Verwechseln wir Stallone nicht – ohne es uns bewusst zu machen – mit seiner berühmtesten Rolle als Rocky Balboa? Sollten wir den echten Sylvester Stallone nicht vielmehr als Künstler auffassen, schliesslich hat er ja das Drehbuch für «Rocky» selbst geschrieben. Wie auch Chaplin den Vagabunden selbst erfunden hat. Ist unsere Überzeugung, ein gutes Double zu sehen, im Grunde nicht ein schlichter Irrtum?

Bei anderen Fotos erweist sich unser Eindruck, dass irgendetwas nicht ganz stimmt, in anderer Hinsicht als Irrtum. Königin Elizabeth II. in einer Bürgerwohnung mit normalen Familienfotos an der Wand? Etwas in uns sträubt sich sogleich, denn wir wissen: Das kann nicht sein. Die Königin wohnt anders, ganz klar. Wir fragen uns, wie sie denn wirklich wohnt. Bestimmt auch mit Bildern von Familienangehörigen an der Wand, aber müssten es nicht grosse und in Gold gerahmte Ölgemälde sein? Das blosse Foto, die Inszenierung, wirkt mit der feinen Komik unmittelbar.

Soweit also Beispiele dafür, dass ein Foto echt wirkt, aber falsch ist, oder ein Foto zwar falsch wirkt, aber dennoch stimmig ist – jedenfalls wenn es darum geht, eine interessante Aussage zu treffen. Wenden wir uns aber nun Luciano Pavarotti in seiner Küche zu. Echt oder Täuschung? Die Küche scheint ein wenig klein geraten, aber Pavarotti war schliesslich als Opernsänger bekannt und nicht als Chefkoch.

Er war berühmt und wohlhabend, musste beruflich viel reisen und besass bestimmt mehrere Wohnungen weltweit. Es besteht kein Grund für unsere Annahme, dass die Küchen in all diesen Wohnungen unbedingt gross gewesen sein mussten.

Hier scheinen wir in dem schmalen Grat zwischen Wahrheit und Täuschung steckenzubleiben, nicht weiter zu kommen. Ist das, was wir sehen, bloss das Porträt eines Mannes, der uns ein wenig an seinem Alltag abseits von Glamour, Karriere und Lifestyle teilhaben lässt? Oder doch etwas völlig anderes?

Wir leben in einer Zeit, in der die Idee der Prominenz omnipräsent ist. Viel zu oft lesen wir Schlagzeilen und Geschichten, die mit ein bisschen Distanz als objektiv absolut wert- und folgenlos erkennbar sind. So liess sich Britney Spears 2007 ihre Haare schneiden und schwupp, schon steht in den Nachrichten auf der ganzen Welt kaum etwas anderes. Zur selben Zeit braute sich aber eine Finanzkrise zusammen, die zur Insolvenz der Lehman Brothers und beinahe zum Zusammenbruch vieler anderer Institutionen führte. Von diesen Geschehen nahm die breite Öffentlichkeit leider kaum Notiz.

Wenn wir die Fotos in diesem Buch mit der richtigen Einstellung betrachten, ergeben sich automatisch Fragen zur Natur der Prominenz und unseres Interesses an ihr. Wir erkennen Angelina Jolie und denken uns: Grossartig, Olivia sieht genau wie Angelina Jolie aus! Indes dürfen wir nicht vergessen, dass Angelina Jolie auch genau wie Olivia aussieht! Ausserdem: Was kümmert uns das überhaupt? Warum ist das wichtig? Welche Bedeutung hat das überhaupt?

Wen sollen wir als Ideale betrachten? Was sollen wir mit uns selbst anfangen? Der Schlüssel zu Spoerris Bildern ist, sich nicht täuschen zu lassen. Wenn wir die Zielstrebigkeit von Rocky Balboa bewundern, sollten wir eigentlich Sylvester Stallone, den genialen Schöpfer der Figur, bewundern und nicht die Person, die ihm zufällig ähnlich sieht. Selbst wenn wir Pavarottis Gesang lieben, sollten wir dabei nicht vergessen, dass auch er manchmal – genauso wie wir – in einer ganz normalen Küche stand,

sich einen Kaffee machte und ein interessantes Buch genoss.

Ich lade Sie also ein, dasselbe zu tun: Geniessen Sie die Fotos, verweilen Sie einen Moment bei jedem von ihnen. Inwiefern ähnelt der Doppelgänger dem Original? Wo sind die Unterschiede, welche interessanten Gedanken kommen uns? Überlegen Sie doch, ob nicht unsere Vorstellung von Originalität grundsätzlich falsch ist. Ahmt ein Imitator von Charlie Chaplin wirklich den Vagabunden nach? Denken Sie an Ihr eigenes Leben, seien Sie mit sich selbst und Ihren Idealen ehrlich. Und vergessen Sie dabei nicht zu lachen! Nach der Lektüre des Buches hat sich Ihre Sicht auf die Welt – hoffentlich – ein klein wenig verändert.

Whose Lookalike?
The Real and the Character

by Jimmy Wales

In 1915, a craze called "Chaplinitis" swept the United States.

Charlie Chaplin had burst onto the scene with what would become his trademark character of the Tramp, in *Kid Auto Races in Venice* from the legendary Keystone Pictures Studio in 1914, and his popularity and celebrity was soon universal.

A part of that craze was the emergence of Charlie Chaplin lookalike contests, in which people would dress up as the Tramp and emulate the classic walk, with cane and moustache. As a joke, perhaps, Chaplin entered such a competition at a San Francisco theatre. History doesn't record how he fared in any detail, but what we do know is that he failed to make the finals, and certainly did not win.

An amusing story, yes, but perhaps even more amusing as we dig deeper. The contest was not to see who looked the most like Charlie Chaplin, the actor, as he would be mostly unrecognized without his trademark costume and walk. Instead, the contest was a lookalike contest to see who could most look like the Tramp, the character. Could the creator most look like his own creation? If God made man in his own image, could God make the finals in a lookalike contest with Adam?

Celebrity imitators mimic elements that are familiar to us, and those elements are often elements of the persona, the character, the image that the creator is trying to create, not of the underlying person. As we view the photos in this book, we feel different emotions, different responses, according to how accurate the copy seems to be, or if inaccurate, how interesting the inaccuracy feels to us.

Sylvester Stallone in a gym. At first glance this seems natural and right. But are we responding to the rightness in our minds of Stallone in the gym, or are we making a mistake and thinking of his most famous character Rocky Balboa in the gym? After all, the real Sylvester Stallone is someone we should perhaps think of as a creative artist, since he actually wrote the original script for Rocky, and created this character in the same way that Chaplin created the Tramp. Is our response that this is a good double in error?

If God made man in his own image, could God make the finals in a lookalike contest with Adam?

In other cases, our feeling that something is 'not quite right' runs in a different direction. Queen Elizabeth II in a middle-class home with ordinary family portraits on the wall? We immediately react to this, knowing something is wrong – the Queen lives differently, we know. We may wonder how she does live, surely with pictures of family members on the wall, but aren't these large oil paintings in gilded frames? We immediately feel the humour of the setting.

So far I have given an example where the photo feels right, but is wrong. And one where the photo feels wrong, but is right – in the sense of making an interesting statement. But now turn to look at Pavarotti in his kitchen. Is it right or wrong? The kitchen seems small, but he's famous for being a great opera singer, not for being a chef. He's a famous and wealthy personality, he must have travelled widely and owned many apartments around the world. There is no reason for us to know or suppose that all of them had grand kitchens.

So here we are stuck in the middle – is this an intimate portrait of a man letting us see a side of his life away from the glamour of his career and lifestyle? Or is it something else?

We live in an era where celebrity is with us always. Far too often the news headlines are filled with stories that, if you step back and view them objectively, are of absolutely no value and no consequence. In 2007 Britney Spears cuts off her hair, and the worldwide news speaks of little else for a week. Meanwhile a financial crisis was brewing that would lead to the collapse of Lehman Brothers and the near collapse of many other institutions, and the public was for the most part sadly unaware.

If we approach it with the right mindset, a reflection on photos in this book leads us to a reflection on the nature of celebrity and the nature of our interest in it. We see Angelina Jolie in the book and we think, wow, look, Olivia looks like Angelina Jolie. But we must also remember that, wow, Angelina Jolie looks like Olivia. And why do we care? Why is it important, what does it mean?

Who should we hold as our ideals? What should we do with ourselves? The key here is to try not to be fooled. If we admire the determination of Rocky Balboa, we should admire Sylvester Stallone the writer and creative genius who created him, and not the person who happens to look like him. If we admire the singing of Pavarotti, we should also remember that he sometimes went into an ordinary kitchen as we do, and made himself a coffee and enjoyed reading an interesting book.

And so I invite you to do the same now: enjoy the photos and linger for a moment with each one. How is the imitator similar to the original? And where there are differences, what interesting thoughts pass through our minds. Think about whether our concept of the original is false – is a Charlie Chaplin imitator really imitating the Tramp? And think about your life, and about being true to yourself and your own ideals. And come away with a smile and hopefully, in some small way, a different view of the world!

Sich aufgeben, um jemand zu sein

Ihre Berühmtheit besteht darin, Berühmten zu gleichen. Das geht für sie nicht ohne Verluste ab. Anmerkungen zur Fankultur im Zeitalter medial verschalteter Originale.

von Jean-Martin Büttner

Dave Kovic lebt in Washington und vermittelt Arbeitslosen eine befristete Stelle. Oder, er versucht es wenigstens. Weil das zu wenig einbringt, hat er einen Nebenjob: Bei Geschäftseröffnungen und anderen Anlässen stellt Dave den amerikanischen Präsidenten dar. Er sieht ihm nicht nur ähnlich; er kann auch seine Stimme imitieren, seine Gestik, den verbindlichen Blick. Dave wird zum Präsidenten, wenn er den Präsidenten nachmacht.

Als er nach einem Auftritt vor einem Supermarkt heimkommt, sitzen zwei stumme Männer in seiner Stube. Dave glaubt, es sei die Steuerbehörde. Aber die Männer sind Spitzenbeamte aus dem Weissen Haus. Und sie wollen Dave nicht verhören. Sie wollen ihn anstellen: Dave Kovic soll für die amerikanische Öffentlichkeit den Präsidenten spielen, wenn dieser gerade anderweitig beschäftigt ist. Zum Beispiel, wenn er unter seiner Geliebten liegt. Oder sonstwo, wo er lieber wäre als bei einem Empfang. Dave wird ins Weisse Haus gefahren, zurechtgemacht und losgeschickt. Er schreitet durch die Menge, winkt den Gästen zu, geht auf die Limousine zu, dreht sich um und sagt: «Gott schütze die Vereinigten Staaten von Amerika!» Alle klatschen, einige jubeln.

Die Auftraggeber sind sehr zufrieden. Eine Limousine fährt Dave wieder heim. Ein Handy läutet, der Begleiter nimmt ab. Der Fahrer wendet das Auto und fährt ins Weisse Haus zurück. Der Präsident hat, im Bett mit der Geliebten, einen Herzinfarkt erlitten. Seinen Beratern passt das nicht, denn sie trauen dem Vizepräsidenten nicht. Sie fragen Dave, ob er seine Rolle etwas ausdehnen könnte. Dave zögert, sagt dann zu: Das Land braucht ihn ja.

So bekommt Dave Kovic, der gutmütige Kleinbürger, die Rolle seines Lebens: Er spielt den amerikanischen Präsidenten nicht mehr, er wird zum amerikanischen Präsidenten. Ein Laiendarsteller wird zum mächtigsten Mann der Welt. Was mehr kann sich so einer wünschen?

Die Komödie «Dave» von Ivan Reitman (1993) mit dem brillanten Drehbuch von Gary Ross denkt den Wunsch des Doppelgängers zu Ende: Dass er dem Original nicht nur gleicht, sondern es ersetzt: Dass die Kopie zum Original wird. Und weil der Film nicht nur als Komödie, sondern als mediales Märchen angelegt ist, erweist sich die Kopie als das bessere Original. Gerade weil Dave nicht vom Parteiapparat pasteurisiert, von seinen Geldgebern gegängelt, von einem endlosen Wahlkampf abgenutzt, von der Realpolitik zerstört wurde, wird er zum bestmöglichen Präsidenten von allen: einem Idealisten mit Einfluss, einem Optimisten mit Erfolg.

Es braucht die Medien als verschaltete Vervielfältigungsapparate, damit sich Originale anbieten können, auf die sich dann die Kopien beziehen. Und es braucht die elektronischen Medien, um den Vorbildern eine Stimme und einen Auftritt zu ermöglichen. Mit dem Internet nähert sich die Reaktion auf die Übertragung faktisch der Echtzeit. Kaum hat ein Politiker seine Rede gehalten, wird bereits schon die Parodie ins Netz gestellt. Als Barack Obama im Wahlkampf bei «Saturday Night Live» auftrat, der amerikanischen Satiresendung, verbarg er sein Gesicht hinter einer Obama-Maske. Und als die Komikerin Tina Fey sich in derselben Sendung über Sarah Palin mokierte, die republikanische Kandidatin fürs Vizepräsidium, zitierte sie wörtlich die Sonderbarkeiten, die Palin kurz zuvor bei CNN deponiert hatte. Die Originale geben sich wie Kopien, die Kopien gleichen immer mehr den Originalen.

Aber wie lange lässt sich das weitertreiben? Und mit welchen Folgen? Was verlieren die Kopien, je mehr sie sich den Originalen nähern? Was haben die Originale, das keine Kopie ersetzen kann? Die erste Antwort hat mit Identität zu tun, die zweite mit Charisma.

Die Porträts von Niklaus Spoerri inszenieren das Dilemma seiner Figuren behutsam, gerade deshalb aber schonungslos. Denn die Doppelgänger wirken deplatziert, eben weil der Fotograf sie inszeniert, umgeben von ihren biederen Einrichtungen, gefangen in ihren Wänden, verraten durch die eigenen Tische, Gartentore, Tierteppiche, Bilder und Lampen. Michael Jackson neben einer Tanne, die ihn noch unwirklicher aussehen lässt; Udo Lindenberg vor einem Zimmer, das überhaupt nichts Lindenberg'sches an sich hat; Bill Clinton vor einem Balkon mit

Einfamilienhäusern; Jack Nicholson vor einer Wohnwand mit Gläsern, auf eine versöhnliche Weise lächelnd, wie sein Vorbild es niemals tun würde. Nicholson lächelt nicht, er grinst, und sein Grinsen sieht aus wie ein Haifischbiss.

Hinter dem Stolz in den Gesichtern, den routiniert eingenommenen Posen macht sich Unsicherheit bemerkbar: Gleiche ich ihm genug? Bin ich ihr wirklich ähnlich? Die Frage zielt auf den Widerspruch derer, die jemand werden, indem sie sich aufgeben. Entweder die Ähnlichkeit ist gross genug, dann aber verschwinden die Kopien hinter dem Original, sie werden jemand, indem sie nicht mehr sie selber sind. Oder die Ähnlichkeit ist nicht gross genug, und die Kopien bleiben Kopien beim Versuch, jemand anderes zu werden. Im einen Fall wird die eigene Identität einer Berühmtheit zuliebe aufgegeben, im anderen drückt die eigene Identität das Scheitern aus, berühmt aussehen zu wollen. «My only problem is that I'm not somebody else», hat Woody Allen einmal gesagt: Mein einziges Problem ist, dass ich kein anderer bin. Die Menschen in den Bildern von Niklaus Spoerri haben das umgekehrte Problem: Ihre Schwierigkeit besteht darin, dass sie, im besten Fall, jemand anderem gleichen.

Die Inszenierungen zeigen aber auch, was die Kopie immer vom Original unterscheiden wird, gerade weil sie sich um Originalität bemüht: Die Doppelgänger oder «Impersonators», wie sie auf Englisch treffender heissen, die Personifizierer bleiben ohne jedes Charisma. Nichts Aufregendes strahlt von ihnen ab, es fehlt die

Aura nicht nur der Berühmtheit und damit der Gewohnheit des Berühmtseins. Sondern die Ausstrahlung, das Zwingende, Dominierende, Unverwechselbare. Der Ausdruck, die Geste, die Stimme, die das Publikum sofort für sie einnimmt. Die Kopien können nichts von dem, was die Originale berühmt gemacht hat. Sie können es auch nicht ausstrahlen.

Charisma ist schwer zu definieren, widersprüchlich, schillernd. Warum ist Charisma ohne Berühmtsein nicht denkbar? Warum spricht man nur bei Männern von Charisma und bei Frauen eher von Ausstrahlung? Warum werden wir uns wohl rasch einig, wer Charisma hat, wissen aber nie genau, wie man es bekommt? Weil Charisma sich nicht über Schönheit und Berühmtheit definieren lässt. Weil es nicht lernbar ist, sondern sich aus dem Talent, dem Ehrgeiz, dem Machtwillen, der Kreativität heraus entwickelt, untrennbar ist vom Willen zu Macht, Einfluss, Erfolg, Ausdruck, Gestaltung. Jeder amerikanische Präsident war eine Zeitlang berühmt, kaum einer hatte das Charisma von John F. Kennedy, Ronald Reagan, Bill Clinton oder, allen voran, Barack Obama. Charisma ist die Eigenschaft eines Menschen, die bei seinem Publikum die Sehnsucht nach seiner Ausstrahlung weckt. Charisma ist körperlich und wirkt auch so. Wer Charismatikern schon begegnet ist, weiss, dass etwas von ihnen ausgeht, das keine Kamera und erst recht kein Doppelgänger wiedergeben kann: Das Selbstbewusstsein des Einzigartigen.

Das muss auch Dave Kovic erfahren, der Präsident gewordene Selbstdarsteller in Ivan Reitmans Film. Als er immer mehr eingeholt wird von den Täuschungen und Betrügereien des Mannes, den er imitiert, inszeniert er vor dem Parlament eine eigene Herzattacke und damit seinen Abgang. Während der echte Präsident ins Krankenhaus gefahren wird, wo er später sterben wird, kehrt Dave Kovic heim und lanciert seine eigene politische Karriere. Als Bodyguard steht ihm der Sicherheitsmann zur Seite, der ihn damals entdeckt hat. Die Kopie, zum Original geworden, erfindet sich neu als Original seiner selbst.

Giving Oneself up to be Somebody

Their fame consists in being the same as famous people. This cannot be done without losses to the self. Notes on fan culture in the age of media-networked originals.

by Jean-Martin Büttner

Dave Kovic lives in Washington and finds temporary jobs for the unemployed. Or tries to, at least. If this doesn't bring in enough money, he has a side job. For business launches and other causes he impersonates the American president. Not only does he look like him, he can also do his voice, his gestures, the intense stare. Dave becomes the president when he impersonates him.

When he gets home from an appearance in front of a supermarket, two surly men are sitting in his front room. Dave thinks it's the tax authorities, but the men are top officials from the White House. And they don't want to interrogate Dave. They want to employ him: the intention is for Dave Kovic to play the president for the American public when the president himself is busy elsewhere, for example when he is lying beneath his lover. Or anywhere else he would rather be than at a reception. Dave is driven to the White House and sent on his way. He strides through the crowd, waves at guests or walks up to the limousine, turns round and says, "God Bless the United States of America" Everybody applauds, some people cheer.

The employers are very pleased. A limousine drives Dave back home. A mobile phone rings, the minder answers. The driver turns the car round and heads back to the White House. The president has just had a heart attack, in bed with his lover. His advisors don't like this, because they don't trust the vice-president. They ask Dave if he could extend his role slightly, Dave hesitates, but then agrees: his country needs him, after all.

And so Dave Kovic, the well-meaning petty bourgeois, gets the role of his life. He no longer just plays the American president, he becomes the American president. A lay actor becomes the most powerful man in the world. What more can you ask?

The comedy "Dave" by Ivan Reitman (1993), with a brilliant screenplay by Gary Ross, plays out the wish of the double to its logical conclusion: he not only resembles the original, but replaces him; the copy becomes the original. And because the film is set up not just as a comedy, but as a media fairy tale, the copy turns out to better than the original. And because Dave has not been homogenised by the party apparatus, suffocated by his sponsors, worn down by an endless election campaign or destroyed by political realism, he becomes the best possible president of them all: An idealist with influence, an optimist with success.

The media, as networked reproduction machines, provide the forum for originals to appear and from which copies can be made. It takes electronic media to give the models a voice and a stage. With the internet, the reaction to the transmission is virtually in real time. Hardly has a politician made a speech than a parody of it is circulated on the net. When Barack Obama appeared during the election campaign on "Saturday Night Live", the American satire programme, he hid his face behind an Obama mask. When comedian Tina Fey made fun of Sarah Palin, Republican candidate for the vice presidency, in the same programme, she quoted verbatim the quirky sound bites which Palin had given to CNN only shortly before. The originals pretend to be copies, the copies ever more resemble the originals.

How long can things go on like this and with what consequences? What do the copies lose the closer they get to the originals? What is it that originals have that cannot be replaced by any copy? The first answer has to do with identity, the second with charisma.

The portraits by Niklaus Spoerri present the dilemma of his figures carefully, but for this reason also unsparingly. The doubles seem to be out of place, since the photographer pictures them in their homes surrounded by their bourgeois trappings, caught within their own four walls, betrayed by their own tables, garden gates, animal carpets, pictures and lamps. Michael Jackson next to a fir tree, which makes him seem even more unreal; Udo Lindenberg in front of a room that has nothing whatsoever Lindenbergish about it; Bill Clinton in front of a balcony with detached houses; Jack Nicholson in front of a wall unit filled with glasses, smiling in a conciliatory manner in a way that his original would never do. Nicholson doesn't do smiles; he grins, and his grin looks like a shark bite.

Behind the pride in the faces, the pose assumed as a matter of routine, uncertainty can be felt: do I resemble him sufficiently? Am I really similar to her? The question is addressed at the contradiction in those who want to become somebody, by giving up themselves. Either the similarity is close enough, but then the copies disappear behind the original. They become somebody by no longer being themselves. Or the similarity is not enough, and the copies remain themselves in the attempt to become someone else. In the one case one's own identity is given up for the sake of somebody famous, In the other, one's own identity expresses the failure of looking famous. Woody

Woody Allen once said, "My only problem is that I'm not somebody else".

Allen once said, "My only problem is that I'm not somebody else". The people in the pictures by Niklaus Spoerri have the reverse problem: their difficulty consists of, in the best case, resembling someone else.

These stagings also show, however, what will always distinguish the copy from the original for the very reason that it tries to seek out originality: doubles, or more appropriately "impersonators": they have no charisma whatsoever. Nothing exciting radiates from them, not only is the aura of fame missing, and thus the familiarity that comes with being famous, but also the vibrancy, the forcefulness, the domination, the unmistakable. The expression, the gesture, the voice, which the public immediately fell for. The copies can do none of these things that have made the original famous. They can also not exude these qualities.

Charisma is difficult to define, contradictory, fickle. Why is charisma not conceivable without being famous? Why is it only men that have charisma, and women have more of

an aura? Why do we quickly agree on who has got charisma, but we never know exactly how it is acquired? It is because charisma cannot be defined through beauty and fame. Because it cannot be learnt, but must be developed out of the talent, the ambition, the willpower, the creativity, and is inseparable from the determination to achieve power, influence, success, ambition. Every American president was famous for a time, but few had the charisma of John F. Kennedy, Ronald Reagan, Bill Clinton or, above all, Barack Obama. Charisma is the characteristic of a person who arouses in an audience the longing for his aura. Charisma is physical, and it feels like that. Anyone who has met charismatic people knows that they radiate something that no camera, and certainly no impersonator, can reproduce: the self-confidence of the unique.

This is a lesson that Dave Kovic is forced to learn, the performer who has become president in Ivan Reitman's film. When he becomes more and more embroiled in the deceits and frauds of the man he is impersonating, he stages his own heart attack, and thus his departure, in front of the Senate. While the real president is driven to hospital, where he will later die, Dave Kovic returns home and launches his own political career. By his side as a bodyguard is the security man who originally discovered him. The copy, having become the original, reinvents itself as the original of itself.

Spiegelei

von Caroline Morpeth

Ich betrachte zusammen mit meiner Tante ein Foto meiner Tochter. Über ihre Stirn fällt ein langer Haarschopf, der hinter das rechte Ohr gesteckt ist. Dunkle, mandelförmige Augen blicken forsch in die Kamera. Sie hat sanfte Lippen, lächelt aber nicht. Plötzlich sagt meine Tante: «Sie ist dein Ebenbild, als du gleich alt warst.»

Ich grüble, was das eigentlich heissen soll. Das Wort Ebenbild, auf Englisch auch «spitting image», wird oft verwendet, wenn eine Person einer anderen physisch sehr stark ähnelt. Aber selbst in der Alltagssprache scheint «spitting image» kurios, wenn man die Wendung ihrer wörtlichen Bedeutung entkoppelt. Der Begriff leistet Widerstand. Etymologisch gesehen ist der Ausdruck eine Verballhornung von «spitten image» oder «the spit and image», letztere ihrerseits Neologismen aus dem 19. Jahrhundert, die aus der Wendung «the spit of», zu deutsch etwa: Ebenbild, aus dem 16. Jahrhundert entstanden sind. Die Phrase «spitting image» ist also eine Tautologie, weil sowohl «spit» als auch «image» Ebenbild bedeuten. Sie ist mithin sogar autologisch, da die Tautologie zusätzlich noch durch eine Verdoppelung auf der Bedeutungsebene gespiegelt wird.

Diese tautologisch-autologische Verbindung gefällt mir. Dennoch versuche ich, sie besser zu verstehen. Wie könnte die Hauptbedeutung von «spit», also Spucke, gleichbedeutend mit Ebenbild sein? Weil Spucke als Körpersekret metaphorisch für den Samen steht, der ja ganz offensichtlich körperliche Ähnlichkeiten von einer Generation zur nächsten überträgt?

Oder kommt das vom altgriechischen Mythos des Kronos, der seine eigenen Kinder nach ihrer Geburt verschlang, damit sie sich nicht gegen ihn erheben konnten, bis Zeus als einziger Sohn, dem die Flucht gelang, zurückkehrte und ihn zwang, ein Kind nach dem anderen wieder auszuspucken? Spucken ist seinerseits doppelt metaphorisch. Man kann ausspucken, um das Glück zu beschwören und damit Unglück abzuwenden, oder um Hass und Verachtung auszudrücken. Als Präsenspartizip, «spitting» für «spuckend», verweist es eher auf die negative Bedeutung. Spucke als aggressiv und gehässig, voll Zorn ausgespuckt – als kämpfe sie gegen den Zwang, ans «image», an ihr Ebenbild gekettet zu sein.

Aber auch das Ebenbild ist verzwickt, fehlt ihm doch die Selbstständigkeit. Immer ist es die Spiegelung von etwas Anderem, immer ist es im Anderen befangen. Nach der Lacan'schen Identitätsvorstellung ist dieses Anderssein indessen der Kern unseres Daseins. Jacques Lacan teilte Freuds Theorie der Kindesentwicklung in drei Stadien ein: Er definierte diese als imaginäres Stadium, Spiegelstadium und symbolisches Stadium. Im Lauf des imaginären Stadiums hat das Kind noch keine Sprache und ist seinen ersten Eindrücken und Trieben gegenüber völlig offen. Es kennt noch keine Grenze zwischen seinem Körper und der Welt. Beim Eintritt ins Spiegelstadium erkennt das Kind dann seine Individualität, die Trennung von der Mutter. Die Welt wird über das Ich hinaus projiziert und als Bild zurückgeworfen. Dies führt aber zum Missverstehen der eigenen Individualität, Ich und Anderer entstehen. Diese Dualität wird dann durch den Spracherwerb in die symbolische Ordnung übertragen. Die Sprache symbolisiert das Reale und verhindert zugleich, dass das Reale repräsentiert werden kann, da sie ihrer Natur nach figurativ ist. Lacan fasste das Symbolische als «*nom du père*» auf, als Name oder Gesetz des Vaters, weil das Erlernen der Sprache den Eintritt in ein, durch die Kultur konstruiertes, patriarchalisches Autoritätssystem bedeutet. Letzteres verzerrt unseren Identitätssinn noch mehr, weil das Subjektive unweigerlich in der Interaktion mit anderen erlebt wird. Die menschliche Identität ist daher immer instabil und unvollständig. Ein Gefühl des Mangels, des unwiederbringlichen Verlusts ersetzt das ganzheitliche Erleben des imaginären Stadiums. In ihrer Lesart der Theorie Lacans führte Julia Kristeva zusätzlich das Konzept des Semiotischen ein, das – als grundsätzlich weiblich, fliessend und verdrängt – dem Symbolischen als Anderes gegenübersteht. Zugleich ist das Semiotische aber untrennbar mit dem Symbolischen verbunden, und ihre Bedeutungen fliessen permanent ineinander.

Wenn Identität also missverstanden und gedoppelt ist, dann gemahnt das Ebenbild, der Doppelgänger, das «spitting image», offensichtlich an die Grenzen der Individualität. Hier ist ein «Ich», das nicht eine, sondern zwei Personen ist. Das Ebenbild überschreitet die Grenze unseres liminalen Eindrucks, dass wir bei der Betrachtung unseres Spiegelbilds sowohl innerhalb als auch ausserhalb des Bildes erscheinen. Wenn wir einen Doppelgänger als Ebenbild betrachten, sind wir durch dessen Doppelidentität gezwungen, uns selbst zu erkennen.

Das Foto eines Doppelgängers kann diese Verschiebung nur verstärken, sind doch alle Fotos Ebenbilder. Die Fotografie kommt nicht über jenes Paradox hinaus, das schon René Magritte in sein Gemälde «La Trahison des Images» fasste. Die Darstellung einer Pfeife wird durch die Worte «*Ceci n'est pas une pipe*» unterlaufen. Jedes Foto strebt nach Transparenz, um das Reale darzustellen. Aber genau das muss scheitern, weil das Reale immer schon ein Bild ist. Dort, wo meine Tochter ein Foto von sich erblickt, sieht meine Tante eine verblichene Erinnerung an mich, und ich sehe ein Palimpsest meiner Tochter, meine Tochter von jetzt, ich damals, ich jetzt. Die fotografierte Person ist nicht bloss zweigeteilt, sondern vervielfacht und letztlich unbegreiflich: *Ceci n'est pas ma fille.*

Bei Fotos von Doppelgängern von Prominenten verschwimmen die Grenzen zwischen Authentizität und Individualität noch mehr. Bei diesen Bildern unterteilt sich das Dreieck Prominente/r, Doppelgänger/in, Betrachter/in (das seinerseits noch die Triade Kamera, Fotograf, Publikum umfasst) zu einem Konglomerat sich überlagernder und doch fragmentierter Identitäten und Erlebnisse. Dennoch ist der Kern des Bildes etwas Abwesendes. Der oder die Prominente ist – und war nie – hier. Doch unser Blick insistiert. Kraft unserer Vorstellung bringen wir das Bild mit Realität und Imitat zugleich zur Deckung. Der Prominente wird immer auf das Foto projiziert. Sein Wegsein wird zu einem (un)sichtbaren Dasein. Der Doppelgänger taucht dermassen in seinen Glanz ein, dass der Betrachter den Eindruck hat, er könne ihn mit den Händen greifen. Doch wir, selbst auch gedoppelt, sind immer im Widerspruch. Obwohl wir uns Ruhm ersehnen, durch das Foto den Ruhm berühren wollen, erkennen wir, dass der Griff über diese Grenze bloss in einen Abgrund, ins Nichts führen würde. Der Ruhm ist ein Miasma, das, gleich einem Sonnenstrahl in der hohlen Hand, nicht durch den Prominenten

Die fotografierte Person ist nicht bloss zweigeteilt, sondern vervielfacht und letztlich unbegreiflich: *Ceci n'est pas ma fille.*

ausgeschöpft ist. Der Glanz des Ruhmes kommt von anderswo, vom Anderen im Spiegel.

In Grossbritannien hat man eine zwiespältige und sarkastische Haltung zum Ruhm. Sie wird am besten durch die Geschichte der Doppelgängerin Chantelle Houghton exemplifiziert, einer hübschen, normalen Dreiundzwanzigjährigen aus Essex, deren Ruhm einzig aus einer starken Ähnlichkeit mit Paris Hilton resultiert. 2006 wurde Chantelle mit einem Sonderauftrag in die Sendung «Celebrity Big Brother» geschickt. Sie hatte eine Woche Zeit, die anderen im Container zu überzeugen, dass sie eine genauso echte Berühmtheit sei wie sie. Sollte sie das nicht schaffen, würde sie wieder hinausgeworfen. Als Mitglied einer fiktiven Mädchenband eingeführt, fragte sie ein Mitbewohner gleich nach dem Hit dieser Band. Chantelle krächzte freundlich ein paar Zeilen dieses imaginären Hits. Dann begann sie zu kichern und strauchelte, während ein paar ihrer Mitbewohner meinten, dass sie sich jetzt natürlich an den Song erinnern könnten. Am Ende der Woche wurden die Teilnehmenden gebeten, sich je nach Berühmtheit einzuordnen. Sollte Chantelle an letzter Stelle sein, hätte sie ihren Auftrag verfehlt. Das Ergebnis der Abstimmung illustriert das unsichere Dasein von Prominenten im England des 21. Jahrhunderts, die sichtlich nicht mehr haben als die berühmten 15 Minuten, von denen Andy Warhol sprach. Das normale Mädchen aus Essex erfüllte nämlich nicht nur ihren Auftrag, weil sie als berühmter als die anderen, angeblich echten Berühmtheiten im Haus durchging. In weiterer Folge gewann sie sogar den ganzen Wettbewerb. Das britische Publikum wählte sie mit Begeisterung und schwelgte geradezu in der Ironie, eine Nichtberühmtheit als Königin der Berühmtheiten zu küren.

Als Chantelle den Big-Brother-Container verliess, war sie ebenso berühmt wie jene, denen sie die Schau gestohlen hatte. Ein paar Monate später heiratete sie sogar Preston, einen der Teilnehmer und Mitglied der alternativen Rockband «The Ordinary Boys». Obwohl sich die beiden schon im folgenden Jahr scheiden liessen, fanden sie sich einmütig im britischen Big-Brother-Finale 2010 – «Ultimate Big Brother» –

ein, um ihren Ehestreit zu einem amüsanten Publikumsspektakel zu machen. In den folgenden Tagen jedoch brach das glitzernde, lächelnde Ruhm-Imitat in sich zusammen. Publikum wie Exmann bekamen Chantelles Leid und Verletzbarkeit zu Gesicht. Letzterer nahm sie in den Arm, als sie verzweifelt schluchzte, und das Publikum lechzte derweil nach Versöhnung. Aber vielleicht spielten sie ja, wie manche glauben, das Liebes- und Trennungsdrama nur vor – zum Nutzen von Publikum, Presse und Ruhm.

Als Chantelle den Big-Brother-Container als «berühmtester Niemand Grossbritanniens» verliess, suchte, so Katy Guest in der Zeitung *The Independent*[1], die Agentur, die sie vorher als Paris-Hilton-Double vermittelt hatte, bereits nach einem Chantelle-Houghton-Double. Der Ruhm im 21. Jahrhundert ist offenbar wie eine Matrioschka-Puppe: Hinter einem kommt immer gleich ein neuer Möchtegern zum Vorschein. In Grossbritannien wird diese Art Ruhm geliebt und gleichzeitig gehasst. Boulevardblätter, Zeitschriften und immer neue Kabelkanäle haben einen unersättlichen Appetit nach Berühmtheiten, aber wie bei Kronos hat die Liebe, die sie den Prominenten schenken, einen Haken. Die Medien schlucken ihre Kinder und spucken sie gleich wieder aus. Chantelles Karriere vom «Niemand» zur Prominenten wurde zum Paradebeispiel der britischen Vorstellung von Ruhm. Das Innere des Ruhmes wurde nach aussen gekehrt, seine Mechanik blossgestellt, seziert und neu zusammengesetzt. Seine unvermeidliche Janusköpfigkeit – Jemand, Niemand, Jemand, Niemand – offenbarte sich.

Gegensätze wie öffentlich/privat, berühmt/unbekannt oder real/fiktiv haben heutzutage ihre Gegensätzlichkeit verloren und sind vollkommen intertextuell. Julia Kristevas Semiotik sperrt sich im Gegensatz zum vorherrschenden symbolischen Modus jeder Systematisierung. Symbolisches und Semiotisches sind im Subjekt untrennbar vereint, sie vereinen Körper und Sprache. Genauso sperrt sich das Bild des Prominentendoubles jeglicher Definition. Zwei Körper werden zu einer intertextuellen Einheit.

Jedenfalls fällt auf den Fotos als erstes die Anspielung auf die Berühmtheit in den Blick,

und Anspielungen sind immer intertextuell. Die recycelten Bilder sind überdeterminiert. Sie verweisen auf das Fehlen einer einheitlichen Realität. Die Realität ist zersplittert zwischen Individuum und den widersprüchlichen Andeutungen, die das Bild evoziert. Doch im Januskopf von Illusion und Anspielung auf die Berühmtheit liegt die Chance auf Kreativität verborgen: Die hybride Persona, die zugleich berühmt und nicht berühmt ist, die zugleich eine private und keine private Person ist, die alles und nichts zugleich ist. In der Kluft zwischen Bild und Wahrnehmung ist die Wirklichkeit aufgehoben.

Nun schon vor 35 Jahren schrieb Susan Sontag: «Der wahre moderne Primitivismus indessen besteht nicht darin, dass man das Bild als etwas Reales ansieht; so wirklich sind fotografische Bilder kaum. Vielmehr wirkt die Wirklichkeit mehr und mehr so, wie das, was uns die Kameras zeigen.»[2] Der moderne Primitivismus von heute bedeutet vielleicht, nichts als wirklich anzusehen. Der Doppelgänger ist bloss ein Tiegel, in dem zwei zu einem, Gewissheit zu Zweifel, Realität zu Fiktion verschmolzen werden. Er ist eine unheimliche Manifestierung schäbiger Nichtigkeit. Doch obwohl uns das Foto eines Prominentendoppelgängers immer tiefer in diesen Tiegel zieht, glitzert auf dessen Boden doch etwas Wertvolles.

Wenn wir nämlich das Bild so betrachten, als sei es ein Spiegel des Ruhmes, als läge seine Bedeutung einzig in dieser kulturell kodierten Oberfläche, dann starrt uns die blosse Abwesenheit ins Gesicht. Das Ebenbild, das «spitting image», ist das Zeichen, nicht man selbst zu sein, das Zeichen, ein Anderer zu sein, das Zeichen der Zersplitterung. Wenn wir auf dem Foto nichts als den Doppelgänger sehen, dann spiegelt uns dieser jenen Mangel, jenen unwiederbringlichen Verlust zurück, der verborgen im Kern jeder Identität schlummert und sich nach dem vorbewussten, ganzheitlichen und für immer verlorenen Sein verzehrt. Wenn wir aber durch den Doppelgänger auf die Essenz des Bildes schauen, können die bedeutungsschweren Voreingenommenheiten der Vorstellung von Ruhm von uns abfallen. Der Blick klärt sich, das Bild wird schärfer. Der Prominente ist gar nicht

das Original, dessen Ebenbild der Doppelgänger liefert. Im Gegenteil: Er ist bloss der einzige Doppelgänger, der als Original gilt. In der Intensität des nüchternen Kamerablicks erkennen wir nicht mehr Gleichheit, sondern Differenz. Jedes Bild enthüllt eine Unzahl winziger Details des Gesichts und des Körpers, die Unterschiede kenntlich machen wie eine Landkarte, die Grenzen zwischen Staaten verzeichnet. Aus dem Schatten des Ebenbildes erhebt sich abermals das Individuum.

Erst in diesem konzentrierten Akt der Dekonstruktion, mit dem «spit» von «image», die Spucke vom Bild getrennt wird, erkennen wir die *différance*. In der Derrida'schen Redeweise verweist das Wort *différance* immer auf zwei Bedeutungen – «defer» (verschieben) und «differ» (sich unterscheiden). Durch die Verschiebung von Bedeutung entsteht die Differenz. Selbst wenn wir uns einen Augenblick von dem gespaltenen Bild abwenden, so ist seine gedoppelte Identität umgehend wieder da, sobald wir wieder hinblicken. Einmal mehr ist der Moment des Verstehens verschoben, und wir müssen sein gespaltenes Sein verstehen, um die Differenz zu erkennen.

Anstatt also vor Wut auf das Double im Spiegel, das uns unsere vermeintliche Identität gestohlen hat, zu spucken, sollten wir lieber ausspucken, um unser Glück zu beschwören. So wie das Semiotische in, um und durch das Symbolische schwappt, formlos und untrennbar, hat das «spitting image» als Ebenbild seine eigene Wahrheit: Das Ich liegt im Anderen.

1 Guest, Katy, «Oh, my God! Oh, my God! Oh, my God!». *The Independent*, Sonntag, 5. Februar 2006.

2 Susan Sontag, 1980, *Über Fotografie* [Orig. 1977], Fischer, Frankfurt am Main, S. 153f.

Spitting in the Mirror

by Caroline Morpeth

We are looking at a photograph of my daughter – long hair looping over her forehead to tuck behind her right ear, dark almond eyes staring straight into the camera, lips soft but unsmiling – and my aunt says, "She's the spitting image of you at that age."

I start to think about what that means. "Spitting image" is a common English expression used to describe a person who bears a strong physical resemblance to another. But even everyday commonplace language becomes strange when one attempts to separate it from its referent, and the concept resists me. Etymologically the expression is a corruption of "spitten image", or "the spit and image", themselves nineteenth-century neologisms of the sixteenth-century usage "the spit of" to denote extreme likeness. So the phrase "spitting image" is a tautology, since "spit" and "image" are both signifiers of physical resemblance, and thus also autological, since the doubleness of the tautology echoes the doubled identity that the phrase "spitting image" references.

In spite of the satisfactory neatness of this tautological/autological symbiosis, though, I am still straining towards understanding. Why should spit act as a synonym of physical doubleness? Is it because, as a bodily excretion, it functions as a metaphor for semen, an evident carrier of physical likeness from one generation to another? Or perhaps it is drawn from the ancient Greek myth of Cronus who devoured his own children at birth so that they could never rebel against him, until Zeus, the only son to escape, returned and forced him to spit them out, one by one. Spit is itself figuratively double: you can spit for luck, to ward off evil; but also to express contempt and hatred. As a present participle, "spitting" is more denotative of spit's negative implied meanings: active and venomous, filled with rage as it fights against the chains linking it to the "image", its own double.

The image too is caught. As image it lacks autonomy: always the reflection of something Other, trapped within alterity. In Lacanian theories of the construction of identity, such Otherness lies at the very heart of our being. Jacques Lacan reinterpreted Freud's theories on child development into three stages that he classified as the Imaginary, the Mirror, and the Symbolic. During the Imaginary stage the infant has no language and is fully open to inchoate sensations and drives, recognising no limits to its own body in its boundless world. The child's emerging realisation of individuality, of separation from the mother, on entering the Mirror stage when the world is projected beyond the self and reflected back as image, leads to a misrecognised identity, simultaneously the self and the Other. This duality is carried into the Symbolic order with the acquisition of language, which both symbolises the Real and prevents its full representation since language is intrinsically figurative. Lacan configured the Symbolic as the "*nom du père*" (law of the father) since the acquisition of language represents entry into a culturally constructed patriarchal authority that further distorts our sense of identity because the subjective is inevitably experienced through interaction with others. As a result, identity is always unstable and incomplete, and a sense of lack, of irretrievable loss, is substituted for the wholeness experienced during the Imaginary stage. Revisiting Lacan's theories, Julia Kristeva introduced the concept of the Semiotic, an essentially female, fluid and repressed Other to the Symbolic but simultaneously inseparable from it, so that meaning flows ceaselessly into the other.

If identity is intrinsically misrecognised and double, then the spitting image signifies an overt reminder of the limits of individuality.

Here is the "I" that is not one person but divided. It drags over the threshold our liminal understanding that when we look into our own reflection in the mirror we are both outside and inside the framed image. When we gaze at the lookalike, at the spitting image, we are forced, through its un-unified identity, into facing our own.

The photographed presence itself can only intensify this dislocation, for all photographs are spitting images. Photography can never escape from the paradox that René Magritte locked into his painting "La Trahison des Images" in which the image of a pipe is undermined by the inscription beneath it: *"Ceci n'est pas une pipe"*. A photograph seeks invisibility, to present the real. But it must fail: the real is always transmuted into image. Where my daughter sees a photograph of a version of herself, my aunt sees a long-gone memory of me, and I see a palimpsest of my daughter then, my daughter now, myself then, myself now, so the person that is photographed is not merely divided but multiple and finally inaccessible: *Ceci n'est pas ma fille*.

The boundaries between authenticity and individuality are dissolved even further within photographs of celebrity lookalikes. In these images, the triangle of celebrity, lookalike and viewer (which in turn encompasses its own tripartite structure of camera lens, photographer and audience) divides and subdivides into a profusion of superimposed yet fragmented identities and experiences. And yet at the heart of the image is an absence: the celebrity is not – has never been – here. But our gaze is too insistent: we reimagine the image into a juxtaposition of reality and impersonation and situate the celebrity firmly inside the photographic frame. The celebrity is transformed from absence into (in)visible presence. The lookalike becomes imbued with the gloss of the celebrity's identity so that the viewer feels that it might almost be possible to stretch out and brush against the fingertips of fame. But, intrinsically double, we are always contradictory. Even as we desire fame and strive to connect with it, we also recognise that if we were to step over its threshold we might find

In the present age, the binary oppositions of public/private, fame/anonymity, reality/falseness have lost their contrariety: they have become ineffably intertextual.

only an abyss, a nothingness. Fame is a miasma that, like a sunbeam between cupped hands, cannot be gripped by the celebrity since it is reflected from elsewhere: it is the Other in the mirror.

The United Kingdom's ambivalent and mordant attitude towards fame is exemplified by the story of celebrity-lookalike Chantelle Houghton, a pretty, ordinary, twenty-three year-old Essex girl whose resemblance to Paris Hilton was her only claim to fame. Chantelle was sent into the Celebrity Big Brother house in 2006 with a special task: she had one week in which to persuade the participants that she was as much of a genuine celebrity as they, and if she failed in this she would be evicted from the house. Presented as a member of a fictitious girl band, she was asked by one housemate to remind him of her band's hit song. Obligingly she performed a few slightly off-key verses of the imaginary hit before giggling and stumbling to a halt, whilst some of her housemates claimed that, of course, now they remembered the song. At the end of the week, the housemates were asked to rank themselves in order of fame: if Chantelle were placed last, she would have failed the task. The result illustrated the slippery identity of celebrity in twenty-first century Britain, its lack of references to anything more concrete than Andy Warhol's fifteen minutes. The ordinary girl from Essex not only passed the test of being acknowledged as more famous than others in the house presumed to have genuine claims to celebrity, but went on to win the entire show; cheered on and voted for by a British public revelling in the irony of crowning a non-celebrity as Queen of the Celebrity Big Brother household.

By the time she left the Big Brother house, Chantelle had acquired as much claim to fame as those she had beaten, and several months later even married one of the celebrities she had upstaged. Although she and Preston, a member of indie band "The Ordinary Boys", were divorced the following year, they both returned to take part in the UK's Big Brother finale in 2010, Ultimate Big Brother, willing to entertain viewers with the fallout of a marriage breakdown played out as public spectacle. Over the following days, the glossy, smiling, simulacrum of fame broke down as Chantelle's pain and fragility were exposed to the viewers and to her ex-husband, who took her in his arms as she sobbed in distress whilst the watching public hankered for a reconciliation. Or perhaps, as some believed, they were merely acting out a simulated drama of love and hurt and rejection for the benefit of the audience, for the benefit of press attention, for the benefit of fame.

When Chantelle first left the Big Brother household as the "most famous nobody in Britain", according to Katy Guest in "The Independent" newspaper[1], the agency that she had formerly worked for as a Paris Hilton lookalike was already looking for a Chantelle Houghton lookalike to put on their books. Like stacking Russian dolls, twenty-first century fame opens up to reveal a wannabe inside. In the United Kingdom such celebrity is both celebrated and denigrated. Tabloid newspapers, magazines, the proliferating cable television channels, have an insatiable appetite for celebrity to feed to their readers and viewers, but the love on offer is always conditional: like Cronus, they swallow and spit out their offspring. Chantelle's trajectory from "nobody" to celebrity became a paradigm of the British relationship with fame, turning it inside out to expose its workings, dissecting and reconstructing it to reveal its mechanical dualism: someone, no-one, someone, no-one.

In the present age, the binary oppositions of public/private, fame/anonymity, reality/falseness have lost their contrariety: they have become ineffably intertextual. Julia Kristeva's Semiotic defies systemisation in opposition to the prevalent Symbolic mode since they are inseparable within the subject, integrating body and language. In the same way the image of the celebrity lookalike also resists definition, instead integrating body and body to produce an intertextual identity.

The initial focus of the photographic image is on the allusive presence of the celebrity. Allusion is always intertextual, its reused imagery powerfully articulate in indicating the absence of a singular reality, as reality becomes fractured amongst the juxtaposition of individual, conflicting presences that allusion evokes. Concealed within the shape-shifting illusion/allusion of the celebrity's presence lies the possibility of creativity: the hybrid persona who both is the celebrity and is not the celebrity; who both is the private person and is not the private person; the persona who is all of these at one time and none. Reality becomes suspended over the chasm that opens up between image and perception.

Thirty-five years ago Susan Sontag wrote that "the true modern primitivism is not to regard the image as a real thing; photographic images are hardly that real. Instead, reality has come to seem more and more like what we are shown by cameras."[2] Nowadays the modern primitivism is perhaps to regard nothing as real. The spitting image seems to be a crucible that distills one into two, certainty into doubt, reality into falsity; an uncanny manifestation of contemptuous nullity. But as we are pulled deeper within the framing lens of the celebrity lookalike photograph, something real shimmers into being at the edge of our vision.

When we look at the image as if it were a mirror of celebrity, as if meaning lies solely on the level of its culturally encoded surface, only absence stares out, for the spitting image is the sign of not being oneself, the sign of being Other, the sign of fragmentation. If we look only for the double, it reflects back to us instead the Lack, the inconsolable loss, which resonates silently at the centre of all identity, yearning for a never-to-be-regained pre-conscious and unified existence. But when we look beyond the double at the presence that is in the picture, the loaded pre-existing meanings introduced by the concept of celebrity can fall away so that the focus sharpens and irrepressibly a new clarity emerges. The celebrity is not the original to the lookalike's spitting image – on the contrary, it is the lookalike who has the only claim here of being the original. And in the intensity of the camera's even gaze, we no longer see sameness, but difference. Each image reveals a myriad tiny details of face and body that chart difference just as a map charts boundaries between countries. Individuality re-emerges out of the shadow of the spitting image.

It is during this concentrated visual act of deconstruction, when the "spit" is separated from the "image", that we encounter *différance*. In Derridean terms, the French word *différance* cannot help but reference two separate meanings – to defer and to differ – so that it is through the deferment of meaning that difference emerges. And so, even if we glance momentarily away from the split image, its doubled identity resurfaces as we look back, and once more the moment of comprehension is deferred and we must renegotiate its un-unified identity to discern difference.

Instead of spitting at the mirror in anger at the double who has stolen our identity, perhaps we should spit for luck. Just as the Semiotic washes in and around and through the Symbolic, formless and inseparable, the spitting image knows its own truth. Within the Other lies the self.

1   Katy Guest, "Oh, my God! Oh, my God! Oh, my God!", *The Independent*, Sunday 5 February 2006.

2   Susan Sontag, 2008, *On Photography*, [1977], Penguin, London.

(Fast) wie ein Ei dem anderen

von Markus Reich

Mal eben mit Queen Elizabeth II. ein Tässchen Tee schlürfen? Oder mit Sophia Loren über den neuesten Klatsch aus dem Showbiz plaudern? Mal eben am Ruhm nippen, an der Aura schnuppern, die von so einem Star ausgehen? Geht nicht? Aber sicher doch! Nun, vielleicht nicht mit dem Original. Aber wer heute etwas von seiner Prominenz hält, beschäftigt ein Double, ein Lookalike, das ihm fast wie ein Ei dem anderen gleicht!

Nicht selten steht ein Prominenter nicht für die Kunden zur Verfügung, heisst es beispielsweise bei der Agentur «doubles.de». Gründe dafür können sein: Zeitmangel, Gagenunstimmigkeiten, uninteressanter Kunde oder einfach Lustlosigkeit. Dies sind Argumente, warum ein Double interessant sein kann. Der Umgang mit Doubles ist oftmals unkomplizierter, sie sind schneller verfügbar, sie setzen Kundenwünsche gerne um, und sie sind um ein Vielfaches günstiger. Doppelgänger haben viele gute Ideen. Ein blosses Nachahmen des Originals wird als langweilig und wenig einfallsreich empfunden. Ein gutes Double muss fast besser sein als sein Vorbild. Neben gut imitieren müssen sie tanzen, singen und moderieren können.

Das Phänomen der Doubles geht zeitlich ganz weit zurück. Denn um den Gedanken der Authentizität war es schon vor langer Zeit nicht gut bestellt. Nicht bloss japanische Fürsten hielten sich Doppelgänger. Auch die österreichische Kaiserin Elisabeth liess eine Hofdame als sie selbst umhergehen und repräsentieren. Wenn sie einen ihrer Migräneanfälle hatte, liess sie sich vertreten. Damals schrieb kein Zeitgenosse und kein Historiker vom drohenden Verfall der Sitten.

Doch nicht nur beim Adel, auch in der Politik sind Lookalikes gang und gäbe. So hat der britische Premierminister Winston Churchill, der 1965 verstarb, einige seiner berühmten Radioansprachen während des Zweiten Weltkrieges nicht selbst gehalten. Er beauftragte den Schauspieler Norman Shelley mit dem Vortrag in der BBC. Churchill liess sich einfach ersetzen. Die Radios rauschten damals noch ordentlich, nur die Wochenschauen zeigten gelegentlich Churchill in Bild und Ton. Kurz, keiner hat etwas gemerkt, und die Regierung hatte nichts gesagt. Nicht immer treten Doppelgänger zum Spass auf. Diktatoren wie einst Saddam Hussein schicken sie an die Medienfront, aus Angst vor Attentaten zum Beispiel.

Zu den gefragtesten Doubles im deutschsprachigen Raum gehören Lookalikes der deutschen Bundeskanzlerin Angela Merkel. Susanne Knoll ist eine der Doppelgängerinnen Merkels und hat von allen Lookalikes die wohl bewegendste Geschichte hinter sich. Sie sagt von sich, dass dieser Job ihr das Leben gerettet habe. Ihre Geschichte ist eine Parabel über die Medien oder über die sehr bizarre Welt der Doppelgänger. Susanne Knoll erzählte in einem Interview mit der «Süddeutschen Zeitung», wie schwer ihre Kindheit in Armut, Streit und Lieblosigkeit war, geprägt von Alkohol und Schlägen. Sie selbst bekam drei Töchter, ihre Ehe belastete sie. Sie erkrankte an Krebs, erlitt mit 38 Jahren einen Schlaganfall. Sie überwand beides. Eines Tages sagte ein Freund zu ihr, dass sie Angela Merkel ähnlich sähe. Ein Agent wurde auf sie aufmerksam. Bald hielt sie vor 100 Leuten eines Energieunternehmens eine Rede, wurde beklatscht. Nach einem Artikel über sie im Nachrichtenmagazin «Der Spiegel» ging es richtig los. Es war wie eine Lawine. Einladungen zu Talkshows, Partys, Parteiveranstaltungen jagten sich. Sie wird behandelt wie die echte Angela. «Darf ich ein Foto machen?» – «Frau Bundeskanzlerin, dass ich Sie hier so einfach treffe!» Natürlich wissen und sehen alle, dass sie nur die Doppelgängerin ist. Aber auch die Doppelgängerin der Kanzlerin ist heutzutage ein Medienstar, eine Prominente. Die Grenzen verschwimmen. Susanne Knoll sagt, die letzten Jahre seien die

besten ihres Lebens gewesen. Sie habe ihre Jugend nachgeholt. Früher habe sie oft an Selbstmord gedacht. «Mit 39 war ich eigentlich tot. Heute bin ich stolz und glücklich. Ich bin dankbar, dass es Angela Merkel gibt. Ich verdanke ihr mein Leben.» Nicht immer gelingt es Lookalikes, mit der eigenen Prominenz umzugehen. Der Doppelgänger von Rocker Ozzy Osbourne zieht sich inzwischen überall die Hosen herunter. Der Doppelgänger von Dieter Bohlen führt sich ordinärer auf als Dieter Bohlen selbst. Manche verlieren die Realität und denken, sie seien es wirklich.

Zeigten die Doubles früher Ehrfurcht vor ihren Vorbildern, so übergiessen sie diese heute teilweise mit Häme und Spott. Ein Leidtragender ist der deutsche Volksmusikstar Florian Silbereisen. Er ist Stammgast in der Pro-7-Show «Switch – reloaded». Sein Doppelgänger äfft seine Mimik nach und verhunzt seine Stimme. Und wie reagiert der Betroffene? Er versucht, es mit Humor zu nehmen, sagt, man müsse doch sehr prominent sein, um überhaupt in dieser Sendung aufzutauchen. Nicht immer geht es jedoch so diplomatisch zu. Eines der Doubles von

«Ich bin dankbar, dass es Angela Merkel gibt. Ich verdanke ihr mein Leben.»

Entertainerin Liza Minnelli beklagt sich immer mal wieder, wenn ihr Vorbild für Eskapaden sorgt. Nach einem Drogenabsturz oder nach Cortisonbehandlungen ändert sich Lizas Aussehen, auf das das Double achten muss. Auch ein neues Hüftgelenk von Minnelli kann kurzfristig für Verwirrung sorgen. Ihr Gang ändert sich dadurch geringfügig.

Auch die Doubles des verstorbenen Popstars Michael Jackson waren und sind einem Wechselbad des Geschmacks ausgesetzt. Es gab schwierige Zeiten, als der Sänger Anfang der 1990er Jahre wegen Kindesmissbrauchs verdächtigt und 2003 sogar angeklagt wurde. In einer Art Sippenhaft wurde keines der Doubles

mehr beschäftigt. Anfragen blieben aus. Kam es doch zu einem Auftritt, wurden die Doubles als Kinderschänder beschimpft. Nach Jacksons Tod brummte das Geschäft wieder. Das zeigt, wie sehr das Publikum oft nicht mehr zwischen Realität und Fiktion zu unterscheiden weiss.

Wie sieht die Zukunft aus? Gefragt sind im Moment vor allem Politiker, in Deutschland speziell FDP-Politiker Guido Westerwelle. Die Schweiz ist zu klein und der Markt zu wenig lukrativ, als dass man eine Vollzeitbeschäftigung als Promi-Double annehmen, geschweige denn von ihr leben könnte.

Und um auf die Queen zurückzukommen, selbst bei ihr gibt es Nachteile, wenn man ihr Double ist. So beklagte sich zum Beispiel Elizabeth Richards über Pech in der Liebe. Männer wagten nicht mehr, sie anzusprechen. Sie hätten Angst vor ihr. Elizabeth Richards ergeht es dann so wie ihrem Vorbild, wenn etwas ungelegen kommt: Sie ist «not amused».

(Almost) alike as two Peas in a Pod

by Markus Reich

How about having tea with Queen Elizabeth II? Or chatting with Sophia Loren about the latest gossip from showbiz? Just enjoy a taste of fame, sample the aura surrounding a star like this? You can't? Sure you can! But maybe just not with the original one. Today, though, anybody who is anybody employs a double, a lookalike, who is almost absolutely identical to him!

It is quite often the case that a celebrity is not available for customers, as we are told for instance by the agency "doubles.de". There can be many reasons for this: lack of time, disagreements about fees, a client seen as offering no benefits to the celebrity, or indeed, simply lack of interest in the event. These are arguments that make using a lookalike quite tempting. Employing a lookalike is often much less complicated; they are available at short notice, they are happy to do what the customer asks of them, and they are a lot cheaper. Lookalikes have many good ideas. Merely imitating the original is considered to be boring and unimaginative and a good double has to be almost better than their model. In addition to impersonating well, they have to be able to sing, dance and host shows.

The phenomenon of the double goes back a long way. Even long ago the outlook for reliable authenticity was limited. Not only Japanese princes kept doubles. The Austrian empress Elisabeth had a court lady who acted as her lookalike, walking around the court: If Elisabeth had one of her migraine attacks, this lady would stand in for her. No contemporaries or historians wrote at the time of the impending decline of morals.

Not only among the nobility, lookalikes are common practice in politics as well. British Prime Minister Winston Churchill, for example, who died in 1965, did not hold all of his most important radio speeches himself. He passed this task on at the BBC to the actor Norman Shelley, who simply became Churchill's substitute. Radios produced a lot of white noise back then, only the newsreels occasionally showed Churchill in sound and motion. In short, nobody noticed anything, and the government certainly didn't let on. Doubles do not always appear as a matter of fun. Dictators such as the late Saddam Hussein send them to media gatherings for example, out of fear of assassination.

Some of the most in-demand doubles in German-speaking countries are lookalikes of German chancellor Angela Merkel. Susanne Knoll is one of Merkel's doubles and has lived through what is probably the most moving story of all lookalikes. She says of herself that this job saved her life. Her story is a parable of the media or of the very bizarre world of the doppelganger. In an interview with the "Süddeutsche Zeitung", Susanne Knoll described what a difficult childhood she had had, with poverty, conflict and a lack of love, marked by alcohol and beatings. She herself had three daughters, but could not cope with her marriage, and fell ill with cancer and suffered a stroke at the age of 38. She recovered from both. One day a friend mentioned that she looked like Angela Merkel. She came to the attention of an agent. Soon she was making a speech in front of 100 people from an energy company and was applauded. Once an article about her had been published in the new magazine "Der Spiegel", things really took off. It was like an avalanche. There was no end to the invitations to chat shows, parties, political party events. She is treated like the real Angela. "May I take a picture?" – "Mrs Chancellor, how nice to meet you here like this!" Of course everyone knows and can see that she is just a lookalike. Yet the lookalike of the chancellor is today herself a media star, a celebrity. The borders are merging. Susanne Knoll says that the last years have been the best years of her life. She has regained her youth. She often used to have suicidal thoughts. "When I was 39 I was just about dead. Today I feel proud and happy. I am grateful that Angela Merkel exists. I owe my life to her." Lookalikes do not always manage to cope with their own celebrity. The double of rock musician Ozzy Osbourne now pulls his trousers down everywhere he goes. The doppelganger of Dieter Bohlen (the German Simon Cowell) behaves more vulgarly than Dieter Bohlen himself. Some people lose sight of reality and start believing they really are the person they are imitating.

Whereas doubles once showed great respect for their models, today some of them pour scorn and ridicule on them. One of the victims of this is German folk music star Florian Silbereisen. He is a regular guest on the Pro-7 show "Switch – reloaded". His double apes his facial expressions and ridicules his voice. And how does the target react? He tries to take things with a smile, and says you have to be a real celebrity to even appear on this programme. But things don't always work out so diplomatically. One of the doubles of entertainer Liza Minnelli always complains when her model hits the headlines. After a drugs overdose or cortisone treatment, Liza's appearance is altered, and the double has to copy this. Confusion is even caused when she has a new hip joint, as her gait changes slightly.

The doubles of deceased pop star Michael Jackson were and still are exposed to emotional roller-coaster rides. They went through difficult times when the singer was accused of child abuse. None of the doubles were employed any more, through a sense of being tarred with the same brush. Invitations stopped arriving. If they did make an appearance, the doubles were insulted as child molesters. After Jackson's death, business boomed again. This shows to what extent the public can often no longer differentiate between reality and fiction.

How will things develop in future? Above all politicians are in demand at the moment, in Germany it is specifically FDP politician Guido Westerwelle. Switzerland is too small and the market is not lucrative enough for a celebrity double to have work full time, let alone live from it.

To come back to the Queen, even with her there are disadvantages in being her double. Elizabeth Richards, for example, complained about being unlucky in love. Men no longer dared speak to her. They were afraid of her. Elizabeth Richards then feels like her role model when something inconvenient happens – she is "not amused".

"May I take a picture?" – "Mrs Chancellor, how nice to meet you here like this!" Of course everyone knows and can see that she is just a lookalike.

Der Ruhm
der anderen

Niklaus Spoerris «Who is Who?» der internationalen Double-Szene

von Rudolf Scheutle

In bravourös einstudierter Manier des Leadsängers von U2 fletscht der Stellvertreter Bonos seine Zähne. Blinkende Pop-Accessoires wie Sonnenbrille, Kreuzanhänger, dicker Goldohrring sind trotz ihres erst auf den zweiten Blick ersichtlichen Fake-Charakters stilgerecht gewählt. Und wäre die Mimik nicht eine Spur zu maliziös, so könnte der Kerl in seiner schwarzen Lederjackenkluft tatsächlich als Rockstar Bono durchgehen. Auch Pseudo-Pavarotti Dieter Wagner scheint trotz passabler Ähnlichkeit mit dem Startenor in der demonstrativen Zurschaustellung seiner Körperfülle im wahrsten Sinne des Wortes etwas dick aufzutragen. Ganz zu schweigen von dem kuriosen Ambiente, das hier wie auch auf den meisten anderen Double-Porträts von Niklaus Spoerri eher dem bürgerlichen Milieu zuzurechnen ist und so in Kontrast zu dem behaupteten Starstatus steht. Während ein falscher Maradona etwa die Fussballposter seines übermächtigen Vorbilds und andere Devotionalien massenhaft an die Wand gepinnt hat, baut sich Dieter alias Pavarotti vor dem Schlauch einer blitzblanken Einbauküchenzeile in Weiss auf. Niklaus Spoerri nimmt die von ihm aufgespürten, professionellen Doubles detailbewusst in ihrem jeweiligen privaten Umfeld ins Visier. Eine geschickte Strategie, weil man dadurch den Gesamtkontext der Porträts wie ein Psychogramm zu lesen und deuten beginnt. Spoerri selbst meint dazu: «Mir geht es in diesen dokumentarischen Porträts darum, nicht einfach den geschminkten Star von der Bühne abzulichten, sondern den Menschen hinter dem Double hervortreten zu lassen: Men-schen, die sonst wahrscheinlich ihr Leben lang medial ‹unsichtbar› geblieben wären.»

Schliesslich fungiert das Double in seinen mehr oder minder geglückten Adaptionsversuchen an den jeweils zum Vorbild genommenen Prominenten als soziale Randfigur des Starkults. Die in totaler Identitätsverleugnung selbst auferlegte Rolle des Imitators resultiert in der Regel bereits aus einer gesellschaftlichen Position, die im Grunde himmelweit von jenen Projektionsfiguren entfernt ist, in der sich unsere kollektiven Sehnsüchte spiegeln. Das heisst, der Ruhm des anderen, der scheinbar überirdischen Gestalt, strahlt mitnichten auf das bezahlte Double zurück. Nur selten dürfte es wie bei dem Anthony-Hopkins-Imitator namens Frank Powell der Fall sein, dass jemand durch die geschickte Assimilation an einen renommierten Schauspieler seinen sozialen Status entscheidend verbessern konnte. Powell jedenfalls gelang es, sich dank seiner täuschenden Ähnlichkeit mit dem britischen Schauspieler aus seiner Arbeitslosigkeit zu befreien – der damalige Hype um die Verfilmung der Horrorgeschichte von Hannibal Lecter beförderte dies natürlich enorm. Gemeinhin umweht die von Spoerri porträtierten Doubles aber ein Hauch von Travestie und Tragikomödie. Der Fotograf Spoerri sagt, dass ihn künstliche Welten schon immer fasziniert hätten: «Wie wenig es braucht, um zu bluffen. Doubles bluffen. Sie sind Menschen, die aussehen wie jemand anderes, wie eine Berühmtheit, ein Star. Aber: Ist das Leben ein anderes, wenn man aussieht wie George Clooney?»

Für sein seit 2007 entstandenes «dokumentarisches Nachschlagewerk der internationalen Double-Szene» hat Niklaus Spoerri über die in dem Sektor sehr rar vorhandenen Agenturen die Fährten aufgenommen. Um hier nur zwei der zentralen Vermittler für Doubles zu nennen: Während in Deutschland Jochen Florstedt von «doubles.de» viele der Star-Nachahmer exklusiv vertritt, betreibt Susan Scott mit «lookalikes.info» die älteste Agentur in England überhaupt und vermittelte Spoerri an die 20 Kontakte. Die stringent konzeptuell angelegte Recherche Spoerris förderte so manche Überraschung zutage. Erst über das langwierige Erwirken eines Vertrauensverhältnisses zu den Agenturen war es ihm möglich, an die Doubles heranzutreten, da sie anders als etwa veritable Schauspieler oder auch umtriebige Starlets eher aus dem Verborgenen heraus ihr Prominentenunwesen treiben. In Spoerris Schweizer Heimat waren zudem kurioserweise so gut wie keine Doubles auszumachen. Dafür gibt es in dem Yellow-Press-Wonderland Grossbritannien eine ganze Reihe von höchst professionell auftretenden Pseudo-Idolen, deren Stärke eher in der schauspielerischen Brillanz als in äusseren Verwandtschaftsverhältnissen mit den populären Berühmtheiten unserer Hochglanzwelt liegt. Entsprechend hoch sind deren Gagen veranschlagt.

Laut Roland Barthes führt der Star der breiten Masse immer wieder einen «gelebten Mythos» vor Augen. In seinem viel rezipierten Buch «Mythen des Alltags» beschreibt der französische Philosoph essayhaft, wie formidabel im eigentlichen Wortsinn der Körper der Celebritys von der Kulturindustrie eingesetzt wird, damit er sich wie ein mythisches Zeichen deuten lässt. In Nachfolge zu der Idealisierung der früheren klassischen Heroen entzünden sich an dem als ausserordentlich empfundenen Schicksal des Stars heute die Phantasmen der Mediengesellschaft. Nicht zuletzt über das Miterleben der aus dem Rahmen des Gewöhnlichen fallenden Persönlichkeit und ihres spannungsreichen Werdegangs werden Brüche, Sprünge in der eigenen Biografie kompensiert, das in jedem profanen Leben gegenwärtige Scheitern übertüncht. Spoerris Fotografien von Doubles zeigen letztlich, wie sich diese Identifikation mit dem übermächtigen Vorbild ins Gegenteil des Auratischen verkehrt. Insofern haben die nur scheinbar sachlichen Porträts mehr mit unseren Höhen und Tiefen als den wie auch immer gearteten melodramatischen Starverhältnissen zu tun.

Je stärker das Ich von einer spezifischen Maske überzogen und einem Idol angeglichen wird, desto grösser sind vermutlich die persönlichen Narben und Fehlstellen, desto übermächtiger die Gespenster in der eigenen Vita. Die Travestie vermag allerdings für Momente, die Kluft zwischen Sehnsucht und Alltag, Anspruch und Phantomschmerz zu schliessen. Und so sieht man in einem relativ unspektakulären Kontrastumfeld eine Dame den «Dynasty»-Vamp Joan Collins mit obligatorischem Champagnerkelch markieren, während einer ihrer männlichen Kollegen im prototypischen Garten eines deutschen Einfamilienhauses das blasierte Laissez-Faire des Skandalprinzen August von Hannover samt Einstecktuch vorgibt. Und auch das in dem aufgewühlten Allerweltsschlafzimmer posierende Double des nahezu kahlköpfigen Tennisstars Andre Agassi spricht von den paradoxen Überbrückungsversuchen zwischen Schein und Sein. Mit seinen nie voyeuristischen, sondern stets von Empathie getragenen Porträts der Star-Wiedergänger hält Spoerri uns letztlich den Spiegel vor: Der übersteigerte Kult um die Celebritys filtert das Defizitäre einer an Originalität und Individualität verlierenden Gesellschaft.

Nicht erst in den letzten zwanzig Jahren erfahren Prominente eine fulminante mediale Aufmerksamkeit. Mit den modernen Medien, also dem Anfang der 1920er Jahre begeistert begrüssten Kinofilm und in die heimischen Wohnzimmer eingezogenen Radio wurde quasi auch die Celebrity-Kultur erfunden, um der breiten Masse ein glanzvolles Spektakel zu bieten. In einer heute wieder grassierenden Hochzeit der Celebrity-Fotografie schleichen sich angesichts der kaum mehr zu stillenden Nachfrage gehäuft auch die Lookalikes in die Boulevardforen ein. Wer würde sich nicht an Michael Jacksons Ablenkungsmanöver mit mehreren seiner Doubles erinnern? Paparazzis lichteten hier und da in ihrem Übereifer tatsächlich den falschen Jackson ab. Die letztendliche Dekuvrierung des Nichtidentischen gehört auch in den Massenmedien mit zum Doppelgängerspiel. Wobei der Doppelgänger vor allem durch die Literatur der Romantik ein Topos der getäuschten Wahrnehmung geworden ist.

Das täuschend, also zum Verwechseln Ähnliche ist allerdings bei einem veritablen Double relativ selten gegeben. Niklaus Spoerris sachliche Porträts enthüllen hingegen, dass der Simulakrum-Effekt weniger von einer an Zwillinge erinnernden, halbwegs identischen Physiognomie herrührt, sondern sich mehr auf die eingenommene Attitüde samt Kleidung, Accessoires und Attributen bezieht. Spoerris Michael Jackson heisst im übrigen Daimyo und lehnt an einem von Nadelholzbüschen gesäumten Gartenzaun, wie er in jeder deutschen Peripherie zu finden sein könnte. An der prekären «Schnittstelle zwischen Privatheit und Öffentlichkeit» wollte der Fotograf seine Porträts ansiedeln: «Deshalb: kein Casting, kein Wettbewerb, keine Bühne, sondern Porträts, die mit dokumentarischem Blick beobachten und eine Geschichte erzählen aus dem privaten Wohnumfeld – so zum Beispiel von Hans aus Pforzheim, der aussieht wie Bruce Willis, oder dem Versicherungskaufmann Heinz-Uwe aus Schwerin, der aussieht wie die provokante Filmfigur Borat.» Der doppeldeutig zu verstehende Titel «Who is Who?» von Spoerris Nachschlagewerk der Double-Szene fordert fast parodistisch auf, das mitunter nicht prima vista zu erkennende Vorbild mit dem jeweiligen Prominenten wie in einem Rätsel zur Deckungsgleichheit zu bringen.

Bei allen subtilen Referenzen zu den Medien, zu ihrem kommerziellen System, ihrer Verführungsstrategie und auch Philosophie gliedern sich Spoerris fokussierte Doubles zugleich historisch in die moderne Porträtfotografie und ihre Klassiker ein. Durch seine Suche nach dem gesellschaftlich Typologischen in einer massenmedial konditionierten Gesellschaft schliesst Spoerri an das von August Sanders «Menschen des 20. Jahrhunderts» geöffnete Album ein weiteres Kapitel an. Auch Sanders vor allem durch das Licht und die Environments geformten Por-

«Aber: Ist das Leben ein anderes, wenn man aussieht wie George Clooney?»

träts verschiedener Berufsstände laden dazu ein, hinter der Klassifizierung zu erforschen, ob die jeweiligen Menschen in ihrer sozialen Situation glücklich oder besorgt sind. Das zwischen Typus und Individualität, zwischen Klischee und Abweichung, zwischen Original und Kopie oszillierende Gepräge von Spoerris Double-Serie führt in den immer schon zwiespältigen Bereich dessen, was die Porträtfotografie an persönlicher Identität überhaupt zu transportieren vermag. Man denke hier auch an Diane Arbus' Bildikone der «Identical Twins» von 1967, die anhand von eineiigen Zwillingsmädchen zu einem vergleichenden Sehen zwang.

Das Überraschende an den Double-Porträts ist, dass sie ungeachtet ihres bühnenreif skurrilen Ausdrucks nicht von Spoerri hinter der Kamera dirigiert sind: «Ich überliess es den Porträtierten, wie viel sie von sich und ihrer Doppelgänger-Figur explizit zeigen wollten und beobachtete, wie sie sich vor der Kamera inszenieren, wie viel und wie wenig Hinweise sie geben, um ‹ihr› Original in ihnen erkennen zu lassen.» In der Gegenwartsfotografie riskierte Daniela Rossell Ende der 1990er Jahre eine vergleichbare Selbstinszenierung der von ihr ausersehenen Personengruppe, als sie mexikanische Superreiche in «Ricas e Famosas» ihre masslose Verschwendungssucht in dem gegebenen opulenten Rahmen zur Schau stellen liess. Und Larry Sultan fotografierte während der Drehpausen von Pornofilmen in San Fernando Valley bei Los Angeles Bilder, die auf ihre Kontrastwirkung zwischen der gemieteten, mittelständischen Location und dem professionellen Erotikgewerbe zugespitzt waren. Aus einer Diskrepanz zweier scheinbar unvereinbarer Sphären bezieht auch Niklaus Spoerris Nachschlagewerk seine konzeptuelle Schärfe: Das medial produzierte Image der Stars fällt an den Körpern der Doubles und ihrer banalen Umgebung wie Talmiglanz ab.

The Fame of the Others

Niklaus Spoerri's "Who is Who?" of the European double scene

by Rudolf Scheutle

In the brilliantly studied manner of the lead singer of U2, Bono's impersonator bares his teeth. Flashing pop accessories such as sun glasses, a cross pendant, a thick golden earring are chosen true to style, despite their obvious fake character when you look closer. And if the facial expressions weren't a trace too malicious, the guy in his black leather jacket really could pass as rock star Bono. And despite a reasonable similarity with the star tenor, pseudo-Pavarotti Dieter Wagner also tends to lay things on a bit thick, in the truest sense of the word in the demonstrative exhibition of his corpulence, to say nothing of the curious atmosphere which here, as in most of the other double portraits by Niklaus Spoerri, can be attributed more to the middle-class milieu that stands in sharp contrast to the alleged star status. Whereas a fake Maradona might pin up masses of football posters and other devotional objects of his all-powerful role model to the wall, Dieter alias Pavarotti presents himself in front of a tiny but spotless kitchenette all in white. The professional doubles that Niklaus Spoerri has tracked down are examined in great detail in their respective private surroundings. A clever strategy, because through this one begins to see and interpret the overall context of the portraits as a psychogram. Spoerri himself says about this: "What I want to achieve in these documentary portraits is not simply to photograph the made-up star as we know from the stage, but to allow the person behind and with the double to reveal himself: people who otherwise would probably have remained 'invisible' in media terms all their lives."

Ultimately, in his more or less successful attempts at adapting to the celebrity on which he models himself, the double functions as a marginal social figure of the cult of the star. The self-imposed role of the imitator, in total denial of his own identity, is usually the result of a social position that is basically light-years away from those projected figures in which our collective longings are mirrored. This means that the fame of the other, the apparently superhuman figure, in no way reflects back onto the paid double. Only rarely is it the case, as with Anthony Hopkins' imitator Frank Powell, that somebody could significantly raise their social status through the skilful assimilation of a renowned actor. Powell managed to escape unemployment, however, thanks to his deceptively similar looks to the British actor – the hype at the time surrounding filming of the horror story about Hannibal Lecter helped enormously, of course. But generally the lookalikes portrayed by Spoerri are surrounded by a whiff of travesty and tragicomedy. The photographer says that artificial worlds have always fascinat-

ed him: "How little is needed to bluff. Doubles bluff. They are people who look like somebody else, like someone famous, a star. But is your life really that different if you happen to look like George Clooney?"

For his "documentary reference work of the international doubles scene", in progress since 2007, Niklaus Spoerri picked up the trail via agencies that are rare in the sector. To name just two of the mediators for doubles: whereas Jochen Florstedt from "doubles.de" in Germany exclusively represents many star imitators, Susan Scott, with "lookalikes.info" runs the oldest agency in England and supplied Spoerri with some 20 contacts. The strictly conceptual approach of Spoerri's research brought to light a number of surprises. A long time was spent establishing a relationship of trust with the agencies before it was possible for him to approach the doubles, since in contrast to real actors or busy starlets, for example, they get up to their celebrity mischief secretively instead. Curiously in Switzerland, where Spoerri lives, there were hardly any doubles to be found. In the gutter press culture of Great Britain, there is a whole series of highly professional pseudo idols whose strength lies more in acting brilliance than in physical similarities with the popular celebrities of our glamour world. Their fees are correspondingly high.

According to Roland Barthes, the star repeatedly presents a "lived out myth" to the broad masses. In his widely discussed book "Mythologies", the French philosopher describes in essays how formidably, in the true sense of the word, the body of the celebrity is used by the culture industry so that it can be interpreted like a mythical sign. Following on from the idealisation of earlier classical heroes, today the fantasies of media society are ignited by the fate of the star, which is felt to be extraordinary. The breaks and gaps in one's own biography are compensated; the current failure that is present in any banal life is glossed over, not least by the experience of the personality of this out-of-the-ordinary personality and his exciting career. Spoerri's photographs of lookalikes ultimately show how this identification with the all-powerful model turns into the opposite of the auratic. In this respect the portraits that are only apparently objective have more to do with our own highs and lows than with any star relationships, however melodramatic they may turn out to be.

The more heavily the ego is covered by a specific mask and made to match an idol, probably the more the personal scars and flaws, and all the more overwhelming are the ghosts in one's own life. This travesty, however, is capable of closing the gap between aspiration and everyday life for a few moments, between pretence and phantom pain. Hence, in a relatively unspectacular contrasting field you see a lady feign the "Dynasty" vamp Joan Collins with the obligatory glass of champagne, while one of her male colleagues reeks of the smug laissez-faire of the scandal prince August von Hannover and his breast pocket handkerchief in the garden of a typical German detached house. Similarly, the double of the almost bald tennis star Andre Agassi, posing in the untidy universal bedroom, reveals the paradoxical attempts at bridging appearance and reality. With his portraits that are never voyeuristic, but always guided by empathy, portraits of star reincarnations, Spoerri ultimately holds up a mirror to ourselves: The exaggerated cult of celebrities filters out the deficiencies of a society that is becoming less and less original and individual.

The exaggerated cult of celebrities filters out the deficiencies of a society that is becoming less and less original and individual.

It is not just in the last twenty years that celebrities have been exposed to resounding media attention. With the arrival of modern media at the beginning of the 1920s, in the form of radio, as it became a feature of most private households, and of course the enthusiastically received cinema, the celebrity was more or less invented to provide mass audiences with a glamorous spectacle. In a society again characterised by an all-pervasive culture of celebrity photography, the "lookalikes" are also increasingly slipping into the gutter media as a result of the demand that can hardly be satisfied any longer. Who can forget Michael Jackson's diversionary tactics with several of his doubles? In their eagerness, paparazzi really did photograph the wrong Jackson now and again. What is ultimately an uncovering of the non-identical is also part of this game of doppelganger in the mass media. Whereas the doppelganger, above all through the literature of Romanticism, has become a motif of deceived perception.

The deceptively similar – the spitting image – is relatively seldom the case with a real lookalike, however. In contrast Niklaus Spoerri's objective portraits reveal that the simulacrum effect has less to do with a practically identical physiognomy, reflecting a twin, than with the acquired mannerisms, combined with clothing accessories and attributes. Spoerri's Michael Jackson, by the way, is called Daimyo, and leans on a garden fence bordered with coniferous bushes, as could be found in any German suburb. The photographer wanted to locate his portraits at the precarious "intersection between private and public life": "for this reason no casting, no competition, no stage, but portraits, which observe from a documentary perspective and tell a story from their private surroundings – for example, Hans from Pforzheim, who looks like Bruce Willis, or insurance broker Heinz-Uwe from Schwerin, who looks like the provocative film character Borat." The ambiguously titled "Who is Who?", Spoerri's reference work of the lookalike branch, the reader is challenged, in what is almost a parody of the conventional puzzle form, to match up the lookalike to the respective celebrity, whereby the similarity is not always immediately obvious.

With all the subtle references to the media, to their commercial system, their strategy of seduction and also philosophy, Spoerri's focused lookalikes at the same time also fit in historically with modern portrait photography and its classic images. Through his search for what is socially typological in a society conditioned by the mass media, Spoerri adds another chapter to the open album of August Sander's "People of the 20th Century". Sander's portraits of various professions, shaped particularly by light and the environment, invite you to look behind the classification and see whether the respective person is happy or worried in their social situation. The character of Spoerri's double series, oscillating between typus and individuality, between cliché and difference, between original and copy, leads into the field that was always ambiguous; of what portrait photography is capable of conveying in terms of personal identity. Here one can picture Diane Arbus' iconic image of the "Identical Twins" from 1967, which uses the picture of identical twin girls to force you into making a comparison.

The surprising thing about the lookalike portraits is that they are not directed by Spoerri from behind the camera, despite the bizarre and stage-worthy subject matter: "I left it up to those being portrayed as to how much they explicitly wanted to show of themselves and of their doppelganger character and observed how they presented themselves in front of the camera, how many or few indications they give to let 'their' original come out in them." In contemporary photography, Daniela Rossell at the end of the 1990s risked a comparable self-staging of a group of people chosen by her when she had the Mexican super-rich portrayed in "Ricas e Famosas", showing off their excessive extravagance in their opulent surroundings. And Larry Sultan took photographs during breaks in shooting porn films in San Fernando Valley near Los Angeles, which were aimed at bringing out the contrasts between the rented middle-class location and the professional business of eroticism. Niklaus Spoerri's reference work also draws its conceptual focus from this discrepancy between two seemingly incompatible spheres. The image of the stars produced by the media falls off the bodies of the doubles and their banal surroundings like cheap glitter.

«You are either professional or not»

Interview mit dem Queen Elizabeth II.-Double
Jeannette Charles

Seit wann spielen Sie die Rolle der Queen?
Seit 1971.

Wurden Sie als Queen entdeckt oder bemerkten Sie Ihr Talent selbst?
Wissen Sie, früher wurden die jungen Prinzessinnen für ihre Bildung in alle Welt geschickt. Unterrichtet wurden sie ausschliesslich im Palast. Es war undenkbar, dass sie sich unter die gewöhnlichen Leute mischten wie die Mitglieder der königlichen Familie heutzutage. Die Prinzen gehen heute ja sogar in öffentliche Schulen!

Als ich 17 Jahre alt war, besuchte ich die Insel Capri. Ein paar Wochen vorher hielt sich die junge Prinzessin Elizabeth dort auf. Zu meiner Überraschung riefen mir die Italiener immer wieder «Prinzessin Elizabeth!» zu und klatschten, wenn sie mich sahen. Ich begriff gar nicht, warum, bis man es mir schliesslich erklärte. Das war das erste Mal, dass ich auf die Ähnlichkeit aufmerksam gemacht wurde. Das zweite Mal passierte das, als ich mit meiner Familie einen Ausflug nach Greenwich machte. Ein Fotograf wollte mich knipsen. Er fragte meine Mutter: «Darf ich ein Foto von Ihrer Tochter machen? Sie sieht aus wie Prinzessin Elizabeth!» Meine Mutter war schockiert. Damals umwehte die königliche Familie noch eine Art mystische Aura.

1971 dann sass ich zu Hause und überlegte, was ich meinem Mann zum Geburtstag schenken könnte. In der Zeitung las ich die Annonce:

«Spezialisiert auf Porträts». Ich schrieb der Fotografin, die die Annonce aufgegeben hatte und liess ein Porträt von mir machen. Sie meinte: «Sie sehen der Queen so ähnlich! Ich schreibe eine wöchentliche Kolumne in der Zeitung. Darf ich schreiben, wie ähnlich Sie der Queen sind?» Ich lachte, weil ich dachte, das wäre ein Scherz. So fing es also an.

Dann kam das Fernsehen, und bald wurden es immer mehr Sender. Zuerst gabs ja nur die BBC. Ich bekam Anrufe. Erst nur aus meiner Stadt und später aus dem ganzen Land. Dauernd Interviews. Schliesslich wurde ich gefragt, ob ich in Fernsehshows auftreten wollte, von denen bekannt war, dass das Zielpublikum vor allem aus Fans der königlichen Familie bestand. Ich trat natürlich in voller Montur auf! Ich fand das lustig. Damals allerdings gab es nur Agenten für Models und Schauspieler. Ich selbst habe für meine Auftritte nie Geld verlangt, hatte aber Verträge mit den Fernsehstudios unterzeichnet – irgendjemand von dort schickte mir immer Geld.

1971 prägte David Thurlow vom «Daily Express» das Wort «Lookalike». Er sagte zu mir: «Sie sind eine Doppelgängerin der Queen.» Ich antwortete, dass ich aber kleiner sei, woraufhin er meinte: «Sie sehen ihr so ähnlich, dann nenne ich Sie eben LOOKALIKE.» So entstand das Wort.

Ich bekam einen Brief von drei Fotografen, die fanden, man könne auch mit Fotos von

anderen Leuten, die Mitgliedern der königlichen Familie ähnlich sähen, Geld machen. Sie nannten das Unternehmen «Lookalike Agency», und das war die erste Agentur dieser Art weltweit. Ich akzeptierte, fuhr nach London, traf die drei in einem kleinen Hinterzimmer und unterschrieb einen Vertrag, der ihnen 20 Prozent der Einnahmen sicherte. Das war 1972.

Ich muss aber hinzufügen, dass ich als junges Mädchen Sprech- und Schauspielstunden genommen habe. Es fiel mir also nicht schwer, als Schauspielerin zu arbeiten.

Arbeiten Sie für eine Agentur?
Ich arbeite seit jeher exklusiv mit einer Agentur. Wie zu Beginn bin ich dort noch immer das Aushängeschild für alle Lookalikes, die heute in der ganzen Welt gebucht werden.

Ich habe in meinem ganzen Leben überhaupt nur mit zwei Agenturen zusammengearbeitet. Ich bin ein loyaler Mensch. Die meisten Doubles organisieren sich jetzt per Internet. Sie brauchen keine Agenturen mehr und zahlen daher auch keine Vermittlungsgebühr. Ich hingegen bin für die Agenturen nach wie vor eine Art Geldanlage, genauso wie die anderen berühmten Doubles.

Bei welchen Veranstaltungen treten Sie auf?
Die Londoner Lookalike Agency von Susan Scott bietet mir passende Jobs an, und ich entscheide dann, ob ich sie annehme oder nicht. Vor ein paar Jahren wurde ich für einen «Ali G.»-Film angefragt, aber ich lehnte ab, weil meiner Meinung nach die Queen darin beleidigt wurde. Dafür hätte ich mich geschämt! Ich lese immer vorher das Drehbuch und entscheide dann. Beim «Austin Powers»-Film zum Beispiel habe ich gerne mitgemacht. Das war ein Heidenspass!

Ich werde gebucht für Familienfeiern, Rollen in Kino- oder Fernsehfilmen, Interviews im Radio oder im Fernsehen, Überraschungsauftritte usw. In diesem Zusammenhang möchte ich betonen, dass ich jederzeit für wohltätige Anlässe zur Verfügung stehe, auch für Auftritte in dem Dorf, in dem ich lebe – wenn nötig sogar im Weihnachtsmärchen. Ich hatte sogar schon einmal einen Gastauftritt bei «Big Brother».

Wissen Sie von irgendwelchen Schwierigkeiten anderer Doubles der königlichen Familie, weil ihr Verhalten beim Königshaus auf Missfallen stiess? Versucht man, Auftritte von Doubles zu beeinflussen oder gar zu verhindern?
Ich arbeite kaum mit anderen Doubles. Über meine Arbeit habe ich bisher nur Gutes gehört. Ich empfinde gegenüber dem Königshaus grossen Respekt, ich denke bei dem, was ich tue, aber auch an meine eigene Familie. Ich wollte immer, dass sie stolz auf mich ist.

Allerdings erinnere ich mich daran, dass mich vor Jahren einmal eine Dame ansprach und meinte: «Ich werde Sie in der Rolle als Queen übertrumpfen!» Sie bekam *einen* Auftrag, glaube ich. Das war's dann.

Wie und wann studieren Sie die Queen? Sicherlich ist da auch schauspielerisches Talent wichtig. Gibt es auch den Ehrgeiz, ihre Sprache und ihren Tonfall, also typische Ausdrucksweisen und Redefiguren, zu imitieren?
Am Anfang schaute ich mir die Weihnachtsgrüsse der Queen im Fernsehen an. Das war alles. Ihre Stimme und Eigenarten konnte ich leicht nachahmen. Auf eine Annonce im «Equity Magazine» hin suchte ich damals einen «Schauspieldoktor» in London auf. Sechs Wochen lang nahm ich wöchentlich eine bezahlte Stunde bei ihm. Ich spielte die Queen und er korrigierte mich. Das war eine Investition. Am Schluss meinte er, ich sei nun perfekt.

Besuchen Sie offizielle Auftritte der Königin? Haben Sie sie jemals persönlich getroffen?
Erste Frage: Nein. Ich kann die Queen im Fernsehen beobachten. Sie wird älter, so wie ich. Zweite Frage: Diese Frage beantworte ich nie.

Ist es nicht kompliziert und auch teuer, sich mit der eleganten Garderobe und den richtigen Accessoires auszustatten? Wie wichtig ist die äusserliche «Verwandlung» für Ihre innere Haltung und als Vorbereitung auf die Rolle?
Viele Jahre lang liess ich Näherinnen die Kleider der Queen, die ich in Zeitschriften usw. fand, kopieren. In den ersten Jahren hatte ich zudem das Glück, dass mich berühmte Modeschöp-

fer ansprachen, die mit Theaterproduzenten in Kontakt waren. Hin und wieder verkaufen Theater nämlich ihr Inventar, und da werde ich im Voraus eingeladen zu kaufen, was ich will. **Ich habe wunderschöne Kleider und Accessoires! Ich besitze auch das Originalkleid aus der «Nackten Kanone». Paramount hat es mir geschenkt.**

Die Fotositzungen mit Niklaus Spoerri verliefen sicherlich anders als Ihre sonstigen Engagements. Was dachten Sie, als Sie von seinem Projekt erfuhren? Waren Sie anfangs skeptisch?
Ich mochte Niklaus und seine Art zu reden gleich bei unserem ersten Treffen. Ich gehe nach meinem Instinkt. Er macht gute Arbeit. Da bin ich nie skeptisch.

Und was dachten Sie über die Idee, in Ihrer eigenen Wohnung als Queen zu posieren?
Das ist nichts Neues. Der Hintergrund ist wichtig. ENTWEDER IST MAN EIN PROFI ODER MAN IST KEINER. Niklaus und ich sind Profis!

Was halten Sie von der Idee, eine Art Verzeichnis von Doppelgängern anzulegen? Kennen Sie Ihre «Kollegen»?
Vor Jahren gab es beim Film und im Theater Doubles, die auftraten, wenn die wirklichen Schauspieler eine Pause machten. Damals gab es dafür nur das Wort «Stand-in». Von dem Augenblick an, als ich mit dem Wort «Lookalike» kam, wurde «Stand-in» plötzlich nie mehr verwendet. Das Wort «Lookalike» gibt es nur wegen mir, verstehen Sie? Ich habe einen nachhaltigen Kult losgetreten, der vielen Menschen Arbeit gibt.

Wie ist im Allgemeinen die Reaktion der Leute, wenn Sie als Queen auftreten? Bemerken Sie Hochachtung oder Respekt, oder verhalten sich die Zuschauer/Besucher eher neutral? Anders gefragt: Haben Sie das Gefühl, dass Ihr Publikum immer klar zwischen Ihnen und Ihrer Rolle unterscheidet?
Die Leute sind einfach fröhlich, sie lachen und wollen mir die Hand schütteln. Ich mache das ja nun schon seit Jahren, und die Leute mögen

mich wirklich. Das ist wunderbar. Ich habe der königlichen Familie immer Respekt gezollt. Ich durfte Leute aus der Oberschicht und dem Königshaus kennenlernen.

Ausserdem bin ich bekannt. Einmal sprach mich eine Dame an und meinte mit einem sehr freundlichen Lächeln: «Jeannette, Sie haben eine Laufmasche in Ihrem Strumpf.» Da ich zu Auftritten immer Ersatzkleidung mitnehme, bin ich mit meiner Assistentin in den Umkleideraum gegangen und habe einfach die Strümpfe ausgewechselt. Ich finde das Publikum immer grossartig, in Grossbritannien und auch im Ausland. Für die Leute bin ich wie eine alte Freundin.

Vor zwei Jahren war ich auf Urlaub in Paphos auf Zypern. Meine Agentin rief mich an und sagte: «Jeannette, da sind zwei Russen bei Ihnen, die Sie interviewen wollen.» Ich konnte es nicht glauben! Swetlana und Pawlow waren den ganzen weiten Weg zu meinem Bungalow in Paphos gereist, machten ein Interview, schossen ein paar Fotos und gingen wieder. Offenbar bin ich auch in Russland berühmt. Ich habe so viel von der Welt gesehen! Ich hatte das Privileg, die Grossen und Wichtigen zu treffen. Ich bin der glücklichste Mensch der Welt.

Die 1927 geborene Britin und ausgebildete Schauspielerin Jeannette Charles ist eine Wegbereiterin der internationalen Double-Szene. Seit 1971 verkörpert sie Queen Elizabeth II. In Grossbritannien ist Jeannette Charles selbst eine Berühmtheit. Sie war schon in zahlreichen Spielfilmen, Fernsehserien und Fernsehshows zu sehen. Den wohl grössten Auftritt ihrer Karriere hatte sie an der Seite von Leslie Nielsen im ersten Teil von David Zuckers Trilogie «Die nackte Kanone». Weiterhin spielte sie in «Austin Powers in Goldständer» und «Hilfe, die Amis kommen» mit Chevy Chase und war zudem in Werbekampagnen, beispielsweise für «The Who», «Status Quo» und «Queen», zu sehen.

Das Interview führte Silvia Jaklitsch per E-Mail, Juli 2011.
Auf den Seiten 67/68 sehen Sie Jeannette Charles.

"You are either professional or not"

Interview with the Queen Elizabeth II lookalike Jeannette Charles

How long have you been playing the role of the Queen?
Since 1971.

Were you discovered as the Queen, or did you recognise your talent yourself?
As teenagers the young princesses were taken to countries around the world in completion of their education. They were taught inside the Palace and did not, as the young royals do today, associate with the public – even attending public schools, as the younger royals do. I went to the Isle of Capri when I was 17 years old, where the young Princess Elizabeth had visited some weeks earlier and, to my amazement, when I was in Italy people called out "Princess Elizabeth" several times and clapped. I just did not understand until it was explained to me. That was the first time. The second time was when I went to Greenwich with my family, and a photographer was filming. He said to my mother, "May I have a photo of your daughter, she is so like Princess Elizabeth". My mother was horrified. In those days there was a mystique about the royals.

In 1971 I was at home deciding what to give my husband as a birthday present, and in the local paper I saw: "Sittings a Speciality". I wrote to the photographer who was advertising, and had a portrait taken. She said to me, "You are
so like the Queen. I write a weekly column in the paper. May I write how alike to the Queen you are?" I laughed, I thought it was funny. So it started.

They were branching out on the TV stations. More and more of them. Up to then it had only been BBC. The phone calls began. Locally and then nationally. Interviews, incessantly. Then I was asked to appear in comedy shows that were known to have royalty as admirers. I was, of course, outfitted with the GEAR. I thought it was fun but at that time the only agents were model or theatrical agencies. I never asked for money but I had contracts signed when I was at the studios, and money was sent to me.

The word "lookalike" was made up in 1971 by a David Thurlow, a journalist for the "Daily Express". He said to me, "You are the double of the Queen". I said I was shorter, so he then said, "you look so much like her I will call you a LOOKALIKE", and that was the first time it was used. I had a letter from three photographers who had decided there was money to be made by photographing other people who looked like members of the royal family, and they said they would call it the "Lookalike Agency", the first in the world. So I agreed, and went to London to meet them in a very small room, and signed a contract that they would take 20 per cent, in 1972.

I must add that as a young girl I had taken elocution lessons and acting lessons so it was easy for me to work in the studios as an actress.

Do you work for an agency?
I do still work with an agency. I am still the Premier Artiste as I began the lookalike work, which has spawned all over the World.

In all of my career I have only ever been involved with two agencies. I am loyal. Most lookalikes, whoever they are, usually do their own thing now using the Internet, doing without agencies as then they do not pay commission. Bit I, on the other hand, represent a kind of investment, just like the other well-known doubles.

What kind of events are you engaged for?
The Lookalike Agency, owned by Susan Scott in London. When she has possible jobs for me I decide if I want to accept. For example, some years ago I was asked to be in an "Ali G."-movie but I declined as I thought the part was demeaning to the Queen, and I would have been ashamed. I always read the script and then I decide, as I did with the "Austin Powers"-movie I was in, "Goldmember". It was fun and I enjoyed it.

Other jobs: Personal appearances at family celebrations, film parts, TV parts, interviews, whether on TV or radio, surprise appearances

etc. I must add that I will always consider charity appearances, or indeed appearances in my local village. If necessary, for example, in the xmas panto. I was even in a "Big Brother" episode.

Do you know of any difficulties that other doubles of the royal family may have had because their behaviour might not be approved of by the royal household? Are attempts made to exert an influence on, or even to prevent doubles' appearances?
I hardly ever work with other doubles. I have never heard of any comment being passed over my work except praise. I have always respected royalty, but I also think of my own family: I have always wanted them to be proud of me.

I do remember that years ago someone came up to me and said, "I am going to be more important than you are acting as the Queen." She did one job, I think, and that was it.

When do you have opportunities to observe the Queen, and how? Do you also try to imitate the language or a certain tone of voice, and use certain typical expressions or figures of speech?
At the beginning I watched the Queen's Christmas message, that was all. I could perfect her voice and mannerisms easily. I also answered an advert in "Equity Magazine" for an "Act Doctor". He was in London and I paid him for an hour every week for six weeks. I performed as the Queen and he helped me with performances. It was an investment. At the end he said I was perfect!

Do you visit official appearances of the Queen? Have you ever met the Queen personally?
1st question: No I do not. I can observe her on TV. She is ageing, as I am.
2nd question: I never answer that question.

Isn't it very complicated and expensive to acquire the appropriate wardrobe and accessories? How important is the external "transformation" for the inner posture and preparing to assume your role?
Over many years I have had seamstresses copy gowns that I have seen in magazines etc. I was also very lucky in the early years to have been spoken to by well-known couturiers who had contact with theatrical producers, and now and again when theatres sell their stocks I am invited to go in advance and buy anything I want. I have the most beautiful gowns and accessories. I also have the original gown from Paramount's "The Naked Gun". They presented it to me as a gift.

The photo session with Niklaus Spoerri was certainly unusual. What were your thoughts when he told you about the project? Were you initially sceptical?
The first time I saw Niklaus I liked him and his way of speaking to me. I go on instinct. He is good at his job. I am never sceptical.

What did you think of the idea of posing as the Queen in your own apartment?
Nothing new in that. It is the background that is important. YOU ARE EITHER PROFESSIONAL OR NOT. We both are.

What do you think of the idea of creating a kind of doubles' directory? Do you know any of your "colleagues"?
Years ago in the film world and on the stage they would have a "stand-in", that was someone who would appear as the actor/actress whilst the genuine artist would have a rest. That was the only word used then, when I used the word "lookalike" all of a sudden the word "stand-in" was never used. You see, the word "lookalike" came about because of me. I started a cult that has carried on and given many people work.

What, in general, is the reaction of people around you when you appear as the Queen? Do you notice something like reverence or respect, or are people more impartial towards you, that is, do they make a clear distinction between your portrayal of the Queen and the real Queen?
People always have a lovely smile on their face and want to shake my hand. I am like an old friend. I have been around for years and people genuinely warm towards me. That is wonderful. I have never been anything but respectful to the Royal Family. I have mixed with the upper classes and with royalty.

I am accepted. Only once did a lady come up to me, and with a very sweet smile said "Jeannette, you have a run in your stocking", and as I always have extra of everything when I work I went with my helper to my room and changed the stocking. I find that people are lovely, whether here or overseas. I am like an old friend.

Two years ago I was holidaying in Paphos, Cyprus, when I had a phone call from my agent. She said "Jeannette, two Russians want to interview you". I could not believe it. Svetlana and Pavlov came all the way to my bungalow in Paphos, had an interview, took a few photos and left. Evidently, I am very well known over there. I have been to so much of the world. I am very fortunate to have been with the great and the important. I am most blessed.

British woman Jeannette Charles, born in 1927 and a trained actress, is a pioneer of the international lookalike scene. She has been impersonating Queen Elizabeth II since 1971. Jeannette Charles is herself a celebrity in Great Britain. She has appeared in numerous feature films, television series and shows. Probably the biggest moment of her career was appearing alongside Leslie Nielsen in the first part of David Zucker's trilogy "The Naked Gun". She also appeared in "Austin Powers in Goldmember" and "National Lampoon's European Vacation" with Chevy Chase, as well as in advertising campaigns, such as for the "The Who", "Status Quo" and "Queen".

Interview by Silvia Jaklitsch via email, July 2011.
On page 67/68 you find the photographies of Jeannette Charles.

Wenn die Menschen sich verdoppeln

von Manfred Prisching

Menschliche Physiognomie: Nase, Ohren, Augen, Haare – eine klare Vorgabe. Umso verwunderlicher ist es, wie viele unterschiedliche Typen, Rassen, Gesichter, Individualitäten innerhalb dieses «Grundmodells» möglich sind. *Jeder ein anderer, jede eine andere.* Freilich ist das Unterscheidungsvermögen durch kulturelle Zugehörigkeit eingeschränkt: Für Europäer sehen die meisten Asiaten ziemlich ähnlich aus. Aber dennoch: Wir halten es grundsätzlich für eine Besonderheit, ja eine Laune der Natur, wenn Menschen einander ähneln. Eineiige Zwillinge fallen auf. Unähnlichkeit ist der Normalfall: Menschen sind unterschiedlich. Sie sind es in Mentalität, Werten, Auffassungen, Weltbildern, aber sie sind es auch im Körperbau und vor allem im Gesicht. Wir nehmen Unterschiede wahr, weil die Verhältnisse der einzelnen Gesichtspartien zueinander verschieden sind. Das Gesicht drückt den Menschen aus, seine Gemütsregungen, durch die jeweilige Kontraktion der mimischen Muskulatur. Das Gesicht ist der «Spiegel der Seele».

Manche müssen ähnliche Seelen haben. Denn einige Personen sind nicht so unterschiedlich. Es gibt Ähnlichkeiten, und diese können manchmal fast zur Gleichheit werden. Doppelgänger ähneln einer anderen Person so stark, dass man sie mit dieser verwechseln könnte. Das mag im Alltagsleben geschehen: Irgendein Passant mag dem Fleischermeister aus der nächsten Strasse so ähnlich sehen, dass man ihn irrtümlich grüsst. Irgendeine Frau mag für jene Lehrerin gehalten werden, die vor zwei Jahrzehnten in der hiesigen Grundschule unterrichtet hat. Aber derlei Alltags-Verwechslungen sind nicht allzu interessant, obwohl berühmte Komödien auf solchen Verwechslungen ihre Geschichte aufbauen.

Prominente Verdoppelungen

In einer spätmodernen Gesellschaft sind es nicht die traditionellen Helden, die imitiert werden. Wenn man *Prominenten* ähnelt, kann man dies zum Geschäft machen. Die Menschen wollen Prominente sehen, und allenfalls sind sie mit deren Imitationen zufrieden. Wo das Doppelgängertum zum Business wird, wissen marktorientierte Doppelgänger um ihre theatralische Aufgabe. Es gibt sie, die «wirklichen» Doppelgänger, die den Originalen ähneln, die sich auch durch ein wenig Nachhilfe Mühe geben, sich den imaginierten Personen anzunähern, bis hin zu den Accessoires. Sie wollen unterscheidbar werden, ohne den Unterschied in der Person zu leugnen. Sie spielen mit der Identität eines anderen, ohne das Spiel zu verheimlichen. Es ist ein gemeinsames Spiel von Imitanten und Zusehern.

Doppelgänger bilden andere Menschen ab – prominente Menschen natürlich, ansonsten würde man sie nicht «erkennen». In einer spätmodernen Gesellschaft, in der jede soziale Übersichtlichkeit geschwunden ist, in einer Mediengesellschaft, in der alles, was von Belang ist, in den – vorzugsweise elektronischen – Medien dargeboten wird und in der alles, was in den Medien vorkommt, von Belang ist, ist Prominenz ein Selektionsmodus: Mit der Ressource Aufmerksamkeit muss effizient umgegangen werden. Prominenz ist üblicherweise von jeder Leistung entkoppelt. *Prominent ist, wer prominent ist* – da gibt es keine Referenzen ausserhalb des «Spiels». Er oder sie muss nichts geleistet haben. Er oder sie kann dumm sein. Er muss auch keinen ganzen Satz herausbringen. Aber prominent ist, wer in «Seitenblicke»-Sendungen einen Platz eingeräumt bekommt, mit Prominenten zu verkehren pflegt oder über den roten Teppich schreiten darf. Prominent ist, wer als prominent eingestuft wird, aus welchen Gründen auch immer.

Die doppelgängerische Imitation von prominenten Personen ist ein Betätigungsfeld, mit Hilfe dessen sich manche Menschen ihren Lebensunterhalt erarbeiten. Sie treten als Reprä-

Das Doppelgängertum findet sich in der eigenen Seele.

sentanten der prominenten Person auf. Es gibt Unternehmen, die Doppelgänger vermitteln. Eine Webseite untergliedert die Kategorien: Promi-Doubles, Royal-Doubles, Politiker-Doubles, Sportler-Doubles, Fussballer-Doubles. Gesonderte Kategorien gibt es etwa für Double-Shows oder Bond-Doubles. Unter den Royal-Doubles sind etwa die englische Königin, Prinz Charles oder Lady Diana gefragt.

Doppelgänger sind als Imitanten gefragt, als Darsteller von Prominenz, die man dorthin einladen kann, wo die Originale nicht hingehen würden – und sie sind billiger. Es wäre ein Kategorienfehler, Madonna zum Feuerwehrfest einladen zu wollen; aber eine Madonna-Darstellerin kann dafür engagiert werden. Beim Feuerwehrfest wird es eher ein DJ Ötzi-Darsteller oder beim Pensionistenausflug ein Roberto Blanco-Imitator sein. Es werden auch Hochzeiten gefeiert, bei denen man sich von Elvis Presley «ansingen» lassen darf – in Las Vegas gibt es eine grosse Auswahl an Hochzeits-Packages mit solchen Höhepunkten.

Doppelgängertum kann für Prominente eine Auszeichnung darstellen: Wenn das Publikum erst einmal ein Double attraktiv findet, dann ist man *wirklich* prominent – was nicht bedeu-

tet, dass die dargestellten Originale nicht auf manche kabarettistischen Darstellungen ihrer Person verzichten könnten. George W. Bush ist nicht stolz auf seine Doubles, und schon gar nicht darauf, was diese bei ihren Auftritten zu bieten haben. Wie immer in solchen Fällen gilt dennoch für viele Prominente, was auch über Karikaturen gesagt wird: Noch schlimmer wäre es, kein Double zu haben. Denn dann ist man nicht wirklich prominent.

Nostalgische Verdoppelungen

Wenn man in Las Vegas über den Boulevard schlendert, begegnet man dem erwähnten Elvis Presley in mehrfacher Ausführung. Die Doppelgänger stehen sich schon im Weg. Es sind nicht Doppel-, sondern Vielfachgänger. Auch wenn wir die Jahrzehnte alten Gerüchte kennen, dass er, der «King», in Wahrheit nicht gestorben sei, werden wir die entsprechenden Gestalten doch als Doppelgänger erkennen. Keinen Augenblick kommt uns die Idee, dass die besagten Gerüchte nun ihre empirische Bestätigung gefunden haben könnten, da wir den Sänger doch leibhaftig vor uns haben. Vielmehr wissen wir, dass wir es mit einem Quasi-Schauspieler zu tun haben, der aus den nostalgischen Gefühlen der Boulevard-Flaneure, die sich mit ihm gerne fotografieren lassen, ein paar Geldscheine lukrieren möchte.

Professioneller sind meist jene Aufführungen, in denen Doppelgänger den Glanz aus alten Zeiten heraufbeschwören, von Marilyn Monroe bis Humphrey Bogart. Das *Rat Pack* aus dem Sands Hotel tritt wieder auf – Frank Sinatra, Sammy Davis Jr. und Dean Martin, manchmal begleitet von anderen «Stars» dieser Jahre. Sie lassen als Doppelgänger die «alten Zeiten» wieder auferstehen. Die ganz grossen Stars sind natürlich bevorzugte ImitationskandidatInnen: Marlene Dietrich, Michael Jackson, Falco, Charlie Chaplin; aber auch Mr. Bean. Wer immer berühmt ist, kann gedoubelt werden: Bruce Willis und Paris Hilton, Adriano Celentano und Tina Turner. Durchschnittspreis bei einer Vermittlungsagentur: 30 Minuten für 1500 Euro; aber es gibt auch niedrigere und höhere Offerten, je nach Qualität, Aufwand und Nachfrage. Wenn

der Imitator von Berühmtheiten auch schon berühmt wird, steigt der Preis.

In den meisten Fällen werden «echte» Personen gedoubelt. Im Fall von James Bond sind es aber Doppelgänger von Schauspielern, die den «echten» James Bond darstellen, die literarische Figur des englischen Geheimagenten, die in den Köpfen des Publikums mit den Bildern seiner Darsteller – Brosnan, Craig, Connery – verschmolzen ist. Da werden dann – bei den Doppelgänger-Auftritten – auch bekannte Szenen nachgespielt: Bond gegen Goldfinger. Der Brosnan-Doppelgänger ist dann der Bond-Doppelgänger, die Simulation des «echten» James Bond.

Gruselige Verdoppelungen

Doppelgängertum hat auch andere Facetten, weniger unterhaltsame. Geschichten werden erzählt, in denen man sich selbst als Doppelgänger erlebt – doch es sind meist keine Geschichten, die man erleben möchte. Im Moment des Todes schwebe man – wie manche, die wider Erwarten noch einmal ins Leben gefunden haben, berichten – aus dem Leib nach oben und sehe sich selbst, gleichsam verdoppelt, auf dem Totenbette oder im zertrümmerten Auto liegen. Abergläubische Menschen wissen von Begegnungen mit Gestalten zu berichten, in denen sie sich selbst erkennen; auch das eine gruselige Sache: Wenn man sich selbst als Doppelgänger identifiziert, gilt das seit jeher als böses Omen. Aber es kann auch gut ausgehen. Auf einer Webseite, die sich mit paranormalen Phänomenen befasst, heisst es: «Unter einem Doppelgänger im esoterischen Sinn versteht man das immaterielle, feinstoffliche Pendant eines Menschen, das häufig völlig unvermittelt auftaucht, oft in Momenten der Gefahr.» Es werden Anekdoten über Menschen erzählt, denen eine solche Begegnung widerfahren ist. Aber es muss nicht jeder an Doppelgänger glauben, die, wie beschrieben, gleichzeitig «feinstofflich» und «immateriell» sein sollen.

Wie viele Personen bin ich? Das hat man sich in Erzählungen schon vor Jahrhunderten gefragt, vor allem dann, wenn der Doppelgänger, das eigene Selbst, ganz anders ist als die

Person, mit der man sonst Umgang zu pflegen glaubt: Wenn das Selbst plötzlich zum Fremden wird, zu einem bösen oder peinlichen Fremden. Da werden das Gute und das Böse, Körper und Geist, Verstand und Leidenschaft abgebildet: Dr. Jekyll und Mr. Hyde. Man erschrickt vor seinem Doppelgänger. Man hätte nicht gedacht, dass auch diese Wesenskomponenten zum eigenen Selbst gehören. Man kann das mythisch betrachten oder – ganz einfach – psychoanalytisch: Sigmund Freud hat eine der grossen Beleidigungen für das Selbstbewusstsein des Menschen geliefert, indem er die Selbsteinschätzung des Homo sapiens in Zweifel ge-

Die Vermehrung der Doppelgänger verdoppelt die Prominenz, aber auch die Prominenz expandiert.

zogen hat. Da mag dieser sich als Höhepunkt der Aufgeklärtheit rühmen – doch es gibt einen «Untergrund», dem Bewusstsein kaum zugänglich, ein psychisches «Schattenreich», in dem Leidenschaften und Grausamkeiten, Emotionen und Unanständigkeiten herrschen. Das Doppelgängertum findet sich in der eigenen Seele.

Auch wenn die Spätmoderne gerne mit mythischen Figuren spielt, mit Hexen und Rittern, mit Vampiren und Werwölfen, sind es doch technisch-elektronische Errungenschaften, die es nahelegen, von der Erschaffung künstlicher Personen zu erzählen; oder von digital konstruierten Individuen, die in einer Welt leben, in der sich der Unterschied zwischen Virtualität und Wirklichkeit nicht mehr ausmachen lässt. Computer können Personen unschwer verdoppeln – oder gar vervielfachen. Science-Fiction-Filme malen genetische Versuche aus, die vor oder nach der Geburt stattfinden können, gesteuert von Geheimdiensten oder potenziellen Welteroberern, Versuche, in denen Doppelgänger, etwa durch Klonen, entstehen – als Super-Menschen, als Kampfmaschinen, als Hybride, mit transnatürlichen Fähigkeiten. Wir sind mit

diesen Doppelgängern in zahlreichen Filmen konfrontiert. Eine spätmoderne Gesellschaft, die auf Identität versessen ist, muss die Verdoppelung einer Person besonders unheimlich finden: eine Entindividualisierung, die das Einzige aufhebt, was die spätmoderne Gesellschaft noch hat – das Selbst, die Einzigartigkeit, die Authentizität.

Praktische Verdoppelungen

Phantasievolle Storys dieser Art sind eine Variante, mit Doppelgängern umzugehen, die Banalitäten der wirklichen Welt sind etwas anderes. «Echte» Doppelgänger, die in der Tat so aussehen wie die jeweils repräsentierten Originale, hatten unterschiedliche Funktionen. Totalitäre Herrscher, denen ein Anschlag vonseiten ihres «geliebten Volkes» drohte, haben sich (angeblich) verdoppelte «Ichs» gehalten – wie dies etwa von Saddam Hussein kolportiert wird. Eine ideale Ausgangssituation, um Verschwörungstheorien zu produzieren.

Schauspieler, die als unersetzlich gelten oder die gut behandelt werden müssen, haben ein Double für gefährliche oder pikante Szenen. Damit sie sich nicht den Hals brechen, werden Stuntmen eingesetzt. Es handelt sich dabei um «Body-Doubles». Es gibt auch «Stimmen-Doubles»: Synchronsprecher wirken ebenfalls im Hintergrund, sie sind nur die Stimme des visuellen Originals. In allen diesen Fällen tritt der Körper- oder Stimmen-Doppelgänger nicht als Doppelgänger auf, ja das Wesen seiner Existenz beruht gerade darauf, dass er gar nicht wahrgenommen wird. Wenn er seine Aufgabe gut macht, wird für Zuseherinnen und Zuseher nicht einmal ersichtlich, dass es einen Doppelgänger gibt. Er verschmilzt mit dem Original. Soweit er – als Gestalt oder Stimme – wahrgenommen wird, wird er – im Film – als das Original gesehen, als Repräsentant einer anderen Person. Es wird verschleiert, dass es sich um einen Doppelgänger handelt. Das unterscheidet sich von jenen Fällen, in denen kein Hehl daraus gemacht wird, dass das Original imitiert, nachgemacht, verdoppelt wird; dass die Echtheit simuliert wird; dass die Besonderheit eben in der Täuschung liegt. Perfekte Täuschung ist perfekte Leistung – zugleich aber ist die Täuschung gar keine Täuschung, weil wir darüber Bescheid wissen. Doppelgänger lügen nicht. Wir wollen den Bluff. Das ist ja auch in anderen Lebensbereichen so: etwa in der Politik.

Phantasievolle Verdoppelungen

Es gehört zu ihren Besonderheiten, dass die Menschen zuweilen von dem Drang überwältigt werden, sich als andere darzustellen, zu dekorieren, zu inszenieren. Menschen lieben *Masken*. Es sind verschiedene Zeiten und Anlässe für die Maskierung vorgesehen – etwa der Fasching. Da treten die Kinder als Seeräuber oder Hexe, als Teufel oder Engel, als Vampir oder Cowboy auf – und die Erwachsenen sind nicht viel einfallsreicher. Sie sind Imitate, aber sie wollen dies auch nicht leugnen. Der kleine Bub verkleidet sich als Winnetou, und auch wenn er sich in seine Rolle hineinlebt, werden weder er noch seine Umwelt auf die Idee kommen, dass es sich um Winnetou – reinkarniert in einem kindlichen Körper – handelt. Der Bub «spielt» Winnetou, er ist die «Darstellung» des Häuptlings – aber er ist ein Imitat, das als solches kenntlich bleibt; kein Replikat, keine möglichst «originalgetreue», «verwechselbare» Kopie, die den Anschein erweckt, Winnetou sei auferstanden; ein Rollenspiel.

Das «Spiel» erlaubt es, in andere Rollen zu schlüpfen. Manche wollen ein attraktives touristisches Umfeld bieten, und so heuern sie Leute an, die sich in die Ritterrüstung werfen und ein Turnier imitieren, auf dass sich das Flair einer mittelalterlichen Burg vertiefe. Da mag auch schon der Doppelgänger des Richard Löwenherz auftreten; was ohne grossen Aufwand deshalb geschehen kann, weil man nicht weiss, wie der «echte» Richard Löwenherz ausgesehen hat – und weil man nicht viel dazu tun muss, um in einer Ritterrüstung die erforderliche «Ähnlichkeit» herzustellen. In den Südstaaten der USA werden von einschlägigen Vereinen Kampfszenen und Schlachten aus dem Bürgerkrieg «nachgespielt», und da mag auch schon mal der «Doppelgänger» von General Lee im Spiele sein. Man legt Wert auf passende Uniformen, Ausrüstung, Accessoires – die Ähnlichkeit zum General wird

angestrebt (und deshalb benötigt der Akteur jedenfalls einen Bart), aber es geht ihm nicht darum, einen wirklich täuschenden Doppelgänger vorzuführen, auf dass ein staunendes Publikum die Wiederbelebung des konföderierten Helden feiere. Die Gegenwartsgesellschaft ist eine visualisierte Gesellschaft, wir leben mit Bildern, und diese führen uns andauernd Personen vor. Wir haben Brad Pitt im eigenen Wohnzimmer, eine Abbildung, eine Simulation, eine Repräsentation von Brad Pitt – und doch das Gefühl, dass wir mit ihm gewissermassen «vertraut» sind. Da ist es nur ein kleiner Schritt zu einer «realistischeren» Brad Pitt-Imagination, wenn der Imitator leibhaftig auftritt.

In der Vertrautheit des Umgangs sind uns die Stars «nahe». «Ich» könnte auch Brad Pitt sein. «Partielle Doppelgänger-Rollen» sind in einer spätmodernen Gesellschaft nicht unüblich, in der jeder zum Star werden möchte, auch wenn er dafür nicht die geringste Eignung besitzt oder die geringste Voraussetzung aufweist. Karaoke, der Gesangswettbewerb für Unbegabte, spielt gleichsam mit der Doppelgängerschaft. Man singt, was üblicherweise ein Star singt, einen bekannten Song, den jeder identifizieren kann; oder man singt das Lied nicht einmal, sondern tut nur so. Man täuscht niemanden, man ist bloss ein Doppelgänger unter Vorbehalt – aber man kann sich doch ein wenig als Star fühlen. Die Verdoppelung findet als solche ihre Wertschätzung: Da es mittlerweile Casting-Shows für alles gibt, gibt es auch eine Doppelgänger-Casting-Show in unterschiedlichen Alterskategorien. Im Aufruf heisst es: «Überzeugen Sie unsere prominente Jury mit Ihrer gesanglichen Leistung! Dann verwirklichen professionelle Stylisten sowie Tanz- und Gesangscoaches Ihre unglaubliche Verwandlung in das Abbild Ihrer Stars.»

Doppelte Verdoppelungen

Gute Doppelgänger – von attraktiven «Stars» – haben ein Problem: ihre Doppelgänger. Der Markt für englische Königinnen und Prinzen ist beschränkt, und es herrscht Konkurrenz zwischen den Darstellern und Darstellerinnen. Da kommt es schon einmal vor, dass ein Anbieter damit wirbt, nur er sei der «echte Doppel-

gänger», alle anderen hätten sich ohne Erfolg redlich oder unredlich bemüht. Auch die Doppelgänger von Prominenten sind um ihre Prominenz bemüht.

Die Vermehrung der Doppelgänger verdoppelt die Prominenz, aber auch die Prominenz expandiert. Wenn Prominenz nur auf (medialer) Bekanntheit beruht, gibt es in der spätmodernen Gesellschaft unter dem Druck von Sensation und Aktualität kein langsames Wachsen von Prominenz mehr, sondern immer mehr bloss die künstliche Erzeugung einer solchen. Nichtssagende Individuen werden – meist nur für kurze Zeit – zur Prominenz gekürt: als Karikaturen einer Prominenz, als Spielmaterial einer zynisch-aufgekratzten Journalistentruppe, als «Prominentenproletariat».

Die künstliche Produktion von Prominenz erfasst immer weitere Personengruppen. Längst bemüht man sich, Fussballer in diese Kategorie einzuschleusen, besonders dann, wenn sie Models oder Starlets heiraten; dann hat man gleichsam Quasi-Prominenz im Doppelpack. Die wechselseitige Attraktivität muss wohl damit zu tun haben, dass die betreffenden Personen in derselben Art von Geisteswelt zu Hause sind. Die Knappheit an potenziellen Gestalten lässt auch auf Rennfahrer, Köche und Friseure zurückgreifen. Es sagt einiges über eine Gesellschaft aus, wenn die Friseure der Stars zu Stars werden. Dies ist nur ein Aspekt der epidemischen Entgeistigung in einer Entertainment-Gesellschaft.

Während die drittklassigen VIPs über lokale Berühmtheit oder kurzfristige «Sternschnupperei» nicht hinauskommen, sind sie normalerweise keine Quelle für Doppelgängertum – nicht einmal dazu reicht es. Die Doppelgänger drängeln sich um die *First Class*-Prominenz. Der Markt für sie ist grösser, die Wiedererkennbarkeit unproblematisch, die Bekanntheit leichter darzustellen.

Kabarettistische Verdoppelungen

Die Doppelgänger prominenter Persönlichkeiten haben unterschiedliche Funktionen. Doppelgänger von Aristokraten oder gekrönten Häuptern werden anders eingesetzt als ein

Doppelgänger von Frank Sinatra. Der Imitator des Letzteren soll tatsächlich imitieren, möglichst ganz genau so singen wie das Original, auf dass das Publikum nostalgisch-romantisch dahinschmelze: *New York, New York.* Man würde die Erwartungshaltungen der Zuseherinnen und Zuseher gravierend verfehlen, würde man Frank Sinatra als miesen Mafioso oder abgewrackten Alkoholiker darstellen. Das Publikum will bewundern, sich sehnen, sich erinnern. Doppelgänger sind häufig Katalysatoren der eigenen Jugenderinnerungen – und der Sehnsüchte ohnehin.

Bei gekrönten Häuptern ist das anders: Wenn der Imitator von Prinz Charles auftritt, wird er nicht eine ernsthafte Rede über Stadt- und Architekturentwicklung von sich geben, sondern eine skurrile Gestalt inszenieren. Auch Politiker-Imitatoren werden meist nicht als «seriöse Vortragende» eingeladen: Die Darsteller von Bill Clinton und George W. Bush werden ihre Gestalten wohl unterschiedlich anlegen, Bush vermutlich mit wenig Verstand und Clinton mit viel Schlüpfrigkeit. Auch «Angela Merkel» wird wohl ein paar belämmerte Reden halten.

Boris Becker mag eine Figur sein, die für einen kabarettistischen Imitator zweifelsohne einiges hergibt. Ansonsten tut man sich bei Fussballern schwerer, sich vorzustellen, was auf der Bühne geboten werden könnte. Von einer Agentur wird angeboten: «Die Beste DJ Ötzi Double Show – Alpenpower Pur Live. Mit zwei hübschen Tänzerinnen in Original Steirertrachten. Die ultimative Partystimmung! Für Ihr Vereins-, Firmen- und Stadtfest. Bei Geschäftseröffnung, Jubiläum, Produktpräsentation und auf dem Messestand.» Gewisse Qualitäten wird auch die Darstellerin von Pamela Anderson aufzubieten haben, und das werden andere sein als bei Hannah Montana.

Marketing-Verdoppelungen

Ein Haupteinsatzgebiet von Doppelgängern ist die Werbung. Der Clooney-Klon ist billiger als das Original (auch wenn der Klon wohl Mühe haben wird, Schönheit und Souveränität des Originals zu erreichen). Werbung mit Prominenten ist üblich und nicht wegzudenken, in manchen Fällen tun es aber auch Doubles. Das erspart Millionen.

Prominenz, Publizität, Aufmerksamkeit – das fliesst zusammen, und es macht einen geldwerten Vorteil aus. Michael Schumacher hat vor etlichen Jahren geklagt, als mit seinem Gesicht – d. h. mit der Person seines Doppelgängers – Werbung gemacht wurde, und das Landesgericht Stuttgart hat ihm recht gegeben, wegen Verletzung seines Persönlichkeitsrechtes. Doch sind nicht alle Doppelgänger-Auftritte untersagt. Nach Ansicht des Landesgerichts fallen solche Aktionen jedoch nicht unter Kunstfreiheit, da die Auftritte des Doubles keine eigenständige künstlerische Leistung seien, sondern eine möglichst genaue Nachahmung des Originals bezweckten. Diese Beurteilung wird freilich den unterschiedlichen Leistungen von Doppelgängern nicht gerecht, insbesondere dann, wenn der Auftritt durchaus originelle (zum Beispiel kabarettistische) Elemente enthält.

Voyeuristische Verdoppelungen

Dennoch bleibt die Frage, was an den Doppelgängern reizt. Man könnte sich ja auch die umgekehrte Reaktion vorstellen: eine Verärgerung des Publikums, das man mit Nachahmung abspeist; der Verdacht, für dumm verkauft zu werden; eine Verstimmung darüber, dass man nicht einmal in die Nähe der wirklichen Prominenz gerät, sondern mit Ersatzlösungen zufriedengestellt wird. Doch das ist nicht der Fall. Doppelgänger befinden sich im Spannungsfeld von *Exhibitionismus* und *Voyeurismus*. Eine gewisse exhibitionistische Ader muss ihnen selbst zu eigen sein, wie allen Schauspielerinnen und Schauspielern; immerhin stellen sie aber nicht sich selbst zur Schau, sondern prominente Personen, denen eigentlich dieser Exhibitionismus in höherem Masse zuzuschreiben ist. Es ist also nur ein abgeleiteter, eben imitierter Exhibitionismus, den die Doppelgänger pflegen.

Der Voyeurismus des Publikums hingegen ist «echt». Man hat sich längst daran gewöhnt, dass in der medialen Welt das Privatleben prominenter Personen vermarktet und skrupellos dokumentiert wird. Die Berichterstattung darüber, wer mit wem ins Bett geht, wer Alkohol-probleme hat, wer sich ein Kind wünscht oder soeben adoptiert hat, wer mit Weinflaschen um sich geworfen hat und wer sich einer Abmagerungs- oder Entziehungskur unterzieht, ist Teil des Spiels. Es ist ein unablässig gelieferter, quantitativ zunehmender Strom von Trivialitäten, die zur Unterhaltung und Erschütterung der Menschen dienen. Die Gesellschaft wird zur Klatschrunde. Zaghafte Versuche, in Einzelfällen dem Publikum seinen Drang zum Voyeurismus streitig zu machen, werden mit Ungnädigkeit beantwortet. Die Visualisierung eines prominenten Lebens ist allgegenwärtig, die Zuseherschaft ist darauf trainiert, prominente Bilder – Bilder von Prominenten in allen Lebenslagen – zu sehen. Die Prominenz flaniert – mit elektronischen Methoden – alltäglich im eigenen Privatleben, als Abbild, Konstruktion, Metapher; eine visuelle Erzählung des wirklichen Menschen, der hinter dem Bild stecken mag. Es sind freilich «Produkte», «Symbole», «Homunculi», die in die Schlagzeilen und Sendungen Eingang finden, doch sie werden als «Menschen» verkauft. Gerade das ist ja Teil der Verkaufsstrategie, dass das Menschliche an den Kunstprodukten, oft gar das Allzumenschliche, herausgestrichen wird. Beim Publikum mischen sich dann Bewunderung und Schadenfreude, Ehrfurcht und Mitleid, und der Neid wird (zeitweise) ein wenig gebremst. Und es gibt eine Moral von der Geschichte: Wie man sieht, macht auch Geld nicht glücklich, selbst der Ruhm sichert kein gutes Leben. Das Märchen ist ein Märchen. Das beruhigt für eine Weile, wenn es auch die Märchenhaftigkeit der eigenen Lebenserwartungen nicht zerstört.

Da ist der Doppelgänger auch nur eine andere Erzählung, ein anderes Abbild, eine andere Version des Transfers von Prominenz und Illusion, Sehnsucht und Märchenhaftigkeit in den Wahrnehmungsbereich der Zuseher. In einer Welt der Bilder wird alles zum Bild. In einer Welt der Simulationen wird alles zur Simulation. In einer Welt der Verdoppelungen sind die Doppelgänger fast schon die Originale.

When People Duplicate themselves

by Manfred Prisching

The parameters of human physiognomy seem very clear: nose, ears, eyes, hair. It is all the more surprising then how many different types, races, faces, and individualities are possible within this basic model. *Every man, every woman is unique.* Of course the ability to distinguish is restricted by the culture we belong to: for Europeans, most Orientals look quite similar. Nevertheless we consider it to be something quite special, even a quirk of nature, if people are similar to one another. Identical twins stand out. Dissimilarity is the norm. Each person is different. They have different mindsets, values, interpretations, views of the world, but they are also different in physique, and above all in their faces. We perceive differences because the proportions of individual facial parts vary. The face is an expression of the person and their frame of mind, as seen through contractions of the facial muscles. It is said that the face is the "mirror of the soul".

Some people must have similar souls then, because a number of people are not very different from each other. They look similar and can sometimes become almost identical. A lookalike appears so similar to another person that they could be mistaken for the other person. This may happen in everyday situations: a passer-by might seem so similar to the butcher from the next street that he is greeted by mistake. A woman may be mistaken for the teacher who taught in the local school 20 years ago. Such everyday mix-ups are not all that striking, even though the plots of some famous comedies are based on such mistaken identities.

Celebrity Doubles

In a late-modern society it is not traditional heroes that are imitated. If somebody looks like a *celebrity* they can make money out of it. People want to see celebrities, and if need be they will make do with imitations of them. When being a double becomes a job, market-orientated look-alikes understand their theatrical task. They exist, these "real" doubles, who resemble the originals, and who make an effort to study the original, coming close to the appearance of the imagined person, right down to the accessories. They want to become indistinguishable, without denying the difference in the person. They play with the identity of someone else without making a secret of it. This is a game played between imitator and viewers.

Doubles represent other people – important people of course – otherwise they would not be "recognised". In a late-modern society in which all social delineations have faded, in a media society in which everything that matters is offered in the – preferably electronic – media and in which everything which appears in the media matters, prominence is a mode of selection: the resource of attention has to be managed efficiently. Prominence is normally separated from any achievement. *A prominent person is one who stands out* – there are no references outside the "game". They do not have to have achieved anything. They can be stupid. They don't need to utter a full sentence. But a prominent person is someone who is allowed to appear in celebrity gossip shows, who is used to mingling with celebrities, who is allowed to tread the red carpet. A prominent person is someone who is rated as prominent, for whatever reasons.

The impersonation of VIPs is a branch of activity in which some people can make a living. They make appearances as representatives of the prominent person. There are companies who act as agents for lookalikes. One website divides them into categories: celebrity doubles, doubles of royalty, politician doubles, athlete doubles, footballer doubles. There are separate categories for lookalike shows or James Bond doubles. Among the royal doubles, for instance, the Queen, Prince Charles or Lady Diana are in demand.

Doubles are in demand as imitators, as impersonators of celebrities, who can be invited to places where the originals would not go – and they are cheaper. It would be a big mistake to want to invite Madonna to the firemen's party, but a Madonna impersonator can be hired. A DJ Ötzi[1] impersonator would go down better for the firemen's party, and a Roberto Blanco[2] imitator would best suit the pensioner's day out. There are also weddings where you can be "serenaded" by Elvis Presley – in Las Vegas there is a large selection of marriage packages with such highlights.

Impersonation can be seen as an accolade for celebrities: when the public finds a lookalike appealing, then you *really are* a celebrity – although the originals concerned might often prefer some of the cabaret-like impersonations of their character not to take place. George W. Bush is not flattered by doubles, still less by what they portray in their performances. As always in such cases, however, the same applies for many celebrities as is said about caricatures: it would be even worse not to have a double, because then you're not really a celebrity.

Nostalgic Doubles

If you walk down the Boulevard in Las Vegas, you can meet Elvis Presley in multiple variations: you can hardly move for doubles. These are not doubles, but multiple replicas. And even though we have heard the decades-old rumours that the "King" is not really dead, we still know that these figures are lookalikes. At no moment do we begin to think that the rumours might be true, that we have the singer standing in person before our eyes. Rather we know that we are dealing with an untrained-actor who wants to earn a few dollars from the nostalgia of those out strolling on the Boulevard and who want to be photographed with him.

Those shows in which lookalikes conjure up the glamour of bygone times, from Marilyn Monroe to Humphrey Bogart, are usually more professional. The *Rat Pack* from the Sands Hotel is again appearing – Frank Sinatra, Sammy Davis Jr. and Dean Martin, sometimes accompanied by other "stars" from those years. As lookalikes they resurrect the "good old days". The really big stars are of course the preferred candidates for impersonation: Marlene Dietrich, Michael Jackson, Falco, Charlie Chaplin, but also Mr. Bean. Anyone famous can be impersonated: Bruce Willis and Paris Hilton, Adriano Celentano[3] and Tina Turner. The average price

It is said that the face is the "mirror of the soul". Some people must have similar souls then, because a number of people are not very different from each other.

at an agency is 1500 Euro for 30 minutes, but there are also lower and higher rates, depending on quality, expenses and demand. If the impersonators of celebrities are themselves already famous, the price goes up.

In most cases, "real" people are doubled. In the case of James Bond, however, it is doubles of actors playing the "real" James Bond, the literary figure of the English secret agent, who in the minds of the public merge with the pictures of his portrayer – Brosnan, Craig, Connery. Then, in the lookalike shows, well-known scenes are also acted out: Bond against Goldfinger. The Brosnan double is then the Bond double, the simulation of the "real" James Bond.

Scary Doubles

Impersonation also has other aspects, less entertaining ones. Stories are told in which one experiences oneself as a doppelganger – but these are not normally stories that you would like to experience. In the moment of death, like some people who against all expectations find their way back to life – you float upwards out of your body and see yourself – duplicated as it were – on the death bed or lying in a smashed up car. Superstitious people talk of meetings with figures in which they see themselves; this is also a spine-chilling affair. If you recognise yourself as a doppelganger, this has always been considered an evil omen. But it can also have a good outcome. One website dealing with paranormal phenomena comments: "Doppelganger in the esoteric sense refers to the immaterial, ethereal pendant of a person which frequently appears completely unexpectedly, often in moments of danger." Anecdotes are told about people who have experienced such encounters. But not everybody needs to believe in doppelgangers, which are supposed to be, as already suggested, simultaneously "ethereal" and "immaterial".

How many people am I? This was a question asked in short stories hundreds of years ago, especially when the doppelganger, one's own self, is quite different from the self that one is accustomed to: This other self suddenly becomes a stranger, an evil or awkward stranger. The polarities of good and evil, body and soul, intellect and passion are portrayed: Dr. Jekyll and Mr. Hyde. One is shocked by one's doppelganger. Who would have thought that these components are also part of your own self. This can be seen in a mythical or – quite simply – a psychoanalytical light: Sigmund Freud provided one of the greatest insults to the self-confidence of human beings when questioning the self-estimation of *homo sapiens*. Man may pride himself on being the pinnacle of enlightenment, but there is also an "underground", hardly accessible to the consciousness, a psychic "shadowy realm", in which passions and cruelties, emotions and obscenities prevail. The notion of a double can be found in one's own soul.

Even if the late-modernists like to play with mythical figures, with witches and knights, with vampires and werewolves, it is technical and electronic advances that encourage us to talk of the creation of artistic persons or of digitally constructed individuals who live in a world in which you can no longer tell the difference between the virtual and the real. It is not difficult for computers to generate an exact image of people – or even multiple copies. Science fiction films depict genetic experiments that have taken place before or after birth, controlled by secret services or potential conquerors of the world, experiments in which doppelgangers are created, perhaps through cloning – as superbeings, as fighting machines, as hybrids, with supernatural abilities. We are confronted with these doppelgangers in numerous films. A late modern society which is obsessed with identity must find the duplication of a person especially uncanny: a de-individualisation that removes the only thing that late modern society still has – the self, uniqueness, authenticity.

Practical Doubles

Stories of this type, full of imagination, are one way of dealing with lookalikes, but the banalities of the real world are quite different. "Genuine" doppelgangers, who really do look like the originals they represent, had different functions. Totalitarian rulers threatened with an attack on the part of their "beloved people", have (allegedly) kept lookalikes of themselves – such as the rumours circulating about Saddam Hussein. It is an ideal starting point for conspiracy theories.

Actors considered to be irreplaceable, or who have to be well-treated, have a double for dangerous or love scenes. Stuntmen are used so that they are not at risk of serious injuries, These are called "body doubles". There are also "voice doubles": dubbing artists who work in the background and are just the voice of the visual original. In all these cases, the body or voice double does not perform as a double. The essence of their existence is that they are not noticed. If they do their job well, the audience will not even realise that there is a double as it merges into the original. If the double is perceived – as a figure or as a voice – they will be understood to represent, to stand in for the original. The fact that a double is used is covered up. This is different from those cases in which no secret is made of the fact that the original is imitated, copied, duplicated, that the authenticity is simulated; that what is special here is the illusion. Perfect pretence is perfect performance – but it is not deception at all, because we are aware of what is going on. Doubles do not lie. We want to be tricked. And this is also the case in other walks of life, such as politics.

Doubles full of imagination

It is one of their peculiarities that human beings are at times overwhelmed by the urge to dress up, to adorn themselves, to present themselves as other people. People love masks. Various times and events are set aside for putting masks on, such as carnival. Children dress up as pirates or witches, as devils or little angels, as vampires or cowboys – and the adults are not much more imaginative. They are imitations, but people don't try to hide the fact. The little boy dresses up as Winnetou[4], and even if he lives out his role, neither he nor the people around him would ever begin to think that this is Winnetou[4] – reincarnated in the body of a child. The boy is "playing" Winnetou[4], he is the "image" of the Indian – but he is an imitation that remains visible as such, not a replica, not a copy "true as possible" to the original that could be "mistaken" for the original, giving the impression that Winnetou[4] had risen from the dead; just a role-playing game.

The "game" enables you to slip into other roles. Some people want to offer an appealing tourist environment and so they hire people to don suits of armour and imitate a tournament evoking the atmosphere of a medieval castle. You might even catch the double of Richard the Lionheart, which could happen without much fuss, because nobody knows what the "real" Richard the Lionheart looked like, and you don't need to do much to create the necessary "similarity" inside a suit of armour. In the southern states of the USA, fight scenes and battles from the civil war are "re-enacted" by the relevant associations, and you might see the "double" of General Lee. Emphasis is placed on the correct uniform, equipment, accessories – similar-

A late modern society which is obsessed with identity must find the duplication of a person especially uncanny: a de-individualisation that removes the only thing that late modern society still has – the self, uniqueness, authenticity.

ity to the General is strived for (which is why the actor at least has to have a beard), but it's not about presenting a double who is really deceptively similar in looks, as if the amazed audience were cheering the reincarnation of the Confederate hero. Contemporary society is a visualised society, we live with images, and these present us continually with people. We have Brad Pitt in our own front room, a copy, a simulation, a representation of Brad Pitt – and the feeling that we are "familiar" with him, as it were. From there it is just a small step to a "more realistic" imagined Brad Pitt when the impersonator appears in person.

Stars are "close" to us in the familiarity of exposure. "I" could also be Brad Pitt. "Partial double roles" are not unusual in a late-modern society, in which everybody wants to become a star, even if they are not suited in the slightest nor have the least qualifications for this. Karaoke, the singing competition for the untalented, could be said to play with looka-likeness. You sing what a star would normally sing, a well-known song with which everyone can identify; or you don't even sing the song, you just pretend to sing. You're not deceiving anybody, you are a double, but you can still feel a bit like a star. The impersonation as such is appreciated. Since there are now casting shows for everything, there is also a doubles casting show, in different age categories. The invitation declares: "Win over our jury of celebrities with your singing! Professional stylists, along with dance and singing coaches, will then make your unbelievable transformation into the copy of your star come true."

Duplicate Doubles

Good doubles – of attractive "stars" – have one problem: their own doubles. The market for English queens and princes is limited, and there is competition between actors. It can sometimes happen that one bidder maintains that only he is the "real double", all the others, for all their efforts, are unsuccessful. Even the doubles of celebrities have to fight for their celebrity.

The increase in lookalikes also doubles the number of celebrities, and in addition, celebrity itself is expanding. If celebrity status is defined by how well-known a person is in the media, the pressure of sensationalism and topicality means that in late-modern society there is no longer a slow growth to prominence; it is more about the artificial generation of such celebrity status. Featureless individuals are elected to prominence – usually for just a short time: as caricatures of celebrity; as the targets for a cynically high-spirited troop of journalists; as a "celebrity proletariat".

The artificial production of celebrity status is now extending to more and more groups of people. For a long time people have been trying to get footballers into this category, especially when they marry models or starlets; then you have a twin-pack celebrity, as it were. The mutual attraction is assumed to do with the fact that the persons involved share the same values. The shortage of potential figures allows even racing drivers, cooks and hairdressers to be included. It surely says quite a lot about a society when the hairdressers of the stars become stars themselves. This is just one aspect of the epidemic of dumbing down that is taking place in our entertainment society.

Third-rate VIPs do not make it beyond local renown, or are very briefly shooting stars, and are not normally a source of impersonation – their moment of fame is not even sufficient for this. The doubles scramble to lay claim to *first class VIPs*. The market for these is bigger; recognisability is not a problem: prominence is easier to impersonate.

Cabaret Doubles

The lookalikes of prominent VIPs have different functions. Doubles of aristocrats or crowned heads of state are used in a different way than a double of Frank Sinatra. The lookalike of the former is really supposed to impersonate, sing as closely as possible to the original, swaying the audience with romance and nostalgia: *New York, New York*. You would seriously disappoint the expectations of the audience if you presented Frank Sinatra as a seedy Mafioso or an alcoholic wreck. The public wants to be thrilled, to yearn, to remember. Doubles are frequently catalysts of one's own youthful memories – and always of yearnings.

With crowned heads of state, things are different. When the impersonator of Prince Charles appears, he does not make a serious speech about urban or architectural development, but plays a bizarre figure. Impersonators of politicians are also usually not invited as "serious lecturers". The lookalikes of Bill Clinton and George W. Bush play their characters very differently: Bush is probably presented as a rather stupid character and Clinton as a slippery one. "Angela Merkel" will also probably make a few idiotic speeches.

Boris Becker may be a character who would without doubt provide material for cabaret impersonators. Otherwise with most athletes, especially footballers, it is difficult to imagine what they could offer on stage. One agency offers "the best DJ Ötzi[1] double show – pure alpine power live. Featuring two pretty dancers in traditional Austrian costume. The ultimate party atmosphere! For your club, company and village party. For the opening of businesses, anniversaries, product presentations and on the trade fair stand." The impersonator of Pamela Anderson will also have certain qualities to offer, and these will be different to what Hannah Montana offers.

Marketing Doubles

One main area where doubles work is advertising. The Clooney clone comes cheaper than the original (even though the clone will find it difficult to match the handsomeness and authority of the original). Advertising with celebrities is normal and can hardly be imagined without them, but in some cases doubles do the job as well. This can saves millions.

Celebrity, publicity, attention – this accumulates and turns into a valuable advantage. Michael Schumacher sued several years ago when adverts were made using his face – that is, with the face of his double – and the Stuttgart District Court ruled in his favour, because of the violation of his personal rights. But not all lookalike appearances are prohibited. According to the views of the District Court, such

actions would not be covered by artistic freedom since the appearances of the doubles are not a separate artistic show, but serve to be as closely as possible an imitation of the original. This judgement, of course, does not do justice to the varied performances of doubles, particularly when the appearance does contain original (for example cabaret) elements.

Voyeuristic Doubles

The question remains, however, as to what attracts us to doubles. You could also imagine the reverse reaction: that the audience is annoyed to be fed imitations; the assumption that they are considered to be stupid; resentment that you are not even close to real celebrity, but are fobbed off with substitutes. Yet this is not the case. Doubles are located in the field of tension between *exhibitionism* and *voyeurism*. They have to possess a certain exhibitionist streak, like all actors and actresses; all the same they exhibit not themselves, but rather VIPs, to whom this exhibitionism is ascribed to a greater extent. So it is only a second-hand and imitated exhibitionism that is cultivated by the lookalikes.

The voyeurism of the audience, on the other hand, is "genuine". People have long become used to the fact that, in the world of the media, the private lives of celebrities are marketed, reported with embarrassing accuracy and scrupulously documented. Reporting on who goes to bed with whom, who has problems with alcohol, who wants to have a child, or has just adopted one, who has thrown wine bottles around, or who is having weight loss treatment or is undergoing withdrawal treatment, is all part of the game. There is an incessantly delivered stream of trivialities, increasing in quantity, which serve to entertain and shock people. Society becomes a round of gossip. Cautious attempts to challenge the audience urge for voyeurism are met with ungracious reactions. The visualisation of the life of a celebrity is omnipresent, viewers are trained to see images of VIPs – images of celebrities in all sorts of situations. Celebrities stroll along every day – with electronic resources – in their own private

lives, as reproduction, construction, metaphor; a visual narrative of the real person who might be hiding behind the image. These are, of course, "products", "symbols", "homunculi" which find their way into the headlines and broadcasts, but they are sold as "people". All this is part of the sales strategy, that the human element in art products, often even what is all-too-human, is deleted. A mixture of amazement and schadenfreude, awe and sympathy, is to be found in the audience, and envy is (for a while) reduced a little. There is a moral to the story: as you can see, money alone does not make you happy, even fame does not guarantee you a good life. The fairy tale is just that. This pacifies for a while, even though it does not destroy the fairy tale-like quality of one's own life expectations.

In this the double is just another narration, another reproduction, another version of the transfer of prominence and illusion, longing and magic into the range of perception of the viewers. In a world of images, everything becomes an image. In a world of simulations, everything becomes simulation. In a world of replicas, doubles are just about the same as the originals.

1 DJ Ötzi is an Austrian DJ and entertainer, well-known in German-speaking countries.

2 Roberto Blanco is a German-speaking Schlager singer and actor.

3 Adriano Celentano is a very popular Italian singer, actor and entertainer.

4 Winnetou is a fictional Native American hero of several novels written by Karl May (1842 – 1912).

Die theatrale Konsequenz des Doubles

Notizen zu Niklaus Spoerris «Who is Who?»

von Jens Groß

Wenn man die Bilder von Niklaus Spoerri betrachtet, besticht sofort die grosse Theatralität der Bilder. Scheinbar bekannte Menschen befinden sich in einer Umgebung, die nicht oder nur bedingt zu ihnen zu passen scheint. Eine Soll-Bruch-Stelle, eine inszenierte, simulierte Situation, die extrem nach Wirklichkeit aussieht und dennoch spürbar falsch ist. Theater. Nur, was ist falsch, was wahr?

Offensichtlich handelt es sich bei den abgebildeten Personen um Doppelgänger oder Doubles. Menschen, die Prominenten ähnlich sehen, oder sich Prominenten ähnlich machen, werden in ihrer individuellen und privaten (und damit plötzlich nicht mehr stimmigen) Umgebung gezeigt. Gleichzeitige Doppelwelten. Durch ein Double wird die Realität ausgelöscht, da ohne mögliche Verifikation der dargestellte Ausschnitt der Welt eine grundsätzliche Illusion sein könnte. Wenn jedoch schon der Schein trügt, verbirgt er deswegen ja nicht unbedingt die Wahrheit.

Die Unterscheidbarkeit von wahr und falsch ist das Zeichen von Simulation, welche eine künstliche Wirklichkeit widerspiegelt, ein Spiel, um die Realität verschwinden zu lassen und neu zu konstituieren. Ein phänomenaler Trick des Fotografen, um unseren Blick auf die Wirklichkeit grundsätzlich zu erschüttern. Er spielt mit Menschen, bekannten Gesichtern und Motiven, die wir aus den Massenmedien kennen. In der Spannung zwischen dem äusseren Erscheinungsbild dieser Masken und der dahinter liegenden Differenz offenbaren sich die inneren Konflikte der Gesellschaft. Die Simulationen sind rückwärtsgewandt, zitieren etwas schon Vergangenes oder wenigstens Bekanntes. Sie artikulieren nicht das Besondere, sondern ein durchschnittliches, wiedererkennbares Bild des Typischen mit kleinen Irritationen. Sterile Illusions- und Scheinwelten. Wunschwelten? Doppelwelten? Doppelgänger. Wer mochte nicht auch schon einmal reich und berühmt sein? Wer nicht einen Prominenten bei sich als Gast haben?

Die als negativ deklarierten Phänomene (des eigenen Selbst) werden im Double ausgeschlossen, die Schattenseiten des Realen unterdrückt. Realität wird als möglicher Schwindel enttarnt. Die durch ein Double (und die unstimmige Parallelwelt) plötzlich ausgelöschte Realität erzeugt grösstmögliche Verunsicherung und bietet Platz für eine dritte Welt: Die Welt des Betrachters, der sich nun entscheiden muss, wem oder was er glaubt.

Der Titel des Buches «Who ist Who?» verweist auf das Phänomen des Doubles und ist nicht von ungefähr gewählt. Das Thema der Doppelung ist seit jeher eines der grossen Themen des Theaters: Parallelwelten und Simulakren, Doppelgänger und Spiegelbilder, Differenzen. Dinge, Figuren, Materialien sind in jeder Inszenierung in ein neues, jeweilig anderes Verhältnis zu den Darstellern gesetzt. Denn die

Die Frage lautet nicht mehr: Wie entkommt man seinem Schicksal? Sondern: Wie entkommt man ihm nicht?

Grenze zwischen diesen «Welten», zwischen der Simulation und dem Simulierten folgt allein der spielerischen Behauptung. In einer solchen Welt ist der Darsteller nicht mehr der auktoriale «Manipulator», vielmehr wird er Teil einer fremden Welt, in der Hoffnung, das «vergessene Menschliche» (Walter Benjamin) der Dinge wahrnehmbar zu machen. Die Archäologie jener Grenze, die Frage nach der Differenz zwi-

schen Körpern und Dingen eignet daher jeder Inszenierung dieses Theaters auf ganz spezifische Weise. Es ist eine Frage, die auch die merkwürdige Eigentümlichkeit des «Doppelgängers» erkundet. Denn wer da wen doppelt, ob «Original» und «Double» überhaupt unterscheidbar wären, oder wie sehr jenen daran liegt, ebensolche Unterscheidbarkeit zu verwischen, ist eine jener konkreten Seherfahrungen, die das Theater mannigfach bereithält, und auf deren Techniken dieser Bildband zugreift.

Duplizität stellt das Ideale und Absolute in Frage. Wenn es zwei gibt, relativieren sie sich und jedes hinterfragt das andere, jedes wird als eine Möglichkeit gesehen, ein neues Drittes wird vorstellbar. Doubles führen die Ambivalenz zwischen Einheit und Doppelung zu vielfachen Lesarten der multiplen Identitäten. Im Gegensatz zur Auflösung und Vermischung stellt Duplizität die gleichzeitige Existenz unterscheidbarer Ganzheiten und Identitäten dar. Damit schafft sie eine Offenheit und Dynamik, die zugleich das Selbstverständnis untergräbt. Das ist der wesentliche Spielraum des Theaters. Das ist ein Grund, warum sich Kunst für dieses Phänomen interessiert.

Doch warum geben Menschen ihre Einzigartigkeit, ihr ständiges Streben danach freiwillig auf? Warum wollen manche Menschen gerne Doubles sein? Ist es die verzweifelte Suche nach einem Selbstverständnis, nach einer Fluchtmöglichkeit vor der eigenen Bedeutungslosigkeit? Vielleicht flüchten Menschen, um der Angst vor dem Tod zu entgehen, vor der Wirklichkeit und beten etwas an, was nicht da ist? Anstelle der Welt wie sie tatsächlich ist, erfinden sie ein «Double», ein Paralleluniversum, das als Phantomrivale zur existierenden Welt fungiert,

als verzweifelter Ausgleich zu den Leiden, die mit der Akzeptanz der Wirklichkeit verbunden sind. Dieses «Double» nimmt alle möglichen Formen an, vom gehörnten Ehemann, der sich, weil er die Wahrheit nicht erträgt, selbst allem Anschein zum Trotz einredet, seine Frau sei treu; über den Globalisierungskritiker, für den eine «andere Welt» möglich ist, bis zum Metaphysiker, der beweist, dass die Wahrheit wie das «wahre Leben» immer «woanders» ist oder dem Pragmatiker, der sagt: «Gebt mir eine andere Welt, oder ich ersticke!»

Es herrscht vermutlich ein archetypischer Kampf zwischen dem Streben aller Kultur nach individueller Freiheit und einer urtümlicheren Abneigung gegen Individualität und Freiheit. Ein unlösbarer Konflikt, der in einen immer stärkeren Selbsthass mündet. Das moderne Individuum hat eine kritische Schwelle überschritten, jenseits derer es in Bezug auf die Gattung zu einem spezifischen Bumerangeffekt kommt, indem die Selbstverleugnung zum letzten Stadium des individuellen Bewusstseins wird. Das Problem der Gegenwart ist nicht mehr das der Freiheit – wie sie erringen? –, sondern eher jenes: Wie ihr entkommen? Wie der grenzlosen Individuation und dem Selbsthass entkommen? Die Frage lautet nicht mehr: Wie entkommt man seinem Schicksal? Sondern: Wie entkommt man ihm nicht? Denn wir haben das Original verloren, den Sinn, warum man sich so anstrengen muss, originär zu sein, wenn eh alles Schwindel sein kann. Es ist nicht mehr nötig, das Leben kontinuierlich zu ändern, um am Leben zu bleiben – es genügt, zwei oder mehrere davon zu haben. Der Wechsel gegen das Werden. Chamäleons. Sie wechseln, aber werden nicht(s).

The theatrical Consequence of the Lookalike

Notes on Niklaus Spoerri's "Who is Who?"

by Jens Groß

Looking at the pictures by Niklaus Spoerri, one is immediately struck by the theatricality of them. Apparently well-known people find themselves in surroundings in which they don't seem to fit, or only partly fit. A staged, simulated situation, which looks extremely like reality, and yet is tangibly wrong. Theatre. Only, which one is true, which one false?

Obviously the people photographed are lookalikes or doubles. People who look very similar to celebrities or transform themselves to look like celebrities are shown in their individual and private surroundings (which then are suddenly no longer right). Parallel double worlds. Reality is obliterated by a double, since without any verification, the detail of the world presented could be a fundamental illusion. But if even appearances are deceptive, this does not mean that underneath definitely lies the truth.

Making a distinction between true and false is a sign of simulation, one which reflects an artificial reality, a game to make reality disappear and be reconstituted. A phenomenal trick of the photographer, which fundamentally disrupts our view of reality. He plays with people, with well-known faces and motifs with which we are familiar from the mass media. In the tension between the external appearance of these masks and the difference that lies beneath them, the inner conflicts of society are revealed. The simulations are backward-looking, referring to something that is already past, or at least well-known. They do not articulate anything special, but rather an average, recognisable image of something typical, with small irritations. Sterile worlds of illusion and make-believe. Desired

"

worlds? Double worlds? Doppelganger. Who wouldn't want to be rich and famous just for once? Who wouldn't want to have a celebrity in their home as a guest?

Those phenomena (of the self) seen to be negative are ruled out in the double, the drawbacks of the real are suppressed. Reality is uncovered as a possible fake. The reality that is suddenly eliminated by a double (and the incongruous setting) generates the greatest possible uncertainty and offers scope for a third world: the world of the observer, who now has to decide in whom or in what he believes.

The title of the book "Who is Who?" refers to the phenomenon of the double and has not been chosen by accident. The issue of duplication has always been one of the big themes of the theatre: parallel worlds and simulations, doppelganger and reflections, differences, things, figures, materials, are set in each production to a new relationship with the actors, one which is different each time. Because the border between these worlds, between simulation and what is simulated, is based purely on the acting performance. In such a world the actor is no longer the auctorial "manipulator", rather he becomes part of an alien world in the hope of being able to make perceptible the "forgotten human side" (Walter Benjamin) of things. The archaeology of this border, the question of the difference between bodies and things, is therefore characteristic of every staging of this theatre in a very specific manner. It is a question that also explores the remarkable peculiarity of the "doppelganger". Because who is duplicating whom, whether there is any distinction at all between the "original" and the "double",

or how important it is for them to blur any such distinctions, is one of those concrete visual experiences that the theatre offers in abundance, and the techniques of which are used in this illustrated book.

Duplicity puts into question the ideal and the absolute. If there are two, they are relative to each other, and each challenges the other, each is seen as just one possibility and a new, third option becomes conceivable. Doubles cause the ambivalence between oneness and duplication to result in several different levels of interpretation of multiple identities. In contrast to dissolution or amalgamation, duplicity represents the simultaneous existence of distinct individuals and identities in all their facets. Thus it creates an openness and dynamic and at the same time undermines the self-image. This is the fundamental scope of the theatre. This is one reason why art is interested in this phenomenon.

But why do people voluntarily give up their uniqueness, their continual striving for this? Why do some people want to be doubles? Is it the desperate search for a self-image, for a means of escape from one's own insignificance? Do people perhaps flee to escape the fear of death, to escape reality, and revere something that is not there? Instead of the world as it really is, they invent a "double", a parallel universe, which functions as a phantom rival to the existing world as a desperate compensation for the suffering that is linked to the acceptance of reality. This "double" takes on all possible forms, from the cuckold who, because he cannot bear the truth, persuades himself that his wife is faithful to him, despite all appearances to the contrary, via globalisation critics

for whom "another world" is possible, down to the meta-physician who proves that truth, like "real life", is always "somewhere else", or the pragmatist who says "Give me another world or I will suffocate!"

Presumably an archetypal struggle is going on between the striving of all culture towards individual freedom and a more primitive aversion towards individuality and freedom. An irresolvable conflict leading to self-hate that becomes ever stronger. The modern individual has passed a critical threshold beyond which a specific boomerang effect takes hold with respect to the species, in which self-denial becomes the last stage of individual consciousness. The problem of the present day is no longer that of freedom – how to achieve it? – but rather that of how to escape it? How to escape the boundless individualisation and the self-hate? The question is no longer how does one escape one's fate, but rather, how does one not escape it? Because we have lost sight of the original, of the sense of why you have to make such an effort to be original, if everything might be fake anyway. It is no longer necessary to continually change your life to stay alive – it is sufficient to just have two of them, or more. Change, in exchange for becoming something. Chameleons. They change, but do not become anything (new).

Because we have lost sight of the original, of the sense of why you have to make such an effort to be original, if everything might be fake anyway.

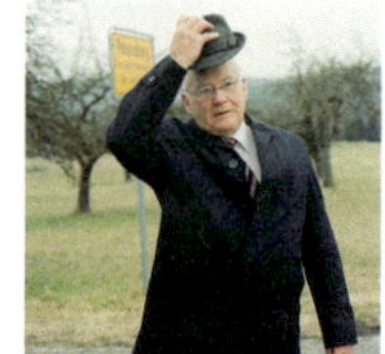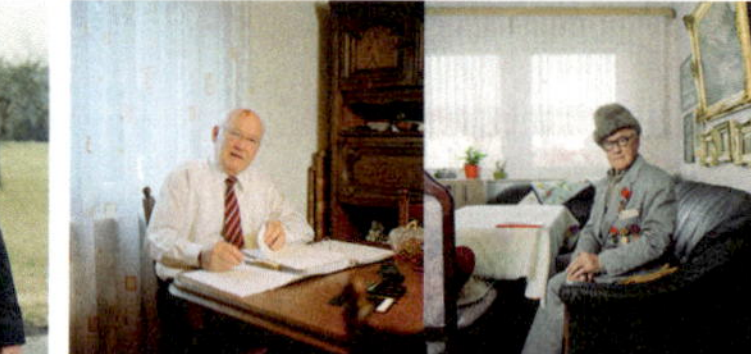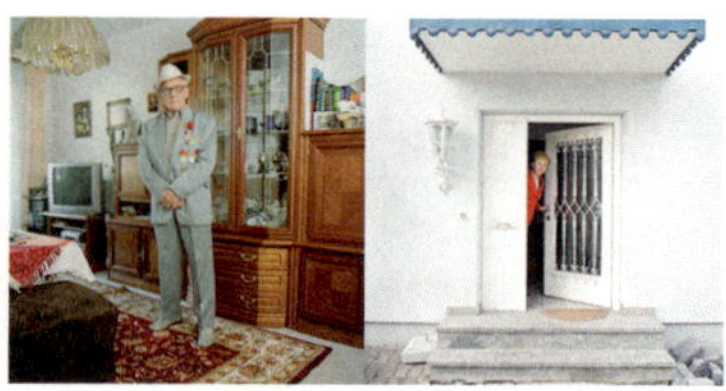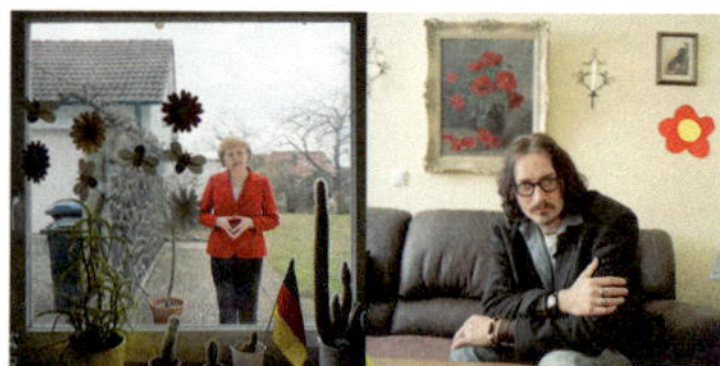

1 Winfried Werner Salmen alias Michail Gorbatschow
2 Winfried Werner Salmen alias Michail Gorbatschow
3 Erich Schmitt alias Erich Honecker
4 Erich Schmitt alias Erich Honecker
5 Marianne Schätzle alias Angela Merkel
6 Marianne Schätzle alias Angela Merkel
7 Michael Reich alias Johnny Depp

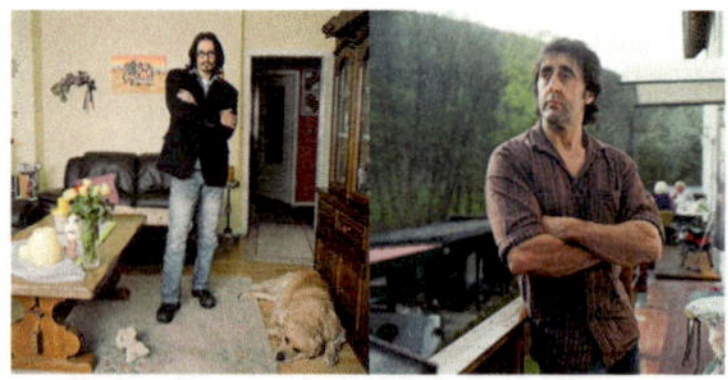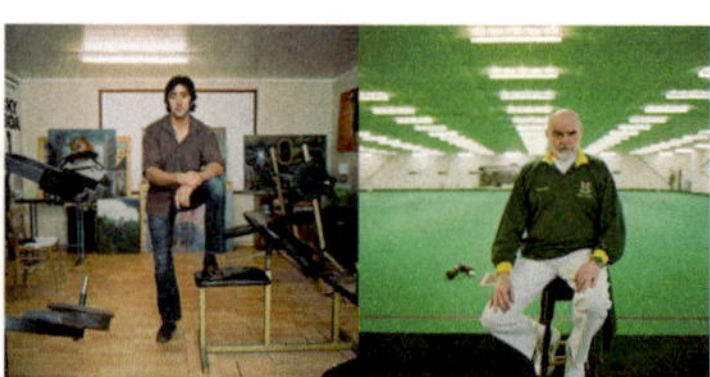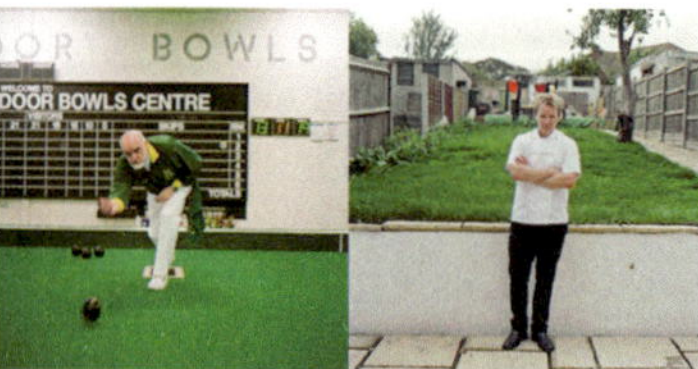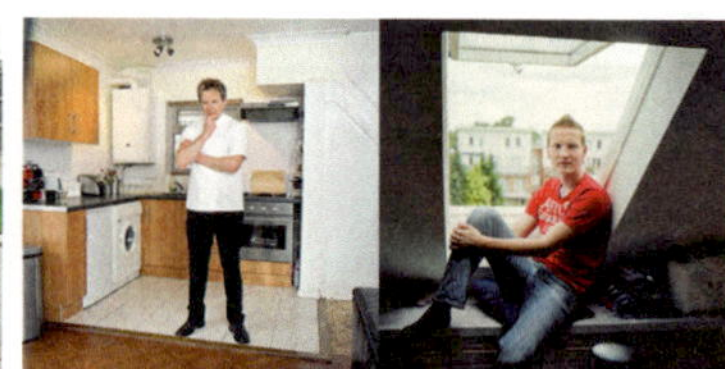

8 Michael Reich alias Johnny Depp
9 Danko Caberica alias Sylvester Stallone
10 Danko Caberica alias Sylvester Stallone
11 Hugh Lewis alias Sean Connery
12 Hugh Lewis alias Sean Connery
13 Martin Jordan alias Gordon Ramsay
14 Martin Jordan alias Gordon Ramsay
15 Benjamin Thoms alias Sebastian Schweinsteiger

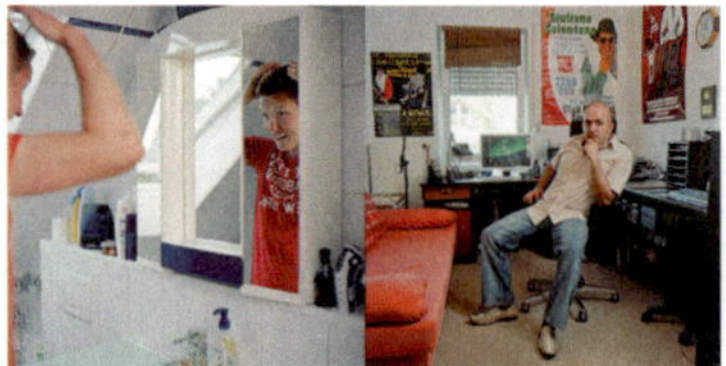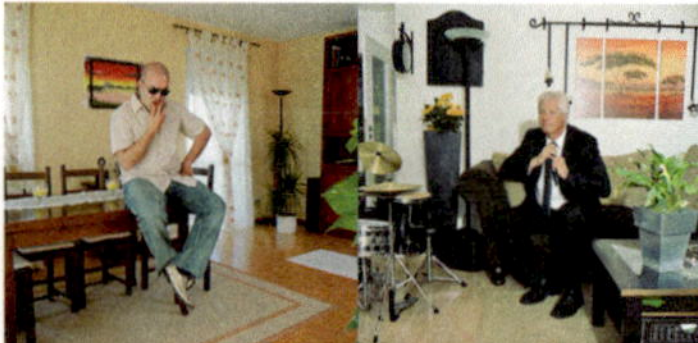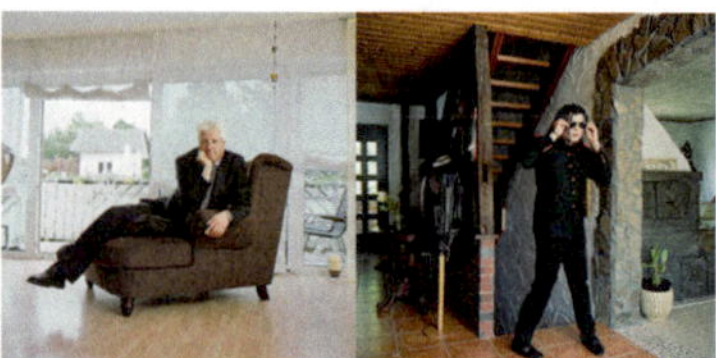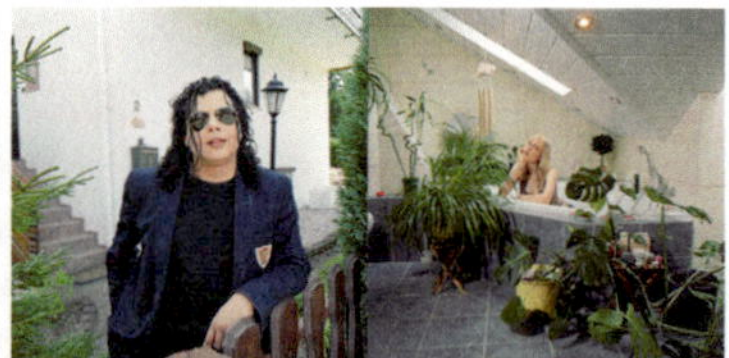

16 Benjamin Thoms alias Sebastian Schweinsteiger
17 Giuliano Camedda alias Adriano Celentano
18 Giuliano Camedda alias Adriano Celentano
19 Rainer Köster alias Bill Clinton
20 Rainer Köster alias Bill Clinton
21 Daimyo Jackson alias Michael Jackson
22 Daimyo Jackson alias Michael Jackson
23 Elischeba Wilde alias Daryl Hannah

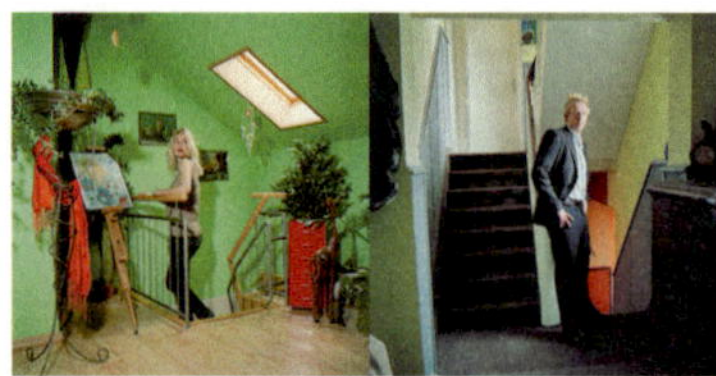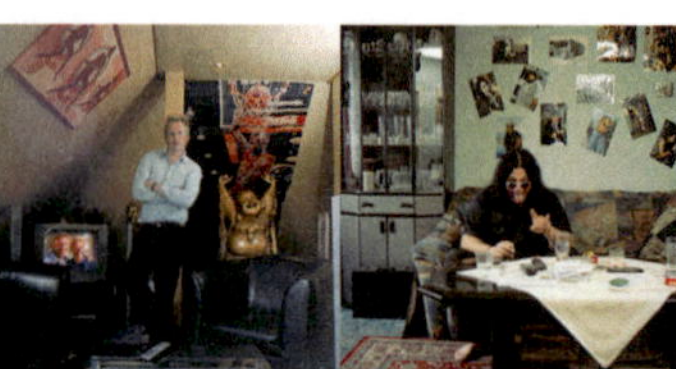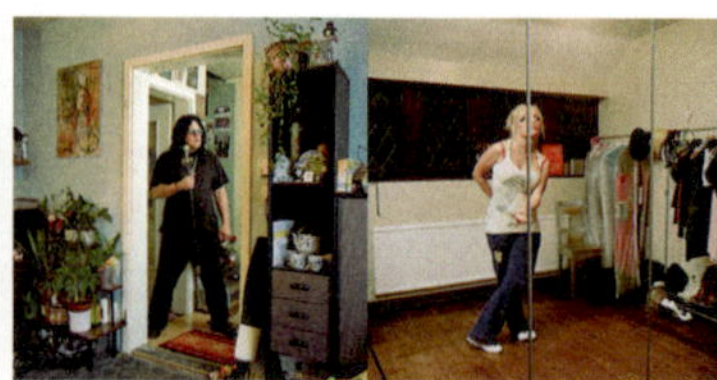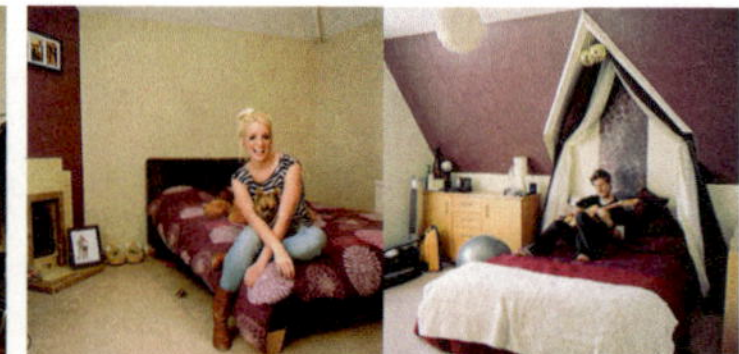

24 Elischeba Wilde alias Daryl Hannah
25 Maik Lohmann alias Boris Becker
26 Maik Lohmann alias Boris Becker
27 Mike Koch alias Ozzy Osbourne
28 Mike Koch alias Ozzy Osbourne
29 Michaela Weeks alias Britney Spears
30 Michaela Weeks alias Britney Spears
31 Andy Harmer alias David Beckham

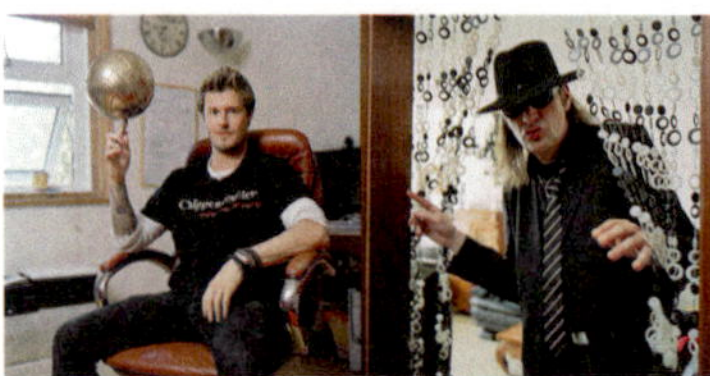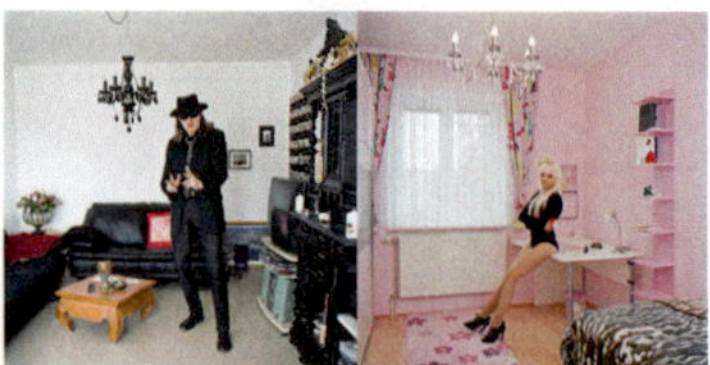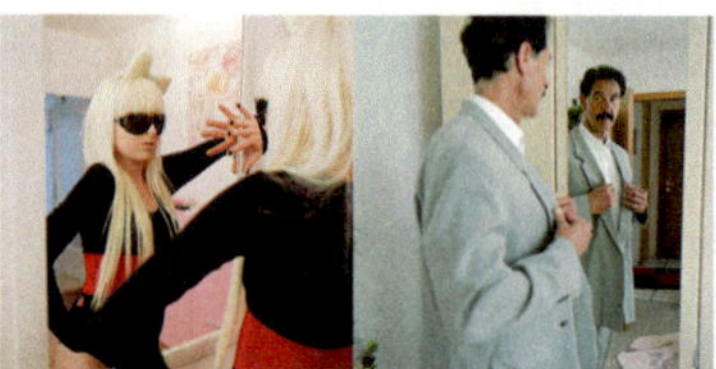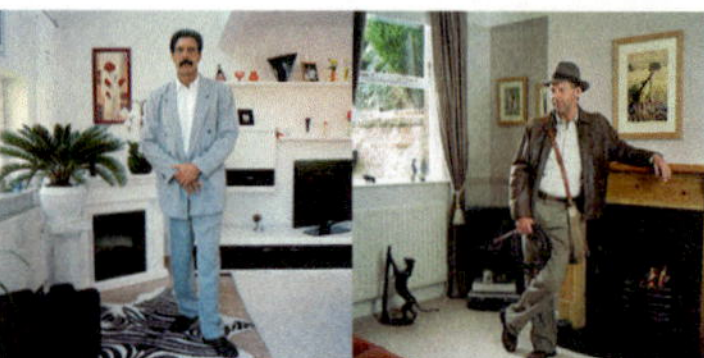

32 Andy Harmer alias David Beckham
33 Ansgar Hüttenmüller alias Udo Lindenberg
34 Ansgar Hüttenmüller alias Udo Lindenberg
35 Nina Berger alias Lady Gaga
36 Nina Berger alias Lady Gaga
37 Heinz Uwe Berg alias Borat
38 Heinz Uwe Berg alias Borat
39 Richie Jones alias Indiana Jones

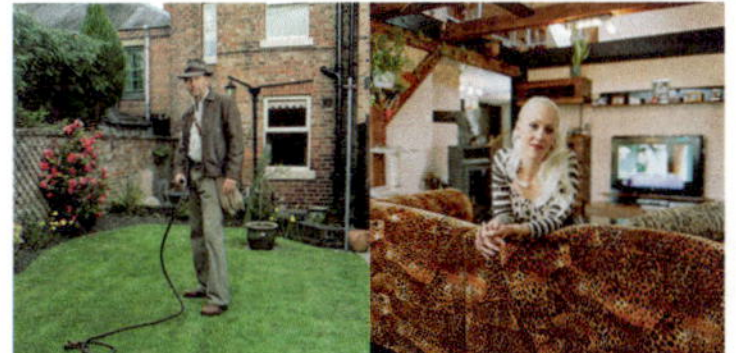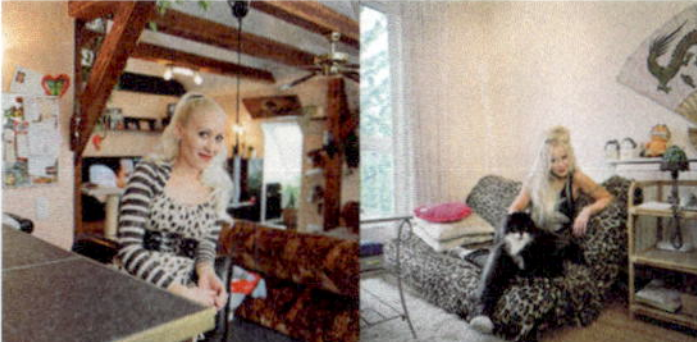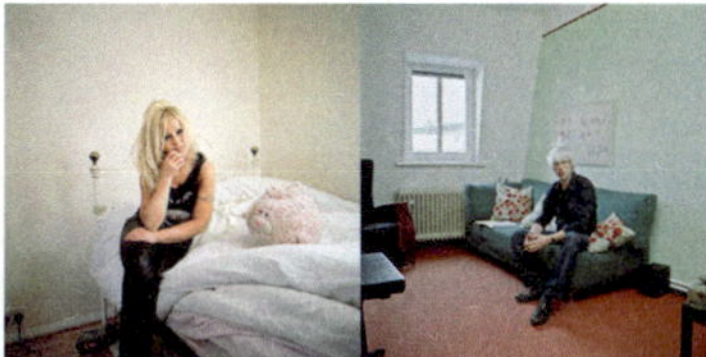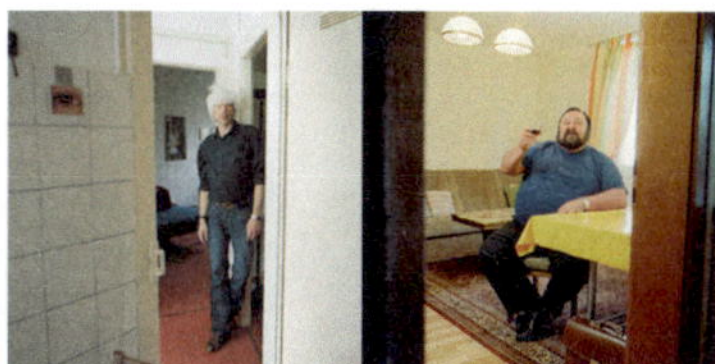

40 Richie Jones alias Indiana Jones
41 Kateryna Zakhavayeva alias Gwen Stefani

42 Kateryna Zakhavayeva alias Gwen Stefani
43 Tanya Christianssen alias Pamela Anderson

44 Tanya Christianssen alias Pamela Anderson
45 Philipp Höhler alias Andy Warhol

46 Philipp Höhler alias Andy Warhol
47 Dieter Wagner alias Luciano Pavarotti

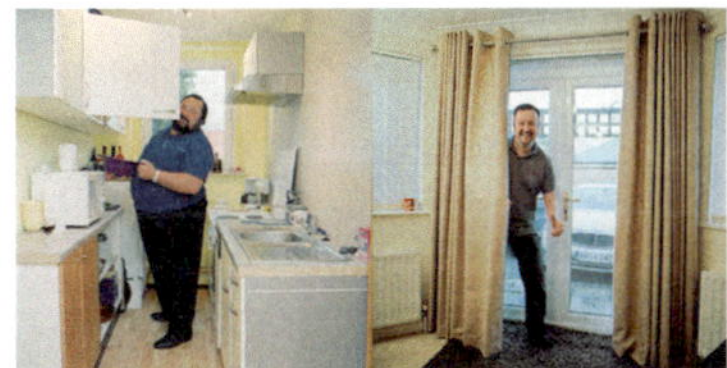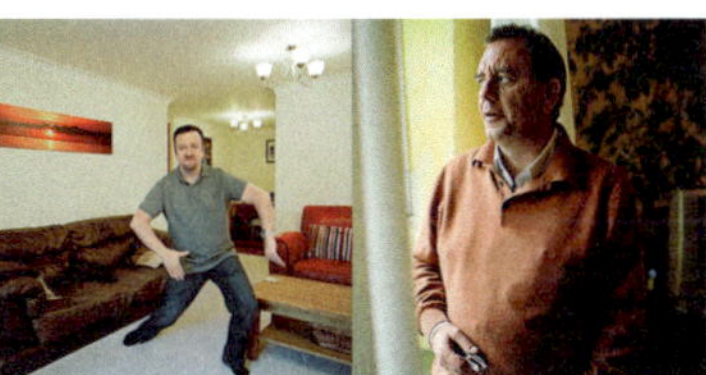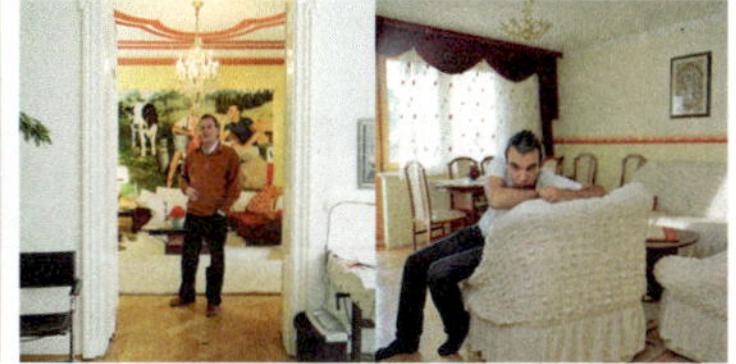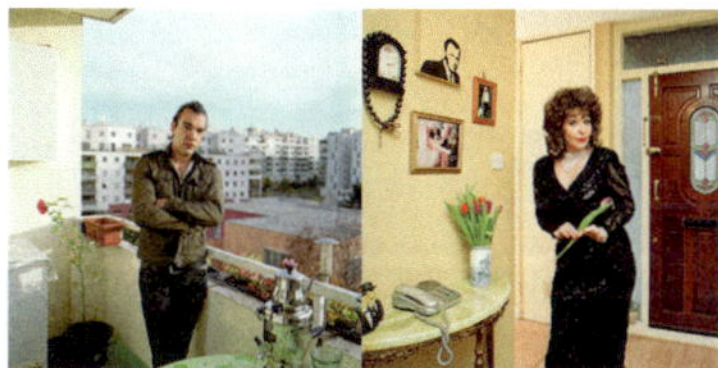

48 Dieter Wagner alias Luciano Pavarotti
49 Tim Oliver alias Ricky Gervais

50 Tim Oliver alias Ricky Gervais
51 Jürgen Piechotka alias Gerhard Schröder

52 Jürgen Piechotka alias Gerhard Schröder
53 Eray Kocak alias Antonio Banderas

54 Eray Kocak alias Antonio Banderas
55 Barbara Kealy alias Joan Collins

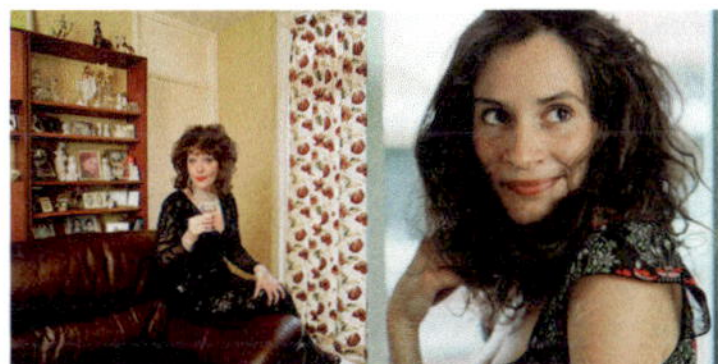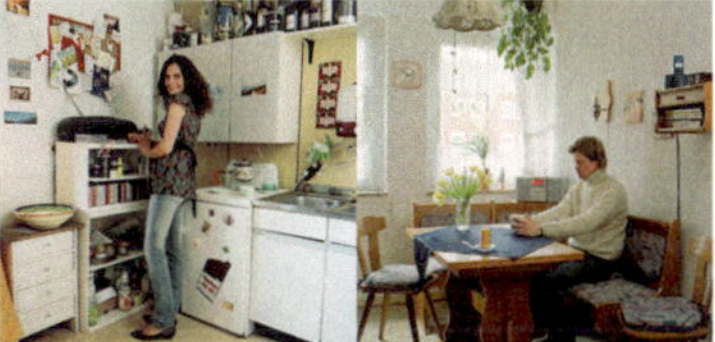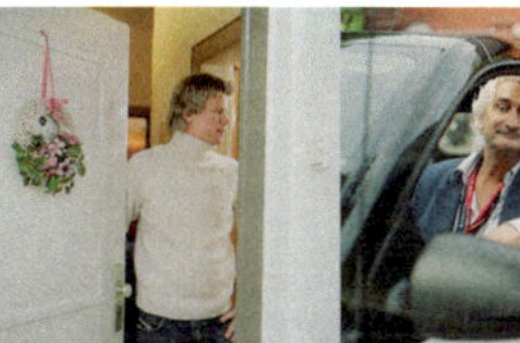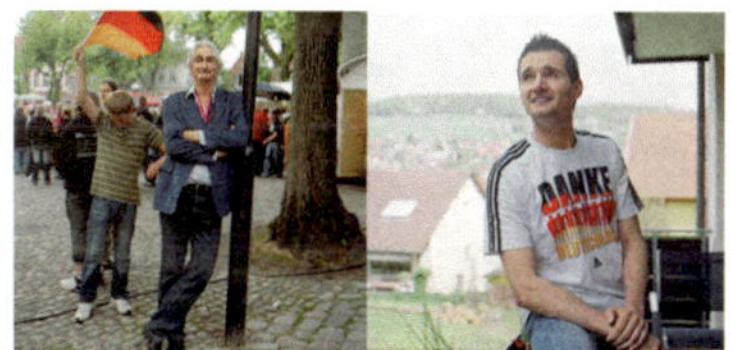

56 Barbara Kealy alias Joan Collins
57 Judith Gresky alias Julia Roberts

58 Judith Gresky alias Julia Roberts
59 Christian Wessel alias Oliver Kahn

60 Christian Wessel alias Oliver Kahn
61 Michael Matthies alias Rudi Völler

62 Michael Matthies alias Rudi Völler
63 Martin Hess alias Miroslav Klose

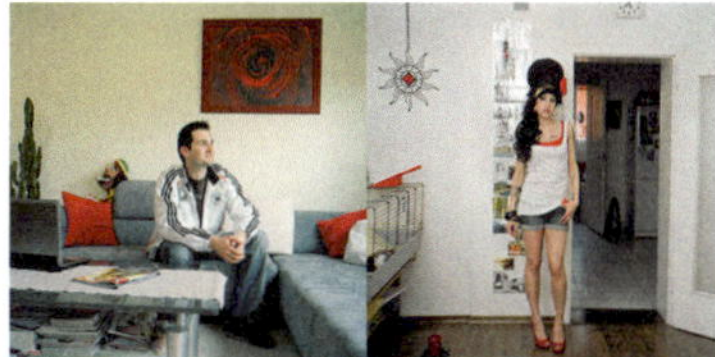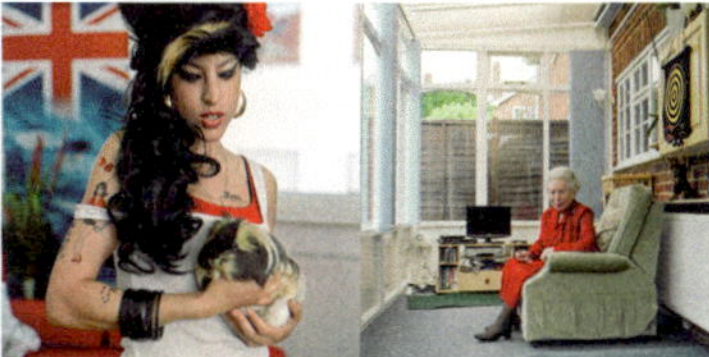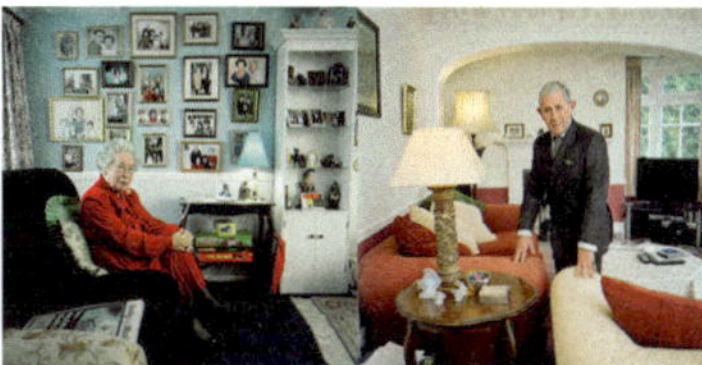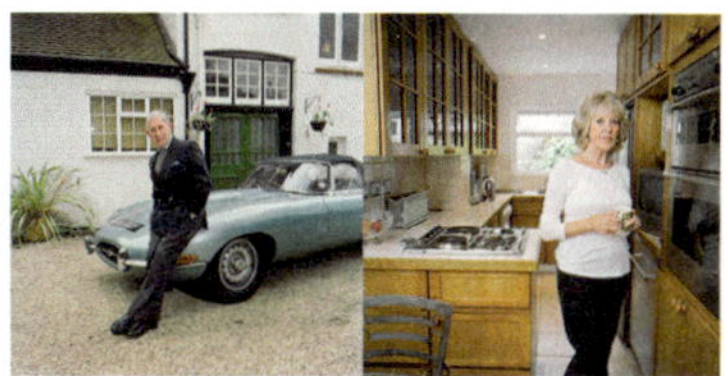

64 Martin Hess alias Miroslav Klose
65 Anna Glück alias Amy Winehouse

66 Anna Glück alias Amy Winehouse
67 Jeannette Charles alias Queen Elizabeth II

68 Jeannette Charles alias Queen Elizabeth II
69 Peter Hugo alias Prince Charles

70 Peter Hugo alias Prince Charles
71 Ann Clifton alias Camilla Parker Bowles

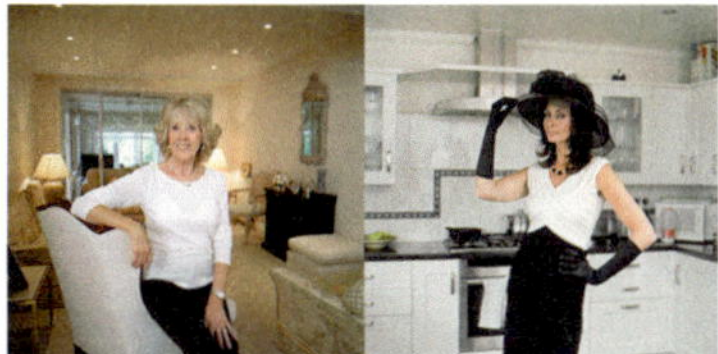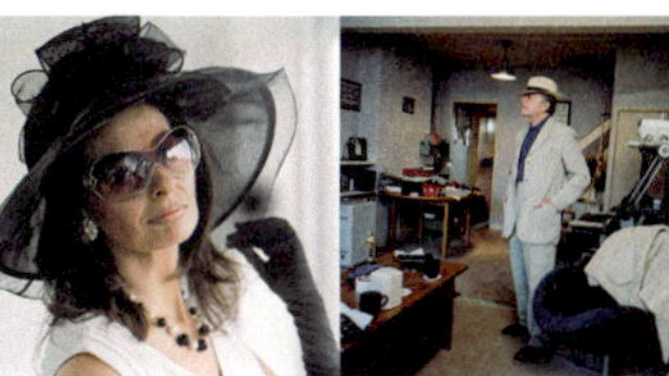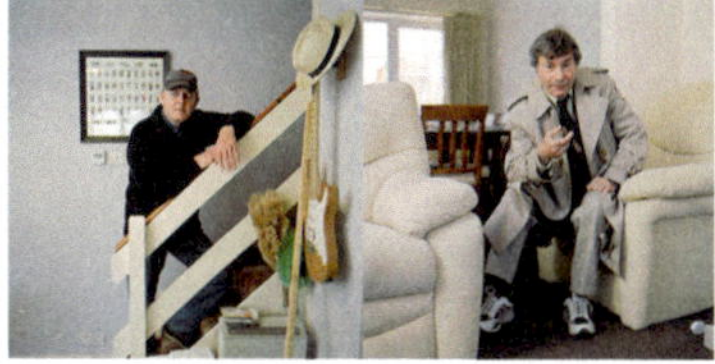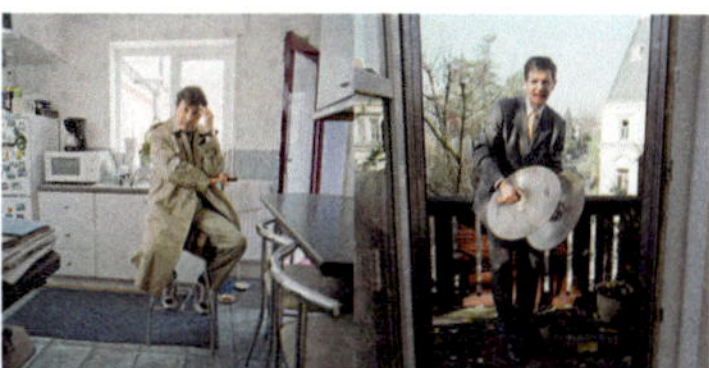

72 Ann Clifton alias Camilla Parker Bowles
73 Elaine Holgado alias Sophia Loren

74 Elaine Holgado alias Sophia Loren
75 Frank Powell alias Anthony Hopkins

76 Frank Powell alias Anthony Hopkins
77 Ralph Berkley alias Columbo

78 Ralph Berkley alias Columbo
79 Andreas Scholz alias Günther Jauch

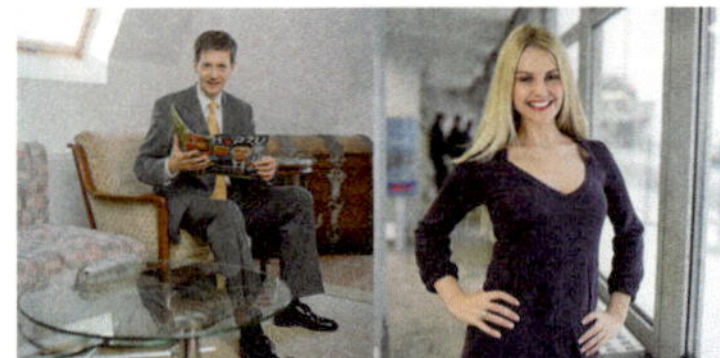
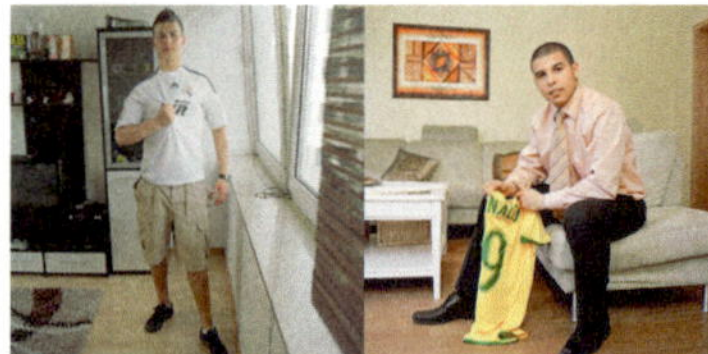
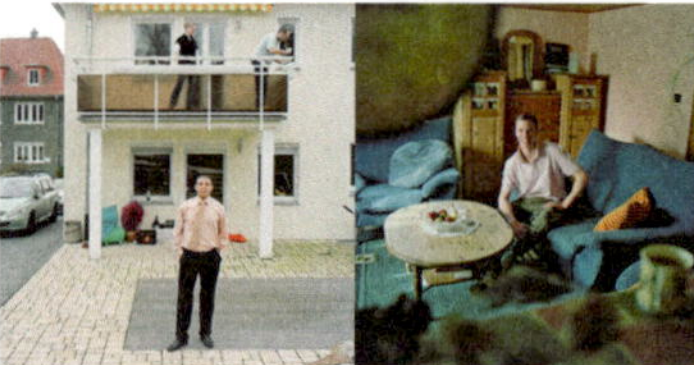
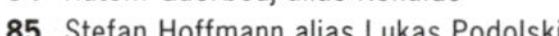
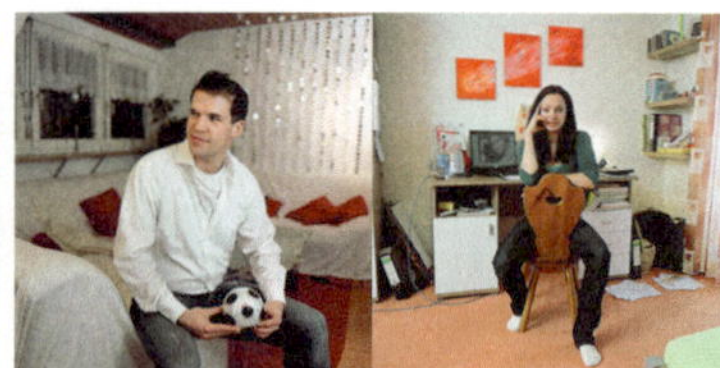

80 Andreas Scholz alias Günther Jauch
81 Vera Buachidze alias Michelle Hunziker

82 Georgius Exouzidis alias Cristiano Ronaldo
83 Hatem Guerbouj alias Ronaldo

84 Hatem Guerbouj alias Ronaldo
85 Stefan Hoffmann alias Lukas Podolski

86 Michael Missale alias Michael Ballack
87 Olivia Preisser alias Angelina Jolie

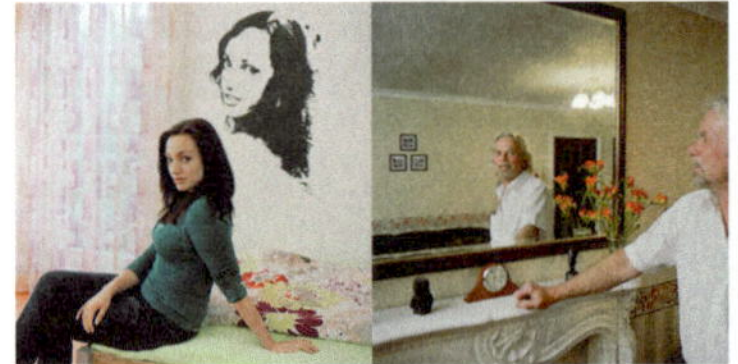
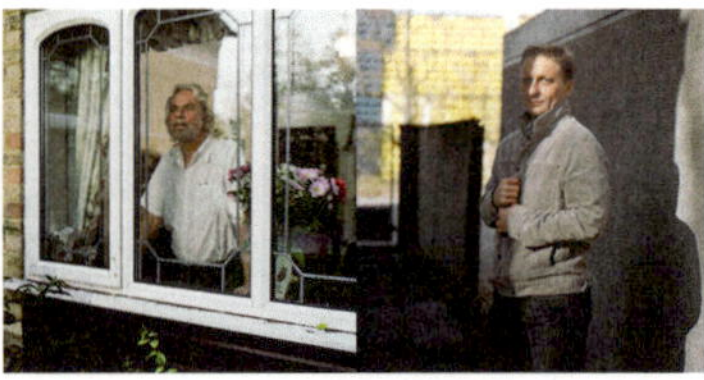
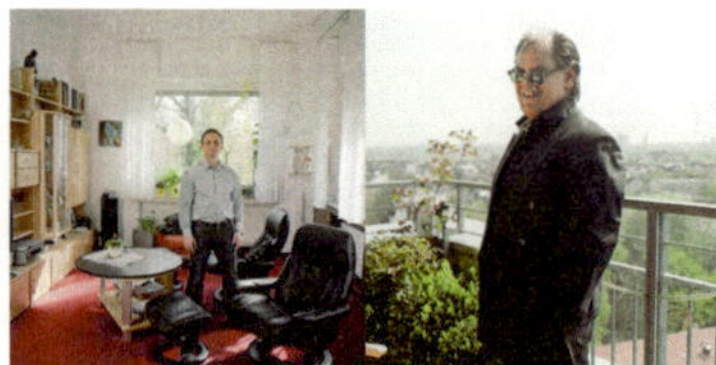
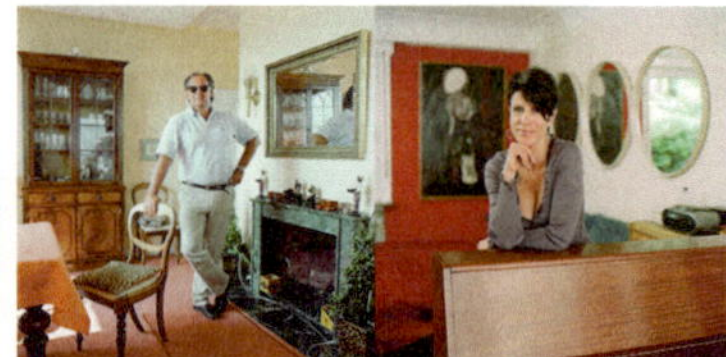

88 Olivia Preisser alias Angelina Jolie
89 Keith Skelsey alias Richard Branson

90 Keith Skelsey alias Richard Branson
91 Reiner Dongmann alias Daniel Craig

92 Reiner Dongmann alias Daniel Craig
93 Thomas Guse alias Jack Nicholson

94 Thomas Guse alias Jack Nicholson
95 Nicole Prinzlau alias Jamie Lee Curtis

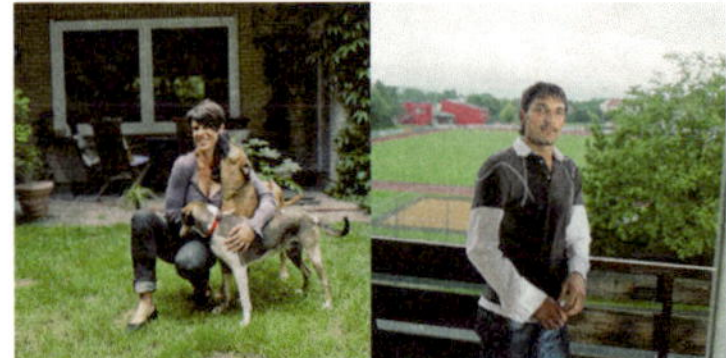
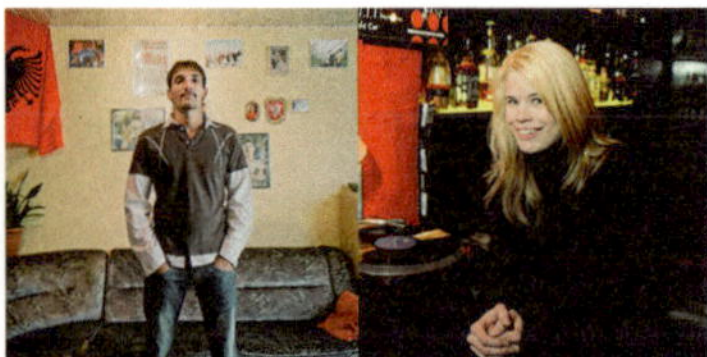
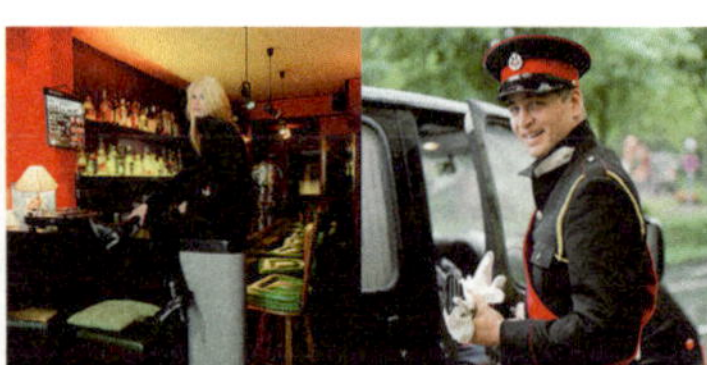
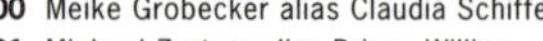
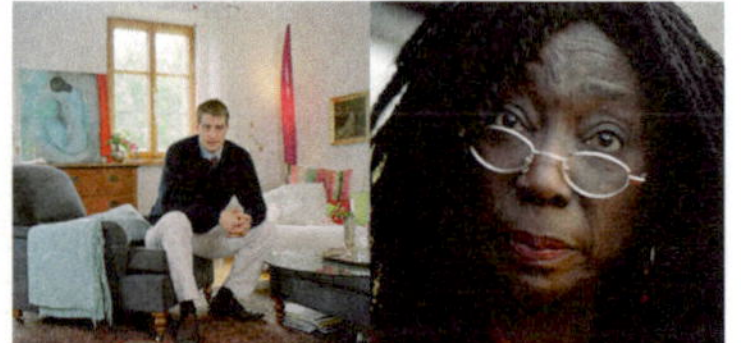

96 Nicole Prinzlau alias Jamie Lee Curtis
97 Sedat Shala alias Kevin Kuranyi

98 Sedat Shala alias Kevin Kuranyi
99 Meike Grobecker alias Claudia Schiffer

100 Meike Grobecker alias Claudia Schiffer
101 Michael Zartner alias Prince William

102 Michael Zartner alias Prince William
103 Melbra Rai alias Whoopi Goldberg

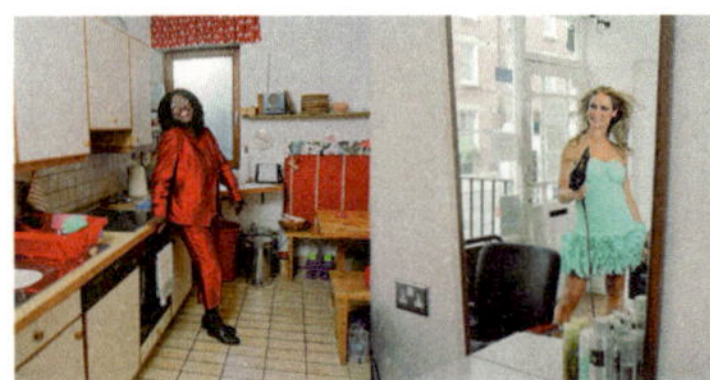
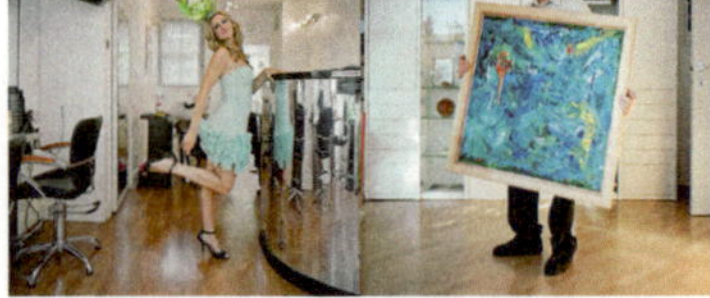
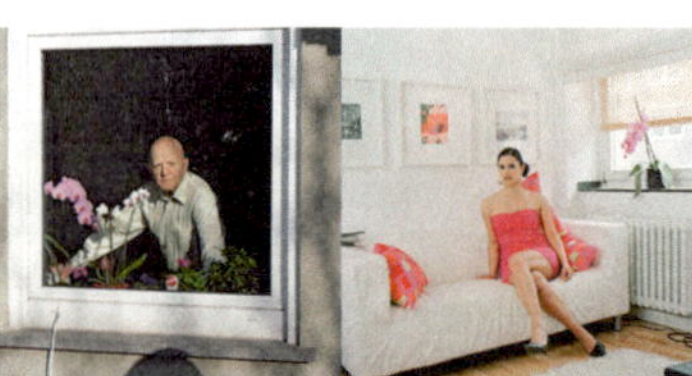
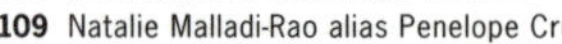
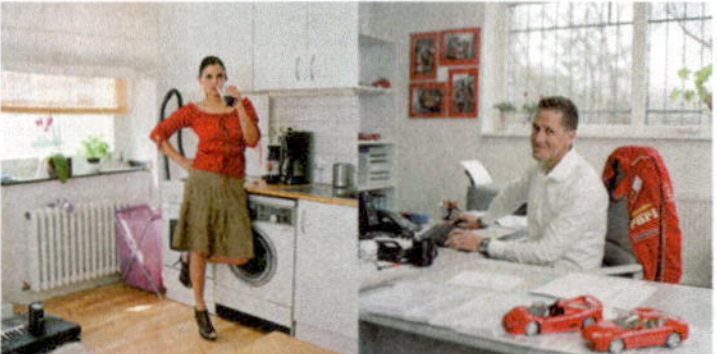

104 Melbra Rai alias Whoopi Goldberg
105 Jemima Slade alias Sarah Jessica Parker

106 Jemima Slade alias Sarah Jessica Parker
107 Hermann Roos alias Pablo Picasso

108 Hermann Roos alias Pablo Picasso
109 Natalie Malladi-Rao alias Penelope Cruz

110 Natalie Malladi-Rao alias Penelope Cruz
111 Frank Saasen alias Michael Schumacher

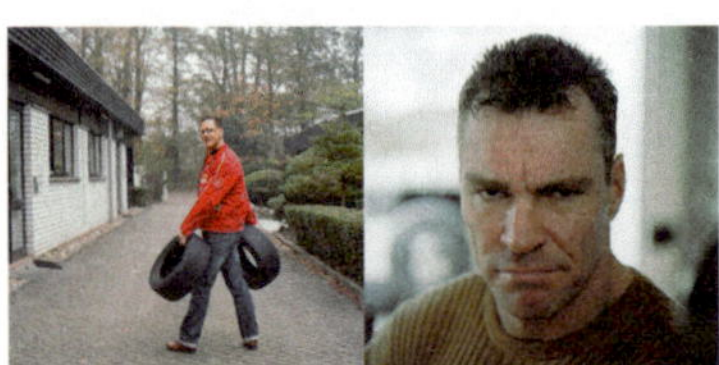
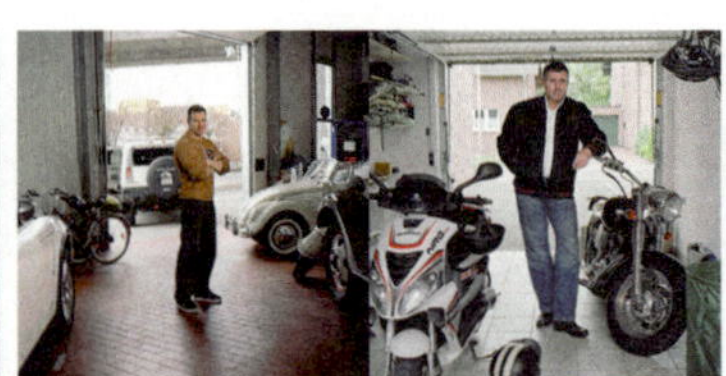
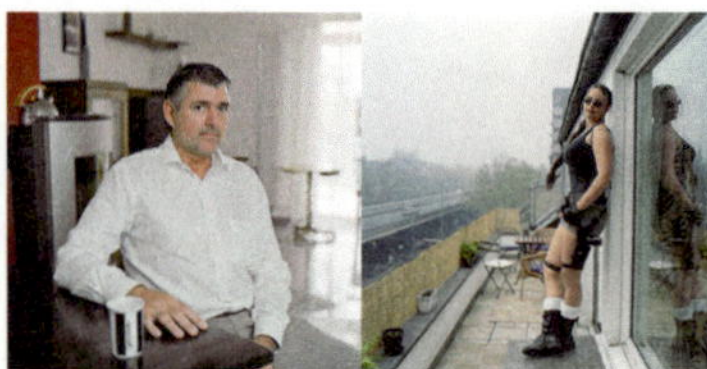
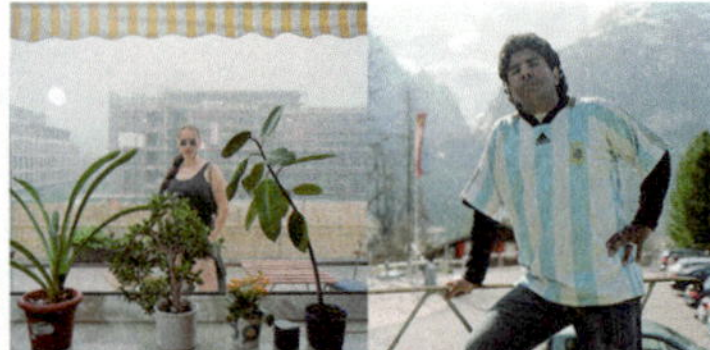

112 Frank Saasen alias Michael Schumacher
113 Thomas Morawek alias Arnold Schwarzenegger

114 Thomas Morawek alias Arnold Schwarzenegger
115 Wolfgang Moll alias George Clooney

116 Wolfgang Moll alias George Clooney
117 Katrin Monsberger alias Lara Croft

118 Katrin Monsberger alias Lara Croft
119 Abi Atici alias Diego Maradona

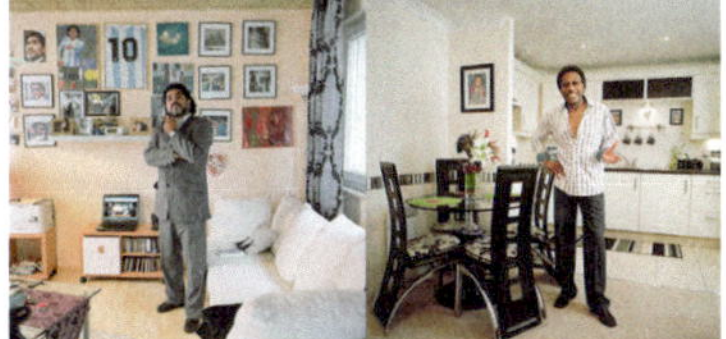 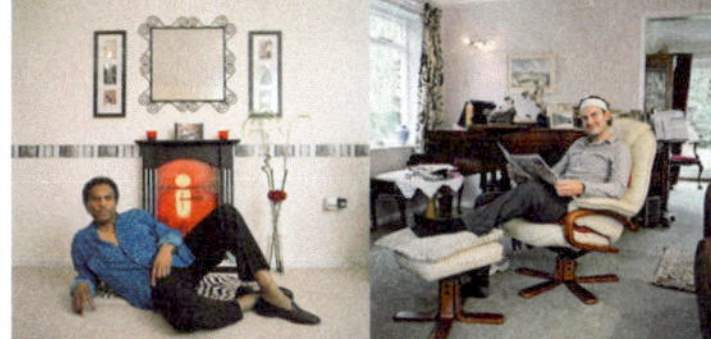 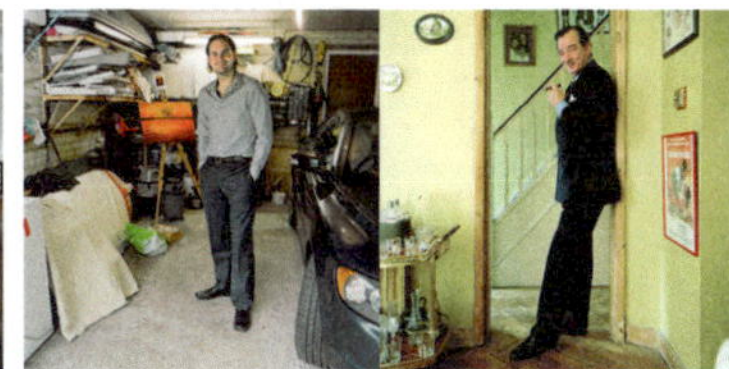 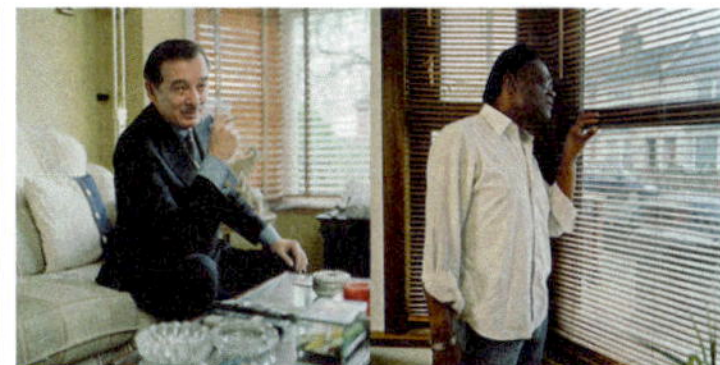

120 Abi Atici alias Diego Maradona
121 Edward Scott alias Lionel Richie

122 Edward Scott alias Lionel Richie
123 Andy Cobb alias Roger Federer

124 Andy Cobb alias Roger Federer
125 Gene Daily alias Clark Gable

126 Gene Daily alias Clark Gable
127 Samuel DeHaney alias Samuel L. Jackson

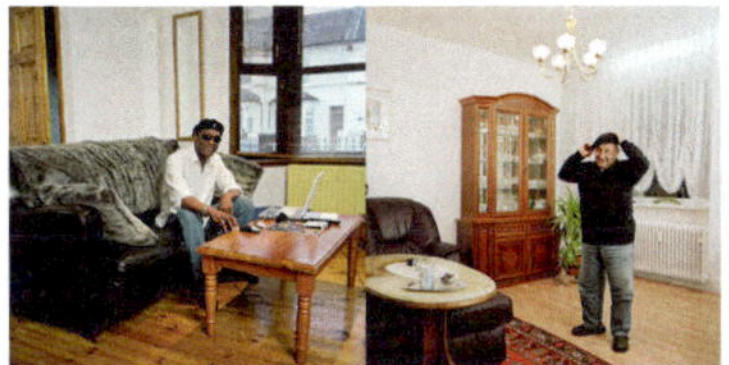 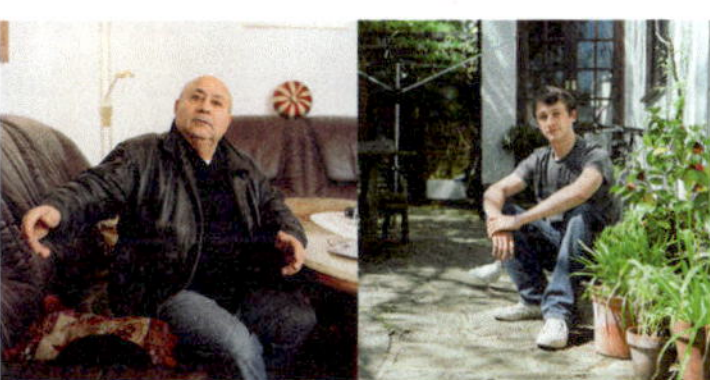 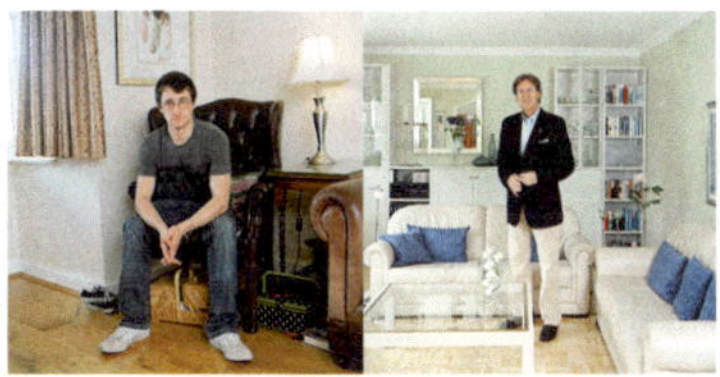 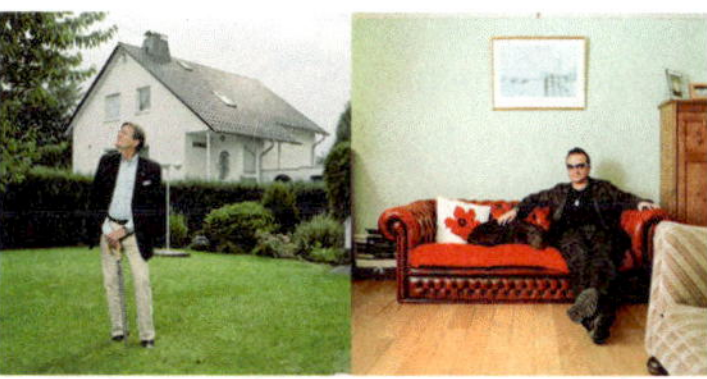

128 Samuel DeHaney alias Samuel L. Jackson
129 Victor El Ari alias Danny DeVito

130 Victor El Ari alias Danny DeVito
131 Luke Williams alias Harry Potter

132 Luke Williams alias Harry Potter
133 Claus Schoenekaes alias Prince August von Hannover

134 Claus Schoenekaes alias Prince August von Hannover
135 Andy Barker alias Bono

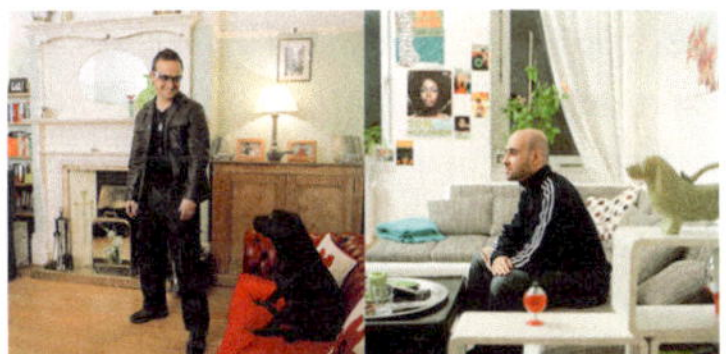 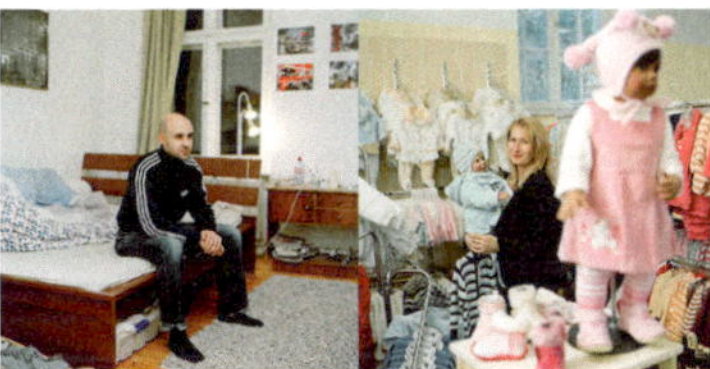 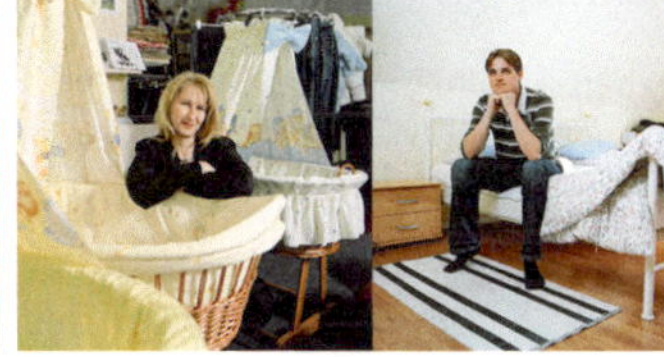 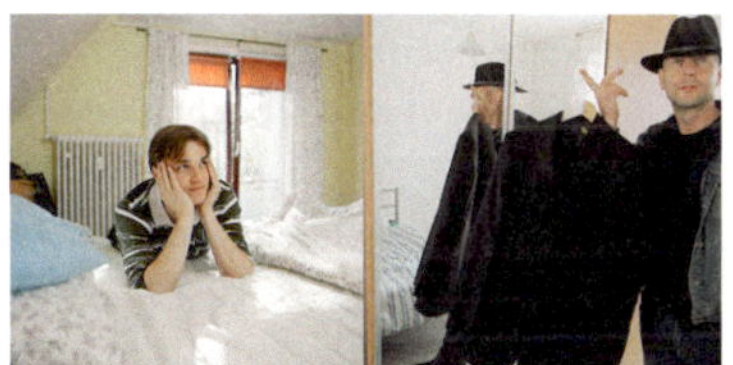

136 Andy Barker alias Bono
137 Christof Weingärtner alias Andre Agassi

138 Christof Weingärtner alias Andre Agassi
139 Ina Bormann alias Steffi Graf

140 Ina Bormann alias Steffi Graf
141 Rainer Roeloffs alias Leonardo DiCaprio

142 Rainer Roeloffs alias Leonardo DiCaprio
143 Hans Plessnitzer alias Bruce Willis

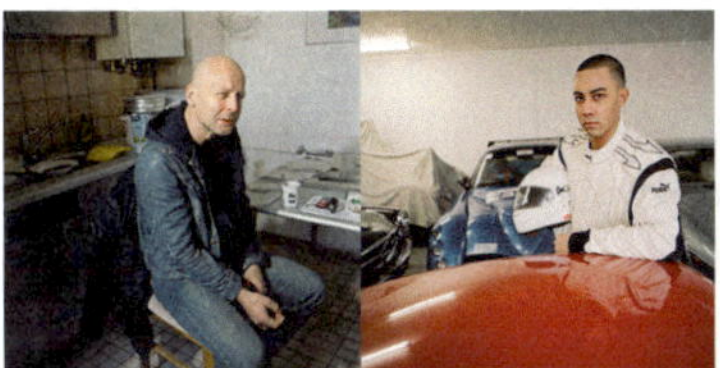 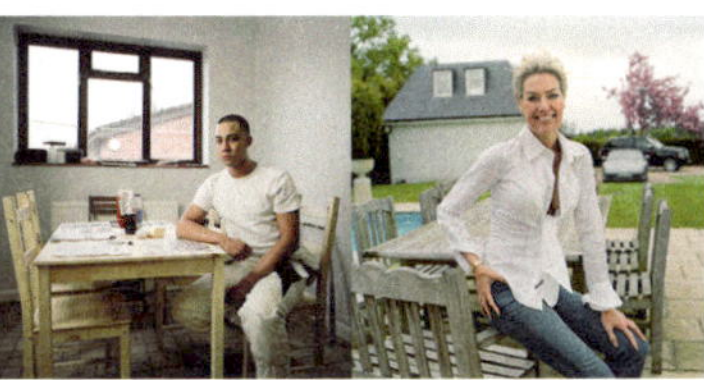 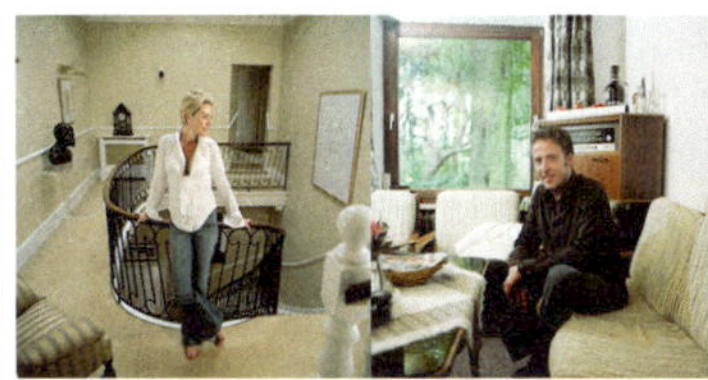 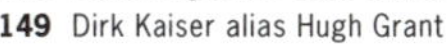 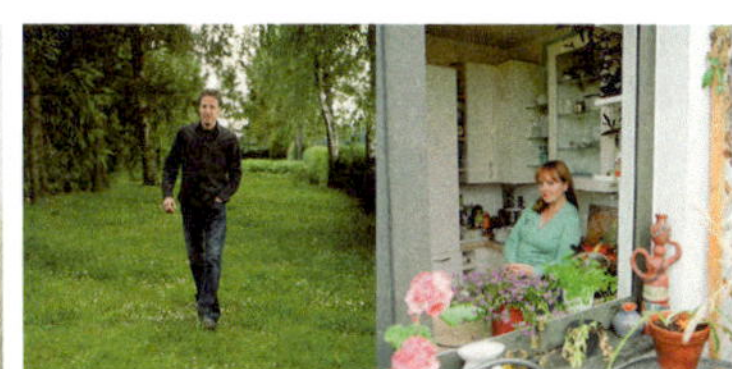

144 Hans Plessnitzer alias Bruce Willis
145 Jay Deakin alias Lewis Hamilton

146 Jay Deakin alias Lewis Hamilton
147 Hazel Englander alias Sharon Stone

148 Hazel Englander alias Sharon Stone
149 Dirk Kaiser alias Hugh Grant

150 Dirk Kaiser alias Hugh Grant
151 Brigitte Rotter alias Sarah Ferguson

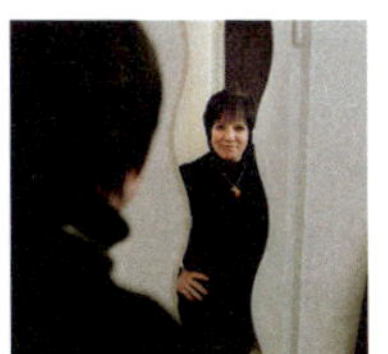

152 Heidi Kelleh alias Liza Minnelli

Biografien/Biographies

Biografie Niklaus Spoerri

Niklaus Spoerri, Künstler und Fotograf (*1965, Zürich) lebt und arbeitet in Zürich.
1986–1990 Fotografie-Ausbildung an der Schule für Gestaltung, Zürich, 1992 Mitbegründer der Fotoagentur Regards in Zürich.

Gruppenausstellungen:
- «Schiffbau, Transformation eines Ortes», Wanderausstellung anlässlich der 10. Theater Quadriennale, Prag 2003
- Auszeichnung für Dokumentation «Arbeitsalltag bei Schweizer Radio DRS» im Rahmen des Wettbewerbs «the selection» der VfG, Zürich 2000
- freie Arbeiten in der Ausstellung «Blind», Nürnberg und Dresden 1992

Beiträge in Publikationen:
- Peter Regli: «Reality Hacking 256–001», Edition Patrick Frey, Zürich 2007
- Titelbilder sämtlicher «Hochparterre»-Ausgaben aus dem Jahr 2005
- «Schiffbau, Transformation eines Ortes», Birkhäuser Verlag, Zürich 2003
- «Emotional Landscapes: Die Architektur von Mateja Vehovar und Stefan Jauslin», Birkhäuser Verlag, Zürich 2002
- Ausstellung für das Rote Kreuz am Bellevue im Rahmen des Projekts «schöneaussichten» 2001
- Fotografische Dokumentation für Fischli/Weiss an der Börse Zürich, Oktagon 1993
- «Blind. Junge Fotografie aus der Schweiz», Verlag für moderne Kunst Nürnberg, Nürnberg, 1992

Biografien der Textautoren

Jean-Martin Büttner, Reporter und Musikkritiker beim «Tages-Anzeiger» (Schweiz): (*1959, Bern) wuchs zweisprachig in Basel auf. Studium der Psychologie, Psychopathologie und Anglistik in Zürich, Abschluss 1986, Promotion 1995 über «Sänger, Songs und triebhafte Rede: Rock als Erzählweise» (Frankfurt am Main: Stroemfeld, 1997). 1987–1988 Volontariat beim «Tages-Anzeiger» und Besuch der Journalistenschule MAZ in Luzern, Abschluss 1988. Seit 1990 Redakteur beim Zürcher «Tages-Anzeiger», zuerst im Ressort Inland, dann in der Kultur. Von 1995 bis 1998 Westschweizer Korrespondent in Genf, dann bis 2004 Bundeshauskorrespondent in Bern. Seit-

her Reporter und Musikkritiker mit Austragungsort Zürich. Zürcher Journalistenpreis 2004 für einen Artikel über Niklaus Meienberg («Was er als Stil betrieb, ist heute eine Marke»). Lebt in Zürich. Dozent am Medienausbildungszentrum, Publikationen auch in «Du», «Zeit» u. v. a. m.

Jens Groß, Dramaturg (Deutschland): seit Sommer 2011 Chefdramaturg am Maxim Gorki Theater Berlin. Werdegang: nach dem Abitur Buchhandelslehre und Schauspielausbildung. 1982–1985 erstes Festengagement als Schauspieler, Regie- und Dramaturgieassistent am Schauspielhaus Wien. 1985–1988 Schauspieler, Dramaturg und Leitungsmitglied des Beinhardt-Ensembles in Wien. 1988–1992 Studium der Germanistik und Philosophie in Regensburg. 1992–1996 Dramaturg am Staatstheater Braunschweig, 1996–1999 Dramaturg am Niedersächsischen Staatstheater Hannover, 1999–2001 Dramaturg am Bayerischen Staatsschauspiel München, 2001–2009 Chefdramaturg am Schauspiel Frankfurt, 2009–2011 Dramaturg am Staatsschauspiel Dresden. Diverse Lehraufträge an der Johann Wolfgang Goethe-Universität Frankfurt am Main (Bereich Dramaturgie) und an der Hochschule für Musik und darstellende Kunst Frankfurt am Main (Bereich Regie). Studioleiter des Schauspielstudio Dresden der Hochschule für Musik und Theater Felix Mendelssohn Bartholdy Leipzig. Gastprofessur am Deutschen Literaturinstitut Leipzig für szenisches Schreiben.

Silvia Jaklitsch, Publikationsmanagement, Lektorin (Österreich): (*1977, Augsburg) studierte Kunstgeschichte und Germanistik in Bamberg und Heidelberg. Seit 2003 freie Mitarbeiterin des Verlags für moderne Kunst Nürnberg. Seit 2006 leitet sie das Wiener Büro und betreut internationale Buchprojekte aus dem Bereich der zeitgenössischen Kunst.

Caroline Morpeth (Grossbritannien): (*1956, Walton on Thames, Surrey/Grossbritannien) lebte u. a. in Frankreich, in einem Kibbuz in Israel und einige Jahre in der Schweiz. Ihr aktuelles Zuhause ist London, wo sie zusammen mit ihrem Mann und ihren beiden Kindern wohnt. Sie arbeitet halbtags für Hachette, eine grosse britische Verlagsanstalt. Sie liest Manuskripte – hofft inständig, eines Tages den neuen Bestseller in Händen zu halten –, lektoriert Proofs und E-Books

und verbessert grammatikalische und inhaltliche Schnitzer. Caroline Morpeth hat einen Abschluss in Literatur und jüngst begonnen, über Kunst zu schreiben und zu veröffentlichen.

Univ. Prof. Mag. Dr. Manfred Prisching, Fakultät der Soziologie der Universität Graz (Österreich): (*1950, Bruck/Mur) Autor des vielbeachteten Buches «Das Selbst. Die Maske. Der Bluff», 2009. Studium der Rechtswissenschaften und der Volkswirtschaftslehre, Universitätsassistent an den Instituten für Rechtsphilosophie, für Volkswirtschaftslehre und Volkswirtschaftspolitik und für Soziologie. Habilitation für Soziologie 1985; ao. Univ. Prof. 1994. 1987/1988 an der Rijksuniversiteit Limburg (Maastricht, NL). 1995/1996 Schumpeter-Gastprofessur an der Harvard University (Cambridge/Boston); 2005/2006 Visiting Scholar an den Universitäten von New Orleans, Little Rock, Las Vegas. 1997–2001 wissenschaftlicher Leiter der Technikum Joanneum GmbH (steirische Fachhochschulen). Korr. Mitglied der Österreichischen Akademie der Wissenschaften. 2010 Grosses Ehrenzeichen des Landes Steiermark, 2011 der Republik Österreich. Viele Buchwerke und wissenschaftliche Aufsätze zur Wirtschaftssoziologie, Ideengeschichte, Soziologie der Politik, Zeitdiagnose. www.manfredprisching.com

Markus Reich, Glückspost/Ringier, Journalist (Schweiz): (*1964, St. Gallen) studierte nach der Matura Englisch und Deutsch. Danach arbeitete er für das Winterthurer «Radio Eulach» sowie für verschiedene Lokal- und Regionalzeitungen. Am SAWI in Biel absolvierte er die Ausbildung zum PR-Assistenten und war danach in Werbeagenturen als Texter tätig. Seit 1992 schreibt er für die Zeitschrift «Glückspost» des Zürcher Medienkonzerns Ringier und berichtet über Prominenz aus Film und Fernsehen.

Rudolf Scheutle, Kurator am Münchner Stadtmuseum/Sammlung Fotografie (Deutschland): (*1964, Deggingen/Baden-Württemberg) ist neben seiner Kuratorentätigkeit Lehrbeauftragter für Fotografiegeschichte an der Hochschule für angewandte Wissenschaften in München. Nach dem Studium der Kunstgeschichte, Theaterwissenschaft und Soziologie in München arbeite er als freier Kurator und Autor im Bereich Fotografie und zeitgenössische Kunst und war Lehrbeauftragter für Fotografiegeschichte an der Staatlichen Fachakademie für Fotodesign, München und an der Universität Eichstätt/Ingolstadt. Zu den von ihm kuratierten Ausstellungen gehören: «Zeitzonen – 3. Triennale zeitgenössischer Kunst Weingarten» (2005), «Last & Lost – Bilder eines verschwindenden Europas» (2006), «Urban Conditions» (2007), «Unlängst im Wald» (2011). Im Münchner Stadtmuseum realisierte er unter anderem «Lehrjahre Lichtjahre – Die Münchner Fotoschule 1900–2000» (2000), «Nude Visions. 150 Jahre Körperbilder in der Fotografie» (2009) und «Industriezeit» (2011).

Jimmy Wales, Gründer der Wikipedia Foundation (USA): Jimmy Wales ist ein amerikanischer Internet-Unternehmer. Seine bekannteste Gründung ist die Wikimedia Foundation – jene Non-Profit-Organisation, die Wikipedia.org betreibt. Zudem ist Wales auch Mitbegründer von Wikia.com.
Wales studierte Finanzwirtschaft. Er erlangte seinen Bachelor an der Auburn University und den Master an der University of Alabama. 2005 war er Forschungsstipendiat am Berkman Center for Internet & Society der Harvard Law School. 2006 wurde er Mitglied im Aufsichtsrat der gemeinnützigen Organisation Creative Commons.
Im Januar 2001 startete Wales die Gemeinschaftsenzyklopädie Wikipedia.org. Wikipedia und Schwesterprojekte sind heute unter den fünf am meisten besuchten Webseiten im Netz. Mitte 2003 gründete Wales in St. Petersburg (Florida) die gemeinnützige Wikimedia Foundation, die wikipedia.org betreibt. Die Stiftung, die heute im Zentrum San Franciscos angesiedelt ist, weist einen Personalstand von fast 30 Angestellten auf, die sich zur Verbesserung der Wikipedia ständig um Fundraising, Technik und Programmierung bemüht. Wales sitzt heute im Kuratorium der Wikimedia Foundation und ist als deren Gründer auch weiterhin einer ihrer wichtigsten Sprecher.
2004 beteiligte sich Wales an der Gründung von Wikia.com, einer eigenständigen Firma, die Nutzergruppen den Austausch von Informationen und Meinungen, die nicht in den Aufgabenbereich einer Enzyklopädie fallen, gestattet. Die Themen der von den einzelnen Gruppen gegründeten Wikis reichen von Videospielen und Filmen bis zu Finanzwirtschaft und Umwelt. Wikias Netzwerk rangiert laut Quantcast.

com unter den Top 75 Webseiten und wächst auch weiterhin stark.
2007 zeichnete das World Economic Forum Wales als einen der «Young Global Leaders» aus. Diese angesehene Auszeichnung ergeht an die 250 wichtigsten Jungmanager für berufliche Leistungen, soziales Engagement und ihr Potenzial zur Gestaltung der Zukunft des Planeten. Zusätzlich erhielt Wales 2006 den «Time 100 Award» als eine der weltweit einflussreichsten Personen in der Kategorie «Wissenschaftler und Denker».

Biografien der Mitherausgeber

Irene Jost/Culture_Art_Communications, Zürich (Hrsg.): www.culture-art-com.ch
(*1966, Wynigen/Bern) Doppelgängerin von der Kunstwelt bis zur wirtschaftlichen Identität: Informationsarchitektin, Markenstrategin und Kommunikationsspezialistin mit Schwerpunkt in CI-CD und Website-/Social-Media-Kommunikation, mit eigener Agentur seit 1998 – Produzentin & Vermittlung von Kunstprojekten, u.a. Monografie von RELAX (chiarenza & hauser & co) «we save what you give» 2006; Vorstand Shedhalle 2007–2010; Organisation der Mitgliederfeste der Shedhalle 2007, 2008, 2009; Medialisierung/Schaffung von Öffentlichkeit für die Sans-Papiers-Kunstaktion «1 SFR = 1 Stimme/1 CHF = 1 Voice» von Andreja Kulunčić/Shedhalle «work to do!»; Publikation «work to do! Selbstorganisation in prekären Arbeitsbedingungen» von Sønke Gau&Katharina Schlieben für den Verein Shedhalle; diverse Ausstellungsprojekte («weisser als weiss», «domestic things», «saisonniers») und aktuelle Publikation «Johnnie Walker on the beach» für Francisco Paco Carrascosa, Zürich.

2. stock süd netthoevel & gaberthüel, Biel (Hrsg.): www.secondfloorsouth.com
Der Gestaltungsbetrieb «2. stock süd» wurde 1990 in der Schweizer Uhrenmetropole Biel am Jurasüdfuss gegründet. Die im Februar 1963 geborenen Grafiker Andréas Netthoevel und Martin Gaberthüel, die sich 1979 an der «Schule für Gestaltung Biel» kennengelernt haben, füllen seit 1995 gemeinsam aus Inhalten Formen für Aufträge, die ihnen aus den unterschiedlichsten Bereichen der visuellen Kommunikation anvertraut werden (Corporate Design, Editorial, Signaletik, Interventionen am Bau). Die beiden

Gestalter erhielten regelmässig nationale und internationale Auszeichnungen, so vom ADC Schweiz und New York; dem Design Preis Schweiz; dem Type Directors Club New York; den The New York Festivals, dem D&AD-Award.

Institut für moderne Kunst Nürnberg (Hrsg.): www.moderne-kunst.org
Das 1967 gegründete Institut ist ein Informations- und Dokumentationszentrum für zeitgenössische Kunst, das vom Freistaat Bayern, dem Bezirk Mittelfranken, der Stadt Nürnberg und privaten Mitgliedern getragen wird. Aufgaben des Instituts sind die Pflege eines Archivs für deutsche und internationale Kunst der Gegenwart, die Konzeption und Durchführung von Ausstellungen sowie die Herausgabe von Publikationen zur zeitgenössischen Kunst.

Biography of Niklaus Spoerri

<u>Niklaus Spoerri</u>, artist and photographer (*1965, Zurich) lives and works in Zurich.
1986–1990 studies photography at Schule für Gestaltung, Zurich, 1992 co-founder of the photo agency in Zurich.

Group exhibitions:
- "Schiffbau. A Site is Transformed", 10. Quadriennal of Stage Design and Theatre Architecture 2003 in Prague
- Award for the documentation "The daily work at Swiss Radio DRS" on the occasion of the competition "the selection" of the VfG, Zürich 2000
- participation in the exhibition "Blind" with several works, Nuremberg and Dresden 1992

Contributions in Publications:
- Peter Regli: "Reality Hacking 256–001", Edition Patrick Frey, Zurich 2007
- Covers of all "Hochparterre"-editions in 2005
- "Schiffbau. Transformation eines Ortes", Birkhäuser Verlag, Zurich 2003
- "Emotional Landscapes: Die Architektur von Mateja Vehovar und Stefan Jauslin", Birkhäuser Verlag, Zurich 2002
- exhibition for Red Cross at the Bellevue on the occasion of "schöneaussichten" 2001
- Photographic documentation for Fischli/Weiss at the Stock Exchange Zurich, Oktagon 1993
- "Blind. Junge Fotografie aus der Schweiz", Verlag für moderne Kunst Nürnberg, Nuremberg, 1992

Biographies of the authors

<u>Jean-Martin Büttner</u>, reporter and music critic of the Tages-Anzeiger (Switzerland): (*1959, Bern) grew up bilingually in Basel. Studied psychology, psychopathology and English in Zurich, graduated in 1986, doctorate in 1995 with a thesis on "Sänger, Songs und triebhafte Rede: Rock als Erzählweise" [Singers, songs and impulsive speech. Rock as narrative] (Frankfurt am Main: Stroemfeld, 1997). From 1987–1988 traineeship at the "Tages-Anzeiger" and attended the MAZ journalism school in Lucerne, graduated in 1988. Since 1990, editor at the Zurich "Tages-Anzeiger", first in the inland department, before moving to the culture desk. From 1995 to 1998 Western Switzerland correspondent in Geneva, later political correspondent in Bern until 2004. Since then reporter and music critic based in Zurich. Won the Zurich Journalist Prize in 2004 for an article on Niklaus Meienberg ("What he set out as a style has today become a brand"). Lives in Zurich. Lecturer at the Media Training Centre, has also published in "Du", "Zeit" and others.

<u>Jens Groß</u>, dramatic advisor (Germany): Senior dramatic advisor at the Maxim Gorki Theater Berlin from summer 2011: after A-levels, apprenticeship in bookselling and drama school. From 1982–1985 first permanent engagement as actor, assistant director and dramatic advisor at the Schauspielhaus Vienna. From 1985–1988 actor, dramatic advisor and one of the management team at the Beinhardt Ensemble in Vienna. From 1988–1992 he studied German and philosophy in Regensburg. From 1992–1996 dramatic advisor at the Staatstheater Braunschweig, from 1996–1999 dramatic advisor at the Niedersächsische Staatstheater Hannover, from 1999–2001 dramatic advisor at the Bayerische Staatsschauspiel Munich, from 2001–2009 senior dramatic advisor at the Schauspiel Frankfurt, from 2009–2011 dramatic advisor at the Staatsschauspiel Dresden. Diverse teaching posts at the Johann Wolfgang Goethe University Frankfurt (in the field of dramaturgy) and at the Frankfurt University of Music and Performing Arts (in the field of directing). Studio head at the Schauspielstudio Dresden at the University of Music and Theatre Felix Mendelssohn Bartholdy Leipzig. Guest professorship at the German Institute for Literature, Leipzig, for stage writing.

<u>Silvia Jaklitsch</u>, editorial services (Austria): (*1977, Augsburg) studied art history and German language and literature in Bamberg and Heidelberg. Since 2002 she has worked freelance for the Verlag für moderne Kunst Nürnberg. Since 2006 she has been in charge of the Viennese branch office and supervises international book projects on contemporary arts.

<u>Caroline Morpeth</u> (United Kingdom): (*1956, Walton on Thames, Surrey/UK) she lived in France, on a kibbutz in Israel and for several years in Switzerland. She currently lives in London with her husband and their two children. Caroline works part-time for a large commercial publishing company, Hachette UK, where she reads manuscripts, hoping to find the new breakthrough bestseller, and checks proofs and E-books for grammatical and narrative howlers. She has an honours degree in Literature and has recently started to write and publish on the arts.

<u>Univ. Prof. Mag. Dr. Manfred Prisching</u>, sociologist (Austria): (*1950, Bruck/Mur) Author of "Das Selbst. Die Maske. Der Bluff", 2009. Studied economics and law, research assistant at the Institutes for Philosophy of Law, Economics and Political Economics, and Sociology. Post-doctoral qualification in sociology in 1985; associate professor in 1994. In 1987/1988 at the Rijksuniversiteit Limburg (Maastricht, Holland). In 1995/1996 Schumpeter guest professorship at Harvard University (Cambridge/Boston); In 2005/2006 Visiting Scholar at the universities of New Orleans, Little Rock, Las Vegas. From 1997–2001 scientific director of the Technikum Joanneum GmbH (Styrian polytechnics). Corresponding member of the Austrian Academy of Sciences. Was awarded the Grand Decoration of the province of Styria in 2010, and that of the Austrian Republic in 2011. Has written many books and essays on economic sociology, the history of ideas, the sociology of politics, diagnosis of our times. www.manfred-prisching.com

<u>Markus Reich</u>, Glückspost/Ringier, journalist (Switzerland): (* 1964, St. Gallen) after A-levels, studied English and German. He then worked for Radio Eulach in Winterthur and for various local and regional newspapers. He trained as a PR assistant at the SAWI in Biel and subsequently worked in advertising agencies as a copywriter. Since 1992 he has been writing for the "Glückspost" newspaper of the Zurich media group Ringier, reporting on celebrities from the world of film and television.

<u>Rudolf Scheutle</u>, curator (Germany): (*1964, Deggingen/Baden-Wuerttemberg) Curator at the Munich City Museum/Photography Collection and lecturer in photographic history at the Munich University of Applied Sciences. After studying art history, dramatics and sociology in Munich, he worked as a freelance curator and writer in the field of photography and contemporary art. In addition he was a lecturer in photographic history at the State Academy of Photodesign, Munich and at Eichstätt/Ingolstadt University. Some of the the exhibitions he has curated:

"Zeitzonen – 3. Triennale zeitgenössischer Kunst Weingarten" [Time Zones – 3rd Triennial of Contemporary Art, Weingarten], 2005, "Last & Lost – Bilder eines verschwindenden Europas" [Last & Lost – Pictures of a Disappearing Europe] (2006), "Urban Conditions", 2007, "Unlängst im Wald" [Recently in the Forest], 2011. His presentations in the Munich Stadtmuseum include "Lehrjahre Lichtjahre – Die Münchner Fotoschule 1900–2000" [Learning Years Light Years – the Munich Photo School 1900–2000], 2000, "Nude Visions. 150 Jahre Körperbilder in der Fotografie" [Nude Visions. 150 Years of Nude Photography], 2009, and "Industriezeit", 2011.

Jimmy Wales, founder of Wikipedia Foundation (USA): is an American Internet entrepreneur best known as the founder of Wikimedia Foundation, the charity which operates Wikipedia.org, and as the co-founder of Wikia.com.
Wales received his Bachelor's degree in finance from Auburn University and his Master's in finance from University of Alabama. He was appointed a fellow of the Berkman Center for Internet & Society at Harvard Law School in 2005 and in 2006 he joined the Board of Directors of the non-profit organization Creative Commons.
In January 2001, Wales started Wikipedia.org, the online encyclopedia that anyone can edit, and today Wikipedia and its sister projects are among the top-five most visited sites on the web. In mid-2003, Wales set up the Wikimedia Foundation, a non-profit organization based in St. Petersburg, Florida, to support Wikipedia.org. The foundation, now based in downtown San Francisco, boasts a staff of close to thirty focusing on fundraising, technology, and programming relating to the expansion of Wikipedia. Wales now sits on the board of trustees of the Wikimedia Foundation, and as founder continues to act as a key spokesperson.
In 2004, Wales co-founded Wikia.com, a completely separate company that enables groups of people to share information and opinions that fall outside the scope of an encyclopedia. Wikia's community-created wikis range from video games and movies to finance and environmental issues.
Wikia's network is now ranked in the top 75 of all websites according to Quantcast.com, and strong growth continues.

In 2007, The World Economic Forum recognized Wales as one of the "Young Global Leaders." This prestigious award acknowledges the top 250 young leaders for their professional accomplishments, their commitment to society and their potential to contribute to shaping the future of the world. In addition Wales received the "Time 100 Award" in 2006, as he was named one of the world's most influential people in the "Scientists & Thinkers" category.

Biographies of Co-Editors

Irene Jost/Culture_Art_Communications, Zurich (Switzerland): www.culture-art-com.ch
(*1966, Wynigen/Bern) she is a doppelganger from the world of art to a business identity: information architect, brand strategist and communication specialist with a focus on CI-CD and website/social media communication, she has had her own agency since 1998 – production and mediation of art projects, including a monograph of RELAX (chiarenza & hauser & co) "we save what you give" 2006; member of board of the Shedhalle 2007–2010; organisation of members' parties for the Shedhalle 2007, 2008, 2009; medialisation/generating publicity for the Sans-Papiers art action "1 SFR = 1 Stimme/1 CHF = 1 Voice" by Andreja Kulunčić/Shedhalle on the occasion of "work to do!", editing the publication "work to do! Selbstorganisation in prekären Arbeitsbedingungen" [work to do! Self-organisation in precarious work situations] by Sønke Gau & Katharina Schlieben for the Verein Shedhalle; various exhibition projects ("weisser als weiss", "domestic things", "saisonniers") and editing of the current publication "Johnnie Walker on the beach" for Francisco Paco Carrascosa, Zurich.

2. stock süd netthoevel & gaberthüel, Biel (Switzerland): www.secondfloorsouth.com
The design company "2. stock süd" was founded in 1990 in the Swiss watchmaking metropolis of Biel in the Jurasüdfuss region. Graphic artists Andréas Netthoevel and Martin Gaberthüel, who were both born in February 1963 and met in 1979 at the "Schule für Gestaltung Biel" [School of Design, Biel], have since 1995 been preparing designs for lectures entrusted to them from a variety of visual communication fields (corporate design, editorial, signage, interventions in construction). The two design-

ers have regularly won national and international awards, such as from the ADC Switzerland and New York; the Swiss Design Award; the Type Directors Club New York; the New York Festivals, the D&AD Award.

Institut für moderne Kunst Nürnberg (Germany): www.moderne-kunst.org
The Institute, founded in 1967, is an information and documentation centre for contemporary art which is supported by the Free State of Bavaria, the District of Central Franconia and by private members. The responsibilities of the Institute lie in maintaining an archive for German and international contemporary art, the planning and presentation of exhibitions, and the publication of works on contemporary art.

Impressum/Imprint

Herausgeber/Editors: **Niklaus Spoerri, Irene Jost/
Culture_Art_Communications, 2. stock süd
netthoevel & gaberthüel, Institut für moderne
Kunst Nürnberg**

Konzept Publikation & Fotografien/Concept & Photos:
© **Niklaus Spoerri, Zürich**
Produzentin & Konzeption/Producer & Conception:
Irene Jost/Culture_Art_ Communications, Zürich
Gestaltung/Graphic design: **2. stock süd
netthoevel & gaberthüel, Biel**
Redaktion/Editing: **Silvia Jaklitsch, Irene Jost**
Autoren/authors: **Jean-Martin Büttner, Jens Groß,
Silvia Jaklitsch, Caroline Morpeth, Manfred Prisching,
Markus Reich, Rudolf Scheutle, Jimmy Wales**

Lektorat/Proof-Reading: **Irene Gaberthüel, Silvia
Jaklitsch, Irene Jost, Jonathan Quinn, Steve Tomlin**
Übersetzung vom Deutschen ins Englische/Translation
from German into English: **Steve Tomlin**
Übersetzung vom Englischen ins Deutsche/Translation
from English into German: **Thomas Raab**
Scans: **Niklaus Spoerri, Zürich**
Litho: **Ringier AG, Specter PrePress, Marcel Bosshard,
Patrick Eberhard**
Druck/Print: **Druckerei Odermatt AG, Stefan Gabriel**
Buchbinder/Bookbinder: **Buchbinderei Burkhardt AG,
Mönchaltdorf**
Schrift/Typeface: **News Gothic Std, Greta Text Std,
Syntax LT Std**
Gedruckt auf/Printed on: **Algro Design, Zellulose-
karton, einseitig halbmatt gestrichen, hochweiss,
holzfrei, FSC zertifiziert, 300 g/m²; Profibulk 1.1,
matt gestrichen, hochweiss, holzfrei, FSC zertifiziert,
150 g/m²; Lessebo 1.3, White, Offset-Preprint, matt,
hochweiss, holzfrei, FSC zertifiziert, CO₂ neutral,
100 g/m²**

1. Auflage/1st Edition: © 2011 für das Buch bei den
Herausgebern/for the book with the editors, Verlag
für moderne Kunst Nürnberg, Niklaus Spoerri
© 2011 für die abgebildeten Werke bei/for the repro-
duced images with Niklaus Spoerri
© 2011 für die Texte bei den Autoren/for the texts
with the authors

Printed in Switzerland

Erschienen im/Published by
Verlag für moderne Kunst Nürnberg
Luitpoldstrasse 5, D-90402 Nürnberg
Telefon +49-911-240 21 14
Fax +49-911-240 21 19
www.vfmk.de

ISBN 978-3-86984-176-2

Bibliografische Information Der Deutschen
Nationalbibliothek
Die Deutsche Nationalbibliothek verzeichnet diese
Publikation in der Deutschen Nationalbibliografie;
detaillierte bibliografische Daten sind im Internet
über http://dnb.ddb.de abrufbar.

Bibliographic information published by Die Deutsche
Nationalbibliothek
Die Deutsche Nationalbibliothek lists this publication in the Deutsche Nationalbibliografie; detailed
bibliographic data is available on the Internet at
http://dnb.ddb.de.

Distributed in the United Kingdom
Cornerhouse Publications
70 Oxford Street, Manchester M1 5 NH, UK
phone +44-161-200 15 03, fax +44-161-200 15 04

Distributed outside Europe
D.A.P. Distributed Art Publishers, Inc.
155 Sixth Avenue, 2nd Floor, New York,
NY 10013, USA
phone +1-212-627 19 99, fax +1-212-627 94 84

"Have you ever met the Queen?" –
"I never answer that question!"

Jeannette Charles alias Queen Elizabeth II

Thank you

Herzlichen Dank an alle, die an mich, mein Projekt und das Buch geglaubt haben!
- SILVIA JAKLITSCH, die sich mit grosser Freude für das Projekt engagierte und es über die lange Zeit hinweg redaktionell begleitete
- IRENE GABERTHÜEL und BETTINA SPOERRI, die all das «Schriftliche», das ein Kunstprojekt zum Durchstarten braucht, in eine überzeugende Form brachten
- FRANCISCO PACO CARRASCOSA, der in allen Projektphasen sein künstlerisches Feedback einbrachte
- SUSANNE HOLZER und RITA und HEINRICH HOLZER, die den Künstlernachwuchs LILLI und JON während meiner unzähligen Auslandsreisen bestens betreuten und mir damit die Arbeit an diesem Projekt möglich machten. PAULA SPOERRI für ihre Geduld und Unterstützung
- JOCHEN FLORSTEDT von doubles.de, der Professionalität bewies und seine exklusiven Doubles zu einem Topauftritt ohne Topgage bewegte
- SUSAN SCOTT of lookalikes.info, who did the same for us in the UK
- FRANK SAASEN von www.carsandstars.nl und RENATE DIETHELM von findaface.ch für die hilfreiche Vermittlung von Kontakten
- ALLE DOUBLES selbst, die sich auf das Projekt einliessen und ihre kostbare Zeit und ihre Privaträume zur Verfügung stellten
- KARSTEN WITZMANN und PHILIPPE PFISTER von der Blick-Gruppe, die der Kunst eine breite Bühne geben
- HILLA und DIETER BERTELSMANN und STEFAN JAUSLIN, die das private Mäzenatentum pflegen und mich wohlwollend unterstützt haben
- All my friends, die sich ebenfalls höchst grosszügig! engagierten: DORINE ABEGG, ANTOINE BUGMANN und PRISKA LUSSI, MERET ERNST, ANNE KASPER und BEAT MAYER, RÖBI KOLLER, RITA und HEINRICH HOLZER, URS STAUBER, ANJA SAUER, BETTINA SPOERRI, BRUNO SPOERRI, MISCHA, YASMINA, DRISS und SAMIR SPOERRI, MARTIN STOLLENWERK, MATEJA VEHOVAR
- Aufgeschlossene und mutige Stiftungen, die einen Sinn für originelle Projekte bewiesen:
  PRÄSIDIALDEPARTEMENT DER STADT ZÜRICH
  GEORGES UND JENNY BLOCH STIFTUNG, Rüschlikon
- Produktive Menschen und Unternehmen, die wertvolle Arbeit geleistet und ihre Zeit investiert haben und all das teilweise unentgeltlich
  2. STOCK SÜD NETTHOEVEL & GABERTHÜEL
  IRENE JOST/CULTURE_ART_COMMUNICATIONS
  BUCHBINDEREI BURKHARDT AG, Mönchaltdorf
  DRUCKEREI ODERMATT AG, Dallenwil
  RINGIER AG, SPECTER PREPRESS
… und IRENE JOST für alles.

A warm thank you to all those who had faith in me, my project and this book!
- SILVIA JAKLITSCH, who worked with great pleasure on this project and spent much time supervising the editorial work
- IRENE GABERTHÜEL und BETTINA SPOERRI, who gathered all the "written material" that an art project needs to get started and put it into a convincing form
- FRANCISCO PACO CARRASCOSA, who gave his artistic feedback in all phases of the project
- SUSANNE HOLZER and RITA and HEINRICH HOLZER, who looked after the artist's children LILLI and JON during my numerous trips abroad, making my work on this project possible. PAULA SPOERRI for her patience and support
- JOCHEN FLORSTEDT from doubles.de, who was most professional and who motivated his exclusive doubles to take part in a first-class appearance without being paid top fees
- SUSAN SCOTT of lookalikes.info, who did the same for us in the UK
- FRANK SAASEN from www.carsandstars.nl and RENATE DIETHELM from findaface.ch for their helpful mediation of contacts
- ALL THE DOUBLES themselves, who got involved with the project and gave their valuable time and made their private homes available
- KARSTEN WITZMANN and PHILIPPE PFISTER from the Blick group, who provide the art with a wide audience
- HILLA and DIETER BERTELSMANN and STEFAN JAUSLIN, who looked after private patronage and who have generously supported me
- All my friends who have also been greatly involved: DORINE ABEGG, ANTOINE BUGMANN und PRISKA LUSSI, MERET ERNST, ANNE KASPER und BEAT MAYER, RÖBI KOLLER, RITA und HEINRICH HOLZER, URS STAUBER, ANJA SAUER, BETTINA SPOERRI, BRUNO SPOERRI, MISCHA, YASMINA, DRISS und SAMIR SPOERRI, MARTIN STOLLENWERK, MATEJA VEHOVAR
- Open and courageous foundations who have shown an appreciation of original projects:
  PRÄSIDIALDEPARTEMENT DER STADT ZÜRICH
  GEORGES UND JENNY BLOCH STIFTUNG, Rüschlikon
- Productive people and companies who have done valuable work and invested their time, and all this without payment
  2. STOCK SÜD NETTHOEVEL & GABERTHÜEL
  IRENE JOST/CULTURE_ART_COMMUNICATIONS
  BUCHBINDEREI BURKHARDT AG, Mönchaltdorf
  DRUCKEREI ODERMATT AG, Dallenwil
  RINGIER AG, SPECTER PREPRESS
… and IRENE JOST for everything.